# Augustine's Political Thought

# ROCHESTER STUDIES IN MEDIEVAL POLITICAL THOUGHT

*Edited by*

Douglas Kries, Gonzaga University
Joshua Parens, University of Dallas

# Augustine's
# Political Thought

Edited by Richard J. Dougherty

UNIVERSITY OF ROCHESTER PRESS

First published 2019

University of Rochester Press
668 Mt. Hope Avenue, Rochester, NY 14620, USA
www.urpress.com
and Boydell & Brewer Limited
PO Box 9, Woodbridge, Suffolk IP12 3DF, UK
www.boydellandbrewer.com

ISBN-13: 978-1-58046-924-1
ISSN: 2380-565X

**Library of Congress Cataloging-in-Publication Data**

Names: Dougherty, Richard J., editor.
Title: Augustine's political thought / Edited by Richard J. Dougherty.
Description: Rochester, NY : University of Rochester Press, [2019] | Series: Rochester studies in medieval political thought, ISSN 2380-565X v. 2 | Includes bibliographical references and index.
Identifiers: LCCN 2019016149 | ISBN 9781580469241 (hardcover : alk. paper)
Subjects: LCSH: Augustine, of Hippo, Saint, 354–430—Political and social views. | Political science—History—To 1500. | Christianity and politics.
Classification: LCC JC121.A8 A95 2019 | DDC 320.01—dc23 LC record available at https://lccn.loc.gov/2019016149

A catalogue record for this title is available from the British Library.

This publication is printed on acid-free paper.
Printed in the United States of America.

# Contents

# Acknowledgments

This volume of essays on *Augustine's Political Thought* appears in the University of Rochester Press's Rochester Studies in Medieval Thought. The series editors, Douglas Kries and Joshua Parens, are to be commended for their efforts in launching the series, and thanked for their encouragement of this volume in particular. My thanks to the dedicated and professional staff at the University of Rochester Press, all of whom were gracious and supportive. Ryan Peterson was instrumental in getting the project off the ground. Sonia Kane, Julia Cook, Jacqueline Heinzelmann, and Tracey Engel have all been tremendously helpful in bringing the volume to fruition. Barbara Curialle was a pleasure to work with, and I thank her especially for her patience in dealing with my technological limitations. Thanks are due also to Mary Misko, Rose Dougherty, Jennifer Fast, and Anna Dean for their help in polishing up the text, and to the anonymous reviewers for the Press. Any mistakes that remain are obviously not the fault of these kindly benefactors.

None of this effort would be possible, though, without the support of my wife, Julie, and our children, all of whom have in one way or another assisted the production—if only in their steady patience with me. To all of you, your advocacy and affection are greatly appreciated.

Two of the included essays have been previously published, and are reprinted here with permission: Michael P. Foley, "The Other Happy Life: The Political Dimensions to St. Augustine's Cassiciacum Dialogues," *Review of Politics* 65, no. 2 (Spring, 2003): 165–83, © The University of Notre Dame, published by Cambridge University Press; and Veronica Roberts Ogle, "Augustine's Ciceronion Response to the Ciceronian Patriot," *Perspectives on Political Science* 45, no. 2 (2016): 113–24, © Taylor and Francis.

This volume is dedicated to three remarkable teachers, all of whom had a significant influence on drawing my attention to St. Augustine's work and in illuminating its importance. Dr. Eugene Thuot first introduced me to *The City of God* as a critical work in the field of political philosophy; I owe him an unpayable debt for his intellectual influence and academic encouragement. Dr. Leo Paul de Alvarez, in his groundbreaking Political Regimes course, took seriously St. Augustine's analysis in *The City of God* of the Roman political order and his confrontation with the classical order; he also painstakingly sharpened my own dissertation, and teaching, on the work. Father Ernest Fortin, A.A., wrote extensively on St. Augustine and became a kind friend and mentor; his influence can be seen throughout the essays contained in this volume.

Feast of St. Benedict
March 21, 2019

# Introduction

## Richard J. Dougherty

The current volume of essays is intended to fill a gap in the scholarly literature on St. Augustine, and to point toward new and fruitful possibilities in the study of St. Augustine's political thought.[1] Significant attention has been paid or repaid to the writings of St. Augustine over the past few decades, and much of it has been quite profitable. This can be seen in the number of volumes that have been produced over that period of time devoted to Augustine's work (and works), perhaps most recognizably in the earlier *Augustine Through the Ages: An Encyclopedia*[2] and the more recent three-volume *Oxford Guide to the Historical Reception of Augustine*.[3] These two works combine serious study of Augustine's work with attention to the many various ways in which his writing and arguments have influenced so much of the development of Western theology and philosophy, among other fields of study. As Ernest Fortin noted a few decades ago, Augustine's works were for centuries "the arch under which philosophers and theologians had to pass, the standard by which they could expect to be judged or against which they sought to measure their achievements."[4]

The contributions to this volume all take as a matter of utmost importance the task of understanding St. Augustine on his own terms, by closely analyzing his textual arguments and the interplay between and among multiple works by Augustine. All of the contributors have significantly benefited from the scholarly work of Ernest Fortin, who authored dozens of essays over the course of his academic career on the thought and influence of St. Augustine. The special mark of the essays in this volume is their affinity for the fundamental concerns of Father Fortin's work—attention to the details of St. Augustine's argument, wide-ranging analysis of multiple original texts, and, most importantly, addressing the writings of St. Augustine as part of an extended conversation with ancient, medieval, and modern writers.

Attention is thus given in the essays to the fundamental works of Augustine that touch on his political teaching in many of the obvious places, especially *The City of God*. But Augustine's comments on politics, the civil order, and the relationship between human nature and political authority also occur in a wide variety of additional texts, from other major works such as the *Confessions* and *Contra Faustum* to *On Free Choice of the Will*. In addition, though, Augustine has much of importance to say about human nature and the political order in numerous other places, such as his early dialogues, letters, sermons, and minor works. The contributors to this volume are interested in the entire corpus of Augustine's writings and are attentive to the important contributions to be found in these relatively less studied corners of Augustine's work.

Each of the essays addresses important themes in Augustine's work and approaches the text with care and precision. The thrust of the essays is not simply putting Augustine into conversation with ancient or modern authors and ideas (though they often do that, as will be seen) but rather first coming to know with as much assurance as possible what Augustine thought about the matters under consideration. To do so, one must honor Augustine's foundational work as much as one can, following the nuances of his argument and often recognizing the interplay between and among multiple texts. Many excellent contemporary studies have the goal of drawing on Augustine to address ongoing modern questions, such as the proper role of religion in the public square, or the meaning of civil society, or the application of Christian principles to the modern liberal democratic state and society. These are important questions and very much worth considering (and many of these works are certainly worth reading), but perhaps too often these studies engage in a rather cursory analysis of Augustine in order to move on to each author's important question, which is often more focused on contemporary questions than on Augustine himself. There is nothing wrong with such an approach, and much rewarding work has been done in this regard, but the focus of this volume is different—its aim is understanding Augustine's own argument comprehensively.

As important as the questions are that each of the essays addresses, it is also the case that most of the issues they raise are not simply new with Augustine, nor are they ignored by subsequent writers in the tradition. Thus, when appropriate, the contributors do put Augustine's argument into context by referring to previous authors (most notably the Platonists) and to modern authors addressing the same or related points. Augustine addresses important perennial questions (e.g., the role of the gods, the legitimacy of human authority in the city) and originates many others (e.g., the role of the will, the serious concern for humility and charity in politics), and the essays deal thoughtfully with many of these issues.

The opening essay, by the editor, takes as its starting point the opening salvo of Augustine's *City of God*, his "magnum opus et arduum," wherein he commences the argument in defense of the Christian religion against those who want to blame it for the weakening of the Roman Empire, resulting in the attack on Rome in 410 by Alaric and the Goths. A significant element of Augustine's argument consists of laying bare the weakness of Roman morals that preceded Christianity's rise to prominence, and that critique includes an attack on the moral and religious principles that animated Rome.[5] This essay focuses especially on Augustine's treatment of the fundamental moral principles that were the basis for Roman politics, beginning with the ever-vexing account of the suicide of Lucretia in book 1. The question of suicide opens Augustine's argument to a fuller assessment of the relationship between pagan and Christian ethics, including the nature of virtue and passion. Special focus is given here to the encounter with Stoic ethics, which Augustine assesses in books 9 and 14 in particular; one of the central concerns is the degree to which the Christian moral code is understandable by natural reason. Augustine's contrast between the Roman political heroes and Christian martyrs is an indication of the limited and limiting character of Roman political ethics.

Michael Foley's essay examines the early dialogues of Augustine as vehicles from which readers can draw political conclusions, even though those dialogues are not ostensibly focused on political teachings. The dialogue format, Foley argues, itself points toward the political and social dimension of Augustine's thought, more than an overtly philosophical tract might do. More important, the substantive discussion, though not immediately or forcefully guiding the audience through first principles of philosophic analysis, provides the occasion for raising such considerations in an open-ended manner that refrains from closing off interesting and important avenues of investigation.

Foley emphasizes that Augustine's primary concern in the dialogues is not a political one; indeed, the dialogues seem on the surface to disparage the mundane concerns of the city, instead focusing the interlocutors' attention on the universal and the transcendent. Arguing that Augustine's early dialogues are modeled Cicero's dialogues, and yet an important corrective to them, Foley focuses on the way in which Augustine's concern with happiness opens the argument to the formation of the soul in such a way that the soul can achieve that happiness. In this sense Augustine follows the Ciceronian political enterprise, recognizing the inherent connection between the promotion of the human good and the concern for law and public order.

In his chapter, Peter Busch considers the important question of the role of peace in Augustine's political teaching, emphasizing the differing ways in which the concern for peace arises and is satisfied. The success of a political order is rightly and routinely assessed in part on whether and to what extent it promotes peace, and Augustine surely recognizes that point. Still, the peace of the earthly city pales in comparison to the eternal peace of the heavenly city, a point Augustine emphasizes in book 19 of *The City of God*. But, the peace of the heavenly city is a model for the earthly city, and is perfectly willing to make use of that earthly peace to provide the occasion for decent living. Busch notes that Augustine says precious little, though, about the particular aspects or qualities of temporal rule, given that the justice it seeks to promote is always limited.

Busch turns then to considering the medieval debate over the relationship between spiritual and temporal authority, analyzing the contributions of Giles of Rome and of Dante as two opposite sides or applications of the Augustinian take on power. Giles' full-throated defense of the superiority of the spiritual power is countered by Dante's defense in his *De Monarchia* of the independence of temporal authority. Both authors draw on some aspect or aspects of Augustine to buttress their argument, though perhaps not with the same degree of directness. Following this debate, Busch returns to a reconsideration of Augustine's own views on the relation between these two powers, focusing on the way in which private and public life intersect in the city.

In her chapter, Ashleen Menchaca-Bagnulo provides a detailed analysis of an often overlooked but critical issue in *The City of God*—Augustine's understanding of the connection between worship and virtue. Throughout the first books of this work, Augustine seems to be fairly explicit that the acquisition of true virtue is intimately connected to true worship, such that one can speak of pagan "virtue" only by way of similitude. Menchaca-Bagnulo considers book 10 of *The City of God*, with its focus on worship and sacrifice, crucial to understanding that fuller concept of virtue that Augustine develops in the work. Here the Roman lust for domination, which Augustine recognizes as a central characteristic of Rome's existence, is transformed by a new understanding of sacrifice, seen now in the Christian dispensation as the seeking of the true good of others. Menchaca-Bagnulo concludes her essay, though, with an analysis of the way in which one can find room in Augustine's account for what looks like virtue, practiced according to reason and the order of nature. A critical part of that reassessment of virtue is seen in Augustine's critique of the apathy of the Stoics; for him, virtue is ordinarily or often accompanied by signs of genuine compassion.

Adam Thomas focuses his essay on the political questions that emerge from what he identifies as Augustine's "treatise on justice" in the *Confessions*. Thomas begins by examining the content and context of the discussion of justice in book 3 of the *Confessions*, where Augustine treats of the recognition of a "true, inner justice" that is a sure guide for human beings. Augustine here considers the various ways in which such justice can be substantively known by human beings, and the extent to which principles of justice must also be applied in particular circumstances. This latter point, so readily recognizable in all manner of human things, including table manners and the rules of poetic construction, can sometimes become a stumbling block to those who are trying to discern the precise guiding principle. Justice for human beings consists in part in the punishment of sin but also in faithfully following the will of God, such that human beings subordinate their own choices and conceptions of the good to God's. But right living, Thomas notes, also requires a legitimate concern for both distributive and retributive justice, as Augustine emphasizes here. And that justice is not unfettered, we see, for it must always be undertaken by a legitimate authority and be fittingly adapted to the good. However, Augustine's account of these issues here is incomplete, Thomas argues, without reverting to additional works by Augustine so as to flesh out the standards for human action and to assess the relative justice of those actions. More particularly, Augustine's *On Free Choice of the Will* is important for responding to the question of what constitutes the origins and character of evil. There he addresses some of the important issues raised in the *Confessions*, but adds a more direct consideration of the relationship between justice and the political order.

The essays in part 2 of this collection address the ways in which Augustine's works constitute a sustained reconsideration of the classical tradition in its interaction with

Christianity.[6] Thomas Harmon examines Augustine's confrontation with the philosophers, especially the Platonists. In both the *Confessions* and *The City of God* we see that Augustine's interest in the question is both experiential and philosophic, requiring a reexamination of his own early commitment to Manicheanism. Both Manicheanism and Porphyrean Platonism were constituted not only by theoretical principles but also by the adoption of a way of life predicated on those principles. Augustine pursues wisdom wherever he might discover it,[7] but the theurgy promoted by the Platonists is incapable of leading everyone to the truth, and, as Harmon notes, Platonism limits access to the human good to the very small group of philosophers. The Christian teaching, especially as seen in the mediation of Christ, is a universal message that addresses the universality of human beings. The universality of that teaching, interestingly, is one of the manifestations of the transpolitical nature of Christianity, and yet at the same time leads Augustine to attach some significance to the role of the political order in human activity. Although the City of God is universal, the earthly city is not, and so there will always be some room for working out the precise relationship between the two orders.

In his chapter, Douglas Kries turns our attention to Augustine's *Confessions* as a source for examining Augustine's political teaching. At of the opening of Plato's *Republic*, the reader is alerted to the problematic aspect of art, especially poetry, in the manner in which it can present an image of disordered souls to the city; for the good of the polity, then, it seems necessary to ban art. Yet we see in the later books of the *Republic* that art makes a return, only now an art that is tutored by philosophy so as to improve the soul of the hearer. Similarly, Kries argues, Augustine in book 1 of the *Confessions* critiques the problematic aspects of art, especially in the works of Terence and Virgil.[8] Yet in imitation of Plato, the latter books of the *Confessions* revivify art by indicating how it can be used to restore a proper understanding of justice. Kries notes that Augustine's knowledge of Plato was likely almost entirely secondhand. Thus he does not attempt to show a line-by-line correspondence between the two authors, but rather that Augustine likely understood the significant consequences of Plato's teaching for politics.[9] Plato and Augustine indicate how art can corrupt the soul, both by displaying bad character and by encouraging or inducing the imitation of such character by the hearer or reader. Such art appeals to the lower parts of the soul, and Kries brings out numerous other striking parallels between the accounts given by the two authors. Augustine's return to the concern of art and its effects in book 9 of the *Confessions* leads him to one of his many considerations of the influence of music, and Kries rightly draws our attention to a similar discussion in Augustine's earlier *De musica*. Finally, Augustine's vision at Ostia, in which he is joined by his mother, Monica, is seen as a parallel of sorts to Socrates' myth of Er and to Cicero's "Dream of Scipio" in the last book of his *De re publica*. Monica, in her attempt to influence her husband (and, one might conclude, their son), is a model of political moderation, in part through her capacity to control the tendency to excessive spiritedness.

St. Augustine has a well-earned reputation as perhaps the leading Western critic of the practice of lying.[10] In his essay, Ryan Balot takes up Augustine's treatment of the question of lying in the opening books of *The City of God*, wherein one finds regular criticism of writers and whole polities that rely on deception as a method of influencing or ruling people. There is a long tradition of writing about and practicing esotericism, the art of concealing the truth behind one's statements, but Augustine's criticism of such concealment is in part a reflection of his recognition of the universal message of Christianity. Augustine sets out to expose the false claims of the pagans in the opening paragraphs of *The City of God*, revealing the deceptive assertions of Roman historical practices and the accompanying theories that perpetuated pagan teaching. Christianity, by contrast, seeks to promote the truth, and its central teachings are available to everyone; these teaching also welcome scrutiny in a way that civil theology does not or cannot, as Augustine points out in his treatment of the discovery of the books of Numa. The unity of the human race, grounded in the recognition that all are made in the image and likeness of God, rejects a fundamental tension between the philosophic elite and the common believer, thus abandoning the necessity of misleading the people through the promotion of falsehoods. By examining Augustine's treatment of figures such as Seneca, Varro, and Balbus, Balot shows Augustine's concern with the false teachings of those who know some teachings are false and yet perpetuate them, either out of their own weakness or out of a sense of the utility of the teaching. Still, as Balot shows, an examination of a variety of Augustine's texts reveals his awareness of the way in which rhetoric can be used to critique some ideas or to present the truth in a particularly useful manner, while at the same time not undermining the commitment to the truth and its ultimate accessibility. Balot concludes his essay by looking at modern theories of concealment, or the rejection of such, and how Augustine's approach would be more useful and more closely attuned to the truth of the human condition.

Veronica Roberts Ogle turns to *The City of God* in order to assess Augustine's own view of one of his most important predecessors, focusing especially on the Ciceronian political teaching he could continue to promote after the advent of Christianity. As Ogle shows, Augustine's writing reveals both an appreciation for Cicero and a meaningful critique of his work. We find in Cicero an encomium to patriotism, a desire to promote engagement with the political order, even or especially among the wise, and Rome's future seems to depend on the willingness of its most prominent citizens to sacrifice for the sake of the public good. The Ciceronian account relies on appeals to an elevated sense of virtue, in particular to the usefulness of praise and blame, glory and pride. Although Augustine has some appreciation for Cicero's promotion of the public good and recognizes the usefulness of civic virtue, in the end he seeks to elevate the concerns of the Christian to a horizon beyond or above the good of the city. By doing so, Ogle argues, Augustine seeks to promote instead an understanding of virtue that transcends the civic good and the accompanying judgment of human beings on that virtue. This reconsideration of the nature of virtue can be seen in

Augustine's recounting in book 5 of the sacrifices made by the Romans for the sake of the city and by contrasting their actions with those of the Christian martyrs, for whom true glory was not bound up with the earthly success of Rome. Ogle thus sees Augustine's argument not as a wholesale rejection of the Ciceronian teaching but as a significant modification of that teaching so as to promote the transpolitical Christian view, in the end a view that would be even more beneficial to the good of the polity Cicero seeks to secure.

In his chapter, Daniel Strand also deals with a topic a number of other essays address, namely religion and the political order, but focuses his attention on the degree to which Roman politics is in fact significantly tied to the religion of the Romans, such that one can hardly disentangle the two concerns. Looking at Roman religion through the lens of sacral politics, Strand shows how Roman religion had a symbiotic relationship with Roman politics; successful religious practice, meaning strict devotion to the determined forms, was understood to result in political success. Strand notes the relative inattention among interpreters to Augustine's serious treatment of Roman religion, including the role that demons play for pagan thinkers, pointing to something of a trivialization of what for Augustine is surely a crucial issue. The Roman perpetuation of its religious practices, perhaps even in the face of an apparent decline in serious attachment to many aspects of its principles, reveals why the rise of Christianity in the fourth century under Constantine and Theodosius was a critical turning point in challenging Roman religion and its politics. Augustine can then work to expose the weaknesses of the Roman political order in large part by exposing the weakness of its religious order; rejecting the pagan religious structure produces the desacralizing effect that must be undertaken to sever the bond between the religious and the political and make way for the new understanding introduced by Christianity. That new teaching, Strand emphasizes, does not amount to a simple rejection of the various elements of Roman religion, but rather, in part, a reinterpretation of some important but misunderstood teachings it propagated. Augustine takes seriously, for example, the question of demons, and attempts to show how a rightful understanding of demons is consistent with, and indeed a central part of, the Christian understanding. But again, that means taking Roman religion seriously, as Strand indicates, and doing so also means taking seriously the Roman politics that was so intimately connected to that religious enterprise.

In the last essay in the volume, Daniel Burns considers the Augustinian response to the Platonic teaching on politics, introduced largely through the early writings of Joseph Ratzinger. Burns indicates the lack of serious attention given in Augustinian scholarship to the work of Ratzinger (a fact pointed out by Ratzinger himself), and sets forth an analysis here of Ratzinger's contributions to understanding the encounter of Augustine with Platonism. That encounter came in the form of a challenge that Christianity presented to the fundamental principles of the political order, with special attention being given to the role the church might play in political analysis. The "two-cities" theme so properly attached to Augustine's work is itself a crucial step in advancing the significance attached to the role of the church in the civil order while seemingly diminishing the importance of the political order more fully. Ratzinger's assessment of the remnants of late antiquity, embodied in Neoplatonism and in forms of civil theology, recognizes the enduring concerns of political philosophy, raising as it does profound questions about the nature of human life and the political order, questions which are not easily dismissed even with the revelation of a religious teaching now grounded in a universal church. Burns points to Ratzinger's attempt to revive serious consideration of Plato's authentic teaching, a teaching that emphasizes the centrality of the concern of justice, or right, and thus the need to return the concerns of political philosophy to a prominent place in Platonic interpretation. Burns's essay concludes with an overview of a number of fertile issues and corresponding Augustinian texts that might more fully flesh out the challenges Ratzinger's work brings to the study of Augustine and to his engagement with classical thought.

The essays in this volume all take as their starting point the serious attention St. Augustine gives to his writing, to his audience, and to the complex religious and political questions raised not just by his own age but also by the confrontation of Christianity with the ancient political, religious, and philosophic order. The challenge of the new order to the old compels Augustine to rethink many of the fundamental principles that animated that older order and to contemplate how Christianity can find its proper role in the new political order. There is no simple answer to that challenge, given the transcendent focus of Christian teaching. In book 5 of *The City of God*, St. Augustine raises a seemingly rhetorical question concerning Christians and the political order: "As far as this mortal life is concerned, which is spent and finished in a few days, what difference does it make under what rule a man lives who is soon to die, provided only that those who rule him do not compel him to do what is impious and wicked?"[11] There is no reason to suspect that St. Augustine does not take the question seriously, compelling the reader to reflect on the relative importance of political orders and influences. A precise answer to the question, though, requires a careful sifting of his argument in this work and in many of his other writings. The essays in the present volume go far in alerting us to the many facets of the work of St. Augustine that would have to be mastered in order to give a full account of the response he himself provides to his important query.

# Notes

1. All but two of the essays in this volume were newly commissioned and have not appeared in print previously.

2. Allan Fitzgerald, OSA, ed., *Augustine Through the Ages: An Encyclopedia* (New York: Eerdman's, 1999).

3. Karla Pollmann and Willemien Otten, eds., *The Oxford Guide to the Historical Reception of Augustine*, 3 vols. (Oxford: Oxford University Press, 2013).

4. Ernest Fortin, "Augustine and the Problem of Human Goodness," in *The Birth of Philosophic Christianity: Studies in Early Christian and Medieval Thought*, ed. Brian Benestad (Lanham, MD: Rowman and Littlefield Publishers, Inc., 1996), 21–39, at 22. This observation is confirmed by Willemien Otten, "The Reception of Augustine in the Early Middle Ages (c. 700–c. 1200)," who notes that Augustine's influence often lay in his simply being cited as an authority by multiple authors, and asserting that "in the early Middle Ages . . . [Augustine] was the era's omnipresent fount of knowledge." *Oxford Guide to the Historical Reception of Augustine*, 1:23–39, at 30.

5. This is not to suggest that there was in fact for Augustine a coherent "Roman" philosophy or theology, only that whatever form it took at any given time was insufficient for forming good moral character.

6. As Fortin notes in the essay cited above, "For more than a thousand years he dominated the intellectual scene, establishing the positions from which others would start and forcing, if not the abandonment, at least a reconsideration of the entire legacy of classical thought." "Augustine and the Problem of Human Goodness," 22.

7. Gerald Phelan notes that after reading Cicero's *Hortensius*, Augustine "was fired with a burning desire to pursue that blessed knowledge. What he yearned for was no mere intellectual insight nor rational explanation of the universe. He sought a truly beautifying wisdom." "Some Illustrations of St. Thomas' Development of the Wisdom of St. Augustine" (Chicago: Argus Press, 1946), 18.

8. One of the underappreciated aspects of Augustine's writing is his use of classical authors such as Terence.

9. In *The City of God*, Augustine does note that Plato made Socrates a speaker in many of his works, indicating that he was aware of dialogues in which Socrates was not a participant (*City of God* 8.4).

10. St. Augustine authored two works on the subject of lying, the early *De mendacio* and the later *Contra mendacium*, and he discusses the problem of lying in numerous other writings.

11. Augustine, *The City of God against the Pagans*, trans. and ed. R. W. Dyson (Cambridge: Cambridge University Press, 1998), 5.17, p. 217.

# Part One

# Politics, Nature, and Virtue

Chapter One

# St. Augustine and the Problem of Political Ethics in *The City of God*

## Richard J. Dougherty

In his *Retractions*, written near the end of his life, St. Augustine recounts the impetus for writing *The City of God*. Augustine relates that he was moved to defend Christianity against its pagan critics, who charged that the abandonment of the worship of the pagan gods by recent Roman emperors was responsible for the fall of Rome in 410.[1] He notes that the work as a whole contains two major parts. The first part constitutes books 1 through 10 and consists primarily of an attack on the Roman pagan religion in its practices and its principles. The second part, books 11 through 22, provides the positive defense of the Christian teaching, largely consisting of an extended account of the foundation and distinction between the two cities, the City of God and the earthly city.[2] The title of the work is often given as *The City of God Against the Pagans*, but that is not Augustine's title, and for good reason; only the first half of the work is aimed at the pagans, while the second half is an extended defense of Christian teaching aimed at strengthening the faith of embattled believers.[3]

St. Augustine's "magnum opus et arduum"[4] is much more than an occasional piece, though. The major concern of this work—the relationship between the City of God and the City of Man—is anticipated in his earlier works, and throughout his works he addresses many of the important concerns of this work.[5] An inventory of the important issues that come to the fore in *The City of God* would include, at least, the Fall and human redemption, the place of Israel in the plan of Divine Providence, pagan heroism in the light of the Christian understanding of virtue, the dangers of civil theology, the authority and persuasiveness of pagan philosophy, and the place of grace and free will in understanding the operations of the human soul. Foremost among the political concerns addressed in this work are the nature of empire, the relative importance of the political order or regime, the founding of political orders, the character of rulers, and the characteristics that bind political communities together.

The thrust of the first ten books of *The City of God* is a critique of pagan teaching and practice, and St. Augustine focuses attention on the limitations of Roman religion, politics, and philosophy. Throughout, Augustine famously challenges the honor accorded various notable Roman heroes, including Romulus and the general Regulus, but perhaps his most notorious criticism is directed at the adulation bestowed on Lucretia, whose suicide precipitated the overthrow of the Roman monarchy and led proximately to the establishment of the Roman Republic.

This essay will focus on one aspect of that account—the tension between the pagan conception of moral life and the Christian understanding Augustine presents by way of contrast. There are many issues which might be addressed in such an analysis, as Augustine treats quite broadly the various elements of pagan life, but we will focus here on the particular question of the Roman view of morality as seen through the treatment of the question of suicide in book 1. The essay will subsequently turn to the contrast between Stoic ethics and the Christian understanding as found in book 14. As we will see, the Stoic teaching was, in part, one of the sources invoked to defend the resort to suicide in the latter period of the Roman Republic.[6]

## Book 1 and the Treatment of Suicide

Augustine commences book 1 with an account of how the attack on Rome in AD 410 differed substantially from the normal course of warfare; instead of the usual practice of engaging in indiscriminate violence, the Goths spared Christians and Christian churches, as well as many pagans who had sought sanctuary in the churches.[7] After some consideration of the universality of the sufferings undergone in this world, affecting the good and bad alike, Augustine embarks on a lengthy treatment of the question of suicide. This discussion can perhaps partially elucidate one aspect of what has been described as a distinctive turn in Augustine's work, the turn away from classical thought. Augustine addresses the suicides of Lucretia, Cato, and Judas, and compares them with the rape of the Christian virgins held in captivity under the Roman Empire.[8] The Christian women, he notes, recognized the fact that true virtue is found in the soul and not in the body, and thus willingly endured the violation of their bodies rather than taking their own lives in a mistaken attempt to escape vice. The body becomes holy by virtue of the holiness of the will, and "while the will remains unshaken and steadfast, nothing that another does with the body, or in the body, that the sufferer has no power to avert without sinning in turn, is the fault of the sufferer."[9] If modesty (or chastity, "pudicitia") is what is being protected, one need not worry about the injustices to which the body may be subjected, since "modesty is a virtue of the soul, and has as its companion a fortitude which resolves to endure any evil rather than consent to evil."[10]

This understanding of chastity, for Augustine, suffices to show that the Christian virgins had no cause to commit suicide and thus would not do so, for their chastity remained inviolate. But that compels one to raise the question of whether a defense could be made in contrast of the suicides of Lucretia, Cato, and Judas.[11] In Augustine's account, Judas simply compounded one crime with another by killing himself, leaving himself chargeable not only with the death of Christ but with his own as well.[12] Cato's suicide is perhaps more defensible as a courageous and noble act in defiance of Caesarian imperialism, but he proved he was not true to his Stoic principles by recommending that his own son cast himself on the mercy of Caesar.[13] More important, when contrasted with the earlier Roman model of Regulus or Torquatus, Cato's actions appear relatively inconsiderable, even if he was frequently praised by Roman authors for his fortitude.[14]

It is the suicide of Lucretia, though, that seems most to capture Augustine's attention.[15] Without doubt she was among the most honored of Romans and considered by many to be the true founder of the Roman republic;[16] but, Augustine asks, what motive could she have had for committing suicide after her violation at the hands of Tarquin? He describes her predicament in striking, indeed deliberately provocative fashion: "For if she is acquitted of murder, she is convicted of adultery, and if she is acquitted of adultery, then she is convicted of murder. . . . One can only ask: If she was an adulteress, why is she praised? If she was pure, why was she slain?"[17] Augustine's interpretation of the death of Lucretia uses the same touchstone as his discussion of the Christian women—the state of her soul after Tarquin violates her. Augustine concludes that Lucretia killed herself because of the outrage carried out against her will; her act against herself was prompted "not from love of modesty, but because of a weakness arising from shame." It was this shame ("pudoris") that drove her to suicide, and her Roman love of praise could not bear the potential of lifelong suspicions about her actions: "Hence, she judged that she must use self-punishment to exhibit the state of her mind to the eyes of men to whom she could not show her conscience."[18] Augustine imputes the Lucretian dilemma not to her alone but to the flawed Roman conception of honor and guilt.[19] Lucretia in this understanding is a parallel to Regulus,[20] the Roman general who had lost his life to the Carthaginians as a result of maintaining his oath to the Roman gods. The Regulus example illuminates the central claim of Augustine in the first five books of *The City of God*—that fidelity to the Roman gods did not provide success in this life.[21]

Yet, one might consider whether this is the only way to judge Lucretia's actions; by considering what the condition of her own will was at that moment. Augustine himself refers to her as "that noble matron of ancient Rome" and she indeed was understood by many to be the crucial figure behind the foundation of the republic.[22] Her suicide, from a different perspective, could perhaps be understood to be a public act, instead of the private act that Augustine makes of it. If Lucretia was most concerned about the future of Rome or the honor of her family, rather than about her own fate or self-honor, it seems not implausible to surmise that her suicide could have been motivated by these factors rather than by her own sense of shame. That is, could not Lucretia's suicide be interpreted as a deliberate act aimed at bringing about the overthrow of Tarquin and the establishment of a republic in Rome? Could it not be that she foresaw the consequences of her action and surrendered her life for the good of Rome, as well as the certain honor it would bring to her family?

There seems to be no place in Augustine's discussion here for the possibility of a justifiable suicide for the public good. Lucretia has earned the honor and praise of all Roman republicans for her heroic role in the overthrow and exile of the tyrannous Tarquin. In Augustine's terms, though, even that great good is no justification for a suicide.[23] His consideration of Lucretia's suicide reveals a turning away from analyzing the public or political results of those acts.[24] The individual soul, rather than the practical or political outcome of the actions taken, is the fundamental locus of concern for Augustine.[25]

Augustine concludes his remarks on suicide by seeking to clarify two points that may be troublesome. First, he argues that the Christian can never commit an evil in order to bring about a good.[26] This clarification may be the response to the seeming political "good" that followed the suicide of Lucretia—even that seemingly good result, the overthrow of the tyranny, does not justify the evil act.[27] Second, Augustine attempts to make clear that particular cases or examples of the actions of holy men and women are not to be followed, such as the apparently deliberate self-imposed drownings of the holy women who threw themselves into a river.[28] Also, others, such as the biblical figure of Samson[29] (and perhaps Abraham[30] and Jephthah[31]), were prompted to their acts by divine wisdom; "he, therefore, who knows that it is unlawful to kill himself, may nonetheless do so if commanded by Him Whose commands it is not lawful to despise."[32] Without that divine sanction, no one can justifiably engage in the act of suicide.[33]

Even with these more complicated cases, though, Augustine avers that some things are certain, including the following teachings:

> (That) no man ought voluntarily to inflict death upon himself, for this is to flee from temporal ills by falling into eternal ones. No one ought to do this because of the sins of another, lest, by doing so, he who would not have been defiled by another's sin incur the gravest guilt of his own. Again, no one ought to do so because of his own past sins, for he has all the more need of this life so that these sins may be healed by repentance. Finally, no one ought to do so out of a desire for the better life which is hoped for after death, for that better life which comes after death does not receive those who are guilty of their own death.[34]

Augustine's four examples successively refer to the suicides of Cato, Lucretia, Judas, and Theombrotus, all of which he has addressed already, and each of whom is blameworthy for extinguishing his or her own life.[35]

The critical rhetorical element of Augustine's argument here seems to offer a degree of solace to the Christian women he begins the analysis with, in chapter 15 of book 1; he praises the women for their steadfastness in the face of extreme suffering and violation of their bodies.[36] His critique of Lucretia, by contrast, appears not so much as a criticism of her different judgment and actions, but rather as a commentary on the character of the Roman customs (including customs of thought) that maintained and perpetuated, indeed glorified, the problematic choice for suicide.[37] The broader context, though, is the extended account in book 1 that explains the universal sufferings visited on human beings in this life and that defends the goodness of creation and even of human possessions, against the exaggerated rejection of material goods by the Manicheans.

## The Controversy over Suicide

The issues at stake in Augustine's treatment of suicide are twofold; the normative question concerning the moral status of suicide and a prudential question concerning the public good that may arise from a particular action such as Lucretia's suicide. To address the latter point first, we might turn to the analysis of the decline of the Roman Republic that Montesquieu provides in his *Considerations on the Causes of the Greatness of the Romans and Their Decline*. In his discussion of the latter years of the Republic, Montesquieu makes two comments that explicitly touch upon the concerns Augustine raises here. The first addresses the reasons that a plethora of suicides seemed to occur at the end of the Republic, including those of Cato, Brutus, and Cassius; as Montesquieu notes:

> Several reasons can be given for this practice of committing suicide that was so common among the Romans: the advances of the Stoic sect, which encouraged it; the establishment of triumphs and slavery, which made many great men think they must not survive a defeat; the advantage those accused of some crime gained by bringing death upon themselves, rather than submitting to a judgment whereby their memory would be tarnished and their property confiscated; a kind of point of honor . . .; finally, a great opportunity for heroism, each man putting an end to the part he played in the world wherever he wished.[38]

Montesquieu provides explanations both theoretical and practical for the rise of suicides, though in this account he reduces almost all of the justifications to personal or private concerns, not the political consequences of the act. He has already addressed this very question in a previous passage in the same chapter of this work, where he contrasts the characters of Cato and Cicero:

> I believe that if Cato had preserved himself for the republic, he would have given a completely different turn to events. Cicero's talents admirably suited him for a

secondary role, but he was not fit for the main one. His genius was superb, but his soul was often common. With Cicero, virtue was the accessory, with Cato, glory. Cicero always thought of himself first, Cato always forgot about himself. The latter wanted to save the republic for its own sake, the former in order to boast of it.[39]

Montesquieu at least reveals here that there might very well be instances in which the ready availability—indeed, the promotion—of suicide could have serious negative consequences for the body politic.[40] One might argue that even if the choice for suicide was animated by political calculation, it is impossible to foresee with any degree of precision what the political consequences of such an act might be.

But for Augustine the former issue—the normative question of the morality of suicide—is a matter of much greater import and of some considerable contestation, including in contemporary political and social debates. Discounting the relative insignificance of the analysis of the prudential fallout of suicide for, say, the Roman Republic, Augustine's primary focus is on the question of the moral justification for this act. The tension between the apparent Roman approbation given to suicide—at least in certain circumstances—and the Christian view propounded by Augustine is palpable, grounded as is on the explicit teaching of the church and also, as Augustine presents it, on reason; we will return to this issue subsequently. And Augustine is not the first Christian author to forward an argument against suicide, as one finds earlier manifestations of the religious claim.[41]

The question of suicide also raises the issue of the binding character on non-Christians of the Christian teaching on suicide and other matters. That is, if suicide is judged blameworthy only because of the Christian prohibition against it, one might consider the degree to which nonbelievers within a political order might legitimately be called on to adopt a presumption against suicide. This question could of course be extended to a consideration of all of the strictures of the Christian teaching in ethics and politics: if one is a non-Christian, can or should one be bound by the laws of a ruler that are passed in accordance with specifically or uniquely Christian revelation? If a regime is based on certain fundamental revealed beliefs, can it sustain itself when there might be those within its borders who are at odds with such beliefs, and who may very well work to undermine the regime? Augustine does not explicitly confront these questions here, for they are not his immediate concern, but they will arise soon historically as Christianity becomes more of a political force.

In a provocative essay on the nature of the Christian moral teaching, Sigrid Undset, in her "Letter to a Parish Priest" remarks that "it is only on the basis of the whole and uncurtailed doctrine of the Christian Church that suicide becomes absolutely iniquitous."[42] Only by accepting the dogmas of the Catholic Church, Undset argues, can one understand why suicide must be a sin. But what if one is not a Christian, she asks? Does suicide become "formal sin" only when the individual *knows* that it is wrong?

The classical statue of a Gallic warrior who has killed his wife and still supports her body with one hand while the other aims the dagger at his breast, is expressive of hero-ism. . . . The point is that the Gaul acts rightly according to his own principles in killing his wife and himself in order to escape slavery. He has never seen a crucifix and does not know what is meant by God ruling from the Tree.[43]

Undset does attempt to find some solace for the relatives of the suicide, based on the hope that the deceased stood outside the church, through no fault of his own; thus the sins he committed were "committed in good faith, in his own eyes they were right and defensible acts."[44] But Augustine does not share Undset's conclusion on this point.[45]

St. Augustine's argument against the moral legitimacy of suicide does certainly rely heavily on the Christian understanding of the soul and the biblical teaching on the preservation of life, including Old Testament injunctions against murder.[46] But scripture is not the sole source of his grounds for criticizing the suicides he treats in book 1 of *The City of God*. For example, he suggests that Plato himself would not have countenanced the suicides in imitation of Socrates' death and could have corrected Theombrotus's misreading of Plato, which led him to com-mit suicide as a way of escaping the confines of the body.[47] In the account of Theombrotus noted above, in book 1, chapter 22, Augustine says that Plato could have told Theombrotus that in committing suicide to arrive more quickly at a better life, "he acted greatly rather than well ("magne potius factum esse quam bene").[48] For Plato, of all people, surely would have been the first to act in the same way had he not, with that mind with which he had seen the soul's immor-tality, also perceived that this should not be done: and should, indeed, be forbid-den."[49] Just as important, Theombrotus might have noted that Plato did not in fact follow this track himself.[50]

In addition to Plato, Augustine cites Virgil as an authority in passing judgment on those who might take the path of suicide, asserting that Lucretia would be con-demned by the "judges of the infernal regions of whom your [Roman] poets sing": "For she is plainly numbered among those who, 'though innocent, laid deadly hands upon themselves, hating the light, and threw away their souls.'"[51] And for these souls, Virgil relates, though they long to escape their condition in the underworld, "fate bars the way."[52] Augustine certainly understands the authority Virgil represents for the Romans, citing him from the very first page of *The City of God* (though, one should note, rewriting him), thus providing here as elsewhere a not so subtle rebuke to the Roman praise for Lucretia on their own terms.[53]

In an earlier work, *On Christian Doctrine*, St. Augustine considers the question of suicide only tangentially, but there his opposition to the practice is grounded not in revelation but in an observation about human nature: "Thus no one hates himself. And, indeed, this principle was never questioned by any sect. Neither does anyone hate his body, and what the Apostle says concerning this is true: 'No man ever hated his own flesh.' And that some say, that they would rather be without a body, arises from a complete delusion: they hate not their bodies, but the corruption and solidity of their bodies."[54] One would suspect that Augustine here has in mind particularly cases such as Theombrotus; the choices people might make in seeking out suicide he attributes to a fundamental misconception they have about nature and the human good.[55]

Indeed, a common Christian conception of the underlying principles of moral action concurs with Augustine's understanding of their continuity with nature and with the Old Testament as well as the New Testament. St. Thomas Aquinas, for example, argues that the moral precepts of the Decalogue are compatible with the natural law: "It is therefore evident that since the moral precepts are about matters which concern good morals; and since good morals are those which are in accord with reason; and since also every judgment of human reason must needs be derived in some way from natural reason; it follows, of necessity, that all the moral precepts belong to the law of nature."[56] Many more recent writers follow this logic: Josef Fuchs, in his *Natural Law: A Theological Investigation*, argues that the scriptural demands are not at odds with the norms available to human reasoning: "The Law of the Old Testament does not simply establish good and evil. It instructed the Jews on what was antecedently good and evil."[57] In a similar fashion, C. S. Lewis describes the relationship between Christian moral teaching and Old Testament and pagan ethics as largely a continuum, not as fundamentally incompatible:

> The idea that Christianity . . . brought a new ethical code into the world is a grave error. If it had done so, then we would have to conclude that all who first preached it profoundly misunderstood their own message: for all of them, its Founder, His precursor, His apostles, came demanding repentance and offering forgiveness, a demand and an offer both meaningless except on the assumption of a moral law already known and already broken. . . . Essentially, Christianity is not the promulgation of a moral discovery.[58]

This account seems to mesh well with that of Aquinas, who cites Augustine in his own treatment of suicide. Aquinas also relies on arguments from nature and reason, along with an appeal to scriptural support. In the *Summa Theologiae*, St. Thomas provides three arguments against suicide. First, he notes that all things by nature seek to preserve themselves. Second, he argues that every part belongs to the whole, and hence every man in a sense belongs to the community. Last, he asserts that only God has power over life and death, and so one who dies by suicide is a usurper of divine authority.[59]

Unlike St. Thomas, Augustine did not have access to Aristotle's moral and political writings, but Aquinas does cite Aristotle in his critique of suicide. In the discussion of the virtue of courage in book 3 of the *Nicomachean Ethics*, Aristotle notes that courageous acts are undertaken because they are noble acts, but not all suffering is undergone for noble reasons: "But dying in order to flee poverty, erotic love, or something painful is not the mark of a courageous man but rather of a coward. For it is softness to flee suffering, and such a person endures death not because it is noble to do so but in order to avoid a bad thing."[60] Here one finds an echo of what Augustine refers to in the passage cited above from book 1 of *The City of God*, where he argues that one cannot undertake an evil deed in order to bring about a good one. Similarly, in book 3 of the *Politics*, Aristotle restates a point he asserted at the outset of this work, that man is by nature a political animal, and that people have a natural desire to live together: "For there is perhaps something fine in living just by itself, provided there is no great excess of hardships. It is clear that most men will endure much harsh treatment in their longings for life, the assumption being that there is a kind of joy inherent in it and a natural sweetness."[61] The idea that there is a "natural sweetness" in human inter-action that would prompt one to seek social bonding and the preservation of one's life is a common refrain in Augustine,[62] and a principle shared by Aristotle[63] and Cicero,[64] among many others.

## Stoic versus Christian Teaching on the Passions

This early treatment of pagan ethics by St. Augustine is not his last word on the subject in *The City of God*. In books 6 through 7, for example, he addresses the dangers of "civil theology," and in books 8 through 10 he critiques the teaching of the Platonist philosophers, responding in both sections to the claim that the pagan gods should be worshiped for the sake of pressing the advantage of the soul in the next life. In the subsequent passages of the work, to which we now turn, St. Augustine examines the connection between pagan teaching and moral action.

In books 11 through 14 of *The City of God*, St. Augustine returns to an extended analysis of pagan ethics, in the context of the coming-to-be of the city of God and the causes and consequences of the Fall. This discussion leads him to consider in book 14 the contrasts between and among the different conceptions of the emo-tions as found in Greek philosophy, Cicero, the Stoics, and Christianity.[65] The affections of the soul, or the emotions, which the Greeks call *eupatheiai* and Cicero calls *constantiae*, are limited by the Stoics to three. In place of desire, the Stoics substitute will; in place of joy, contentment; and in place of fear, caution. They deny that there is sickness or pain (or, as Augustine prefers, "sorrow," for sick-ness and pain usually refer to bodily suffering); these cannot exist in the mind of the wise man since they are connected with evil.[66] Only the wise man "wills, is contented, uses caution," whereas others desire, rejoice, fear, and are sad. Cicero calls these first three affections *constantiae* and the last four *perturbationes*, though many call the last four "passions"; the Greeks call the former *eupatheiai*, the latter *pathe*.[67]

Christianity marks a radical break from this understanding, though, in St. Augustine's view. Contrary to the Stoic presentation of the wise man who escapes desire and sorrow, in the Christian teaching:

> [G]ood and evil men alike feel desire, fear, and joy. But the good feel these emotions in a good way, and the bad feel them in a bad way, just as the will of men may be righteous or perverse.[68] Also, although the Stoics find nothing in the mind of the wise man corresponding to grief, we discover that even this is used in a good sense, and especially in our own Scriptures.[69]

All men, in this view, share in the emotions or affections of the soul, including those who are admired above all others, the citizens of the holy city of God:

> Such citizens feel fear and desire, pain and gladness, but in a manner consistent with the Holy Scriptures and wholesome doctrine; and because their love is righteous, all these emotions are righteous in them.[70] They fear eternal pain and desire eternal life. They feel pain at the present time, because they are still groaning within themselves. . . . They rejoice in hope. . . . Again, they fear to sin, and they desire to persevere. They feel pain for their sins, and gladness in their good works.[71]

These affections or emotions will not be suffered eternally, but instead "belong to this life."[72] We often yield to these affections against our own will, but overcoming them with complete finality, becoming free from the emotions—which are "contrary to reason and which disturb the mind"—that is, to achieve the state that the Greeks call *apatheia*, is desirable but is not possible in this life.[73] True or complete *apatheia* would consist in the establishment of a condition in which there is no sinfulness, but this is not possible here and now: "At the present time, we live well enough if we live without blame. But if anyone supposes that his life is without sin, he does not avoid sin, but rather forfeits pardon."[74] The blessed will continue to experience love and joy in the life to come, but they will no longer experience fear and grief along with them.[75]

Undoubtedly in this life some people will attempt to restrain and temper their passions, but because of their "ungodly pride" their corruption is greater to the extent that their pain is less.[76] "Some of these, with a vanity as monstrous as it is rare, are so entranced by their own self-restraint that they are not stirred or excited or swayed or influenced by any emotions at all. But these rather suffer an entire loss of their humanity than achieve a true tranquility. For a thing is not right merely because it is harsh, nor is stolidity the same thing as health."[77] Augustine makes much the same point in regard to the proper use of virtues such as continence, which is a true virtue only if it is practiced for the proper reasons, with the proper end in mind: "For continence is not a good thing, except when it is practiced in the faith of the highest good, that is, God."[78] Otherwise virtuous actions or habits not directed to the end of true virtue, such as the possession of political power, one might say, are more problematic for the capacity they give the possessor.[79] As Charles McCoy puts it, "Desiring the virtues for their own account and not referring them to God is not 'honest morality' because the mean of virtue is taken according to various circumstances."[80]

The significance of Augustine's rejection of the ethics of Stoicism lies in part in his emphatic denial that true happiness can be achieved in this life. The Stoic wise man is a figment, and Augustine had argued earlier[81] that in reality the Stoics agree with the Platonists and the Peripatetics that the wise man is in fact subject to the perturbations of the soul, but that he is capable of mastering them through the exercise of moderation and reason. Augustine uses the example of Aulus Gellius, who, on a voyage with a Stoic philosopher, became terrified at the possibility of the ship's capsizing. Augustine then reports what Gellius says he read in a book by Epictetus: "[T]hat the soul experiences certain mental images, which [the Stoics] call *phantasiae* ["phantasias"], and that it is not in our power of the soul to determine whether and when these shall strike the soul."[82] These impressions affect the wise and the unwise, the difference between the two consisting in the fact that the wise are able to use their reason to bring their passions under control, whereas the fool cannot do so.[83] As he puts it in his commentary on the Gospel of St. John: "Away with the reasons of philosophers, who assert that a wise man is not affected by mental perturbations. God has made foolish the wisdom of this world;[84] and the Lord knows the thoughts of men, that they are vain."[85]

Augustine thus draws the conclusion that there is a common foundation for the Stoic, Platonic, and Peripatetic teachings, all of which hold that the wise man does not suffer perturbations that prevail over his reason, but that the weaker parts of the soul are in fact assailed by such perturbations. This enduring presence of the perturbations of the soul leads Augustine to conclude that there is no complete happiness in this life but that the undisturbed blessed life of the soul can be achieved only in the next life, through citizenship in the City of God.[86] That happiness is a true and complete happiness, unlike the Stoic vision; as G. E. Evans has described it, "The Stoic is a happy man in a cage, a man who dare not look up, in case he sees a possibility of happiness beyond his present imagining."[87] Only in the heavenly city can the soul be free of the passions and emotions that it is subject to and that threaten to bring it harm—perhaps the ancient maxim that one cannot be called happy until he has reached his death has some salience.[88]

The story Aulus Gellius tells about the Stoic on shipboard is all the more powerful in this context when contrasted with the account in scripture of Christ calming the seas. Christ was with the disciples at sea, already asleep, when the storm struck. But St. Matthew relates that the disciples had to awaken Jesus, who, unlike the Stoic, was not disturbed by the arrival of the storm.[89] The disciples, on the other hand, understandably experienced anxiety about their situation. By contrast, the Stoics "esteem truth to be vanity, regard also insensibility as soundness," not realizing "that a man's mind, like the limbs of his body, is only the more hopelessly diseased when it has lost even the feeling of pain."[90]

## Conclusion

St. Augustine's concern with the problem of suicide, which he dwells on at some length in the opening book of *The City of God*, does address the problematic Roman accommodation and even support for this practice, but his nuanced treatment of the issue also assists in clarifying the Christian perspective on suicide. Augustine is clearly concerned not only with Lucretia and the Roman moral and philosophical position but also with how Christian believers should assess the actions of their predecessors who had seemingly surrendered their lives for the faith, or indeed seem to have more actively precipitated their deaths.[91] Consideration of the actions of the martyrs was perhaps part of the driving force for examining biblical precedents in this regard, including the discussion of Samson treated above.[92] In addition, part of the significant thrust of book 1 constitutes a defense of the good of this life, including the goods of life and property. In a sermon on Saints Perpetua and Felicitas, Augustine underscores the natural attachment of the human soul to life: "So great is the strange charm of this life, which is yet so full of wretchedness, and so strong the natural horror of death in all the living, that even those who, through death, go to that life where one can never die, do not want to die."[93] That natural desire to preserve one's life extends, he notes here and elsewhere, even to those who find themselves in undesirable straits.[94]

In book 2 of *The City of God*, where St. Augustine introduces the role of the philosophers in the context of his critique of the Roman religious teachings and practices prior to the rise of Christianity, he raises an objection to his own claims. It may be true that the Roman religion encouraged or required licentious behavior, he notes, but perhaps the Romans could at least point to their philosophers as having sought to promote moral living. Yet Augustine asserts that just as the pagan religion never attempted to introduce true holiness into the lives of the Romans,[95] neither were the philosophers efficacious in their ethical teachings. This latter situation is partially accounted for by the fact that the philosophers were Greek rather than Roman, yet even as the Greek thinkers came to influence the Romans, their teachings lacked authority, because they were "still not the precepts of the gods, but the inventions of men."[96]

The philosophers were in fact moderately successful in their pursuit of the truth and were able to exercise their rational powers in an attempt to discover what is hidden in nature, "what should be desired and shunned in the sphere of morals, and what, in the field of logic, is entailed by strict deduction and what does and does not follow from given premises."[97] Some of the philosophers were able to discover important truths, but their understanding was hindered—and thus their pride restrained—by their human frailties.[98] Even so, the truths that the philosophers unearthed that could possibly serve as precepts for the moral formation of the Romans were still not acknowledged by the people, for they were not promulgated or sanctioned by the gods.[99] The philosophers' lack of authority points, in

Augustine's presentation, to the inefficacy of purely human efforts and the relative inadequacies of human efforts in persuading others to follow principles of moral action. One cannot rely solely on the pronouncements of thoughtful writers and eloquent speakers if one is to convince people of their moral duties; one must also often be able to make an appeal to the divine in order to indicate the seriousness of the matter, and to make known the rewards and punishments that await those who defy public law.[100] This principle seems to underlie much of what Augustine presents of the moral order and suggests the dependence of the human mind on God and the necessity of properly ordering one's will in order to more fully comprehend and be receptive to the divine order.[101]

As Charles McCoy has described Augustine's approach, "[I]f the political philosophy of Plato and Aristotle had taught that there is a dimension of life beyond the political, which sets limits to political authority, this philosophy had gone much beyond classical Greek and Roman practice."[102] St. Augustine goes beyond the classical view not by fully rejecting it but by embracing the principles it shares with such practices and by providing a broader foundation for both those principles and practices.[103]

Augustine highlights many of the deeds of the Romans who sacrificed much, including their lives, for the good of Rome, in large part as a way of encouraging Christians to endure whatever troubles they may encounter for the sake of eternal life. But he stops short of praising the Roman suicides, instead critiquing the injustice of the act and the base effect it might have on others—including Christians. To be sure, it is not the death of the suicides that is problematic, nor their willingness to suffer death, but their manner of effecting that death. After all, the Christian martyrs also die, undergoing suffering for the sake of something greater than mere life; what, then, separates the two? Answering that question provides a further connection between the treatment of the teaching of the philosophers and the opening account of suicide in book 1.

In his extended treatment of the Platonist philosophers in books 8 through 10, Augustine notes that the internal inconsistencies of their teaching would be resolved by embracing the Christian teaching. Porphyry refused to take this step, even though he understood that no other system had yet been discovered through which the soul could be delivered. Part of the reason for his refusal to accept Christianity, Augustine opines, was that at the time he wrote Christianity was still being persecuted, and he concluded that it probably would not survive.[104] But Porphyry was misled by these persecutions, for rather than being a danger to the survival of Christianity, the persecutions "served only to establish it more firmly and commend it more strongly."[105] The piety of believers is the only way to combat the workings of the demons. Indeed, the power of demons is not merely harmless to true believers but can even be a source of strength for the Church, in that it produces martyrs as citizens of the City of God. Piety establishes martyrs as illustrious in the eyes of the church and is the obstacle to the temptations of the devil. The martyrs, in turn, serve the purpose of providing examples for other believers and can be of greater inspiration than the angels themselves, for they have engaged in the human struggle for virtue and holiness in a way that angels cannot.[106] The martyrs provided the faithful with tangible evidence of the connections between God and man in a way that no angel could; they provide, that is, another, and more accessible, mediation between God and man.[107] Through their greater attachment to a profounder good, the Christian martyrs have now taken the place of the Roman "heroes" of the first five books of the work.[108]

In Augustine's account, the martyrs do not undertake suffering for their own glory or for the good of the political order, but to give glory to God.[109] Thus they were not seeking death in the manner of the Roman suicides, even if death found them; if they could avoid death and glorify God, that would in itself be acceptable.[110] Augustine also notes that the goal of the Christian martyrs was not to effect change or reform in the political order.

> [J]ust as our martyrs, when the Christian religion, by which they knew they were made safe and most glorious for all eternity, was charged to them as a crime, did not choose to evade temporal punishment by denying it. Rather, by confessing, embracing and proclaiming it, and for its sake enduring all things with faith and fortitude, and by dying with godly assurance, they shamed the laws by which it was forbidden, and caused them to be changed.[111]

Augustine distinguishes the deaths of other figures among the Romans and among his contemporary Donatists from those of these Christians by the fact that the martyrs die for the love of God and build up the church that they serve.[112] By contrast, in book 5 Augustine notes the remarkable efforts of the Romans to promote the interest of worldly imperialism:

> The Decii devoted themselves to death, consecrating themselves after a certain fashion and by means of certain words, in order that, when they fell and appeased the anger of the gods with their blood, the Roman army should by this means be delivered. But if the Romans could do this, then by no means should the holy martyrs be proud, as though of something worthy of a share in that fatherland where happiness is eternal and true, if, even to the shedding of their blood, loving not only the brethren for whom it was shed, but also the enemies by whom it was shed, as they were commanded, they have striven to surpass one another in the faith of love and the love of faith.[113]

Considerations of the Roman heroes' sacrificing for the public good brings us back finally to the opening discussion in *The City of God* and St. Augustine's account of the distinction between the pagan qualities that brought Rome tremendous earthly success and the pursuit of Christian virtue, which looked to an eternal reward. The Roman patriots pursued an earthly good, and their self-sacrifice secured that earthly success for Rome. Precisely for that reason, even Marcus Regulus, who appears as perhaps the apex of *exempla* for Christians among the early Romans, is at best a limited model, given his attachment to the pagan gods.[114] In any case, as St. Augustine notes in his assessment of suicide in book 1 "sound reason is certainly to be preferred to examples."[115] And we are not forced to choose between the two, though, because "in this case, the examples are in harmony with reason, and the more excellent in godliness they are, the more worthy are they of emulation."[116] In what amounts to an important addition to the Regulus story, we discover in book 3 that this same Regulus, an "entirely great man," could have brought the First Punic War to an end "had not his great avidity for praise and glory induced him to impose upon the weary Carthaginians conditions harsher than they could bear."[117] Even the best of the Romans could not escape embracing the Roman love of praise, being overcome by the dominant Roman characteristic of the *libido dominandi*.[118] Regulus thus reveals the failure of the Roman gods to protect their most faithful worshipers and the failure of pagan virtue to promote sound politics in the Republic.

# Notes

1. Augustine, *The Retractions*, trans. Sr. M. Inez Bogan, RSM (Washington, DC: Catholic University of America Press, 1968), 2.69.1–2, pp. 209–11.

2. The fact that the whole second half of the work is devoted to a positive articulation of the Christian teaching indicates that understanding the work as being written "against the pagans" limits the scope of the author's intention.

3. On the title of this work, see Gerard O'Daly, *Augustine's "City of God": A Reader's Guide* (Oxford University Press, 1999), 273–74. O'Daly notes that in the *Retractions*, Augustine refers to the work three times as *De civitate dei*.

4. In the preface to book 1, Augustine uses this phrase himself to describe the work ("magnum opus et arduum, sed Deus auditor noster est").

5. For example, one finds discussions of the distinction between the two cities in Augustine's *De catechizandis rudibus* (19.31) and *De genesi ad litteram* (11.15.20).

6. See two essays by Miriam Griffin, "Philosophy, Cato, and Roman Suicide: I," *Greece & Rome* 33 (1986): 64–77; and "Philosophy, Cato, and Roman Suicide: II," *Greece & Rome* 33 (1986): 192–201.

7. *De Civitate Dei* (*The City of God Against the Pagans*), ed. R. W. Dyson (Cambridge: Cambridge University Press, 1998), book 1, ch. 1–7 (hereafter *DCD*). All quotations from the text are taken from Dyson, with some alterations in the translation. The Latin text used is *De ciuitate dei Libri I–X* and *De ciuitate dei Libri XI–XXII*, ed. Bernardus Dombart and Alphonsus Kalb, Corpus Christianorum Series Latina, vols. 47, 48 (Turnhout: Brepols Publishers, 1955).

8. *DCD* 1.26, 16.

9. *DCD* 1.16, 26. See *On Free Choice of the Will* 1.5.38: "As to chastity, who indeed would doubt that it is fixed in the spirit itself, since it is a virtue? Hence, not even chastity can be taken away by a violent assailant," trans. Anna S. Benjamin and L. H. Hackstaff (Indianapolis: Bobbs-Merrill, 1964), 12.

10. *DCD* 1.18, 27: "Sed cum pudicitia virtus sit animi comitemque habeat fortitudinem, qua potius quaelibet mala tolerare quam malo consentire decernit."

11. Augustine's treatment of these suicides is significantly different from the one found in Dante's *Commedia*; see, for example, Leah Schwebel, "The Pagan Suicides: Augustine and *Inferno* 13," *Medium Aevum* 87 (2018): 106–32.

12. *DCD* 1.17, 27, and *DCD* 1.23.

13. *DCD* 1.23, and *DCD* 19.4; Mary Louise Carlson notes a tradition of Christian writers, including Lactantius, who are critical of Cato's suicide: "Pagan Examples of Fortitude in the Latin Christian Apologists," *Classical Philology* 43 (1948): 93–104, at 101. For a treatment of the Stoic teaching on suicide, see J. M. Rist, *Stoic Philosophy* (Cambridge: Cambridge University Press, 1965), 233–55.

14. See Carlson, "Pagan Examples," 100–101.

15. On the multiple interpretations and uses of the Lucretia story, see, e.g., Eleanor Glendinning, "Reinventing Lucretia: Rape, Suicide and Redemption from Classical Antiquity to the Medieval Era," *International Journal of the Classical Tradition*, 20 (2013): 61–82; Glendinning includes an overview of the various early Christian interpretations of Lucretia (68–73).

16. See, for example, Plutarch's account of the Lucretia story in his "Life of Poplicola"; he notes also the important role played by Junius Brutus in the overthrow of Tarquin.

17. *DCD* 1.19, 30–1 ("nec omnino invenitur exitus, ubi dicitur: 'Si adulterata, cur laudata; si pudica, cur occisa'?").

18. *DCD* 1.19, 31: Shakespeare's "The Rape of Lucrece" provides a poetic reconstruction of the motives of Lucretia. On the significance of the role of the conscience, see Ernest L. Fortin, "The Political Implications of St. Augustine's Theory of Conscience," *Augustinian Studies* I (1970), 133–153 (reprinted in *Classical Christianity and the Political Order*, ed. Brian Benestad, Lanham, Maryland: Rowman & Littlefield Publishers, Inc., 1996, 65–84).

19. Augustine repeatedly emphasizes the proper understanding of conscience and moral action as a fundamental point of distinction between the two cities; see, for example, book 14.28.

20. The Regulus story is told in book 1.15, and his heroism is noted again in 2.23 and 5.18; his fidelity is noted in 3.20, but he is criticized in 3.18, as discussed below in the conclusion.

21. As Gerard O'Daly notes, if Regulus is understood as acting for an eternal reward he can be more of an *exempla* for Christians (*Augustine's "City of God,"* 78–79). O'Daly does suggest that the Regulus story may have been an invention (79n10).

22. *DCD* 1.19 ("matronem nobilem veteremque Romanam"). For Livy's account of Lucretia, see *Early History of Rome* 1.57–59; Livy has Lucretia assert her innocence (Livy 1.58: "Quo terrore cum vicisset obstinatam pudicitiam velut vi victrix libido"). Two prominent suicides bookend the Republic—Lucretia's, for the sake of honor, establishes the Republic, whereas Cato's, for his philosophic principles, illustrates in a way the decline of the Republic.

23. Louis J. Swift puts it in the following terms: "For Lucretia the knowledge of her own innocence did not suffice; her good conscience had to be confirmed by public approval. Her own individual 'gloria' was the sole matter of concern and was unrelated to a larger purpose" (517). Swift also considers the tenor of the discussion here: "The gingerly manner in which he treats Lucretia's personal responsibility in the affair with Tarquin indicates that Augustine knew what a strong current he was bucking. Not only history but the whole rhetorical tradition was against him." Swift, "Pagan and Christian Heroes in Augustine's *City of God*," *Augustinianum* 27 (1987), 509–22, at 516n28.

24. As Fr. James Schall puts it, "Augustine's desire for the Eternal City often inclined him, however accurate his descriptions of the Earthly City were, to a kind of indifference to civil society, or at least a realism that did not promise what it could not deliver." *Reason, Revelation, and the Foundations of Political Philosophy* (Baton Rouge: Louisiana State University Press, 1987), 80.

25. This point is especially clear in the discussion in books 11–14 of *The City of God*, with its extended analysis of the role of the will in human action.

26. *DCD* 1.25, 38; Augustine is here likely following Romans, ch. 3: "For if the truth of God hath more abounded through my lie, unto his glory, why am I also yet judged as a sinner? And not rather (as we are slandered, and as some affirm that we say) let us do evil, that there may come good? whose damnation is just. What then? Do we excel them? No, not so" (Rom. 3:7–9).

27. In a provocative essay on Shakespeare's treatment, Harry V. Jaffa argues, "Professor Platt [in his *Rome and Romans According to Shakespeare*] has observed that, had Lucrece been a Christian, she would have decided the choice offered her by Tarquin differently. She would have preferred to keep her chastity intact in the eyes of God, rather than her reputation before men. Moreover, she would have been forbidden by God to take her own life. . . . Lucrece's suicide, defines the spirit of Roman matriotism—which is the foundation of Roman patriotism." "The Unity of Tragedy, Comedy, and History: An Interpretation of the Shakespearean Universe," in *Shakespeare as Political Thinker*, ed. John E. Alvis and Thomas G. West (Wilmington, DE: ISI Books, 2000), 46–48.

28. Here, Augustine may be drawing on the story of Domnina of Antioch, found in Eusebius's *Ecclesiastical History* 8:12, 3–4: "For, she [Domnina] said, that to surrender their souls to the slavery of demons was worse than all deaths and destruction; and she set before them the only deliverance from all these things—escape to Christ. They then listened to her advice. And after arranging their garments suitably, they went aside from the middle of the road, having requested of the guards a little time for retirement, and cast themselves into a river which was flowing by." Eusebius, *Church History*, trans. and ed. ed. P. Schaff and H. Wace, Nicene and Post-Nicene Fathers, 2nd ser. (Reprint: Grand Rapids, MI: Eerdmans, 1955), 1: 32–33.

29. See Judges, ch. 13–16 on the life of Samson.

30. See Genesis 22 on the sacrifice of Isaac.

31. See Judges 11:31–40 on Jephthah's sacrifice of his only daughter to fulfill a vow. Jephthah is seemingly praised in scripture, in spite of what seems his rashness (see 1 Kings [1 Sam.] 12:11, Hebr. 11:32).

32. *DCD* 1.26, 39. Augustine says of Samson that in killing himself along with his foes he is not "excused other than by the fact that the Spirit Who had been performing miracles through him, secretly (*latenter*) commanded him to do this" (*DCD* 1.21.34)—secretly, because the command is not mentioned in the biblical account. In Hebrews 11:32, Samson is praised along with other Old Testament figures, including Jephthah.

33. The subsequent section of my essay elaborates on this question, and with the text extends beyond the issue of divine support or command. P. W. Van der Horst, discusses the views of Augustine and Macrobius, noting that both hold out an exception that allows suicide under a divine command. "A Pagan Platonist and a Christian Platonist on Suicide," *Vigiliae Christianae* 25 (1971): 282–88, at 287.

34. *DCD* 1.26, 39–40.

35. On Theombrotus, see 1.22, 34; Augustine's source for the account of Theombrotus (Cleombrotus) is likely Cicero, who refers to him as Theombrotus in *Tusculan Disputations* 1.84 (though many texts "correct" the reference); Cicero, *Tusculanae disputationes*, Perseus Latin Texts and Translations, accessed February 8, 2019, http://perseus.uchicago.edu/perseus-cgi/citequery3.pl?dbname=LatinAugust2012&query=Cic.%20Tusc.&getid=0). See G. D. Williams, "Cleombrotus of Ambracia: Interpretations of a Suicide from Callimachus to Agathias," *Classical Quarterly* 45 (1995), 154–89n39.

36. On this point, see, for example, Melanie Webb, "'On Lucretia who slew herself': Rape and Consolation in Augustine's *De ciuitate dei*," *Augustinian Studies* 44 (2013): 37–58, at 57: "No philosopher prior to Augustine had ever taken rape as an occasion warranting consolation."

37. Miriam Griffin argues that for the Romans suicide "when performed in the right circumstances, was highly esteemed; and what is esteemed will often be imitated." "Philosophy, Cato, and Roman Suicide: II," 200.

38. Montesquieu, *Considerations on the Causes of the Greatness of the Romans and Their Decline*, trans. David Lowenthal (Cambridge, MA: Hackett, 1999), chap. 12, 117.

39. Montesquieu, *Considerations*, chap. 12, 116.

40. Montesquieu notes earlier the influence that the schools of Stoicism and Epicureanism exercised in the declining years of the Republic: "I believe the sect of Epicurus, which was introduced at Rome toward the end of the republic, contributed much toward tainting the heart and mind of the Romans. The Greeks had been infatuated with this sect earlier and thus were corrupted sooner. Polybius tells us that in his time a Greek's oath inspired no confidence, whereas a Roman was, so to speak, enchained by his." *Considerations*, chap. 10, 97.

41. See, for example, the remarks by Lactantius, in the *Divine Institutes* 3:18, specifically addressing the Pythagorean and Stoic defenses of suicide: "For if a homicide is guilty because he is a destroyer of man, he who puts himself to death is under the same guilt, because he puts to death a man. Yea, that crime may be considered to be greater, the punishment of which belongs to God alone." *Divine Institutes*, trans. William Fletcher, Ante-Nicene Fathers, vol. 7 (Buffalo, NY: Christian Literature Publishing Co., 1886), available online via New Advent, accessed February 8, 2019, http://www.newadvent.org/fathers/07013.htm.

42. Sigrid Undset, "Letter to a Parish Priest," in *Modern Catholic Thinkers: An Anthology*, ed. A. Robert Caponigri (New York: Harper and Brothers, 1960), 587–606, at 589.

43. Undset, 591.

44. Undset, 591.

45. On Augustine's understanding of natural law, see Richard J. Dougherty, "Natural Law in Augustine," in *Research Handbook on Natural Law Theory*, ed. Jonathan Crowe and Constance Youngwon Lee (Cheltenham, UK: Edward Elgar Publishing, forthcoming).

46. See, for example, Gen. 9:5–6, Ex. 20:13, and Prov. 6:17.

47. The ancient accounts refer to Theombrotus's committing suicide after reading the *Phaedo*, Plato's dialogue on the immortality of the soul. Theombrotus (or Cleombrotus) is mentioned at the outset of the dialogue as having been absent when the discussion recorded therein took place (*Phaedo* 59c).

48. *DCD* 1.22, 34–35.

49. *DCD* 1.22, 35: "Quod tamen magne potius factum esse quam bene testis ei esse potuit Plato ipse."

50. Plato's presentation of this question is famously thorny, both in the *Phaedo* and in the *Apology of Socrates*; see, for example, Murray Miles, "Plato on Suicide (*Phaedo* 60c–63c)," *Phoenix* 55, no. 3/4 (2001): 244–58.

51. *DCD* 1.19, 30.

52. *DCD* 1.19, 30. See Virgil, *Aeneid*, 6.434ff: "Next were those sad souls, benighted, who contrived their own destruction, and as they hated daylight, cast their lives away. How they would wish in the upper air now to endure the pain of poverty and toil! But iron law stands in the way, since the drear hateful swamp has pinned them down here, and the Styx that winds nine times around exerts imprisoning power." Trans. Robert Fitzgerald (New York: Random House, 1983), 175.

53. Augustine's rewriting of Virgil is seen in criticizing the Roman appropriation of God's providence, in its claim to "spare the humble and subdue the proud" (*DCD* 1. Preface, citing Virgil's *Aeneid* 6:853), contrasted with James 4:6: "God resisteth the proud and giveth grace to the humble."

54. *On Christian Doctrine*, 1.24.24, trans. D. W. Robertson (Upper Saddle River, NJ: Prentice-Hall, 1997), 20; internal citation to Ephesians 5:29.

55. This purpose is perhaps reflected in the passage in Cicero's *De re publica*, in "The Dream of Scipio" in book 6; Scipio is told "both you and all pious people must keep your soul in the guardianship of the body, and you must not depart from human life without the order of him who gave you your soul: you must not seem to run away from the human duty assigned by the god" (6.15), Cicero, *On the Commonwealth and On the Laws*, ed. James E. G. Zetzel (Cambridge: Cambridge University Press, 1999), 97.

56. Thomas Aquinas, *Summa Theologiae*, trans. Fathers of the Dominican Province (reprint: Westminster, MD: Christian Classics, 1948), 1–2, q. 100 a. 1 *corp.* (2:1037). St. Thomas holds that all the precepts of the Ten Commandments, for example, are knowable by reason, except for the prescription of keeping the Sabbath holy.

57. Joseph Fuchs, *Natural Law: A Theological Investigation* (New York: Sheed and Ward, 1965), 19.

58. C. S. Lewis, *Christian Reflections*, ed. Walter Hooper (Grand Rapids, MI: Eerdmans, 1967), 46.

59. *Summa Theologiae* 2-2, q. 64 a. 5 *corp.* (3:1462–64). Aquinas cites Augustine as his authority in the *sed contra* of the question, from *DCD* 1.20. Aquinas also discusses numerous unjustified defenses of suicide, tracking the passage quoted above from *DCD* 1.26, where Augustine lists four unpersuasive cases.

60. Aristotle, *Nicomachean Ethics*, trans. Robert C. Bartlett and Susan D. Collins (Chicago: University of Chicago Press, 2011), 3.7, 1116a 13–16 (p. 57).

61. Aristotle, *Politics*, trans. Carnes Lord, 2nd ed. (Chicago: University of Chicago Press, 2013), 1278b26–29 (p. 72).

62. See, for example, *DCD* 12.28 ("For there is nothing so social by nature as this race" [p. 539]), and the passages noted above.

63. See Aristotle, *Nicomachean Ethics*, 9.5, on goodwill and its connection to friendship (1166a30ff), and his *Politics* 2.5.9–10, on the need to possess private property in order to exercise liberality toward one's friends (specifically, 1263b5–13).

64. See Cicero, *De re publica* 1.39, for Scipio's account of the formation of the first societies: "The first cause of its assembly is not so much weakness [*inbecilitas*] as a kind of natural herding together of men; this species is not isolated or prone to wandering alone [or: "for man

is not a singular or solitary species"], but born with such a nature that not even under conditions of great prosperity of every sort [is he willing to be isolated from his fellow humans]"; in *On the Commonwealth and On the Laws*, ed. James E. G. Zetzel (Cambridge: Cambridge University Press, 1999, 18). See also Scipio's comment at *De re publica* 4.3 that the "first cause of the creation of society" is "to promote the citizens' shared association in a happy and honorable way of life" (Zetzel, 80).

65. Augustine has already raised this question in book 9; that discussion will be addressed below.

66. *DCD* 14.8, 593.

67. *DCD* 14.8, 593–94.

68. Robert Wilken indicates Lactantius's strong defense of the passions: "Even anger, when properly used, can contribute to virtue: 'Without anger there can be no virtue.'" Wilken, *The Spirit of Early Christian Thought: Seeking the Face of God* (New Haven: Yale University Press, 2003), 297–98; citing Lactantius, *Divine Institutes* 6.15.

69. *DCD* 14.8, 596: "[C]upiunt timent lateanturet boni et mali; sed illi bene, isti mali, sicut hominibus seu recta seu perversa voluntas est. Ipsa quoque tristitia . . . reperitur in bono et maxime apud nostros." Consider here Aquinas's discussion of the connection between moral virtue and passion: "Accordingly, if, as the Stoics held, the passions be taken for inordinate affections, they cannot be in a virtuous man, so that he consent to them deliberately. But if the passions be taken for any movements of the sensitive appetite, they can be in a virtuous man, in so far as they are subordinated to reason." *Summa Theologiae* 1–2, q. 59 a. 2 *corp*. One need only consider the biblical account of Christ in the garden to recognize this departure from the Stoics; it is difficult to conceive how one can declare that,"My soul is sorrowful even unto death" (Mark 14:34) and be the epitome of the wise Stoic.

70. As Wilken notes, "The movements of the soul are the springs of activity that move the will to the good." *Early Christian Thought*, 304.

71. *DCD* 14.9, 597; internal citations to Rom. 8:23 and 1 Cor. 15:54 omitted.

72. *DCD* 14.9, 599.

73. *DCD* 14.9, 600.

74. As we find in the first letter of John, "If we say that we have no sin, we deceive ourselves, and the truth is not in us" (1 John 1:8).

75. As, also, there will no longer be faith or hope, only love: see Augustine, *Enchiridion* 121.

76. In connecting this defect of pride to the Roman heroes treated in Augustine's earlier books, John Cavadini notes that the failure of the empire "is due to the way in which pride, manifested as the love of praise over virtue, means the loss of any place to stand from which one could be self-critical, as glory becomes detached from conscience." Cavadini, "Pride," in *Augustine Through the Ages: An Encyclopedia*, 681.

77. *DCD* 14.9, 602: "Et si nonnulli tanto inmaniore, quanto rariore vanitate hoc in se ipsis adamaverint, ut nullo prorsus erigantur et excitentur, nullo flectantur atque inclinentur affectu: humanitatem totam potius amittunt, quam veram adsequuntur tranquillitatem. Non enim quia durum aliquid, ideo rectum, aut quia stupidum est, ideo sanum."

78. *DCD* 15.20, 506. Compare Aristotle's *Nicomachean Ethics* 3.11 on temperance: "Those who are deficient when it comes to pleasures and enjoy them less than they ought do not arise very often, because this sort of 'insensibility' is not characteristically human. . . . And this sort of person has not obtained a name because he does not arise very often."

Trans. Robert C. Bartlett and Susan D. Collins (Chicago: University of Chicago Press, 2011), 1119a6–11 (p. 65).

79. Aristotle expresses a similar concern about human qualities in the *Politics*, noting the important role that the founders of political orders play in introducing law and justice. *Politics* 1.2.15–16, 1253a30–37.

80. Charles R. N. McCoy, "Christianity and Political Philosophy: The Relation of Church and State," in *The Structure of Political Thought: A Study in the History of Political Ideas* (New York: McGraw-Hill, 1963; reprint: New Brunswick, NJ: Transaction Publishers, 2017), 79, 81–93.

81. In book 9, in the context of dealing with the Platonist philosophers, Augustine introduces the question of Stoic ethics, to which he returns in the passages analyzed here from book 14.

82. *DCD* 9.4, 363: "In eo libro se legisse dicit A Gellius hoc Stoicis placuisse, quod animi visa, quas appellant phantasias nec in potestate est utrum et quando incidant animo."

83. Cf. Plato, *Republic*, 439e–441a, on the internal struggle of the soul. Aristotle discusses the question of the power of phantasms and the human response to them in *Nicomachean Ethics* 3.5 (114a33–1114b26).

84. 1 Cor. 1:20.

85. Augustus on John 13:21, in *Tractates on the Gospel of St. John*, 60.3, trans. John Gibb, in *Lectures or Tractates on the Gospel According to St. John*, Nicene and Post-Nicene Fathers, series 1, vol. 7 (Reprint: Peabody, MA: Hendrickson. 1995), 309.

86. John Sellars notes Augustine's critique of the Stoic view that "through the power of individual reason alone one may become completely virtuous, free, and happy. . . . [T]his is the height of arrogance and in sharp contrast to his own emphasis on our dependence on God for our virtue and happiness." Sellars, "Stoic Tradition," in *The Oxford Guide to the Historical Reception of Augustine*, ed. Karla Pollmann and Willemien Otten (Oxford: Oxford University Press, 2013), 2:1775–79, at 1776.

87. G. E. Evans, *Augustine on Evil* (New York: Cambridge University Press, 1982), 151. As Evans subsequently puts it, the Stoics "have not looked up and tried to conform their wills, not to things as they are, but to things as they ought to be" (153).

88. On Augustine's view of the meaning of death, see, *inter alia*, *DCD* 13.11. On the question of achieving happiness in this life, compare this with Aristotle's *Nicomachean Ethics*, 1.10–11 (1100a10–1101a20); and Herodotus, 1.32.7, on Solon's comment to Croesus to call no man happy before his death, but of the man who has much in this life "one should rather call him lucky." Robert B. Strassler, ed., *The Landmark Herodotus* (New York: Random House, 2007), 21; and Juvenal, *Satire* 10.274–275.

89. Matt. 8:23–27.

90. Augustine, *Tractates on the Gospel of St. John*, 60.3 (309).

91. Alexander Murray discusses the concatenation of concerns Augustine had in mind, expressed in *DCD* and other writings, in his *Suicide in the Middle Ages: The Curse of Self-Murder* (Oxford: Oxford University Press, 2000), 2:113–21.

92. Murray also connects this biblical analysis with a subsequent concern that Augustine had to address with a group of Donatists threatening to commit suicide in their church; in *Contra Gaudentium* (Gaudentius was the Donatist bishop of Thamugadi), Augustine asserts, "By trying to make yourselves martyrs, by burning yourself on the altar of Christ, you will in fact make yourselves a sacrifice to the Devil" (1.27.30; quoted in Murray, 2:109n47). On the

Gaudentius controversy, see also Serge Lancel, *St. Augustine*, trans. Antonia Nevill (London: SCM Press, 2002), 359–60; and Webb, "On Lucretia," 38–39.

93. Cited in Lancel, 442.

94. See *DCD* 11.27, 485–86.

95. *DCD* 2.6, 57.

96. *DCD* 2.7, 58.

97. *DCD* 2.7, 58; Augustine returns to these three concerns of philosophy in the treatment of the Platonist philosophers at the opening of book 8.

98. Augustine's account of pride is routinely tied to the pursuits of the philosophers, although it also extends to others, including political entities such as Rome. Richard Price notes that in the *Confessions* Augustine "attributed the same vice to pagan Platonism: it was a man 'swollen with monstrous arrogance' who had introduced him to the books of the Platonists (*Conf.* 7.9.13), and it was the reluctance of the philosophers to imitate the humility of the incarnation that closed their minds to faith in Christ (7.20.26–21.27)." "Pride," in *The Oxford Guide to the Historical Reception of Augustine*, 3:1600–1603, at 1600.

99. *DCD* 2.7, 58.

100. This is one reason, perhaps, that Augustine addresses the issue of divine providence in book I, in the context of the manner in which the regenerate and unregenerate respond to the vagaries of this world. This question also touches on a matter beyond our scope here, the proper role of rhetoric in Augustine's understanding; see, for example, Ernest Fortin, "Saint Augustine and the Problem of Christian Rhetoric," *Augustinian Studies* 5 (1974): 85–100.

101. This concern may also lead us back to the consideration in book 1 of the relationship between Christian ethics and non-Christian ethics. For later developments of this question, see especially St. Thomas Aquinas, *Summa Theologiae* 1–2.94.2 (*inter alia*); Francisco Suárez, *On God, and God the Lawgiver* 2.6; and Grotius, *On the Law of War and Peace* Prol. 11. But it also raises the general question of the efficacy of human efforts in the moral sphere, an issue addressed in part by the myth of Er in Plato's *Republic* and "The Dream of Scipio" in Cicero's *De re publica*; both works conclude with reference to the divine order.

102. McCoy, *The Structure of Political Thought*, 78.

103. Charles Norris Cochrane notes the relationship between authority and reason for Augustine: "While . . . authority is prior in time to reason, reason is prior to authority in fact. Such is the constitution of human nature that, when we undertake to learn anything, authority must precede reason. But this authority is accepted only as a means to understanding." *Christianity and Classical Culture: A Study of Thought and Action from Augustus to Augustine* (Oxford: Clarendon, 1940; reprint: Indianapolis: Liberty Fund, 2003), 444 (internal notes omitted).

104. *DCD* 10.32, 443. Augustine's interest in the question of the fate of the church in the earthly city leads him to critique the Eusebian conflation of Rome and the church, and Jerome's lamentations following the attack on Rome in AD 410; see Richard J. Dougherty, "The Fall of Rome," *Augustine Through the Ages*, 352–53.

105. *DCD* 10.32, 444.

106. One of Augustine's concerns in books 8–10 is with the demonology of the Platonists; in noting the need for a mediator between God and human beings, they don't recognize Christ as that Mediator (see *DCD* 10.19ff.).

107. Peter Brown has given the following description of these passages in book 10: "The cult of the martyrs, therefore, presented a paradox that enabled Augustine to invert the

traditional hierarchy of the universe. Men who had shown themselves, as martyrs, to be true servants of God, could bind their fellow men even closer to God than could the angels. . . . Augustine's solution summed up a drift in Christian sensibility: the need for intimacy with a protector with whom one could identify as a fellow human being, relations with whom could be conceived of in terms open to the nuances of known human relations." (*The Cult of the Saints: Its Rise and Function in Latin Christianity*, Chicago: University of Chicago Press, 1981, 60–61).

108. Robert Dodaro notes that Augustine's use of the word *hero* is reserved for those who become deified by the Romans; Augustine more commonly refers to "vir optimus." *Christ and the Just Society in the Thought of St. Augustine* (Cambridge: Cambridge University Press, 2004), 36–37n42.

109. "As members of the body of Christ, Christians participate in his triumph over death. They act corporately: 'not for [their own glory], but for God's glory' (1 Tim. 1:17)." Carole Straw, "Timor Mortis," in *Augustine through the Ages*, 840; Straw refers to Augustine's *Epistle* 186.2.

110. For Augustine, the martyr's death serves to glorify God (*Sermon* 319.1).

111. *DCD* 8.20, 340.

112. On this point see Straw, "Martyrdom," *Augustine Through the Ages*, 538–41.

113. *DCD* 5.18, 221.

114. As Robert P. Kennedy aptly notes, in the account of Regulus "we find a high virtue that rings hollow," given his worship of the pagan gods. "Truthfulness as the Bond of Society," in *Augustine and Politics*, ed. John Doody, Keven L. Hughes, and Kim Paffenroth (Lanham, MD: Lexington Books, 2005), 35–52, at 47–48.

115. *DCD* 1.22, 129; we learn this lesson, in fact, from examining Plato, the patriarchs, the prophets, and the apostles (1.22).

116. *DCD* 1.22, 129.

117. *DCD* 3.18, 124. This passage is especially important because at the end of his account of Regulus in book 1, Augustine is relatively ambiguous about the status of Regulus's virtue.

118. Augustine introduces the "libido dominandi," or lust for ruling, at key points in the text, representing the true character of Roman political life; see, e.g., *DCD* 1.Preface, 3.14, 14.15, 14.28.

Chapter Two

# The Other Happy Life

## The Political Dimensions to
## St. Augustine's Cassiciacum Dialogues

### Michael P. Foley

Though they are often overlooked or studied for different reasons, St. Augustine's Cassiciacum dialogues have a subtle yet important political dimension. Much of Augustine's conversation with his interlocutors implicitly hinges on matters concerning political philosophy, as does the very dialogue format Augustine chooses. Yet on the other hand, the focal points of the dialogues are essentially nonpolitical, and some of Augustine's statements can be construed as hostile to civic life and to any thoughtful reflection on the best political order. This essay argues that these apparent inconsistencies are not signs of a contradictory attitude but reveal a three-pronged strategy by Augustine to forge a properly Christian attitude toward political life, a strategy that involves (1) debunking patriotic fervor, (2) inflaming the love of truth, and (3) reengaging the *civitas* from a higher perspective.

Any attempt to cull a cogent political theory from St. Augustine's first four extant writings (commonly referred to as the Cassiciacum dialogues[1]) is bound to be met with a justifiable dose of skepticism. Following J. N. Figgis,[2] scholars have tended to focus on *The City of God* for an understanding of Augustinian politics, while even those endeavors to extricate Augustine's political thought from the whole of his works generally ignore the early dialogues. Herbert A. Deane, in his *Political and Social Ideas of St. Augustine*, makes only cursory references to them,[3] as do Robert A. Markus[4] and R. W. Dyson.[5] Other, less conventional treatments of the topic, such as John Milbank's provocative *Theology and Social Theory*[6] and Jean Bethke Elshtain's self-reflective *Augustine and the Limit of Politics*,[7] have not changed this basic taxonomy.

A preoccupation with *The City of God* is certainly understandable. Augustine's magnum opus is also a magnes opus, a majestic magnet drawing the politically minded reader to itself. Nevertheless, as this essay will attempt to demonstrate, there remain compelling reasons for reassessing the value of the Cassiciacum dialogues as windows into Augustine's political thought. Such a renewed appreciation is particularly important given the likely prospect (which it is also the burden of this essay to demonstrate) that these dialogues are not fully intelligible unless they are viewed in light of classical political philosophy and Augustine's conversation with it. To justify these claims, we will first offer a crude overview of the ways in which the Cassiciacum dialogues may or may not be deemed "political." This overview will indirectly reveal a rather fascinating strategy of Augustine's to forge a properly Christian attitude toward political life, a strategy that will thus occupy the concluding sections of our essay.

## Sketch of the Cassiciacum Dialogues

The Cassiciacum dialogues do not, at first blush, evince any serious concern about either civic life or political philosophy. When "Reason" asks Augustine in the *Soliloquia* whether he wants to know anything more than God and the soul, Augustine exclaims, "Absolutely nothing!" ("Nihil omnino!").[8] Transcribed from private conversations in a friend's villa soon after Augustine's own resignation from public teaching in the fall of AD 386, these four works focus on questions of truth or knowledge rather than on statesmanship or civic responsibility. The *Contra Academicos* ("Against the academic skeptics") determines the knowability of truth, while the *De beata vita* ("On the happy life") explores the relation of truth to human happiness. The *De ordine* ("On order") attempts to discover the truth about the underlying unity of reality, while the *Soliloquia* ("Soliloquies") searches for self-knowledge, the elusive truth about oneself. The theme of each dialogue, in other words, is essentially apolitical. Loving the truth does not require loving one's homeland or one's regime, nor does it demand honorable sacrifice for the sake of a greater cause, such as the common good. It would not even seem to entail any thoughtful reflection on the optimum political order.

In fact, one of the main goals of the Cassiciacum dialogues appears to be the disparagement of a life lived comfortably within the conventions of public duty and opinion. It is not coincidental that two of the three men to whom Augustine has chosen to dedicate the dialogues—Romanianus and Zenobius—are at the time embroiled in great political distress.[9] Augustine has sent them these works to encourage them to flee, at least inwardly, their entangled public lives for the bosom of philosophy.[10] In perhaps one of the dialogues' most revealing characterizations, Augustine refers to the pure and private love of wisdom as "the other happy life, which alone is happy" ("beata alterius uita, quae sola beata est"),[11] implying in one breath that although the life of the noble, public-spirited citizen is the only great alternative to the life of truth seeking, this powerful competitor for the hearts of decent men and women is ultimately a sham.

Perhaps it is this apparent hostility to the "other happy life" of patriotic, magnanimous action that has led most scholars to deemphasize or altogether overlook the interplay between the author of the Cassiciacum dialogues and classical political philosophy.[12] Nonetheless, almost everything that transpires in the Cassiciacum dialogues betrays a rather keen sensitivity to the "political," which I take to mean not only the difficult master art of ruling and perfecting citizens through law and leadership—and not only the often equally difficult art of discerning the limits to and character of civic obedience and public-spiritedness—but also that discovery of human nature that never abstracts from the native political context of either subject or object. To begin with, Augustine's choice of genre, the Ciceronian philosophical dialogue, is not without significance. Although the Ciceronian tenor of the Cassiciacum dialogues has been widely acknowledged in magisterial tomes such as Maurice Testard's *Augustin et Cicero*,[13] most comparisons have focused largely on matters of style and rhetoric rather than content. Robert O'Connell discounts Cicero's substantive influence on Augustine on the grounds that the former could not have provided the latter "a comprehensive philosophic matrix." "Cicero," O'Connell asseverates, "not only does not know the answer to such questions, he wonders whether man can ever know them."[14] Harald Hagendahl, another prominent Augustinian scholar, concurs, arguing that Augustine used Cicero primarily for patterns of literary composition and for obtaining information about ancient philosophy.[15] And yet Hagendahl also notes the curious fact that only one out of seven of Augustine's allusions to Cicero's writings is to a speech or an oratorical work; the rest—that is, the overwhelming majority—are to his philosophical dialogues.[16] This leaves Hagendahl unable to answer his own question: "Why did Augustine, the former rhetor, avail himself so little of Cicero's speeches in comparison with the philosophical dialogues?"[17]

As Hagendahl's statistic would suggest, closer scrutiny of Augustine's interaction with Cicero reveals much more than an interest in style or format. Not only are the Cassiciacum dialogues redolent of the aromatic cedar of Cicero's *gymnasia* (as Augustine puts it[18]) but, as I have argued elsewhere,[19] they are specific responses to Cicero's philosophical dialogues: Augustine's *Contra Academicos* is a response to Cicero's *Academica*; his *De beata vita* is a response to Cicero's *Definibus* and the *Tusculanae disputationes*, which treat of the *summum bonum*[20] and the art of "living blessedly" ("ad beate uiuendum"),[21] respectively.[22] Also, Augustine's *De ordine*, which deals with the question of Providence, is a response to the *De natura deorum*, *De divinatione*, and *De fato*, a trilogy of Cicero's dealing with the same question.[23] Augustine's Cassiciacum conversation with Cicero can be indirect, as in the *De beata vita* and the *De ordine*; or it can be more obvious, as in the *Contra Academicos*, a dialogue that is constituted of a prolonged examination of Cicero and his academic skepticism. And although it is beyond the scope of this essay to do justice to the depth of Augustine's engagement with Cicero, it is at least important to note that Augustine's choice of Cicero as his primary interlocutor implies a sustained interest not just in philosophy but also in political philosophy.

Second, although it is true that the Cassiciacum dialogues are primarily concerned with the pursuit of truth, it is misleading to characterize this pursuit as having no political bearings. One of the areas in which the political dimension of Augustine's quest for truth may be discerned is in his vehement desire for happiness. As Augustine J. Curley persuasively argues, the *Contra Academicos*—which is mined these days primarily for clues into Augustine's so-called epistemology—is driven more by Augustine's concern for authentic human happiness than by a desire to logically refute academic skepticism.[24] Such a concern is only fitting for, as Curley notes, Cartesian skepticism may aim at certainty, but ancient skepticism aims at happiness.[25] And what can be said about the *Contra Academicos* in this regard can safely be said of the other three dialogues. The *De beata vita* is, as its title suggests, centered on the question of happiness; indeed it portrays philosophy as compelling only because of philosophy's capacity to arrive at true happiness.[26] Likewise, the *De ordine* and *Soliloquia* are both designed to help the wavering reader navigate past the "rocks and storms of this life" ("scopulos uitae huius et procellas") to noetic and emotional serenity.[27]

Although the theme of happiness is not considered by all to be political in nature (Epicurean thought being the notorious counterexample), it remains the central driving question for the political philosophy promulgated by Cicero and others and emulated here in part by Augustine, for classical political philosophy takes its origin in wonder about the best way to live one's life.[28] Cicero tells the readers of the *Tusculanae disputationes* that his book is about "living happily" ("ad beate uiuendum"),[29] and Seneca titles one of his works on political philosophy *De vita beata*. Augustine has these thinkers in mind when he takes up similar questions and adopts identical titles. Like those of his philosophical forebears, Augustine's answers to the question of happiness are ultimately apolitical (in the sense that happiness is discovered to be something lying outside the *polis*). Yet also like his forebears, he still attends to the social or political repercussions of these answers, no matter how ethereal the theorizing.

A telling example of this political mindedness occurs in *Contra Academicos* 3.16.35, the passage that contains Augustine's most impassioned condemnation of the New Academy's skepticism.[30] Significantly, this critique is made in reference not to the deficiencies of the skeptics' cognitional theory but to the impact of their thought on public life. Illustrating the disastrous effects of radical doubt on right action, Augustine derisively paints the picture of a courtroom imbued with skeptic philosophy. A defendant is charged with adultery, which he probably committed but is not certain, since he cannot trust his senses. For that matter, the cuckolded husband cannot be certain that he is sleeping with his wife. The judge has no choice but to find the defendant "probably guilty," while the hapless defense attorney must now convince his client that they really won: the defendant only dreamed that he was convicted. This farcical scene is prefaced by Augustine with a direct address to Cicero: "It is you, you I am consulting, Marcus Tullius. We are dealing with the life and morals of young men, and all of those writings of yours have vigilantly aimed at educating and instituting these things."[31] Augustine is obviously discrediting Cicero's adherence to the New Academy, but the way he does so not only meets Cicero on his own ground but willingly concedes the importance of that ground.

The sustained search for happiness, with its personal and political facets, also accounts for Augustine's attentiveness to the formation of his pupils at Cassiciacum. One of the more telling passages in which this attentiveness emerges is Augustine's discourse on the "order of life" ("ordo uitae")[32] as a crucial pedagogue to the "order of education" ("ordo eruditionis").[33] Notably, the order of life as described by Augustine contains virtues that can be exercised only in a political setting. When Augustine advises his students not to be "excessive when they sue or stinting when they forgive" ("cum uindicant ne nimium sit, cum ignoscunt ne parum"), he presupposes a legal environment in which even a Christian disciple must sometimes bring lawsuits against his neighbor. And when he urges obedience in serving and kindness in ruling with the words, "let them so serve that one blushes to order them around, and let them so order others around that it is a delight to serve them" ("ita seruiant, ut eis dominari pudeat, ita dominentur, ut eis seruire delectet"), he is presupposing a political hierarchy in which Christian citizens are to participate fully.

Moreover, Augustine exonerates in this same passage the desire to "administer the republic" ("rem publicam . . . administrare"), so long as the person in question is sufficiently mature. This last piece of advice, in fact, reemerges at the end of the dialogue as the capstone to the entire discussion. When Pythagoras's name is introduced into the conversation, Augustine praises him not for his mathematical or metaphysical insights, but for his "teaching the discipline of ruling the republic last, to his disciples who were already learned, already perfect, already wise, and already happy" ("quo regendae rei publicae disciplinam suis auditoribus ultimam tradebat iam doctis, iam perfectis, iam sapient bus, iam beatis").[34] Such an affirmative evaluation of participation in the public forum is echoed in the *Contra Academicos*, where Augustine goes so far as to praise acts of patriotism and denounce acts of treachery. At one point he refers to Catiline's coup against the Roman republic (which he labels "parricide" ["parricidium"]), as "a crime in which all other crimes are included" ("quo uno continentur omnia scelera");[35] at another, he lets stand unchallenged one of his pupils' depiction of Cicero during the Catiline conspiracy as the paragon of the cardinal virtues.[36]

## Augustine's Theological-Political Strategy

As can be seen from this odd gallimaufry of positive and negative remarks, Augustine's various allusions to politics seem to hang in tension, if not outright opposition, with each other. It is thus tempting to join Dennis Trout and others in interpreting this string of rebukes and praises as the sign of a contradictory attitude in Augustine toward "wealth and temporal fame," an attitude dictated by the "intellectual and social constraints" of his time.[37] I would like to suggest, however, an alternative reading. What the aforementioned traits of the Cassiciacum dialogues reveal is a three-pronged pedagogical strategy on Augustine's part, one designed to fulfill the Gospel injunction to render to both God and Caesar their due.

Debunking Patriotism

The first prong of Augustine's strategy is to strip patriotic thought and action of their seductive qualities by demoting the supremacy of political life. Living according to a complete and unconditional love of one's country, Augustine implicitly charges, is inherently tragic and unfulfilling, for the love of anything temporal is, on account of its fortuitousness, rife with uncertainty, instability, and the fear of loss.[38] Hence, although Augustine does on occasion use the powerful Latin name for the fatherland (*patria*) in reference to one's homeland or country,[39] he more often uses this word to denote a destination utterly beyond the physical, let alone political, world.[40] Conventional patriotism can never evoke our full potential for excellence or make us truly happy, because our nation, people, or clan is not, strictly speaking, our true point of origin or return. It is not our home and must not be loved as such.

Augustine's debunking of unbridled patriotic loyalty may be seen more clearly in his treatment of political virtues ("uirtutes ciuiles") which, significantly, he relegates to the shadowy world of appearance and opinion.[41] In contradistinction to Aristotle, who makes some allowance for genuine nonphilosophic virtues, Augustine takes a hard Platonic line: if moral virtues are not grounded in a clear knowledge of the ultimate end to which they are ordered, then they are not, strictly speaking, virtues.[42] Augustine's source for this understanding of political virtue is most likely Plotinus,[43] but Augustine's rationale bears an important difference. For Plotinus, political virtues are not true virtues because they are closer to matter than to form, to the body than to the soul.[44] But for Augustine, political virtues are not authentic because of their association with disordered desire, a condition that has more to do with the soul's rebellion against the good than its bodily dwelling. Augustine makes this connection explicit in one of his polemics against the Pelagian sympathizer Julian when he characterizes some of Rome's greatest patriots as men who have shown a Babylonian love for their earthly fatherland and who have served demons or human glory by political virtue, which is not true [virtue] but similar to it ("istis qui exhibuerunt terrenae patriae babylonicam dilectionem, et uirtute ciuili, non uera, sed ueri simili daemonibus uel humanae gloriae seruierunt").[45]

Though political virtue may be impressive in many respects, its subordination to a warped zeal like self-glorification renders it an imitation of genuine virtue rather than an exemplification of it.

The *Contra Julianum* was written near the end of Augustine's life, but the germ of his mature thinking on political virtue and its relation to concupiscence may be found in his earlier works as well. This germ is particularly prevalent in Augustine's treatment of the three basic kinds of human desire, known in the Platonic tradition as the three parts of the soul. Augustine's use of this tripartite division of eros as a principal lens through which human behavior, excellence, and happiness may be properly surmised is so pronounced that it functions as one of the seminal *topoi* of his thinking. In the *Confessions*, for example, the threefold longing for physical pleasure or satiation, glory or prominence, and knowledge or truth forms the warp and woof of his narration. It is here that Augustine identifies three main sources for, or "heads of" (*capita*), sin: the *libido sentiendi*, the lust for carnal experience; the *libido principandi*, the lust "for being first"; and the *libido spectandi*, the lust "for looking," that is, the desire for a pernicious knowledge.[46]

The point of this erotically focused theology of sin is not to condemn human desire—on the contrary, Augustine affirms the goodness of all three basic longings[47]—but to underscore the importance of directing these desires toward their true fulfillment. Augustine succinctly summarizes his thinking on the matter when describing his own downward spiral away from God: "In this I sinned, in that I sought pleasures, lofty things, and truths, not in [God] but in his creatures, myself, and others, and thus I rushed into sorrows, confusions, and errors." ("Hoc enim peccabam, quod non in ipso sed in creaturis eius me atque ceteris uoluptates, sublimitates, ueritates quaerebam, atque ita inruebam in dolores, confusiones, errores."[48]) It is only when desires are loosed from their proper ends and seek their satisfaction in lesser substitutes that they become destructive and self-defeating.

Of these three cardinal lusts, the one that Augustine finds especially worrisome is the second, the *libido principandi* or *ambitio saeculi*.[49] Contrary to what many expect from Augustine, whose own conversion seemed to hang so precariously on his deliverance from disordered sexual appetite, Augustine treats not carnal lust but the imbalanced desire for prominence, applause, and mastery as the chief enemy of the good life. When examining his conscience in book 10 of the *Confessions*, Augustine depicts the love of praise (which springs from the second, or thymotic, part of the soul, as the Greeks would call it[50]) as the greatest threat to his postbaptismal happiness.[51] And in the *De vera religione*, Augustine opines that someone who can resist the "pleasure of the flesh" ("cupiditas uoluptatis") and the "allure of curiosity" ("curiositatis inlecebra") may still be overcome by the "haughtiness of temporal domination" ("dominationis temporalis fastus").[52] Augustine is especially suspicious of an unruly *thymos*, most likely because it is from this head that the mother of all sins first emerged: pride.[53] But whatever the reason, it is this kind of disordered desire that shares a special affinity with political virtue. What is called the *dominationis temporalis fastus* in the *De vera religione* and the *libido principandi* in the *Confessions* is the *libido dominandi* famously identified in *The City of God* as the arrogant lust that dominates the earthly city,[54] the pride that in its most aggravated condition seeks unity and absolute power over all things temporal.[55]

The same tripartite hermeneutic of desire that we have been tracing in Augustine's thought as a whole may also be discerned in the Cassiciacum dialogues. When, for example, Augustine outlines the chief threats to happiness in the *De beata vita*, he mentions the seducing calm of "pleasures and honors" ("fallacissima serenitas uoluptatum honorumque")[56] as well as intellectual vainglory.[57] Moreover, the dialogues reflect Augustine's vigorous concern about the effects of *libido principandi* and his subsequent desire to purge it from the souls of his interlocutors and readers.

This is particularly obvious in an incident recorded in the *De ordine*. When the pupils under Augustine's charge begin laughing derisively at each other over missteps made during a philosophical discussion, Augustine berates them so severely that only his own tears prevent him from proceeding further:

> O if you could see . . . in what dangers we lie, and what insanity of disease this laughing indicates! O if you could see, how quickly, how suddenly, and how much longer you would turn it into weeping! Wretches, do you not know where we are? . . . You are trying to introduce and disseminate into philosophy and into the life which I rejoice at last to have embraced a pest, lowest in rank yet more injurious than all others: that of toxic emulation and inane boasting.[58]

Augustine's denunciations would be disproportionate to the transgression were it not for the more serious danger underlying this juvenile schadenfreude. Emulation, boastfulness, and any number of *thymos*-related vices are pernicious precisely because they jettison objectivity when personal or communal reputation is at stake. In defiance of the example Augustine is trying to give—and in these dialogues he states that if a truth-seeking pupil conquers him in debate, no greater triumph could be given to him[59]—Augustine's pupils are fixated on scoring self-aggrandizing polemical hits, with justice and truth becoming ancillary concerns. Nor does Augustine allow us to dismiss this phenomenon as a youthful aberration. Commenting on their behavior, he states that his students were acting "in the manner of boys, or rather of men and of—O the horror of it all!—virtually everyone" ("puerorum scilicet more uel potius hominum—pro nefas!—paene omnium").[60] The words of Artemidorus in Shakespeare's *Julius Caesar* could easily be his: "My heart laments that virtue cannot live/Out of the teeth of emulation."[61]

The Cassiciacum dialogues thus attempt to indirectly break the spells of personal and civic pride that are behind political virtue by exposing their link to such disordered desires as *libido dominandi* and *libido principandi*, desires that are beneficial neither to the individual nor to the *civitas*. Similarly, Augustine demotes the *civitas*, or regime, as the supreme *telos* of human endeavor by demonstrating how all temporal realities are unworthy of our ultimate allegiance. Augustine's rhetoric in both cases can be sharp, but it is not without its value. As Hiram Caton puts it, Augustine's unceremonious demythologizing of the body politic "is useful in dispelling the blindness induced by infatuation with the glamour of great politics."[62]

Inflaming the Love of Truth

Dispelling blindness is a helpful activity, especially when there is something worth seeing. The first prong of Augustine's strategy is preparatory to his second, that of arousing the heart and mind for the truth (the object desired by the third part of the soul). Nothing less than a life defined by a passion for wisdom, Augustine charges, will put one on the path to happiness. This passion finds its true fulfillment in the knowledge and love of the Triune God,[63] for the soul's nourishment consists not only of an understanding and knowledge of things,[64] but of union with a divine reality that cannot be taken away.[65] Augustine is at his most eloquent when he describes the incredible beauty of humanity's ultimate terminus (that is, temporal and eternal ends) and the eyes that are worthy to behold it:

> But when [the soul] has composed and ordered itself, and has rendered itself harmonious and beautiful, it will now dare to see God, the very Fount whence all truth flows and the very Father of Truth. O great God, what eyes those will be! How healthy! How decorous! How strong! How constant! How serene! How happy! But what is it that they see? What, I beseech? What should we imagine it to be? What should we surmise? What should we say? Everyday words present themselves, but all have been made sordid by the basest things. I shall say nothing more, except that to us is promised a vision of beauty, by whose beautiful imitation, by whose comparison, all other things are foul.[66]

Seen from this perspective—the perspective that Augustine insists we must always keep in mind—acting for the sake of anything less than a union with the God of truth appears ridiculous.

Furthermore, in addition to its intrinsic beauty, truth is a perfectly shareable good, accessible to all. Augustine makes this point in a vivid, if not risqué manner, years later:

> Here, therefore, is something which we can all enjoy equally and in common. Here there are no restrictions, and nothing in her is deficient. She receives all her lovers (who are by no means envious of each other), sharing with all in common and yet chaste to each. No one says to another: "Stand back that I too may approach!" or "Remove your hands that I too may embrace!" All cleave [to the same wisdom], all touch her. . . . For nothing at any time ever belongs to one man or to any group of men as their own [proprium], but the whole is common to all at the same time.[67]

Truth's chaste promiscuity contrasts sharply with the unshareability constitutive of the proud "pest" Augustine has been trying to exorcise from his young co-retreatants. Unlike the limited goods of honor, power, and victory that so easily arouse thymotic aggression and assertion, truth draws to herself lovers who exhibit no possessiveness. Consequently, in the soul aflame with the love of truth, the detached and disinterested zeal for an infinitely shareable and objective knowledge of the highest things trumps the tribal fealties that cling to the narrowly defined interests of oneself or one's group. This is significant, for according to Socrates in the *Republic*, it is the "loyalty to one's own"—the blind allegiance to something for no other reason than that it belongs to you or you to it—that is responsible for all injustices in the city.[68] In elevating the soul beyond its attachment to unshareable goods so that it may love the truth, Augustine is thereby also producing citizens who are free from one of the city's greatest evils.

Re-engaging the *Civitas*

Since the unshareable love of one's own is not limited to the strictly personal but easily encompasses the larger spheres of familial, partisan, and national identities, the very idea of patriotism, which takes its beginnings in the pride of belonging to this country and not to that one, would seem to be incorrigibly opposed to the shareable pursuit of the truth that Augustine is so assiduously advocating. As we saw in his critique of *libido principandi*, however, Augustine's objections are not to civic-mindedness or patriotic fervor per se, but to the egocentric or irrational impulses all too often undergirding them. This, in effect, means that if political life can at least be theoretically separated from the motivations of right opinion, transient glory, or self-interest, then it is, so to speak, redeemable. Such is the third prong of Augustine's strategy. Having broken the mesmerizing allure of political virtue and having replaced it with the desire to live according to what is highest in us and in itself, Augustine is able to reground civic-mindedness on the love of wisdom rather than personal or corporate ambition. The result of this grafting is a solicitous will-ingness to serve one's country and to participate in one's regime that is informed by the selfless and sober considerations of justice and truth.

In other words, the best kind of political involvement, according to Augustine, comes from the top down rather than from the bottom up, from the height of the eternal to the depth of the particular. This is ironic, since it essentially means that only those who desire something infinitely greater than governing are fit to govern and that only those who have understood the highest of principles are capable of competently affixing quotidian policies. Certainly, the kind of public-spiritedness to arise from this paradigm will be less boisterous and less ensconced in the instinctive attachments to hearth and home that usually drive political realities; nevertheless, as we intimated earlier, it would ultimately be more reasonable and just, for it will be more responsive to reason's dictates as well as to justice's demands for impartiality and self-sacrifice. Augustine's demotion of politics thus has the paradoxical effect of purifying it, liberating it from its tragic and biased pride, rather than denigrating or abandoning it.

And if the best kind of political involvement comes from the top down, one of the best things to ensure the right direction of its flow is education. Education is crucial in tempering vainglory and in ordering man's noble impulses toward a truly noble end because education cultivates, among other things, the honor-seeking part of the soul. This is one of the reasons that Augustine devotes the latter half of the *De ordine* to the subject of education. It also is why he is at such pains to show "that not by faith alone, but by certain reason" (non iam sola fide sed certa ratione)[69] does one ascend to the happy life. By using the phrase, "certain reason," Augustine is implying that there is such a thing as uncertain reason, that is, a rational and possibly brilliant faculty unhinged from its proper use and not directed toward its objective fulfillment. Education is necessary in preventing such an unfortunate derangement. The proper formation of reason involves a careful harmonizing of human passions, with the desire for truth leading and conducting this orchestra of *eros* and the moderation of spiritedness, or *thymos*, playing a key role. Augustine thus refers frequently to moderation (*moderatio* or *modestia*) and limit (*modum*) in the Cassiciacum dialogues, since both tie into the theme of synchronizing desire.[70] Education not only holds forth the ultimate priority of wisdom but also moderates and modulates personal and political ambition so that wisdom's overwhelming desirability can be fully grasped. Once this reorientation of desires—or to use Augustine's terminology, "conversion"—is complete, the educated man may then participate more intelligently and justly in the civic arena precisely because he knows something better than it.

Education is, therefore, a crucial tool in effecting the transition from a Babylonian to a wholesome love of one's earthly *patria*. But as fond as Augustine is of the liberal arts, he does not consider them a panacea to the problems inherent in political life. R. A. Markus is, in my opinion, hasty in concluding that both Plato and Augustine believe that the "social order" is "secured by making sure of the perfection of the ruler."[71] Although Augustine does put down as a general rule that those bereft of a liberal arts education can never be truly happy in this life,[72] he finds at least one notable exception to this rule—his mother, Monica.[73] The divine authority of the sacred mysteries[74] and the simple power of prayer[75] are, in the final analysis, more important than the perfection of reason through education. In any case, there is no suggestion in the Cassiciacum dialogues (or in any of Augustine's other works) that a perfect Christian ruler can single-handedly transform society or even that a critical number of Christian citizens can bring about a utopian polity or the kingdom of God through their own initiative. The public forum is to be entered because of its importance and for the sake of exercising virtue and bearing witness to the truth, but without expectations of complete success.

Finally, Augustine's strategy of subordinating the political life to the philosophical does much to explain his reluctance in the dialogues to condemn the former tout court; and it also sheds light on his otherwise unusual remarks, such as his approval of Cicero's political valor and his censure of Catiline's political perfidy. As we saw from his comments to Julian, the older Augustine is careful to distinguish sinful from salubrious forms of civic-mindedness: when he condemns those who have a Babylonian love for their country, he is effectively stating that there is such a thing as a "non-Babylonian" kind of patriotism and politically oriented magnanimity. It is no doubt this same, philosophically inspired sense of civic duty that the younger Augustine has in mind at Cassiciacum when, for example, he lauds Pythagoras for teaching statesmanship last. The gist of the compliment is that political rule is so commendable yet complicated that only the very best kind of citizen—the wise man—should be entrusted with it.

## Conclusion

Augustine's variegated approach to politics illustrates the depth of his conversation, even at this early stage of his thinking, with classical political philosophy. By transfusing political life with the love of wisdom rather than the lust for power or loyalty to one's own, Augustine is appropriating the strategies found in Plato's *Republic*, Cicero's *De re publica*, and even, it may be argued, Aristotle's *Nicomachean Ethics*. What separates Augustine from his philosophical predecessors is not so much his analysis of the limitations of political life as his understanding of where the Christian subject or citizen stands vis-à-vis those limitations. One of the effects of the Word becoming flesh is that it enables not just the few but the many to reach that intelligible realm where only the philosopher, if anyone, could reach. The divine intellect taking on our humanity delivers redeemed man from the "multiform darkness of error" ("multiformibus erroris tenebris") so easily caused by a thymotic self-love.[76] The Incarnation heightens the faithful's thirst for wisdom as well as their transcendence from any political order at the same time that it enjoins them to render honest service to whatever regime into which they have been providentially placed.

Whatever else separates Augustine from his philosophical predecessors remains debatable. It may, for example, be potentially misleading to characterize the Augustine that emerges in the Cassiciacum dialogues as a political philosopher at all. Studying political philosophy, understanding it, and even using it well are not identical to following it as the supreme guide. Nor are the Cassiciacum dialogues "political" in the sense that they articulate an elaborate theory of the *civitas* per se or offer a detailed analysis of political rule or citizenship. It is on these grounds that some scholars have concluded that at no point in his life did Augustine have what we would call a "political theory,"[77] or if he did, it was (as opposed to the meatier, "thick" treatments of St. Thomas Aquinas), rather "thin."[78]

On the other hand, the dialogues can be called political in the sense that they presuppose a dynamic of Christian service to one's country that is earnest and informed. Further, they are political in their constant sensitivity to humanity's political nature and in their recognition that divine revelation does not abrogate this constitutive element of human living. That the Incarnation provides a transpolitical solution to the human condition robs political philosophy of much, but not all, of its exigency. This creates a broader ambivalence within Christianity that no doubt accounts for a good deal of the Cassiciacum dialogues' complexity. Though Augustine holds that the *polis* is not, ultimately, "another happy life," a source of human perfection and completion, he also realizes that it is an object worthy of serious attention and care. Consequently, he does not abstract from the difficulty of reconciling the Gospels with the often dirty demands of daily political life; nor does he ignore the powerful sway that patriotism holds over the hearts of honorable citizens. The Cassiciacum dialogues do not resolve these dilemmas, of course, but neither does *The City of God*, which is not so much Augustine's grand solution to the so-called theological-political problem as it is his greatest articulation of that problem. What the dialogues do provide is a foundation for avoiding the pitfalls of political immersion and antipolitical disengagement. As Augustine's nuanced conversations at a villa in Cassiciacum attest, moral, intellectual, and religious conversion do not so much provide the answers as give one the wherewithal to ask the right questions. And it is the way in which these questions are developed that proves to be one of the more fascinating undercurrents of Augustine's first fruits as a Christian.

# Notes

1. In the order they were intended to be read, these are: the *Contra Academicos* ["Against the academic skeptics"], the *De beata vita* ["On the happy life"], the *De ordine* ["On order"], and the *Soliloquia* ["Soliloquies"]. All of them were written at Cassiciacum, in northern Italy, in the tradition of a philosophical dialogue, some time after Augustine's conversion in the summer and autumn of 386 but before his baptism in April 387.

2. John Neville Figgis, *The Political Aspects of S. Augustine's "City of God"* (London: Longmans, Green, 1921).

3. Herbert A. Deane, in his *Political and Social Ideas of St. Augustine* (New York: Columbia University Press, 1963), cf. pp. 253n35, 267n47 (on the *Contra Academicos*), and pp. 281n36, 296n20, 305n78 (on the *De ordine*). All of Deane's references to the Cassiciacum dialogues are found only in footnotes.

4. Robert A. Markus, *Saeculum: History and Society in the Theology of St. Augustine* (Cambridge: Cambridge University Press, 1970), 78, 80.

5. R. W. Dyson, *The Pilgrim City: Social and Political Ideas in the Writings of St. Augustine of Hippo* (Woodbridge, NJ: Boydell, 2001), 73.

6. John Milbank, *Theology and Social Theory: Beyond Secular Reasoning* (Oxford: Basil Blackwell, 1990).

7. Jean Bethke Elshtain, *Augustine and the Limit of Politics* (Notre Dame, IN: University of Notre Dame Press, 1995).

8. *Soliloquia* 1.2.7. All translations in this essay are mine.

9. Romanianus, to whom the *Contra Academicos* is dedicated, was Augustine's lifelong friend and patron. At this time, Romanianus was in Milan trying to protect his interests at the emperor's court (*Conf.* 6.14.24), because many (unspecified) misfortunes had recently befallen him (*Contra Academicos* 1.1.2). Zenobius, to whom the *De ordine* is dedicated, was another close friend of Augustine. He was currently in a kind of self-imposed exile "somewhere beyond the Alps" (*Sol.* 2.14.26) as a result of the Arian attempt to take over the

Catholic basilicas in Milan in the spring of 386, a disturbance that had rendered Milan a "city terrified and tumultuous" (*Conf.* 9.7.15).

10. *Contra Academicos* 1.1.1–3; *De ordine* 1.2.4; compare Augustine's description of his own retreat from public life, *De beata vita* 1.4.

11. *Contra Academicos* 1.1.2.

12. Cf. Peter Brown, *Augustine of Hippo* (Berkeley: University of California Press, 2000). Brown construes Augustine the convert's recent deliverance "from the cares of a public career" as an intention "to live a secluded life" (108,125), and after translating the phrase "otium liberale" as "cultured retirement," he outlines Augustine's early "intellectual programme" at Cassiciacum without any reference to the civic strains of that program or even the sections concerning character development (108,115). Cf. also R. J. Halliburton, "The Inclination to Retirement—the Retreat of Cassiciacum and the 'Monastery' of Tagaste," in *Texte und Untersuchungen zur Geschichte der Altchristlichen Literatur*, Band 80 (reprint: Berlin: Akademie-Verlag, 1962), 329–40, where Halliburton follows up on a line of thinking developed by A. J. Festugière, O.P., in his *Personal Religion Among the Greeks* (Berkeley: University of California Press, 1954), 53ff. My contention is not that Brown et al. believe that the early Augustine was antipolitical or held no political opinions (in fact, scholars such as R. A. Markus argue—incorrectly, I would say—that Augustine held Eusebian views of a Christian empire at this time), but simply that in light of their portrayal of Augustine during his catechumenate and neophyte periods as reclusive and disenchanted with the public forum, it would be understandably tempting for the reader to conclude that Augustine was not interested in engaging in political life or political philosophy at this stage of his life.

13. Maurice Testard, *Augustin et Cicero* (Paris: Études Augustiniennes, 1958).

14. Robert O'Connell, *St. Augustine's Early Theory of Man, A.D. 386–391* (Cambridge, MA: Harvard University Press, 1968), 4, 3, resp. O'Connell's judgment of Cicero, it should be noted, is in diametric opposition to Augustine's, not only with respect to Cicero's value (cf. *Contra Academicos* 3.16.36) but also to Cicero's alleged subscription to skepticism, which Augustine spends most of book 3 of the *Contra Academicos* boldly arguing is more apparent than real. See especially 3.17.37ff and Epistles 1 and 118, where Augustine contends that Cicero and/or the Academics only publicly professed the doctrine of skepticism, privately concealing a much different position. Augustine also alludes to this esotericism in *Conf.* 5.10.19, where he states that he—along with many others—thought that the Academics affirmed that no truth could be grasped because at the time he did not yet understand their real meaning (cf. 5.14.25).

15. Harald Hagendahl, *Augustine and the Latin Classics* (Göteborg: Almquist and Wiksell, 1967), 2:483.

16. Hagendahl, *Augustine*, 481. According to Hagendahl, Augustine quotes twenty-nine passages from Cicero's speeches and 203 passages from Cicero's philosophical writings.

17. Hagendahl, 483.

18. *Confessions* 9.2.4.

19. Foley, "Cicero, Augustine, and the Philosophical Roots of the Cassiciacum Dialogues," *Revue des etudes augustiniennes* 45, no. 1 (1999): 51–77, 63ff.

20. Cf. *De fin.* 3.1.1.

21. *De div.* 2.1.2.

22. It should be noted that Cicero saw these two dialogues as related, one being the foundation for the other (cf. *De div.* 2.1.2).

23. That Cicero expected these three works to be read as a trilogy can be seen from *De div.* 2.1.2.

24. Augustine J. Curley, *Augustine's Critique of Skepticism: A Study of Contra Academicos* (New York: Peter Lang, 1996), xviff.

25. Curley, *Augustine's Critique*, 12.

26. *De beata vita* 1.1.

27. *De ordine* 1.1.1.

28. Cf. Cicero's portrayal of Socrates as the first political philosopher (*Tusc. disp.* 5.4. 10–11).

29. *De divinatione* 2.1.2.

30. The Third, or New, Academy, which was founded by Carneades (ca. 213–129 BC), in response to Stoic epistemology, espoused a form of skepticism about knowing the truth. Its most famous adherent was Cicero (see Cicero, *Academica*).

31. "Te, te consulo, Marce Tulli; de adulescentium moribus uitaque tractamus, cui edu-candae atque instituendae omnes illae litterae tuae uigilauerunt": *Contra Academicos* 3.16.35). Furthermore, when Cicero defends the Academics and Augustine attacks them, both are actu-ally pursuing the same goal of fostering civic mindedness. Cicero's promotion of skepticism was designed in part to attenuate political fanaticism by weakening its foundations in certainty. Augustine's assault on skepticism, on the other hand, is designed in part to promote moral action by expunging from the body politic the cynical inaction bred by systemic doubt. See Foley, "Cicero, Augustine, and the Philosophical Roots of the Cassiciacum Dialogues," 59–61, 64).

32. *De ordine* 2.8.25.

33. *De ordine*, 2.9.26–15.42.

34. *De ordine*, 2.20.54. Significantly, Augustine's praise occurs after his discourse on education, wherein he shows his reader how to become "learned, perfect, wise, and happy." Augustine, in other words, is replicating Pythagoras's pedagogical economy.

35. *Contra Academicos* 3.16.36.

36. *De ordine* 2.7.22.

37. Dennis Trout, "Augustine at Cassiciacum: *Otium honestum* and the Social Dimen-sions of Conversion," *Vigiliae Christianae* 42 (1988): 132–46, at 138, 141, resp.

38. *De beata vita* 2.11.

39. Cf. *Contra Academicos* 3.16.36.

40. Cf. *De beata vita* 1.2, where Augustine twice uses *patria* to denote the beatific harbor of philosophy.

41. *Contra Academicos* 3.17.37.

42. I say "some" because like Plato, Aristotle also uses the adjective "political" to denote quasi or pseudo virtues (*Nicomachean Ethics* 3.1116a17).

43. *Ennead* 1.2.

44. *Ennead* 1.2.2, 3, esp. 1.2.2. 15–25 and 1.2.3. 10–20.

45. *Contra Julianum* 4.3.26.

46. *Contra Julianum* 3.8.16. Augustine elsewhere labels this third type of vice *curiositas*. On this point see 1.10.16 and 10.30.41ff, as well as for more references to the three parts of the soul.

47. *Contra Julianum* 1.20.31: "I avoided pain, despair, ignorance—is this not admirable and praiseworthy in such a living being?" ("Fugiebam dolorem, abiectionem, ignorantiam. quid in tali animante non mirabile atque laudabile?")

48. *Contra Julianum.* at 13.21.30, where Augustine interprets the beasts, cattle, and serpents mentioned in the Genesis account of creation as mystical representations of the three parts of the soul.

49. *Contra Julianum*, 10.30.41. The phrase is from I John 2:16.

50. Note that *libido principandi, ambitio saeculi*, etc., are not synonymous with *thymos* (the spirited or irascible part of the soul) but are one of several possible results of *thymos* when it is in a sinful, disordered state.

51. Cf. *Conf.* 10.38.63, where Augustine describes the temptation of loving praise ("amor laudis") as the most dangerous ("periculosissimam").

52. *Conf.* 10.38.71. I say "presumably" because Augustine does not explicitly state that the lust for temporal domination is stronger than the allure of curiosity, though the passage, in my opinion, implies it.

53. *Conf.* 10.38.71, where Augustine equates the "dominationis temporalis fastus" with "superbia," and *Conf.* 10.44.85, where Augustine describes this "fastus" in terms of the Fall.

54. *De civitate Dei* 1.30 and prologue, resp.

55. *De vera religione* 45.84.

56. *De beata vita* 1.2.

57. *De beata vita* 1.3. Cf. *Contra Academicos* 2.2.3.

58. "O si uideretis . . . in quibus periculis iaceamus, cujus morbi dementiam risus iste indicet! O si uideretis! quam cito, quam statim quantoque productius eum uerteretis in fletus! Miseri, nescitis ubi simus? . . . In philosophiam et in eam uitam, quam me tandem occupasse laetor, aemulationis tabificae atque inanis iactantiae ultimam sed nocentiorem ceteris omnibus pestem introducere ac proseminare conamini. *De ordine* 1.10.29, 30 (emphasis added).

59. *De ordine* 1.7.20.

60. *De ordine* 1.10.29.

61. *Julius Caesar* II. iii. 13, 14.

62. Hiram Caton, "St. Augustine's Critique of Politics," *New Scholasticism* 47 (1973): 433–57, at 441.

63. *De beata vita* 4.35, 36.

64. *De beata vita* 2.8.

65. *De beata vita* 2.11.

66. *De ordine* 2.19.51: "Cum autem se conposuerit et ordinarit concinnam pulchramque reddiderit, audebit iam deum uidere atque ipsum fontem, unde manat omne uerum, ipsumque patrem ueritatis. Deus magne, qui erunt illi oculi, quam sani, quam decori, quam ualentes, quam constantes, quam sereni, quam beati! Quid autem est illud, quod uident? Quid quaeso, quid arbitremur, quid aestimemus, quid loquamur? Cotidiana uerba occurrunt et sordidata sunt omnia uilissimis rebus. Nihil amplius dicam nisi promitti nobis aspectum pulchritudinis, cuius imitatione pulchra, cuius conparatione foeda sunt cetera."

67. *De liberio arbitrio* 2. 14. 37: "Habemus igitur qua fruamur omnes aequaliter atque communiter: nullae sunt angustiae, nullus in ea delectus. Omnes amatores suos nullo modo sibi invidos recipit, et omnibus communis est, et singulis casta est. Nemo alicui dicit: Recede, ut etiam ego accedam; remoue manus, ut etiam ego amplectar. Omnes inhaerent, idipsum

omnes tangunt . . . non enim aliquid ejus aliquando fit cujusquam unius aut quorumdam proprium, sed simul omnibus tota est communis." Truth as the highest and only truly shareable object of our longing is acknowledged in a briefer but equally eyebrow-raising passage in the *De ordine*, where Augustine describes Christ avidly seeking souls worthy of his marriage bed (1.8.24).

68. *Republic* 462b,c; 464a,c. Augustine's judgment that a loyalty to one's own is inherently problematic is reflected in the tension between Augustine and his pupils (Trygetius and Licentius) in the *Contra Academicos*, *De beata vita*, and *De ordine*. He also explains the problem more explicitly in *De vera religione* 46.88ff.

69. *De ordine* 2.20.50.

70. Cf. *De beata vita* 2.8, 4.30–32. Augustine portrays moderation not in terms of abstinence or suppression, but in terms of balance, "right measure," and equanimity. He also uses the concept of moderation rather broadly, extending it beyond the perfection of the appetitive part of the soul to include the spirited, or thymotic, part as well. Cf. *De beata vita* 4.33, where immoderation is described as leading not only to *luxuria* but *dominatio* and *superbia*.

71. Markus, *Saeculum*, 78.

72. *De ordine* 2.9.26.

73. Cf. *De beata vita* 2.10; *De ordine* 1.11.32, 2.1.1.

74. *De ordine* 2.9.27.

75. Cf. *De ordine* 2.19.51, where Augustine attributes his love of truth not to his education but to his mother's prayers.

76. *Contra Academicos* 3.19.42.

77. On this point see, among others, Michael White, "Pluralism and Secularism in the Political Order: St. Augustine and Theoretical Liberalism," *University of Dayton Review* 22, no. 3 (1994): 137–53, at 144–45; Elshtain, *Augustine and the Limits of Politics*, 22; Dyson, *The Pilgrim City*, xi.

78. White, "Pluralism and Secularism in the Political Order," 145. This topic also ties in to the debate over whether Augustine's judgment of political life is pessimistic or positive (see below for examples of both sides of this argument). Though it is outside the scope of this essay to scrutinize these conclusions, I would like to suggest that broadening the examination of Augustine's political thought beyond *The City of the God* to the Cassiciacum dialogues may lead to a more nuanced evaluation of Augustine's thought and effect a mild reconciliation between proponents of his alleged negativity of the *civitas* and political life on the one hand and defendants of his affirmative political assessments on the other. For examples of the former position, see Deane, *Political and Social Ideas of Saint Augustine*, chap. 4; George J. Lavere, "The Political Realism of Saint Augustine," *Augustinian Studies* 11 (1980): 134–44, at 136, 144; White, "Pluralism and Secularism in the Political Order," 144; Paul J. Weithman, "Augustine and Aquinas on Original Sin and the Function of Political Authority," *Journal of the History of Philosophy* 30, no. 3 (July 1992): 356–60; Caton, "St. Augustine's Critique of Politics," 457; Dyson, *The Pilgrim City*. For the latter position, see James V. Schall, "Political Theory and Political Theology," *Laval Théologique et Philosophique* 31 (1975): 25–48, at 27; P. J. Burnell, "The Status of Politics in St. Augustine's *City of God*," *History of Political Thought* 13:1 (1992): 13–29; Jeanne Marie Heffernan, "The Nature and Origin of Political Authority in Augustine and Aquinas" (master's thesis, University of Notre Dame, April 1995); Elshtain, *Augustine and the Limits of Politics*, esp. pp. 93ff.; John von Heyking, *Augustine and Politics as Longing in the World* (Columbia, MO: University of Missouri Press, 2001).

Chapter Three

# Peace in the Order of Nature

## Augustine, Giles, and Dante

### Peter Busch

Nine hundred years after Augustine, in the region of the West that still called itself the Roman Empire, fellow citizens and fellow Christians quarreled as partisans of two rival powers, the emperor and the pope. Each of these powers had its own intellectual defenders. Among those arguing for papal supremacy, perhaps the most important was Giles of Rome, bishop of Bourges and author of the treatise *On Ecclesiastical Power*. For the other side, Dante Alighieri wrote *Monarchy* to defend the right of the emperor to establish universal peace in the world.

In their very opposition, Giles and Dante are both attempting to answer the question of the best regime. That, of course, is something that political philosophers had been trying to do since classical antiquity. Not even the dispute over papal supremacy is wholly new, for Aristotle himself had given priests a certain role in his teaching on the best regime (*Politics* 1329a27–34). What sets Dante and Giles apart from classical political philosophy is the idea that rulers ought to rule for the sake of peace rather than for the cultivation and exercise of virtue. That claim goes beyond the teaching of Aristotle; its source is rather Augustine. In book 19 of *The City of God*, Augustine declares peace to be the natural aim of all human beings, and he describes peace as existing in various forms throughout the order of nature. Giles and Dante both retain this aspect of Augustine's teaching; in that respect, they agree with one another. Where they disagree is on which power, the spiritual or the temporal, is ultimately responsible for defending the peace.

One naturally wonders what Augustine thought of the latter issue. The answer is far from obvious, however, for book 19 contains statements with very different implications about who should rule; some passages seem to anticipate Giles's side of the argument, but others call Dante to mind. It is unclear, indeed, whether the question that exercised Augustine's successors was especially important to Augustine himself, for the very terms "temporal power" and "spiritual power" are absent from *The City of God*. But if Augustine is neither defending nor subverting certain political institutions—if he is not offering his own answer to the best regime—what *is* he doing?

That is what I will investigate in the course of my essay. I begin with an analysis of Augustine's account of peace in the order of nature and note some important ambiguities as he draws on that account to explain the life of Christians in the "earthly city." Next, I show how those ambiguities allowed Giles and Dante to use certain aspects of Augustine's thought in support of their respective positions in the medieval controversy. Finally, I return to Augustine and bring to light what is distinctive in his own political teaching. In my view, Augustine's account of peace is not intended as the foundation of a regime that humans are to institute on earth, but the standard that exposes all earthly regimes in their failure to attain true and complete justice. Augustine's aim is to practice what he has described as the activity of heavenly citizens. It is by illuminating, and even heightening, his readers' restlessness amid the structures needed for earthly peace that Augustine calls us out of the earthly city and into natural citizenship with one another.

# Augustine

Augustine teaches that all human beings, whether as individuals or in community, seek peace. He distinguishes, however, between two basic kinds of peace, each of which defines its own kind of politics—or rather, its own city. "In the earthly city . . . the whole use of temporal things is directed toward the enjoyment of earthly peace. In the Heavenly City, however, such use is directed toward the enjoyment of eternal peace" (*CG* 19.14; see also 14.1).[1] In book 19 Augustine not only distinguishes between these two cities but defends the heavenly city against philosophers and other proponents of the earthly city. In order to do so effectively, he must reach beyond the faithful and address his arguments even to unbelievers (19.1). The centerpiece of his discussion is a theoretical account of peace whose cheerful, contemplative spirit transcends even his polemical purpose.

## Naturally Ordered for Peace

Augustine's account of peace runs through the middle section of book 19. He argues, first, that the *desire* for peace is evident in everything we do as human beings, for anyone "who joins me in an examination, however cursory, of human affairs and our common human nature will acknowledge that, just as there is no one who does not wish to be joyful, so there is no one who does not wish to have peace" (19.12). Augustine can claim such universality because the apparent exceptions actually prove the rule. Even the wickedest of men want peace rather than war for themselves and their households. After all, if the wildest beasts nuzzle their own offspring, "[h]ow much more strongly . . . is a man drawn by the laws of his nature, so to speak, to enter into a similarly peaceful association with his fellow men, so far as it lies within his power to do so?" Pride itself, the root of all rebellion against God, does not seek conflict for its own sake; it rather seeks the peace of ruling in God's place (19.12).

If peace were only desired without actually existing in this world, one could perhaps go only so far in calling it natural. Augustine does think that peace is manifest for us, albeit in differing degrees and kinds according to the justice that makes, or injustice that mars, our relationships with one another and with God. "[H]e who has learnt to prefer right to wrong and the rightly ordered to the perverse, sees that, in comparison with the peace of the just, the peace of the unjust is not worthy to be called peace at all." Once again, the exception helps prove the rule. "Even that which is perverse . . . must of necessity be in, or derived from, or associated with, and to that extent at peace with, some part of the order of things among which it has its being or of which it consists. Otherwise, it would not exist at all" (19.12).

Augustine illustrates this idea in a surprising manner, by describing in bizarre detail what would happen if a man were to be hung upside down. Such a "perverted" orientation would be painful because it disturbs "the peace of the flesh." Nevertheless, the very suffering that the prisoner feels would be impossible if he were not alive; for now, his breath is still at peace with the body. Of course, his breath *will* go eventually: he will die. But when that happens, there will still be peace in his body that keeps it from falling apart. True, in time his body *will* fall apart, but when it does, the parts that fall will be at peace, lying on the ground rather than suspended in the air. Then, if embalming fluids are applied, the body parts will retain their integrity; if not, they will disintegrate, and that will be the end of his body—but not the end of peace, as the bits get eaten by little animals whose bodies are peacefully subservient to their souls. And so on. Through it all, the flesh, in every conversion and transformation, "still finds itself subject to the same laws: to the laws which are distributed throughout the universe for the preservation of every kind of mortal creature, and which give peace by bringing suitable things suitably together" (19.12).

Thus Augustine's gruesome reflections open the way to a beautiful vista in which many natural types of peace are arranged from lowest to highest: peace of the body, peace of the irrational soul, peace of the rational soul, peace of the body and soul, peace among human beings generally, peace in the household, peace of the city, and peace of the heavenly city. Above them all is the peace uniting all things with God, the source of their being. What these many forms have in common is the "peace of all things," which Augustine defines as "tranquility of order"; order, in turn, is "the disposition of equal and unequal things in such a way as to give to each its proper place" (19.13).

Augustine delights in seeing the harshest things redeemed, or at least mitigated, by their place in this natural order, and he invites readers to share his experience. But since no one should be so consumed by the joys of contemplation as to neglect the burdens of justice (cf. 19.19), Augustine returns to practical considerations. He does so, however, with support from the theoretical discussion that he has just made. The heavenly city can now be described and defended as the community whose life fully accords with nature.

The Peace of a Pilgrim

Augustine ascends through the several types of peace, beginning with bodily peace and proceeding with the peace of the irrational soul, the peace of body and soul, and so on. These varieties are enjoyed by all the animals, and in the subhuman ones they are sufficient unto themselves. In a human being, however, these lower varieties should be ordered and maintained for the sake of a higher peace, the peace of the rational soul, which Augustine has defined as "the rightly ordered relationship [*consensio*] of cognition and action" (19.13). For this purpose, a human being "should wish to be neither distressed by pain, nor disturbed by desire, nor extinguished by death, so that he may arrive at some useful knowledge and regulate his life and morals according to that knowledge" (19.14).

There is nothing in what Augustine has said to this point that could not be accepted in the highest reaches of the earthly city, among the philosophers in particular. But, Augustine continues, the rational soul must itself be at peace with the *whole* of nature, which includes the ordering of human beings and God. That is a problem, because human reason is insufficient for attaining knowledge of God. "[F]or as long as he is in this mortal body, he is a pilgrim, far from the Lord; and so he walks by faith, not by sight. That is why he refers all peace, whether of body or of soul, or of both, to that peace which mortal man has with the immortal God, so that he may exhibit an ordered obedience, in faith, to the eternal Law" (19.14). Whereas the philosophers suppose that the soul can be ruled by reason, Augustine confesses that reason is not always to be trusted. A human being "has need of divine guidance," he declares, "which he may obey with confidence, and divine aid, so that he may obey it freely. Otherwise, in his zeal for knowledge, he may fall into some deadly error because of the infirmity of the human mind" (19.14).

Even in its insufficiency, however, the human mind may still be capable of acknowledging a crucial difference that reflects the natural superiority of the Christian life.[2] "[T]he earthly city, which does not live by faith, desires an earthly peace, and it establishes an ordered concord of civic obedience and rule in order to secure a kind of co-operation of men's wills [*quaedam compositio voluntatum*] for the sake of attaining the things which belong to this mortal life" (19.17). That is to say, the earthly city is founded on a salutary compromise or agreement—what others will call a social contract—that gives divergent wills reason to get along. In contrast, heavenly citizens, though wandering as pilgrims, are oriented by their shared love of God and united by their common love of neighbor as oneself, and they live in joyful hope for the full completion that surpasses the things of this life. Such is the peace that fully and truly accords with nature.

How in the meantime do pilgrims live out their lives in the earthly city? Augustine's first word is that they ignore the rules and distinctions on which ordinary political loyalties are founded. "While this Heavenly City . . . is on pilgrimage in this world, she calls out citizens from all nations and so collects a society of aliens, speaking all languages. She takes *no account* of any difference in customs, laws, and institutions, by which earthly peace is achieved and preserved" (*CG* 19.17, emphasis added). It is important to appreciate how scandalous, even seditious, this statement could seem. Imagine strangers raised in different customs, laws, and institutions, stealing across the border in the night, answering the call of Christians who see *them* as their true fellow citizens! Augustine diminishes the scandal by hastening to qualify what he has said: "not that [the Heavenly City] annuls or abolishes any of those, rather she maintains them and follows them (for whatever divergences there are among the diverse nations, those institutions have one single aim—earthly peace)." Does this mean that Christians offer aliens a path to heavenly citizenship while rejecting them in earthly terms? Although Augustine does not enter into this thicket here, he does make clear that heavenly citizens offer no more than conditional support for the customs, laws, and institutions of the earthly city. These things should only to be supported for the earthly peace, and even then only so long as they present "no hindrance . . . to the religion which teaches that one supreme and true God is to be worshipped" (19.17).

Thus, Augustine's remarks on the conduct of heavenly citizens living in the earthly city leave much to be explained. What does it look like to follow or support institutions without taking them seriously for their own sake? In what manner does the heavenly city summon its citizens out of many different nations? What consequences for ordinary political loyalties should be accepted or even welcomed as one performs that duty? What sort of hindrance to religious observance would induce heavenly citizens to resist the customs, laws and institutions of their country? Rather than elaborating, however, Augustine leaves us pondering the implications of his tantalizing statement.

The Case of Rome

Even if Augustine says nothing further about policies, rules, or institutional boundaries to be observed by heavenly citizens in general, he soon considers a case that is bound to shed light on the matter. Rome is the city that grew into an empire that dominated the world for centuries, the empire, moreover, in which Augustine himself and his contemporaries happen to live; it is the city, finally, whose humiliation at the hands of the barbarians has caused a backlash against Christians and provoked Augustine's thousand-page defense. As such, Rome, albeit a particular city among countless others, stands for the earthly city. Many of the questions that we have been asking can be summed up in this one: What is Rome to a Christian?

Augustine's discussion of Rome does not eliminate the perplexities with which we have been struggling, but it does clarify them in a sense, by highlighting a specific tension. Two passages, separated by only a few pages, draw very different conclusions about Rome because they proceed from very different notions of a "republic" (*res publica*). The first discussion (19.21) recalls a definition from Cicero's *Republic*, in which Scipio Africanus at first identifies a republic as that which a people holds in common, but in subsequent conversation Scipio argues that nothing is truly common— strictly speaking, there is no "people" at all—without justice.[3] The conclusion offered in Cicero's text is that Rome, having sunk to the depths of moral corruption, has ceased to exist as a republic.[4] Augustine proceeds even further. If justice depends on more than the earthly peace—if it depends on direction and assistance from a being who ensures that the just ultimately prosper—then of course it matters what one has faith *in*. It was great hypocrisy in Porphyry, for example, to think he could admire the Law of Moses for its justice while ignoring the commandment "You will have no other gods before Me" (*CG* 19.23). One really cannot say that the Romans were just if they worshiped demons rather than serving the true God (19.21, 19.25). Thus, the Roman republic did not merely cease to exist: it never existed in the first place (19.21; cf. 2.21).

But this first statement on Rome is soon followed by a second one, in which Augustine identifies pagan Rome as a "republic," after all. Although the Romans were never united for the sake of anything public in the fullest sense, they did form an alliance to obtain things that they loved separately, especially wealth and honor (19.24). It was for such things that they exerted themselves mightily and successfully in defending the peace of their city (5.12–13). Other peoples, meanwhile, have united under kings for the sake of other particular ends. One also could count such realms as republics after all if one were to define a "people" in different terms, not as a multitude united by justice but as "an assembled multitude of rational creatures bound together by a common agreement as to the objects of their love" (19.24). This second definition was declared the serious or final version by Robert Markus. As Markus argues quite reasonably, such a definition would be recommended insofar as one acknowledges the importance of earthly peace—as even heavenly citizens do.[5]

Taking these two statements together, one is left in a condition that Pierre Manent has memorably termed "seeing double."[6] On the one hand, one cannot ignore Augustine's ascent from mere compromise to the more satisfactory forms of peace that exist only in the city of God. On the other hand, Augustine does not rest satisfied with defining a republic in these terms; in order to preserve the appearances of politics as ordinarily practiced in this life, he also defines republics down to the alliance that preserves the minimum of earthly peace. He could even seem to prefer the second definition, for all its flaws, inasmuch as he speaks of it as "our definition."[7]

If this duality prevents us from giving a satisfactory account of pagan antiquity, could it be resolved in Christian Rome? Although Augustine denies the justice of the so-called republic of centuries before, he does not similarly denounce the empire of his own day. On the contrary, he praises the present emperor, Theodosius, as well as the first Christian emperor, Constantine (see 5.25–26). These men apparently stand above the likes of Julius Caesar or Augustus in Augustine's estimation. If that seems ridiculous to anyone dazzled by the empire's glory under the latter sort of emperor, it is consistent with a Christian understanding of the righteousness and peace that humans can hope for in this life.

> That peace which is our peculiar possession . . . is ours even now, with God by faith; and we shall enjoy it eternally with Him by sight. But the peace which we have here, whether shared with other men or peculiar to ourselves, is only a solace for our wretchedness rather than the joy of blessedness. Our righteousness also [*ipsa quoque nostra iustitia*], though true righteousness insofar as it is directed toward a good end, is in this life such that it consists only in the remission of sin rather than in the perfection of virtue. (19.27)

As Robert Dodaro has noted,[8] Augustine praises Theodosius not as a great leader but as a man who repented when confronted about his sins by Bishop Ambrose. This is evidently as it should be, for Augustine declares (19.19) that bishops ought to view their positions as offices in which they are duty bound to oversee the flock that has been entrusted to them. Could this shared responsibility between emperor and bishop be the pattern of a community that practices justice by providing for earthly peace while praying for the remission of sins?

Augustine constantly leaves room for this possibility without ever affirming it. He says nothing to institutionalize the relationship between bishop and emperor, nothing to require that bishops oversee the emperor's actions and occasionally over-rule them for the sake of true religion. By the same token, however, Augustine says nothing to make clear that bishops should *not* have such authority over secular rulers, though one could expect such a conclusion from the need to provide for earthly peace. Anyone who reads his thousand-page text seeking explicit guidelines for the relation among temporal and spiritual powers is bound to be disappointed.

## The Medieval Controversy

If Augustine is reluctant to lay down such guidelines, others are not always so. Giles of Rome is happy to help Augustine draw the conclusion that temporal rulers ought to submit to the spiritual authority of the church. Dante argues, to the contrary, that if the emperor is to defend the peace, he must be free to wield his sword without priestly interference.

### Giles: Spiritual Power for Spiritual Peace

Perhaps the most famous declaration of papal supremacy is *Unam sanctam* (1302), issued by Pope Boniface VIII; a more substantial argument, however, is made in *Of Ecclesiastical Power*, written by Giles the previous year.[9] Not only was Giles in a position to exercise considerable influence in Boniface's court but he was also the leading Augustinian of his day.[10]

Giles follows Augustine in denying that earthly powers can be judged merely with a view to earthly ends. Like Augustine, he acknowledges the possibility of an earthly justice, but only if it is guided by faith and hopeful for completion in the heavenly peace. As Giles presents the argument, the earthly and heavenly cities differ in being "material" and "spiritual," the former being understood as wholly for the sake of the latter.

> The whole duty of the earthly power is to govern and rule these external and material goods in such a way that the faithful are not impeded in the peace of conscience and in peace of soul and in tranquility of mind. For, in this way, not only have justice and peace kissed in those things which are of God—since unless we live justly with God we shall not have peace with Him—but also justice among these external goods conduces to tranquility of soul and to peace of mind. (*EP* 2.6)

Thus Giles recalls what Augustine had called "the peace of the rational soul" and, like Augustine, insists that it flows as it ought to when the soul is properly subordinated to God. He also catches hold of Augustine's important proviso that laws, institutions, and customs must not be honored when they interfere with the worship of the faithful. And as these Augustinian ideas appear on the page, Giles's prose, which can otherwise be rather turgid, is graced by the image of justice and peace uniting in a kiss.

Where Giles extends on Augustine is in arguing that the work of earthly justice requires priestly supervision. He is not the first medieval writer to take this step; especially important to him was Hugh of Saint Victor. In the fourth chapter of part 1 of his *Of Ecclesiastical Power*, Giles develops Hugh's statement that "spiritual power must both institute the earthly power and judge it if it is not good."[11] Giles finds it necessary, however, to answer the counterargument that the judgment in question should be limited to spiritual matters and thus exclude temporal ones. In his view, limiting the spiritual power in this way would be inconsistent with the divine order that ranks temporal below spiritual things, placing the one sword below the other.

That this is, in fact, required by the divine order is argued in the next chapter (*EP* 1.5), where Giles makes four arguments in favor of the position "that priestly power precedes royal and earthly power in dignity and nobility." The third and fourth of these arguments, to which Giles devotes the most space, are as follows: priestly power was established in the Bible directly by God, while kingly power came only afterwards and through Samuel, a priest; and as lower bodies are ruled by higher bodies and the corporeal realm by the spiritual, so should it be among human beings, with temporal powers governed by the spiritual and ultimately by the pope.

In making both of these arguments, Giles draws explicitly on Augustine. Anticipating the objection that God elsewhere established kings first and priests second—Rome being the prime example, of course—Giles argues that kingdoms believing in other gods lack justice and hence are no more than bands of brigands. As we have seen, this is the fundamental challenge issued in *City of God* 19.21. And again Giles describes an orderly universe with God at the peak of all nature, just as Augustine had in 19.13.[12]

When it comes to drawing political conclusions, however, Giles radicalizes the original teaching of book 19. Augustine, we recall, had stressed that the heavenly city generally obeys and supports the laws, institutions, and customs of the earthly city and that it values earthly peace especially as the opportunity for turning its mind to God (19.17, 19.26). Giles, in contrast, is sufficiently concerned about the connection between temporal and spiritual things that he abandons this general policy of restraint. Since disruptions in the temporal peace have spiritual costs, the spiritual power must be prepared, when the need is great, *to defend the peace by wielding the spiritual sword* (*EP* 2.10, 2.14). Just as an evacuated cup, when pressed against the skin, will draw the flesh into it, so will war or strife, which is a "spiritual vacuum," draw the spiritual power into temporal affairs.

> Therefore, just as among natural phenomena it rests with heavenly power to attract things in order to prevent discontinuities, so in the government of men it rests with heavenly or ecclesiastical power, which is catholic and universal, to draw factions and disputes together, lest wars arise, and lest peace, which is the bond of love and which unites the faithful, be destroyed, so that the ecclesiastical prince may fully govern and rule them. (*EP* 3.6)

But although much in these lines, including their beauty, reminds us again of Augustine, we should note one crucial difference in Giles's discussion. Giles says that "the government of men under some ruling power is natural and laudable when it imitates the government of the whole world or the government of natural things under the one Ruling Power, that is, under the one God" (*EP* 3.6). He apparently does not mean, after all, that peace is natural in the sense that it abides in the whole order of nature, *despite* the disruptions introduced by human beings. What was distinctive and surprising in Augustine's account is subtly dropped by Giles.

To be sure, Giles says nothing explicit to admit that he has radicalized Augustine's argument. If he is aware of the shift, perhaps his explanation would be as follows: Augustine's version is at least misleading, for it could be taken to imply that earthly peace is not only good in its own right, but knowable by and serviceable to earthly rulers. One might then suppose that kings are self-sufficient, able to establish or maintain peace on their own and thus to exercise their own justice in the earthly city. That, of course, would contradict Augustine's own challenge to the pagans. Perhaps the consistent Augustinian position, therefore, is to describe the true ends of government as entirely spiritual, whereas the secular objects are only material. Once this is granted, it is hard to resist the conclusion that kings should submit to the spiritual power (*EP* 1.5). Thus Giles presses Augustine into serving the cause of Boniface VIII.

Dante: Universal Peace and Imperial Rule

Meanwhile, Dante Alighieri entered the fray on behalf of the emperor, writing a work less famous than a certain poem you might have heard of, but one sufficiently interesting to make it on the Vatican's list of spiritually dangerous books.[13]

Dangerous or not, *Monarchy* is certainly an odd book, filled with strange assertions and even stranger arguments. For example, Dante boasts at the beginning (*M* 1.1)[14] that his is the first book ever written on "temporal monarchy"; no reader can be unaware, however, that kingship was certainly discussed by Aristotle, who is mentioned on most pages of Dante's treatise. Dante goes on to explain that the monarchy in question is "commonly called 'empire'" and consists of political supremacy "among and over all things that are measured by time," but although this explanation does indeed point well beyond the monarchies discussed in Aristotle's *Politics*, it only plunges us further into perplexity, for how could a human being exert such authority at all, let alone justly? Nevertheless, Dante's thesis is that all mankind should rightfully be ruled by an earthly emperor. Nothing is more likely to make *Monarchy* seem to us irrelevant at best, dangerous at worst.[15]

Much of this book's strangeness can be explained by the political dysfunction of Dante's time. Ostracized himself as a result of quarrels among the various parties in Florence, Dante sees every day what happens when religious and secular authorities contend for supremacy. In response, he emphatically denies that the Gospels represent spiritual and secular powers as "two swords" that both ultimately belong to Peter (*M* 3.9). Neither can this teaching be found, as some would allege, in Genesis. If the pope, as the spiritual power, may be compared to the sun,[16] the emperor as the moon does not shine only by reflected light; he has some light of his own (*M* 3.4). Or as Dante puts it even more boldly in the second book of his *Comedy* (where the words are safely deposited in the mouth of a dead man): "Rome, which made the world good, used to have / two suns; and they made visible two paths – / the world's path and the pathway that is God's" (*Purgatory* 16.106–8).[17] Nothing is more opposed to Giles's political Augustinianism than the image of an emperor shining like the sun.

But as we have seen, Giles modifies the argument set forth in *The City of God*. Could Dante have understood himself to be restoring Augustine's teaching to its unpoliticized original? It is true that in *Monarchy*, as elsewhere, Dante says nothing but kind things about Augustine. Referring to the writings of Augustine and the other doctors of the church, Dante declares that "anyone who doubts that they were aided by the Holy Spirit has either never seen the fruit of their teachings at all, or if he has seen it, has by no means tasted it" (*M* 3.3). If that statement is as positive as it seems, it is all the more amazing that Dante quotes Augustine only twice in the entire book (both times in *M* 3.4) and even then only regarding methods of biblical interpretation. He is utterly silent about Augustine's distinction between the heavenly and earthly cities, his account of peace, and his views of the Roman Republic or Empire.

Now, regarding the last of these, at least, there can be no doubt of Dante's opinion. Book 2 of *Monarchy* is entirely devoted to the argument that the Romans came to rule the world *not* as a gang of thieves, but with justice. In *M* 2.6, Dante quotes the lines of Virgil in which Anchises urges his son Aeneas, "remember though, O Roman, to rule the nations with thy sway—these shall be thine arts—to crown peace with law, to spare the humbled, and to tame in war the proud."[18] These very words are quoted at the beginning of *The City of God* in order to declare that what they describe is not the prerogative of Rome, after all, but of God. Dante, in contrast, wants to show that in order for rulers to be just, it is enough for them to promote the earthly peace; no reference to God is needed at all. But the poet who dares condemn Boniface to the eighth circle of hell also knows how to keep silent: his disagreement with Augustine is left implicit.

Dante begins his treatise by announcing (1.2) that its whole argument rests on a first principle—which, in a political inquiry like the present one, is a practical end that sets everything else in motion. The first portion of book 1 is dedicated to establishing that principle, and at the end of that discussion he gives what appears to be a simple answer. The goal of politics is "universal peace," or an earthly peace that extends to include all of mankind (1.4).

Augustine, we recall, had likewise stressed the importance of peace among all human beings; for him it consists of an ordered concord that, in its fully natural manifestation, is established by God and animated by love; as one usually finds it on earth, however, such peace is attenuated by sin and consists only of a kind of compromise among wills. Giles, meanwhile, effectively reduces all forms of earthly peace to a means; such peace is an ordering of material things for either worldly or spiritual purposes. Dante likewise modifies Augustine's original account, but instead of downplaying the sufficiency of earthly peace, he amplifies it to the point of reversing the teachings of Giles.

According to Dante's account, each species of animal is made by God to perform an activity that distinguishes it from all other beings. Humans differ from the other animals, on the one hand, in their capacity for intellectual understanding, and from the angels, on the other, in having no more than a *possible* intellect (*M* 1.3). Our intellects have to be actualized, and that is why we need peace. This human need for peace is different from an animal's; what we desire is *not* mere safety, Dante stresses, but a tranquility that allows us to exercise our intellectual awareness (*M* 1.4). It follows that for Dante universal peace is the end in one sense but not another. It is effectively the goal of politics, but it is not simply the goal of all human activity. In fact there are two such goals, an earthly one and a heavenly one, and the earthly *is attainable in this life*.[19]

Thus Dante downplays the tension between leisured contemplation and righteous engagement in affairs, which Augustine himself felt as a bishop and had accentuated in his remarks about a Christian life (*CG* 19.19). By the same token, he is more confident than Augustine is regarding the powers of human understanding.

As we recall, even as Augustine disagrees with the Academic skeptics' claim that nothing can be known with certainty, he also insists that the just man walks by faith and "we do not yet see our good" (cf. *CG* 19.18 with 19.4). Dante's remarks seem to strike a similar balance but really are far more optimistic. On the one hand, the intellect "cannot be completely actualized at any given time by one man or by any one of the particular communities" such as a household, a city, or a particular kingdom. On the other, the intellect can be, and is, actualized by the human race as a whole. "This is so, just as a multitude of generable things is necessary so that the entire potential of prime matter can be actualized all the time. The alternative is to admit that pure potentiality can have a separate existence, which is impossible. And Averroes agrees with this view in his commentary on the *De anima*" (1.3). Although this passage is rather obscure, its meaning becomes clear if we note that the "separate existence" in question would be with God and the angels in heaven rather than among human beings in this life. Dante is claiming that the human race gains access to the truth in the theoretical sciences such as physics or metaphysics. He goes on to assert, however, that "the intellective power I am talking about deals not only with universal forms or species but also with particular ones by a kind of extension." Practical activity is directed either by "political prudence" or "the craftsman's skill," and these in turn "are controlled by speculation, which is as much as to say that they serve the highest goal for which the First Goodness brought mankind into being" (1.3).

Those who actualize the intellect, therefore, will know best how to guide earthly politics to its destination. "This now makes clear that remark in the *Politics*, namely that men of strong intellect naturally lead other men" (1.3).[20] Of course, a given monarch would be only one man and not necessarily a man of intellect, but Dante envisions one with suitable advisors or other guidance. At the end of the treatise, he writes that the emperor "directs the human race to temporal happiness by means of philosophic doctrines" (3.15).

We have seen that Giles's position depends on his appropriation of Augustine's claim that pre-Christian Rome was merely a gang of thieves, for instead of serving any true public good, they maintained an alliance only for the sake of wealth or glory. This argument must somehow be answered if Dante is to defend earthly politics against the claims of the church hierarchy. Book 2 as a whole is dedicated to arguing that the Romans came to rule the world by right and not merely by force. At the center of this argument, and indeed of *Monarchy* as a whole, are the contentions that the Romans ruled by right because they succeeded in serving the common good (*M* 2.5) and not just any such good, but the natural end of humanity (2.6).

In 2.5, Dante begins with the assumption—which Augustine accepts, following Cicero—that "the goal of every law is the common welfare"; whatever does not promote the welfare of those who are subjects is a law in name only. "It is therefore clear," Dante continues, "that whoever intends the common welfare also intends the goal of law." Next he argues that republican Rome did, in fact, intend the common welfare. "These Romans attempted to increase the common good by their sweat, poverty, and exile; for this cause they suffered loss of children, loss of limb, and finally loss of their own lives." The point is illustrated with a torrent of examples, including Cincinnatus, Fabricius, Camillus, the first Brutus, Mucius, the Decii, and above all, Cato the Younger. Dante praises not only the deeds of these men but also the eloquence of Cicero in recalling their example; he implicitly rejects Augustine's contention that Roman virtue was rotten from the beginning. With this preparation, Dante proposes the following syllogism: "Whoever intends the goal of law proceeds in accordance with law; in subjecting the world to its rule, the Roman people intended the goal of law . . . therefore, in subjecting the world to its rule, the Roman people proceeded in accordance with law. Consequently, the Roman people claimed imperial status for itself by lawful right." But as Dante acknowledges, one premise in this syllogism has certainly not been established, even if one grants everything else he has said to this point. Is it not possible to intend what is right without actually *doing* what is right? Any number of incapacities could make the difference, but especially important is this consideration: could one not intend what is right in a general way while being dead wrong in what constitutes the right?

Dante's whole discussion can seem less than serious—rather a satire on the laborious scholasticism of his opponents than a serious argument of his own. There may be some truth to that impression.[21] Nevertheless, Dante seems not to hesitate here[22] on the question of whether human beings need to walk by faith in order to achieve peace among themselves; neither does he seem to think that philosophers need divine direction to avoid going wrong in their political teachings. Dante asserts that when Roman citizens believed themselves to be serving the common advantage or upholding the rule of law, they were in fact doing so. The advantage that they served was universal peace, which is understood and justified by the intellectual contemplation that stands as the true end of earthly existence. The political justice that rests on this basis is sufficient, it seems, without the higher peace that would come in relationship with God.

## Reconsidering Augustine

One may say, therefore, that Giles and Dante clarify the otherwise perplexing features of Augustine's teaching on peace by dividing those features between themselves. Each author offers a portion of that teaching as his own, but with heavy filtering that clears away its ambiguities and aligns it with his own political priorities. Nowhere is this more evident than in the way Giles implicitly embraces the first and rejects the second of the two definitions of "republic" in book 19 (19.21, 19.24), whereas Dante does just the opposite.

And why not? Given the tension between those two definitions, would it not be necessary to pick one or the other? If, on the one hand, all of God's creatures owe him obedience and worship, if the just man walks by faith, and if happiness lies in the peace with God that awaits the faithful, why not conclude that bishops should supervise not only the practice of Christian worship, but the conduct of citizens and rulers? Or, on the other hand, if the peace among human beings—the tranquility of command and obedience that exists in the established political community—is a natural form of peace and sufficient reason for obeying the law, why not identify such peace as the "universal peace" for the sake of which all laws are enacted? Indeed, a ruler who rules on this basis, assisted by sound philosophy in upholding the laws, would appear to rule *by right*.

Instead of taking either of these positions, Augustine leaves his readers suspended uneasily between them. He gives us to understand that the laws and institutions of the particular city where one lives are binding, *even though* true justice is not to be found there. For all the frustrations of trying to see with double vision, Augustine thought it better to offer two doctrines that sit uneasily with one another rather than limiting himself to just one. Does he have good reason for doing so?

Let us first remind ourselves of the conditional nature of Augustine's remarks in *The City of God* 19.17:

> [The heavenly city] takes no account of any difference in customs, laws, and insti-tutions, by which earthly peace is achieved and preserved—not that she annuls or abolishes any of those, rather she maintains them and follows them (for whatever divergences there are among the diverse nations, those institutions have one single aim—earthly peace), provided that no hindrance is presented thereby to the religion which teaches that one supreme and true God is to be worshipped.

In this general statement, Augustine combines provision for the civil peace with adher-ence to a peace that is not only higher, but transcendently so. In order to do both at once, Christians ought to tolerate a great deal of misplaced seriousness about a great many things; thus "a harmony is preserved between [the two cities] with respect to the things which belong to this condition" (19.17). Having said this much, however, Augustine does imply that certain customs, laws, or institutions would need to be ignored or opposed if they presented a hindrance. Thus far we have stressed the frus-trating ambiguity of Augustine's statement. We can add, however, that this proviso seems to be guarding against interference from earthly rulers rather than demanding a priestly blessing or authoritative guidance. What Augustine stresses here is the need to abide by the laws of the earthly city.

But even as Augustine encourages his readers to preserve harmony between the two cities, he understands how disjointed they can be, and how keeping peace between them may require one to live with unsatisfying choices in lamentable cir-cumstances. To see this, let us consider what Augustine says in a portion of the text that we have, thus far, skipped over: his discussion of the household (*CG* 19.14–16).

## Slavery in the Household

Augustine's stated reason for treating the household before the city proper concerns the commandment to love our fellow humans: "for the order of nature and of human society itself gives [a human being] readier access to [its members], and greater opportunity for caring for them" (*CG* 19.14). No doubt this is true of the relationships between parents and children as well as between spouses, and so we are likely to expect them to be the focus in these chapters. But Augustine spends much more time discussing a part of the household that others would wish to pass by in silence: the relation between masters and slaves.

It is hard to imagine a reader who would not be perplexed and troubled by Augustine's discussion of slavery. Much of the ancient world would seem to be implicated as he denies that slavery is natural; indeed, he goes so far as to declare that God "did not intend that His rational creature, made in His own image, should have lordship over any but irrational creatures: not man over man, but man over the beasts" (19.15). Yet despite this, and to our own dismay, Augustine issues no categorical denunciation of slavery; he applies the love commandment to everyone in the household, including masters and slaves. In a sense, such a teaching is more radical than a call for emancipation would have been, for it demands what could seem the impossible. Following Paul, Augustine teaches slaves to serve "not with cunning fear, but in faithful love, until all unrighteousness shall cease, and all authority and power be put down, that God may be all in all." As for masters, they too must love:

> In the household of the just man . . . who "lives by faith" and who is still a pilgrim on his way to that Heavenly City, even those who command are the servants of those whom they seem to command. For it is not out of any desire for mastery that they command; rather, they do so from a dutiful concern for others: not out of pride in ruling, but because they love mercy. (19.14)

In the way of the world, it is no surprise when rulers indulge their pride or their lust for domination, or when slaves resent their servitude and hate their masters in return. Christians, however, are bound by God's law to walk a different path.

One must ask, however, how mastery could *ever* be an act of mercy if, as Augustine has indicated, slavery is contrary to the nature of the rational soul. The most important answer for Augustine must be that masters ought to raise their slaves as Christians, for loving other humans as oneself means teaching them to love God. But surely such mercy is better shown by helping them become freemen rather than keeping them as slaves?

Augustine denies that this is necessarily so. Although slavery is introduced as a result of sin, it is also a *punishment* for sin, in his view, in order to correct human pride (19.15). Moreover, the slave who accepts his situation and loves even his master is free in the most important respect, whereas the master who delights in ruling is actually enslaved in the worst way. From these considerations, Augustine draws a conclusion that is hard to accept: it is a *duty*, he says, for masters to enforce the obedience of slaves, by corporal punishment if necessary (19.16).

It is no surprise that modern readers should be anxious either to play down the importance of this lesson (for example by contextualizing it) or else to condemn it along with Augustine himself.[23] What *is* surprising is that Augustine was also dissatisfied and showed his dissatisfaction in deed. In 428, he wrote his friend Alypius, an old friend and fellow bishop with connections in Rome, to request legal help. Several members of his church were now exposed to lawsuits because they had boarded a ship and helped free more than a hundred prisoners who were to be sold into slavery. Although Augustine is careful to say that he himself was not there in person, he also goes out of his way to show his solidarity. For as he remarks, the action was done knowing "*our* practice of performing acts of mercy in such cases."[24] This story is remarkable in many ways, but we highlight this fact in particular: Augustine expresses not even a little disappointment that the former prisoners are missing out on their lifelong lessons in humility. How is he not contradicting his own teaching in book 19?

Augustine himself would hardly claim immunity to mental or moral dissonance regarding slavery or any other matter. But the tension is at least qualified, if perhaps not resolved, by a third consideration. Augustine's intervention in the case of the slave traders was made possible by the fact that snatching free Africans and selling them into slavery was illegal.[25] Hence, although his congregation took some personal risks in order to save the prisoners, they were still upholding the law in their work of mercy. Merely keeping slaves in one's household, however, was quite legal. To seek the liberation of *all* slaves would mean opposing the domestic, economic and political institutions of their time in a broader and more fundamental way.

Rule and obedience in the household are not isolated from those of the city, in Augustine's view. Domestic peace depends on the civil peace, and Augustine was very impressed by the need to keep that peace.

> A man's household . . . ought to be the beginning, or a little part, of the city; and every beginning has reference to some end proper to itself, and every part has reference to the integrity of the whole of which it is a part. From this, it appears clearly enough that domestic peace has reference to civic peace: that is, that the ordered concord of domestic rule and obedience has reference to the ordered concord of civic rule and obedience. Thus, it is fitting that the father of a family should draw his own precepts from the law of the city, and rule his household in such a way that it is brought into harmony with the city's peace. (19.16)

Thus we might try to explain Augustine's apparent inconsistency in the following way. Where there is an opportunity to arrange for legal emancipation, even at considerable expense or risk to oneself, he gives his bishop's blessing. Where he sees no such opportunity, Augustine finds a necessity that all must endure with patience, not because slavery itself is just but because law and custom maintain the civil peace. Everyone should also remember, however, to worship God and love all human beings, beginning with the very household whose members are so divided by the legacy of sin. Since this is such a great demand, everyone, including the masters, ought to long for a blessed existence in which no human being commands another (19.16).

Augustine's actions regarding slavery are hard to categorize; they seem to fit neither the authoritative intervention that Giles reserved for "spiritual powers," nor the deference favored by Dante. Augustine was quite ready to be an activist in his own way, leading his congregation in spirit (if not in person) as they intervened to save prisoners from the yoke of slavery. This could well be described as entering worldly affairs on behalf of justice. He only did so, however, when such activism could claim support of the law, not to overrule the laws or undermine the rulers who made them. Rather than take such action, Augustine took an obedient stance more in keeping with Dante, even as he encouraged a kind of community that goes far beyond what Dante or anyone else expected from ancient Rome.

Although Augustine's treatment of the household appears to be a digression, less important than the discussion of the city that immediately follows, it is in fact illuminating even of that subsequent discussion. It affords a concrete sense of how heavenly citizens might act in the earthly city with attention to *both* of the upcoming definitions of a republic—and by the same token, to *neither* of them simply. The household is indeed the beginning of the city.

## Calling Citizens from the Earthly City

Augustine teaches his readers to support the most basic elements of the civil peace, and this means upholding inequalities that frustrate our rational natures but are dictated by prevailing customs, laws, and institutions. He does not teach them to be satisfied with such compromises, however. On the contrary, his aim is to encourage their dissatisfaction.

Whether Augustine was writing in half-hearted support of slavery or taking measures to prevent it, his actions were at best imperfect. Such imperfection, and the great anxieties and miseries that attend it, is the theme of the chapters (19.4–11) that immediately precede his account of peace. In a relentlessly depressing polemic, Augustine surveys every good that philosophers have ever identified as an end, and he declares them all to be so transient, so uncertain, so flawed, that none of them could possibly be enough for human happiness. This section sharpens readers' yearning for a peace that surpasses all mortal things—or rather, it reminds them of a yearning that is ever present but often buried.

In one of its most memorable passages, Augustine describes a "wise judge" who, despite his wisdom, can never really be certain of the truth when he condemns prisoners or tortures witnesses. The judge is duty bound to take the seat, and Augustine says that he does indeed do so. But even if that is true, should one also say that such a man lives a happy life? Augustine answers on his behalf: "Surely, it would be more compassionate, and more worthy of the dignity of man, if he were to acknowledge that the necessity of acting in this way is a miserable one: if he hated his own part in it, and if, with the knowledge of godliness, he cried out to God, 'From my necessities deliver Thou me'" (19.6; cf. Ps. 25:17). In his only remarks on the office of a bishop, which we have already had occasion to consider, Augustine speaks in similar though not identical terms. Delightful though it is to live the life of contemplation, one may find that "just employment" (*negotium iustum*) has been "imposed" upon oneself. In that case, the burden is to be borne. "Love of truth desires holy leisure," he writes; "the necessity of love undertakes just employment."[26]

No doubt, Augustine's description here is less bleak than his earlier portrait of the wise judge. We have seen enough, however, of his own work as a bishop to grasp why Augustine would think that his position ought to be borne as a duty rather than sought out as a privileged opportunity. He judges the peace that is normally attainable among human beings by a heavenly standard, a tranquility of order that exists only among those united by love for God's sake. When such love is deficient, as it so often is, one may be left spackling over cracks and fissures that are beyond human power to mend. Augustine has a more chastened opinion than Giles does of what bishops are generally able to accomplish.

And if that is true of bishops, who after all preside over houses of worship, such shortcomings are all the more obvious among political officials and the societies over which they hold sway. That is the great incompleteness that Augustine keeps before the reader's eyes by maintaining two definitions of a republic, one founded on the justice of serving God, the other only on the more basic civil peace. One can understand how the tension that Augustine maintained would provoke attempts to resolve it, either by a bishop who claims formal political authority for the spiritual power, or a philosophic poet who defines justice down to the peace that a worldly prince might keep.

Augustine hopes for a different response. By awakening his readers to their dissatisfaction with the justice of their households and communities, he places them in a position to appreciate how the just man necessarily walks by faith, not by sight. In this way, he carries out the work that he shares with all the heavenly city, which "calls out [*evocat*] citizens of all nations and every tongue, and brings together a society of pilgrims" (19.17). This, then, is Augustine's most important intervention in politics: an education of souls that uproots their ordinary political allegiances, but teaches them to find the ultimate fulfillment of temporal justice in "perfectly ordered and perfectly harmonious fellowship in the enjoyment of God, and of one another in God" (19.13). This is the peace that fully accords with nature, even if it surpasses what any earthly city can provide.

# Notes

1. Augustine, *The City of God Against the Pagans*, trans. R. W. Dyson (Cambridge: Cambridge University Press, 2010). Parenthetical references to this work (abbreviated *CG*) are to book and chapter number. When it is necessary to amend the translation or supply Augustine's Latin, I use the critical texts of *De ciuitate dei Libri I–X* and *De ciuitate dei Libri XI–XXII*, ed. Bernardus Dombart and Alphonsus Kalb, Corpus Christianorum Series Latina, vols. 47, 48 (Turnhout: Brepols Publishers, 1955).

2. Just because reason needs guidance does not, in Augustine's view, mean that everything is uncertain; unlike the Academic skeptics, Christians think that some things are *known* (*CG* 19.18).

3. This passage in Augustine returns to an argument that he had begun back in book 21 (2.21). In response to those who said that the Christians caused the decline of Rome, Augustine had answered that republican virtue was long since dead by the time Christ came along. But Augustine had also promised to go further, and that argument is what we find now in 19.21–24.

4. Cicero, *Republic* 2.42.

5. Robert Markus, *Saeculum: History and Society in the Theology of Augustine* (Cambridge: Cambridge University Press, 1970), 67–71. Rowan Williams has responded with the acute observation that Augustine's list of peoples who meet this new definition includes the ancient Babylonians. If Babylon was a republic, what would despotism be? The alliance that Augustine describes in his second definition is no different from that which unites a criminal with his fellow gangsters; without the justice that comes only with the true faith, ancient Rome simply was a gang of thieves (*CG* 19.12, 4.4). See Rowan Williams, *On Augustine* (London and New York: Bloomsbury), 113; also John Milbank, *Theology and Social Theory*, 2nd ed. (Malden, MA: Blackwell, 2006), 404–7.

6. Pierre Manent, *Metamorphoses of the City* (Cambridge, MA: Harvard University Press, 2013), 22, 214–15.

7. "Secundum istam definitionem nostram Romanus populus populus est et res eius sine dubitatione res publica" (*CG* 19.24). Also consider John von Heyking, *Augustine and Politics as Longing in the World* (Columbia: University of Missouri Press), 88. In commenting on 2.21, where Augustine speaks of "more plausible definitions [*probabiliores . . . definitiones*]" that allow for Rome to have been a republic, von Heyking understates how problematic such "more plausible" definitions really are for Augustine, but like Markus he helps us see that 19.21 is not the whole story.

8. Robert Dodaro, "*Ecclesia* and *Res publica*: How Augustinian Are Neo-Augustinian Politics?" in *Augustine and Postmodern Thought: A New Alliance against Modernity?* ed. L. Boeve, M. Lamberigts, and M. Wisse (Leuven: Peeters, 2009), 237–71, at 244.

9. References to *Ecclesiastical Power* (*EP*) will be to part and chapter of the work. Quotations in English will use *Giles of Rome's* On Ecclesiastical Power: *A Medieval Theory of World Government*, trans. and ed. R. W. Dyson (New York: Columbia University Press, 2004), which also includes the Latin text. I have also consulted *On Ecclesiastical Power*, translated and introduced by Arthur P. Monahan (Lewiston, NY: Edwin Mellen Press, 1990).

10. In his translator's introduction (xxvii), Monahan convincingly argues that *Ecclesiastical Power* was a source text for *Unam sanctam*.

11. Giles is quoting Hugh's *On the Sacraments of the Christian Faith* 2.4.

12. Giles's argument regarding the order of the universe also refers to Augustine's *On the Trinity* (3.4.9) and *Enchirideon* (3.10).

13. "Dantis Monarchia" was included in the first edition of the *Index* (1559). See Roman Office of the Inquisition, *Index Librorum Prohibitorum*, Bayerische Staatsbibliotek, accessed February 8, 2019, http://daten.digitale-sammlungen.de/bsb00001444/image_22.

14. Parenthetical references to Dante's *Monarchy* (*M*) will cite book and chapter numbers. I use *Dante's* Monarchia, trans. and intro. Richard Kay (Toronto: Pontifical Institute of Mediaeval Studies, 1998).

15. Although this book gets some attention from Dante scholars in literature or theology, it is generally ignored by political theorists. An important exception is Larry I. Peterman, who wrote commentaries on the *Monarchy* and used Dante as a foil to reveal what is distinctive in Machiavelli's political philosophy. See "An Introduction to Dante's *De Monarchia*," *Interpretation* 3, no. 2 (1972): 169–90; "Dante's *Monarchia* and Aristotle's Political Thought," *Studies in Medieval and Renaissance History* 10 (1973): 3–39; "Machiavelli's Dante and the Sources of Machiavellianism," *Polity* 20, no. 2 (1987): 247–72.

16. Dante does not mention the source of the allegory of the sun and moon. For a useful summary of the scholarship on this question, see Kay's n4 to *M* 3.4.

17. Dante Alighieri, *Purgatorio*, trans. Allen Mandelbaum (New York: Bantam Classics, 1984).

18. Virgil, *Aeneid* 6.847–53, in *Virgil: Eclogues, Georgics, Aeneid*, trans. H. R. Fairclough (Cambridge, MA: Harvard University Press, 1916), 1:567.

19. Dante essentially modifies Augustine's earthly peace, therefore, by directing it far more consistently toward the Aristotelian end of contemplation. In the *Metaphysics* (980a) Aristotle declares that all human beings by nature desire understanding, and in his works of political philosophy this natural concern always takes the stage sooner or later. Book 10 of the *Nicomachean Ethics* (1177a12–78a33), for example, identifies contemplation as divine inasmuch as it is the only activity that is truly for its own sake. Book 7 of the *Politics* encourages readers to understand the political life not as one that seeks mastery and plunder through war, but as patterned after a self-sufficient life of study, fit for a god but practiced even here by philosophers (1325a33–b29). Dante strikes a similar note: "The beatitude of this life," he says, can be reached "by means of philosophic doctrines, provided that we follow them by practicing the moral and intellectual virtues" (3.15).

20. Cf. Aristotle, *Politics* 1252a31–32.

21. It seems that Dante relies in these chapters on the sort of political science he describes in book 1: he refers his readers to a teleological order discovered through a sort of theoretical speculation. His argument is a brilliant performance, but it is unlikely to convince anyone of anything. In 2.5, Dante argues that "as everything has a goal appropriate to it, so every goal has an appropriate thing of which it is the goal." It follows, he says, that where there is the goal of law, there is also law itself. Moreover, since there cannot be a consequence without an antecedent, it is impossible for people to intend the goal of law without there already being law. "Hence it is abundantly clear," Dante concludes, "that one who intends the goal of law must necessarily intend it in accordance with what is right, just, and lawful." Dante continues in the same vein in the next chapter (2.6), where he again appeals to a teleological account in order to prove the legitimacy of Rome. Law, he says, is endowed with its power in order for nature to achieve the end of all humanity; for this to happen, there must be a people fitted by nature to rule others. Such people have existed, he asserts, and they were the Romans.

22. How the protoliberalism and incipient secularism of *Monarchy* is to be squared with the opposite impression one gets from much of the *Comedy* must be examined, but it lies beyond the scope of this study.

23. See, e.g., Eric Gregory, *Politics and the Order of Love: An Augustinian Ethic of Democratic Citizenship* (Chicago: University of Chicago Press, 2008), 54 for a brief discussion that notes, on the one hand, that Augustine was not an abolitionist but suggests, on the other, that Augustine's "lack of institutional analysis may have less to do with his theology of love and more to do with his limited experience of political reform."

24. Emphasis added. Augustine's letter to Alypius is Letter 10*, which is among the collection of letters discovered a few decades ago by Johannes Divjak. It appears in *Augustine: Political Writings*, trans. and ed. E. M. Atkins and Robert Dodaro (Cambridge: Cambridge University Press, 2001), 43–47.

25. There is no necessary contradiction between this information and the fact that the Galatians who were waiting for the prisoners hoped to recoup their losses in court.

26. "Quamobrem otium sanctum quaerit caritas veritatis; negotium iustum suscipit necessitas caritatis" (my translation).

Chapter Four

# Deeds and Words

## *Latreia,* Justice, and Mercy in Augustine's Political Thought

### Ashleen Menchaca-Bagnulo

The number of interpretations of Augustine's political theory testifies simultaneously to the depth of his text and to its moments of ambiguity. Depending on whom you read, Augustine is a political thinker and practitioner impeded by his longing for the next world,[1] a forerunner of Hobbesian regimes,[2] or an early pluralist whose skepticism and theory of conscience contribute to modern and postmodern political projects.[3] In John Milbank we see a theocratic Augustine who casts the church as the *societas perfectas,* whereas both Gilbert Meilander and Jean Bethke Elshtain emphasize instead the limitations of earthly politics that exist alongside the political obligations of a Christian.[4]

Pierre Manent presents us with a portrait of Augustine as a theorist of the "science of the Romans"; Manent's reflections are, for our purposes, the most relevant starting point. For Manent, Augustine is one of the last thinkers in the Western canon to recognize both "the passionate interest in this world as expressed in active participation in the common thing" and "the passionate interest in the eternal and the infinite as expressed in the postulation of another world."[5] Augustine is trying the "old city by the new," and in doing so characterizes the operation of the passions for liberty, domination, and glory involved in Roman politics, passions that recur for Augustine in political practice generally.[6] In contrast to the problematic dynamic that these competing desires cause for Roman conceptions of virtue, in Augustine's estimation "true virtue, the virtue that does not lie, the virtue that does not make believe it conquers when it is defeated, must, so to speak, integrate the fact that humans cannot be completely happy in this life."[7] According to Augustine, true virtue is a powerful concept, bridging this world and the next, relating virtue to the emotional life in a way that causes men and women both to process and to accept the situation of incomplete happiness they can possess on earth and to be conformed to the good in this life.

Robert Dodaro, Eric Gregory, and John von Heyking, in their works on Augustine, all point toward book 10 of *The City of God* as an interpretive key for understanding what Augustine's full teaching of virtue is, and how it relates to his ethical and political theory. Importantly, Dodaro, Gregory, and von Heyking also all highlight the integration of the properly ordered emotional life as an essential portion of true Augustinian virtue.[8] If we are to take up the thread of Augustine's account of true virtue, we will need to focus on the concept of *latreia* (right worship)—the bedrock of book 10—and the fullness of Augustinian justice. In unpacking *latreia*'s significance, we will find ourselves in a nuanced position. *Latreia*, right worship and the act due God alone, is also *misericordia*, mercy, the virtue due our neighbor. Augustinian *misericordia* is closely related to the capacity for fellow feeling, the feeling of another's sufferings as one's own, that is the hallmark of a properly ordered emotional life.[9] Someone with a healthy emotional life will feel compassion in the right way, and will therefore perform deeds from "out of mercy's innermost marrow" (Ep. John 5.12), deeds that are a component part of *latreia*. This empathic identification with another's sufferings is fueled by the virtue of charity, but it is made possible only by the virtue of humility, which clears the path for being able to see in another person a dignity and worth equivalent to one's own.

This relationship among justice, mercy, and humility is modeled in Augustine's Eucharistic theology, the concluding focus of book 10. The Eucharist as an act of worship becomes not only the final elucidation of what Augustine takes *latreia* to be, but also the means by which Christians are transformed into persons capable of *latreia*. This does not mean, however, that in order to perform acts of mercy one must participate in the Eucharistic sacrifice of the Mass, but rather, one approaches virtue more closely, the more one resembles the crucified Christ—a resemblance that is possible through the practice of latreia, a virtue available to pagans and Christians alike.

In this essay I begin with a reflection on the relationship between right worship and politics, and will then offer an exegesis of book 10, highlighting the various and multi-valenced meanings of *latreia* in *The City of God*. Finally, I will use the lens of *latreia* to identify pagan and Christian actors that Augustine finds praiseworthy, offering a sketch of Augustinian political theory governed by the insights of book 10.

## The Nexus of Worship and Politics

Scholars note what is sometimes called the "democratic aspect" in Augustine's thought, that is the idea that many different kinds of people, of numerous characteristics and nations, fall under the same law and the same grace, a law that is attainable and discernible, and a grace that is mysteriously unrelated to classical conceptions of merit. All are united by the obligation of the "law of love," and no one escapes the title of "sinner."[10] Eric Gregory points us toward one of the most egalitarian lines in *The City of God*: "The law of God should be given not to one man or to a few wise men, but to a whole nation and a great people, by the awesome proclamation of angels, the great things which were done on Mount Sinai were done before the whole people."[11]

Importantly, this line occurs in book 10 of *The City of God*, the book that I, among others, claim is central to interpreting Augustine's most considerable political work and that compels us to consider how we reconcile the idea that many nations and persons will be a part of the City of God with the everyday experience of reasoning toward shared moral precepts in a pluralistic society. One response is to suggest that Augustine believes that knowledge of the good comes from revelation alone; the angels gave the law on Mount Sinai, and Christ proclaimed the good news. In this case, there would be a close (but not complete) identification between the Christian religion and the membership of the City of God. Knowledge of the true religion is a necessary but not a sufficient condition for membership in the City of God.[12]

If this is the case, it would appear that the prospect of membership in the holy city in pre-Christian cultures outside of the Hebraic tradition would be vastly limited, and most certainly, the splendid vices of the ancient Romans would be the best the individual members of a pagan civilization could hope for. Sabine MacCormack writes of the central concept of *latreia*: "True virtue and piety, as Augustine saw matters, could exist only when they were focused on the worship of the one God, even though this God had also aided the 'Romans who were good according to certain measure of the terrestrial city.'"[13] Dodaro echoes the sentiment, albeit in a qualified manner, when he argues that although Augustine neither imagines that Christianity will accomplish major political or social improvements, nor advises as essential the adoption of a full-fledged Christian political agenda, "Augustine holds that the fullest implications of justice, prudence and other virtues required for political decisions are only are knowable in the form of religious mystery, and that the process for arriving at a fuller understanding of the implications of these virtues for just government requires the gradual transformation of the statesman through his practice of true piety."[14]

Dodaro and MacCormack bring us to an important point of reflection on the nature of *latreia*. Dodaro's case for the Christian statesman as Augustine's political ideal is very strong, because Christ alone mediates true virtue by "acting through the human soul."[15] True virtue for Augustine most certainly is a matter of the mediation of Christ and Christ alone, so the argument that Augustine's political theory establishes an essential link between acceptance of revelation and political virtue on earth is compelling.[16]

On the other hand, John von Heyking identifies passages that suggest that a strong link for Augustine between *latreia* and natural reason. An important example of natural knowledge of right worship in Augustine is found in Abraham, who "could not have gained the wisdom he derived from God's revelation about Israel or the Resurrection on his own, but it would have been *intelligible for someone with natural knowledge of latreia.*"[17] For Augustine, Abraham—the father of the Jews and the Gentiles descended from Ishmael—could interpret God's promise to him about his progeny and the seemingly contradictory order to sacrifice Isaac in light of a natural, rationally discerned concept of *latreia*. Augustine points out that this capacity in Abraham existed prior to God's revelation concerning the divine plan of the nation of Israel or of the miraculous resurrection of the body; we know this about Abraham because he could understand what von Heyking calls the "general requirements of *latreia*, of offering up one's first fruits."[18] Von Heyking buttresses this observation with an interpretation of Augustine's treatment of the Platonists as figures responsive to the natural intelligibility of the divine nature and the superlative character of the obligations that derive from such knowledge.[19]

This portrait of *latreia*'s natural accessibility fits with the emphasis that von Heyking, Dodaro, and Gregory place on the significance of the *ordo amoris* for interpretations of Augustinian politics. In book 14 of *The City of God* Augustine writes, "When a man lives according to man and not according to God, he resembles the devil. . . . When a man lives according to truth, then, he lives not according to self, but according to God; for it is God who has said 'I am the truth.' When he lives according to self, however—that is, according to man, and not according to God—he then lives according to falsehood."[20] The "border" between members of the City of God and the City of Man is the difference between love of God and love of self, the choice between the true good of the eternal and the false good of temporal security or respectability; this is the reason that the Roman heroes are not good in the sense that the Christian are.[21] If we can identify pagan persons capable of rightly ordered loves, then the vision of right worship as an exclusively Christian activity is more complex. Such persons make their appearance in book 18 of *The City of God* in the figures of Job, Melchizedek, the Erythraean Sibyl, and even people of the city of Babylon, figures who are able to demonstrate rightly ordered love amid cultural or religious circumstances that might seem to limit them in this regard.[22] For Augustine, the primary way we see rightly ordered loves is in deeds of mercy. As Ernest L. Fortin writes, in contrast to pagan philosophers, "conscience as Augustine understands it is not just an innate moral sense found in all or most men or a general awareness of certain broad limitations to which human conduct is subject." Instead, Augustine's characterization of conscience is one by which "man's life as a whole is governed by rational principles that are natural known and universally valid even under the most extreme cases."[23] Right worship, then, appears to be a virtue accessible through natural reason and therefore possible in many nations and circumstances, even circumstances that are not privy to revelation.

Von Heyking's enlisting of Jonah, Job, Melchizadek, and others as examples of pagans possessing *latreia* is underdeveloped albeit textually substantiated by Augustine's own reliance on these figures as virtuous pagans; therefore, it is worth developing further, as these figures' significance for Augustine sets groundwork for the understanding of *latreia*. The danger of a lack of development in von Heyking's position is that the reader perceives a deficiency in the full complexity of Augustine's claims about human psychology, moral behavior, and ultimately, eternal salvation. There are two modes of *entrée* for our inquiry. One is through the figures of Jonah, who is sent to save the pagan Ninevites, and of the pagan Job, the Edomite whose sufferings introduce perhaps the greatest theodicy in the West. The other opportunity is through a brief detour into Augustine's reappropriation of the Oracle of Delphi's command to "know thyself," an inquiry that adds another dimension to the question of how persons such as Job, Melchizadek, or the prostitute Raheb could show through their actions the properly ordered soul that is the consequence of *latreia*.

The figures of Jonah and Job are inverse figures—they represent separate but equally important responses to the question of divine justice; Jonah represents the believer who would fail to understand *latreia* as an act possible for pagans through the path of humility and sacrifice, and Job represents the pagan who understands humility and sacrifice.

Jonah, sent to the Ninevites, is angry over their repentance, and his anger is a lesson in the ways that an understanding of natural justice coalesces with authentic religious practice, and that religious practice that does not reflect the insights of natural justice is itself deficient. An exegesis of the story of Jonah is useful in illustrating the point.

Rabbi Hayyim Angel suggests that "Jonah was unwilling to accept God's mercy even to the most ethically perfected pagans because that manifestation of mercy was antithetical to Jonah's desired conception of God."[24] While the Ninevites themselves represent the pagan who possesses the humility to turn toward the Lord, Jonah is reprimanded by the Lord for lacking the humility to rejoice with him in the return of the Ninevites. By contrast, the Ninevites have the humility to repent, though it seems clear that they give up their vicious social practices without converting to the Jewish religion; in fact, they later play a role in the destruction of Israel.[25] For this reason, it is fair to view the story of Jonah as a prophecy for the Jewish people but also as an exploration of the spiritual life of the pagan in the time preceding Christ.

The momentum of the story occurs through continuous and implicit comparisons of the behavior of the pagan and of the believer,[26] and in interpretative traditions shared in *Midrash Jonah*[27] and the New American Bible, revised edition (NABRE). The sailors aboard the ship on which Jonah is a stowaway toss God's prophet overboard after Jonah discloses that he is running from the Lord, and they encourage him to reach out to his God and seek God's forgiveness.

In chapter 2, Jonah reminds God that he is a Hebrew and that he offers "true sacrifices," presumably in comparison to the false sacrifices offered by the pagan sailors. However, in certain moments the pagans actually play the role of the prophet. When Jonah is asleep during the storm, a sailor finds him below deck and exhorts him to wake up and pray to his Lord, saying "Perhaps the god will be kind to us and we will not perish."[28] Nineveh's king also speaks like a prophet: "Let everyone turn back from his evil ways and from the injustice of which he is guilty. Who knows but that God may turn and relent? He may turn back from His wrath, so that we do not perish." By contrast, Jonah's message to the Ninevites is only a declaration of the ruination of the city, without the typical prophetic qualification that salvation would come with repentance.[29] Similarly, while the Ninevites don sackcloth and ashes and fast and weep for their sins, after completing his mission, the reluctant Jonah lies on the ground and tells God that he wants to die of anger over his experience of the Ninevites' salvation.[30]

The portrait that emerges is of a Nineveh that responds to God's call, albeit without converting to Judaism, and a Jew who disobeys God out of disappointment in his mercy, saying to God, "I have a right to be angry—angry enough to die." The Lord responds to Jonah's anger over the gourd that he used to cover his head as shelter while he awaited Nineveh's destruction: "You are concerned over the gourd plant which cost you no effort and which you did not grow; it came up in one night and in one night it perished. And should I not be concerned over the great city of Nineveh, in which there are more than a hundred and twenty thousand persons who cannot know their right hand from their left, not to mention all the animals?"[31] The NABRE offers this gloss: "A selfish Jonah bemoans his personal loss of a gourd plant for shade without any concern over the threat of loss of life to the Ninevites," after the gourd is destroyed by a "morning-worm." It appears that for Jonah, "true justice required punishing even the penitent Ninevites, because they still were pagans."[32] A similar interaction between the Lord and Jonah occurs after Jonah's encounter with the pagan sailors, when he prays to the Lord, "Those who worship worthless idols abandon their hope for mercy. But, I, with thankful voice, will sacrifice to you."[33] The structure of the story of Jonah causes us to wonder which character is guilty of worshiping an idol in his heart.

Of Jonah, Augustine says that "he . . . was grieved at the salvation of the Ninevites, that is, at the redemption and deliverance of the Gentiles, from among whom Christ came to call, not righteous men but sinners."[34] He notes that Jonah even built himself a "booth" outside of Nineveh out of a desire to witness its destruction, not understanding the importance of the "salvation of the Gentiles and of the penitent" to the Lord.[35] When Jonah grieves at the destruction of the gourd that covered his head, consumed by a "morning-worm," Augustine interprets this worm to signify Christ and his devouring of Jonah's hope that others might not be saved.[36] Augustine uses Psalm 22 to describe the Christ worm. In him, "All the ends of the world shall *remember*, and turn unto the Lord; and all the kindreds of the nations shall worship in His presence. For the Kingdom is the Lord's and He shall govern among the nations."[37] According to Augustine, the "Ninevites *remembered"* and "turned unto the Lord." What did they remember?

For Augustine, there is not an Old Testament economy of salvation and a New Testament economy of salvation. Augustine's soteriology predicates that one long strand connects the two periods; in any time in history, "the faithful were members of the *novum.*"[38] In fact, although Augustine regards the appearance of Christ as a "decisive caesura" in time, it is not "an absolute one": "For salvation did not begin with the coming of Christ; it had been present throughout the history of mankind. The incarnation was preceded by periods of salvation which were all determined by Christ, which all to Him, all derived their meaning from Him. . . . [L]ong before the birth of Christ there was the earthly history of the City of God."[39]

The "earthly history of the City of God" is filled with persons who remember the mercy of God and act accordingly, offering sacrifices of confession to him, what I suggest is the "inner treasure" no man can steal.[40] This is most clear in the person of Job, the foil of Jonah, whose heart was not capable of mercy and who claimed to offer sacrifices to God when he could not accept that mercy is the sacrifice desired by God.[41] Augustine himself draws our attention to Job, who like the Ninevites "was neither an Israelite by birth nor a proselyte: that is, a convert to the people of Israel." Instead, he came from "the race of Edom; he was born there and he died there," yet "no man of his time is his equal in righteousness and piety." Surely, then, while "there was no other people who might truly be called the people of God . . . the Jews cannot deny that in other nations also there have been some men who belonged, not by earthly but by heavenly fellowship" as "citizens of the supernal fatherland."[42]

In his sermon on Psalm 55, Augustine depicts Job as a man who responds to tragedy with the sacrifice God most desires. "Everything had been taken away and Job remained alone; but inside himself he had those sacrifices of praise that he could offer to God." Satan had sought to destroy Job through destroying his inheritance and his family, not realizing that Job's greatest possession was in his heart. From this we learn the following: "What God seeks from you is praise. Your confession is what God demands of you. . . . What do you have that you did not receive? Will you give him treasures from your heart? He gave you faith and hope and charity; this is what you must present, this you must offer in sacrifice." Job offers true sacrifices, a species of "every work done in order that we may draw near to God in holy fellowship: done, that is, with reference to that supreme good and end in which alone we can be truly blessed."[43]

Job, the pagan, possesses faith, hope, and charity from the Lord. The sacrifice he offers is pleasing to God; in fact, it is normatively representative of what a true sacrifice would be. Jonah, a prophet who speaks with God, rebels against the true sacrifice that is required of him—mercy. How do we find ourselves in such a position? The beginning of the answer is perhaps best captured in the Delphic oracle's command to "know thyself," reconstituted by Augustine as a form of "Remembering the Lord."

For the pagan, the path to true justice is predicated on self-knowledge; however, knowing oneself is something that is within the reach of every person, not just the philosopher, and is dependent on the virtue of humility—a virtue that fulfills "all justice."[44] What Job and the Ninevites share is the willingness to entertain the idea of their finitude and sinfulness, for "to admit one's inability, to shed tears of confession" is "to take the humility of the divine logos as a model and become weak oneself."[45] Augustine claims in *Confessions* and *De trinitate* that this humility is the first step toward fulfilling the Delphic command.[46] When we seek self-knowledge, the disparity between ourselves and the good becomes clearer, and the humility this insight brings opens the door for the divine strength to move us toward the good.[47] While showing us our limitations, this introspection reveals what is most valuable in us—the image of God, which is placed in us as a means of constantly calling us to "be mindful of the divine presence"[48]—to *remember* God as the Ninevites did. In this sense, the oracle's command leads us to remember the image of God, which we encounter when we look inward and find both our own limitations and God's goodness: "I believe that [the soul] should think about itself and live according to its nature. . . . [U]nder him [God] it should be subject to and over all it should govern. . . . [I]ndeed it does many things it does through perverse desires as if it had forgotten itself."[49] By contrast, a fractured soul results from the forgetting caused by desire; "this entanglement in illusion" leads to self-forgetting.[50]

The Ninevites hear about their coming destruction and know that this punishment is the cost of their transgressions.[51] When God asks Job where he was when the world was created, Job knows that God is reminding him of the difference between himself and his creator. His suffering, intelligible in the light of the God's providential difference from man, becomes a source of renewed praise for Job.

This clear-sightedness can also take a more pragmatic form, as is evident in the person of Rahab the prostitute, another figure Augustine chooses as an example of a virtuous pagan in book 17 of *The City of God*. At great risk to herself, Rahab hides from the king of Jericho the spies sent by Joshua. When confronted by the king's spies, she protects the Israelites yet again by lying to the king. When she lowers the Israelites down from the city wall, she tells them:

> I know that the LORD has given you the land, that a dread of you has come upon us, and that all the inhabitants of the land tremble with fear because of you. . . . [E]veryone is utterly dispirited because of you, since the LORD, your God, is God in heaven above and on earth below. Now then, swear to me by the LORD that, since I am showing kindness to you, you in turn will show kindness to my family.[52]

Sinful Rahab, prompted by fear, makes a true confession of the power of the God who is a stranger to her, and trusts that he can save her with a receptivity indicative of humility. She among all those in Jericho does not cling to her own gods, but clearly assesses the power of the true God and serves him. Jonah, on the other hand, lacks humility, and therefore the revelation he is privy to is unintelligible to him. Jonah actually speaks to God, yet he cannot act with mercy or with justice. When he is required to act with mercy toward others by calling the Ninevites to repentance, and with justice toward God by obeying his command, he fails. How could one who spoke to God fail to understand the contours of justice? And how could those outside the sphere of revelation be able to follow what justice demands and act with mercy toward others? Those who follow the path of humility and in turn receive and practice mercy are the ones who remember God, and are the ones that are best able to offer *latreia* to the Lord.

Part of the reason for the lack of clarity about the possibility of true virtue outside of the Christian religion is a result of the complex nature of *latreia* itself. The entirety of book 10 of *The City of God* is an attempt to synthesize the multiple aspects of what it means to practice right worship, harmonizing our duty toward God and neighbor in a way that makes them inseparable from one another. In *The City of God* 10.1, Augustine embarks on an attempt to determine precisely what the relationship is between religious practices and the true good for men and women. The outcome of this inquiry is extremely important, because depending on the relationship between religious practices and the good, the availability of the way of true virtue to humanity both prior to and following the Incarnation and the Resurrection is broadened or limited. Augustine begins by contemplating the relationship of *eusebia* (the Greek term for "piety") to the good and finds the term wanting, because he "holds that the worship of God cannot be separated from the 'works of mercy' or 'acts of compassion' because "God especially commands the performance of such works, and declares that he is pleased with them instead of, or in preference to sacrifices."[53] There is some relationship between pious practices and the human good, but the concept of *eusebia* does not capture the full picture. By contrast, *latreia* (right worship) more fully encompasses the relationship between the worship of God and love of our neighbor. With von Heyking, Gregory locates *latreia* as a form of loving God *through* loving one's neighbor; this virtue is most precisely a species of justice.[54] In this term, then, Augustine unites the dual commandment to love God and love one's neighbor as oneself, showing the unbreakable bond between our duties to God and our duties to society, and clearly demarcating the path of the good to include persons who can love their neighbor authentically as a way of loving God. "To put it bluntly, Book 10 of the *City of God* is the basic text for Augustinian politics: the heart of Augustine's account of the true worship of the crucified God and the charitable service of neighbor in collective *caritas*."[55]

Yet again, however, we must ask what *kind* of knowledge of the Crucified God is required for true virtue. If the rubric for genuine Augustinian political action is centered on the model and mediation of Christ, does that mean only Christians can act with authentic virtue in the political realm?

## *Latreia* as Sacrifice

Let us begin our inquiry by considering Augustine's theory of sacrifice. One of Augustine's most developed discussions of sacrifice occurs in book 10 of *The City of God*. Augustine begins with a discussion of *latreia*, the fitting worship to God. In chapter 2, he writes that *latreia* is demonstrated through sacraments or individual persons, "for we are his temple, each of us and every one of us together."[56] Significantly, then, the starting point in our inquiry into sacrifice bridges the gap between the individual and the community—together and as individuals we offer fittings sacrifices to God. These sacrifices include lifting our hearts to him, burning with love of him, and devoting ourselves and all our talents to him.[57] Sacrifices are not necessary to him, however;[58] instead, they purify us so that we may cling to him, which is our final good. In clinging to him, our "soul is, if one may so put it, filled up and impregnated with true virtues." Yet it is also an act of true love for ourselves, because a person who loves himself seeks his or her own good.[59]

Augustine claims that through our clinging to God, virtue is grown within us. Moreover, the true worship of God is to cling to him and to lead one's neighbor to do the same. Incidentally, this also demonstrates the link between following the commandment to love God and the ability to follow the commandment to love our neighbor as ourself. Augustine calls the combination of cohering to God ourselves and causing others to do the same "the worship of God . . . the true religion . . . the right piety . . . the service which is due to God alone."[60]

It is possible to infer that these virtues, imparted from our nearness to God, become a part of our worship of him because they make us capable of bringing others to him. Corrigan argues that this passage, in light of other passages from the *De trinatate*, shows Augustine understood that our cohering to God allows us to recognize beauty in others and the beauty in ourselves, because in relation to God an authentic beauty emerges. The same may be said of the virtues.[61] By clinging to God, we are given the tools to love our neighbor. In this way, the Christian's pursuit of love for God can never be individualistic; the true pursuit of union with God inevitably leads to a concern for one's community,[62] which leads to an action. This is our first intimation of the political nature of *latreia*, a way of acting in the politics that stands in contrast to the lust for domination and the love of glory.

In this light, it is interesting that Augustine uses the word *virtus* for "strength" when he discusses the command to love God with everything we are capable of.[63] *Virtus* in this regard is not a tool of power subject to the *libido dominandi*; on the contrary, it is the path to virtue, because in powerfully clinging to God, we are equipped with the characteristics to enable us to love others. Canning interprets this passage to mean that "associated with the meaning of loving God with all one's strength, is the injunction to refrain from using that power to lord it over others and to use it rather to bring others to their only Lord."[64] Within Augustine's conception of sacrificial worship as anything that causes us and others to cling to God is the foil of the Roman lust for domination. For Augustine, clinging to God and receiving the love of God in order to bring others is a sacrifice because it is the offering of "ourselves and his gifts in us."[65] Yet Augustine describes sacrifice in another way in book 10, chapter 5: sacrifice is a broken and repenting spirit; this spirit is what the outward symbol of a sacrifice (for example, the animal offerings we find in the Old Testament) is intended to represent. Outer sacrifice does not matter if the inward sacrifice of self does not occur. This inner sacrifice is not just a contrite spirit but a contrite spirit understood as a merciful one because "mercy is the true sacrifice" according to Augustine's citing of Hosea 6:6: "For I desired mercy, and not sacrifice."

Another aspect of sacrifice, then, is interior contrition for one's sins and a spirit of mercy toward others that grows from the understanding of one's own limitations and failings, inspired by a contrite heart. A contrite heart is possible through the example of the crucifixion of Christ, the sinless man who teaches sinners how to die to themselves. The crucifixion of the Lord is both a model for and an inroad to the sacrifice of a broken heart. In *De trinitate*, Augustine compares a repenting spirit to the crucifixion of the inner man and to the inward death of inappropriate self-love. Christ's death is a model of sacrifice; as we meditate on it, we inwardly undergo a purifying death to self-love and outwardly are prepared to give up our bodies in an act of martyrdom.[66]

Again, Augustine's understanding of sacrifice is the very opposite of the Roman *libido dominandi*. Contrition is an act of humility because in order to repent, one must admit error; people must acknowledge an external rule to their own will that they must live by. Moreover, if true sacrifice is mercy, mercy desires to lift others up, rather than subject them to one's own will. Finally, a contrite heart opposes the lust for domination because contrition is derived from the example of the greatest act of humble mercy in history, the death of sinless Jesus for the sake of sinful man.

When we act in accord with love for God and perform acts of mercy, we are offering sacrifice to God.[67] As Augustine says above, every action of ours can become a type of worship of God, but is it possible to imagine that all actions are types of worship of some kind, whether of God, evil spirits, or oneself? Demons want to be worshiped (hence, for Augustine, the existence of pagan religions) because in enticing men to worship them, demons prevent men from making offerings of themselves to God.[68] Are our actions that are discontinuous with love of God acts of worship of self or of evil spirits? If we grant this line of argument, we again see the polar relationship between real sacrifice and *libido dominandi*. In opposition to Christ, demons seek worship in order to prevent the human supplicants from finding their true good; instead of leading humans to cleave to God, they are deliberately frustrating humans' relationship with God. All acts of domination of another are instances of denying them the conditions for their flourishing. All sin is a frustration of union with God, and hence a prevention of real sacrifice, so acts of sin could be considered acts of inappropriate worship—either worship of evil forces or worship of oneself and one's own will.

Combining the two meanings of sacrifice (first understood as cleaving to God/leading others to cleave to him and secondly understood as offering acts of mercy/contrition), Augustine writes that "a true sacrifice, then, is every work done in order that we may draw near to God in holy fellowship: done, that is, with reference to that supreme good and end in which alone we can be truly blessed. . . . [E]ven the mercy which we extend to men is not a sacrifice if it is not given for God's sake."[69] Yet he has not finished defining the meaning of sacrifice.

In book 10, chapter 6, Augustine takes these two properties of sacrifice and begins exploring their Christological and Eucharistic explanations. His argument is complex but important. The shift in his presentation of sacrifice from discussions of goal-directed actions toward heavy theological concepts such as the body of Christ and the sacrifice of the Eucharist is quick and compact. Granting that works of mercy directed toward complete union with God are sacrifice, Augustine next claims it consequently follows that all of the City of God becomes a sacrifice to God through the person of Christ the High Priest, who "offered even Himself for us in the form of servant, so that we might be the body of so great a head." This offering through the person of Christ becomes the "sacrifice of Christians" and is evident to this day in the "sacrament of the altar."

Augustine makes three leaps in this passage: from the definition of sacrifice as works of mercy in instances of cleaving to God and leading others to him, to the person of Christ as mediator and victim, and finally to the existence of the redeemed City as the body of Christ, one with the offering of Christ. How does he substantiate this? The answer is found in the nature of Christ. John Cavadini claims that it is the unity of Christ's two natures, representative of his solidarity with the plight of mankind and under the form of a historical person, that makes Augustine's understanding of suffering operate.[70] In chapter 20 of book 10, Augustine explains that Christ is at once priest, victim, servant, and God. In a sense, as a person of the triune God he is the recipient of the sacrifice of the Mass, but with the humility of a servant he chose to be the victim in the offering. Moreover, because we know from the scriptures that we are members of the body of Christ, when he is offered as a sacrifice we are offered as well because we are a part of him and he is the victim.[71] Similarly, we are also a part of his body as he performs the actions of a priest. In this way, we are at once God's most "wonderful and best sacrifice"[72] and also pupils of Christ in how to offer ourselves to God: "for the Church, being the body of which He is the Head, is taught to offer herself through Him."[73] It is the will of Christ that "there should be a daily sign of this in the sacrament of the Church's sacrifice," the daily Mass. Here Augustine offers yet one more definition of sacrifice; the daily sacrifice of the Mass becomes "the supreme and true sacrifice all false sacrifices have yielded."[74]

An exegesis of book 10 leaves us with three definitions of sacrifice. Sacrifice is the act of cleaving to God and leading others to cleave to Him. The fruits of mercy grow in our hearts when we unite ourselves to God and hence we are able to perform the second definition of worship, acts of mercy performed with a contrite spirit. Finally, sacrifice is Christ's self-offering as both priest and victim, wherein the people of God are offered to the Lord because they are parts of His body. This sacrifice is the sacrifice that takes place in the Eucharist.

Yet how does Augustine reconcile these claims, especially since it appears that deeds of mercy, such as almsgiving or leading others to God, are not the same as ritual sacrifice? In book 10 the "supreme and true sacrifice" is still a rite shared by a community rather than a more conventional act of mercy, such as feeding the poor or burying the dead. According to Alexander Schmemann, the concept of liturgy initially was understood as "an action by which a group of people become something corporately which they had not been as a mere collection of individuals."[75] Through the Eucharist, the community becomes Christ. Augustine's response again relies on the unity of priest and victim in the person of Jesus Christ. Adding another dimension, Augustine extends the offering of Christ in the Eucharist to an offering of self, as the Christian members forming the body of Christ are offered up to God with him in the sign of Christ's merciful deed during the Mass.[76] In this way, the ritual sacrifice is a symbolic representation of love of God and neighbor, both in the person of Christ and in the Christian community's *participation* in the merciful deed, not just the *reception* of its benefits.[77]

It follows that a connection exists between the central sacrifice of the Mass and the conforming of Christian hearts toward acts of mercy. Augustine quotes St. Paul from his letter to the Hebrews which warns believers "To do good and to communicate,[78] forget not: for with such sacrifices God is well pleased."[79]

Performing acts of mercy and participating in the liturgy are both pleasing to the Lord, and even a merciful act becomes a sacrifice of praise and an act of worship to God. In fact, one may assume that the two are connected. As the Christian communicant is offered as a member of the body of Christ, she is also transformed by Christ's atonement on his behalf, receiving the grace of Christ's sacrifice in her soul. The more the communicant is open to the grace of Christ, the more she is conformed to him. Hence, she is better capable of performing merciful acts because of her participation in the most merciful act in all of history.

The sacrifice of the Mass as a cleaving to God causes the fruit of merciful acts to grow in the participants' hearts—they are "impregnated with the virtues," as mentioned earlier. In this way, they can nourish and tend to everyone around them. Similarly, they are more and more conformed in unity with one another. An explanation from a sermon to the newly baptized during Easter demonstrates the way Augustine envisioned the sacrifice. Prior to their entry into the church, they were disparate grains "threshed" when they heard the Gospel, and then stored away during their period as catechumens. Exorcism and fasting ground them, the water of baptism made them dough, and confirmation in the Holy Spirit baked them into a loaf of bread. Moreover, the wine is also a symbol of the faithful's unity because they are like grapes pressed together to make a wine. In this way, they are the body of Christ, but they are also the body of Christ present on the altar.[80]

Besides unifying the faithful, the Eucharist also sanctifies their offerings of deeds of mercy. In the context of fallen human nature, no merciful act is performed without some purpose besides union with God, whether it is union for ourselves or for another. The Eucharist makes up for this shortcoming by forming us into the body of Christ, which is itself the very compassion of God.[81] This is a primary sense in which "Christ communicates virtue to the soul," the way in which Christ is the only mediator, as Robert Dodaro emphasizes in his contemplation of what political virtue entails for Augustine.[82]

We are now prepared to understand more fully how Augustine's definition of sacrifice completely challenges the *libido dominandi*. It is useful to quote Cavadini at length here:

> When we act out of compassion toward a neighbor, and our compassion is progressively formed by our participation in the Eucharist, we are reclaiming that neighbor from the identity the empire would impose, as simply another vehicle for its glory. We are reinvesting the world, and each creature in it, with the glory of God, and so the character of compassion as *latreia* or worship of God is vindicated. Our devotion to Christ, visible outwardly as works of mercy, becomes a practice of critique, a dismantling of the body politic's hegemony over meaning or, at least, over opinion.[83]

The Eucharist is the ultimate example of an act of mercy—the torture and death of the sinless for the sinful, a sacrifice offered in perfect obedience and humility. Inspired by reception of the Eucharist and the example of Christ, people can be liberated from the oppression of estrangement from Christ and recognize that their identity and salvation is in Christ, not the state; through acts of mercy, they can understand justice as "the glory of God over all."[84] The lust for domination is replaced by the proper worship of God, which is also the true sacrifice—the pouring out of self in compassion for the good of another. Eric Gregory describes the multiple components of *latreia* aptly: "It is this vision of love—in piety, worship and service that characterizes Augustine's formation of one's character and the true end of virtue." Eucharistic politics, the idea that the just worship of God is mercy shown to one's fellow men and women, is the antidote to the *libido dominandi* for Augustine, because intrinsically in the order of nature, we can find no right to dominate another person when the divine order itself is built upon a sacrificial and merciful God who requires as his due that we imitate acts of mercy. Eucharistic politics also serves as an antidote to the desire for glory. Glory can only be a pseudo-virtue because it replaces the love of the good with the "worship of false gods of self-interest and dominion, which become ends in themselves." This is the essence of Augustine's critique of the Pax Romana.[85]

However, my exegesis of book 10, because of its culmination in an extended reflection on the Eucharistic sacrifice of the Mass, appears to take us *further* away from the notion that *latreia* is a path of true virtue that may be encountered independently of revelation, though I will argue that cleaving to God and performing acts of mercy, properly understood, are within the realm of possibility for persons who are not acting from the commands of revelation. For the remainder of this essay, I will attempt to interpret *The City of God* through the lens of the component parts of *latreia*—acts of mercy predicated on the virtue of humility, Eucharistic ritual, and the transformation of the emotional life.

### The Path of True Virtue: The Predecessor Culture and *Latreia*

I maintained earlier that in book 10, Augustine offered not only a conception of sacrifice but also a model for human action for the members of the City of God. Eucharistic politics *is* that model of true virtue and right action, but Eucharistic politics does not require direct participation in the Eucharist for its practice. What we are left with at the end of book 10 is an emphasis on the healing of the human heart through the directing of our wills toward the right objects of love, a healing that takes place when our intellect and will turn toward the good.[86] This healing, which requires the submission of our intellect and will to a source of good and truth— distinct from and often opposed to our own desires and will—is predicated on the presence of the virtue of humility, which permits us to turn to the good, and also to see the need of another and to feel that need has a significance as weighty as our own need. Christ is the source of this healing and the model for virtuous human behavior, but for reasons I will elaborate on in greater detail, a person can approach this model and find this healing of the affections without explicit knowledge of Christ, through humbly following natural reason's path toward *right worship*.

Augustine is aware that the search for the ritual healing, or ordering, of the affections is a quest that the Platonists also pursued, and his assessment of their teaching makes up a significant portion of book 10.[87] Augustine shows us that the Platonists are correct when they think they must order their affections, and they are even more correct in identifying political virtue as a domain connected to that purification, yet they cannot identify the real source of true healing, because of their pride.

Augustine's account in book 10 begins with a reflection on theurgy. Certain philosophers and practitioners in the Platonic school believed that in order to overcome temptations, the evil spirits had to receive homage before good spirits could intervene in the ordering of the soul, and therefore the philosophers offered sacrifices of worship to mediating spirits.[88]

Porphyry is right to correct the earlier tradition, and deny that offering sacrifice to earthly things like the sun or moon purify us from our sins or bring us closer to the divine, and he suggests instead that when we offer sacrifice to the *principia*, or the God, and the Intellect that emanates from Him, we are purified.[89] However, even Porphyry could not depart from the theurgists' practice of accepting that mediating spirits in theurgic rites should receive worship, placing them "among [his own] starry gods," insulting "even the stars themselves."[90] In doing so, he permits the offering of *latreia*, which is the highest act a human can perform toward the divine, to something lower than the divine. Augustine points out that this error seems especially confusing, given what he takes to be the Platonists' prideful refusal to accept the Incarnation out of concern that the higher (Christ) takes on the lower (human flesh) in this doctrine.[91]

In contrast to the Platonists' prideful theurgic arts, which honor the lower with what is higher, Augustine argues that it is only "grace which heals the weak, who do not proudly boast a false blessedness of their own, but rather humbly confess their own true wretchedness."[92] However, the impulse of the Platonists is not a misguided one. In the writings of Porphyry, Plotinus, and Iamblichus, the idea that the soul needs a path to deliverance reflects what for Augustine is a certain truth. Our souls must be purified to be able to love the good. The ordering of the emotional life is a central part of this because our emotions are often the unruliest part of our souls, effortlessly loving what it is not good, or just, to love. Ritual practices, particularly those that rely on some means of mediation between the higher and the lower, are an essential part of the transformation of the soul toward loving the good, both for the Platonists and the Christians. In addition to this proper insight concerning theurgic rites, the Platonic school also acknowledges the purification that can occur through the practice of political virtue, a philosophical insight that is a significant inheritance for Augustine's political theory. Dodaro rightly calls our attention to this, reminding us that it was Plotinus who taught that "to the degree that the political virtues regulate the soul's desires and lead it to prefer the truth to false opinions, they can be said to mark the beginning of the soul's assimilation to God."[93] Though the political virtues are lower, our status as bodily creatures requires that purification begins with the science that most pertains to our bodies.

Porphyry, in turn, interprets Plotinus's commentary on the centrality of the political virtues to mean that there are corresponding virtues to the cardinal virtues— hope (*elpis*), truth (*aletheia*), love (*eros*), and faith (*pistis*). These virtues are related to the process of assimilation to God and together make up "true piety," further concretizing the relationship in Neoplatonism between politics and authentic worship.[94] He also suggests that humans might eventually obtain a "definitive purification." In *De mysteriis*, Iamblichus further systematizes Plotinus's insight about the relationship between political virtue and politics by uniting the practice of *elpis*, *eros*, and *pistis* with theurgic prayers.[95]

Therefore, although the theurgists can be critiqued for a mistaken conception of *latreia*, an error partly based on a lack of humility, they rightly identify a connection between the realm of the political and the soul's assimilation to the divine nature. The argument of book 10, therefore, relies in large part on the parallel Augustine draws between the Platonists and the nature of authentic worship.

The Stoics, like the Platonists, seek a path to the ordering of the affections. Augustine scrutinizes their path of purification in *The City of God*, notably in books 9 and 14, depicting the Stoics as individuals searching for release from the tumult of human emotions by denying "that there can exist in the wise man's mind anything corresponding to distress or pain."[96] However, Augustine writes, only those who live "by the standard of man" are "shaken by these emotions as by diseases and upheavals"; those who possess a well-ordered soul know that emotion is an important part of the ethical life, albeit one that needs to be guided by virtue.[97] It turns out that Augustine's most powerful condemnation is not directed at the Platonists. He particularly notes Porphyry for his merciful desire for a *universal* way of salvation, one that is not open to philosophers alone.[98] He praises Plotinus for his insight that the rational soul "cannot be its own light but shines by its participation in another and true light."[99] Their insights reflect, in the former case, a capacity for mercy, and in the latter, a capacity for humility, both instrumental for the performance of *latreia*.[100] Augustine's harshest criticism is reserved for those who claim to feel no emotion, for their actions are so monstrous that they actually destroy their own humanity through their pride. Such people

> are so arrogant and pretentious in their irreligion that the swelling of their pride increases in exact proportion as their feeling of pain decreases. Some of those people may display an empty complacency, the more monstrous for being so rare, which makes them so charmed with this achievement in themselves that they are not stirred or excited by any emotions at all. . . . [T]hey rather lose every shred of humanity than achieve a true tranquility. For hardness does not necessarily imply rectitude, and insensibility is not a guarantee of health.[101]

*Apatheia*, when defined as a state of being where no emotions disturb the mind, is for Augustine "the worst of all moral defects."[102] In a world that is filled with suffering, mourning is not only legitimate but in some cases just; even the pagan Romans discerned that it was right to praise the general Marcus Marcellus when he wept at the sacking of Syracuse.[103] Persons who seek *apatheia* mistake hardness of heart for virtue, and in doing so, they show an improper ordering of their souls and indeed a lack of humanity "because it is human to intervene."[104] By eschewing some of the emotions that are essential parts of compassion, the Stoics, according to Augustine, render themselves incapable of performing the types of merciful actions that are an essential part of *latreia*.

## Augustine and the Centrality of the Emotional Life

As Augustine condemns the Neoplatonists for seeking a pathway to purifying the emotions that misdirect right worship, even while they manage to focus on the relationship between politically virtuous acts and the divine will, he condemns the Stoics for seeking a purification of emotions that seriously impairs the human capacity for mercy, an essential part of right worship. Both condemnations spring from his understanding of *latreia*: the Platonists are idolatrous in their theurgic practices, and in this way they do not offer fitting sacrifice to God, whereas the Stoics are idolatrous in their attempt to stifle the fellow feeling that leads to the divine tribute of *misericordia*.

In contrast to his philosophical predecessors, Ernest Fortin reminds us, "Augustine was intent on preserving or restoring human wholeness by directing all of the individual's activities to the goal or goals to which they are intrinsically ordered," a healing that renewed all the faculties of man, and that did not bar individuals from the path of healing and integration because of their lack of capacity for philosophy.[105] Augustine writes in book 10, chapter 32:

> This then is the universal way of the soul's deliverance, which the holy angels and the holy prophets first foretold where they could among those few men who found the grace of God. . . . This way cleanses the whole man, and prepares each of the parts of which a mortal man is made for immortality. We need not seek one purification for the part which Porphyry calls intellectual, and another for the part he calls spiritual, and another for the body itself; for our most true and mighty purifier and savior took upon himself the whole of human nature.

This healing begins, in a sense, with an encounter with the world itself, a world that is good by creation, but marred by evil. Augustine recognizes that the Platonists and the Stoics were right to begin with the question of appetite and the soul when trying to imagine how the process of assimilation to the divine operates, but it seems that their conceptions of the process were too narrow. Augustine begins more broadly, in part because of his democratic conception of virtue's accessibility, and in part because of his account of the goodness of creation, an account which in a sense fundamentally raises the role of the emotions in the ethical life. For Augustine, the soul, encountering the created world, relies on sense perception, which eventually produces an emotional reaction: "Sensation may therefore be defined as a '*passio corporis per se ipsam non latens animam*,' 'a stimulation of the sense organs sufficiently powerful to register in consciousness.' As such it is immediately translated into an emotion in which form it gives rise to movements of appetition or aversion."[106]

These movements of aversion or appetite are desire, fear, joy and sadness, the four emotions that become the centerpiece of Augustine's treatment of the will in *The City of God*, book 14. The key to judging an emotion lies not in the emotion itself but in the orientation of the individual's soul that causes the emotion: "[T]he question is not *whether* the devout soul is angry, but why; not whether it is sad, but what causes it sadness; not whether it is afraid, but what is the object of fear."[107] Healing the emotions begins with the recognition that all the emotions have a role to play in the ethical life of a member of the City of God; in fact, Augustine says that the scriptures train the Christian's passions to be "instruments of justice," and he specifically praises compassion as an emotion in accord with true religion,[108] a "kind of *fellow-feeling* [my emphasis] in our hearts for another's misery."[109] Emotion, therefore, is concretely related to *latreia*, because it facilitates compassion, and for this reason it is important to assess more fully precisely how the emotions relate to the ethical life for Augustine.

The proper functioning of the emotions is the path that people, without revelation, can take to become truly virtuous, if they become oriented toward the good in such a way that they are able to practice right worship through acts of mercy. This path ostensibly is open to all, because we all engage with the world through our senses and can respond to the needs that we see in it. In other words, the path of universal salvation that Porphyry sought and that he knew related to the emotions can be open to anyone who develops rightly ordered loves and can act from what Augustine calls "the marrow of mercy."

In book 14, we understand more fully how well-ordered emotions relate to the ethical life. According to Augustine, the emotions of fear, desire, joy, and sadness are understood by some ancient thinkers as disturbances (from Cicero) or as passions.[110] Augustine's understanding of the emotions relies on their end, and the selection of the end is achieved by the human will. In book 14, he echoes his statement from book 9, chapter five, that to determine the rightness of a human emotion, one must know the direction of the will. In fact, Augustine says that all four of these emotions are "essentially acts of will": desire and joy are actions of assent to what we wish for, fear and grief are acts of dissent from what we reject. Desire is the pursuit of our wish, joy is the "satisfaction in the attainment."[111] Fear is the disagreement that emerges in response to something we anticipate but have yet to experience; and grief is the will's response to an occurrence that has happened or is happening.

Note that each of these emotions is described in relation to its object, granting a soaring range of flexibility for Augustine's theory. The will is allured or repulsed by the perception of various objects and this action of repulsion or attraction in the will "turns into feelings of various kinds." But what does a good or bad will consist of? A good will exists when a man or woman is determined to love God, his or her neighbor and his or her self, according to the standard of truth.[112] When men and women are lovers of the good and haters of what is evil, they will experience fear, desire, joy, and grief in a praiseworthy way and in doing so will live the right kind of life.[113] By contrast, a bad will is a will formed around what Augustine calls a lie, a false standard that man has chosen for himself, like the love of glory or the love of domination. When one is ruled by this false standard, he will not feel the emotions of grief, joy, desire, or fear in an ordered way. For Augustine, "A righteous will, then, is a good love; and a perverted will is an evil love."[114]

When a well-ordered will becomes the criterion for virtue, its effect on questions of politics is a universalizing one. The will is involved in all emotions; indeed, the emotional life is nothing more than the movement of the will.[115] When we are directed by the right love for self and for others we will desire, fear, grieve, and rejoice in accordance with what seeking the good of ourselves or of another demands—the cleaving to God.[116]

In addition to finding that true virtue is more universally accessible in Augustine's political philosophy, our study of *latreia* also shows us that for Augustine, mercy is intimately connected to justice. Giving God his due requires that we show others mercy. The beginnings of the story of the Incarnation, for example, prove the intimate link between justice and mercy; St. Joseph's refusal to disgrace the Virgin Mary by denouncing her for adultery when he discovers she is pregnant is "an act of mercy counted as justice."[117] Humans owe God most of all right worship. Thus the man or woman who offers him fitting worship is therefore practicing the virtue of justice. But the worship that God requires, as book 10 of *The City of God* tells us, is the sacrifice of humility, a sacrifice that enables men and women to feel compassion, and that in turn directs them toward offering the fitting worship of merciful deeds, which help move the recipient of mercy toward God.

Importantly, God does not require mercy *from* us toward *him;* rather, he is mercy's origin.[118] God needs nothing from us, but it is fitting to offer him the worship he deserves; the justice we owe to God and its identity with the mercy we owe to others reflects the important difference between our nature and God's nature for Augustine, the asymmetry between our human sinfulness and weakness and divine perfection and strength. "For with God there is no injustice; he possesses supreme power, he not only sees what everyone is like but even foresees what they will be like; he alone can judge infallibly, he cannot be deceived in what he knows."[119] In contrast, we humans are constantly confronted by our limited nature and deeply aware of our own imperfections. When God who is perfect shows us mercy, we have no reason to abstain from showing mercy to other fallible creatures because, Augustine reminds us, "you are in the need of the mercy that you are offering."[120] Mercy is motivated out of rightly ordered loves, and as such it is confined to the boundaries of truthful action. Authentic mercy does not forget the justice of truth. A rightly ordered love sees clearly, and desires for others what it hopes for itself, union with the source of truth and goodness.

Notable members of the City of God are able to achieve the fine balance of compassion and truth that characterizes authentic Augustinian mercy, interceding for their community in moments where they can "put whatever pressures they can bear on the structures of the fallen world" from the vantage point of the role they serve in their regime.[121] At this point, let us briefly turn to models from *The City of God* who help concretize our discussion of *latreia* and its political aspects. The human hero for Augustine is someone who understands that true virtue does not "protect . . . against suffering any miseries" but seeks to do what is right in the midst of them.[122] The heroic man or woman is also someone whose humility grows out of an understanding of their own failures in the commission of their own heroic deeds.[123] In other words, Augustinian heroism is rooted in the contrite spirit that is necessary to his theory of sacrifice. I will offer five textual examples to buttress my argument about true sacrifice as merciful political action in *The City of God*: three pre-Christian and two post-Incarnation, and I will situate them in a discussion of two examples of Roman vice: the destruction of Roman war, and the already mentioned monstrosity of *apatheia*. It is important to remember that Augustine's account of emotion models the purification that takes place in his account of sacrifice; when human beings turn to God as their object, their capacity to love themselves and another is purified.

## The Political Practice of *Latreia*: Examples from *The City of God*

Brian Harding claims that the earliest books in *The City of God* confine themselves to pagan examples so Augustine can present his arguments to non-Christians.[124] Augustine finds Alexander the Great an insufficient model of heroism, and he also finds in the Republican Brutus the distasteful motive of love for domination; he even rejects Regulus because of an excessive desire for glory that caused him to be too harsh with the Carthaginians.[125] The two models of pre-Christian action that Augustine upholds are not conceived of as heroes in their own society, but rather victims of the political deeds of others: the Sabine women and the sister of the heroic Horatii brother who defeated the Albans.

In book 3 of *The City of God*, Augustine chronicles the audacity of the Romans who forcibly carry off the Sabine women. After their abduction, horrible battles ensue between these women's family members and their new husbands, who "imbued with the blood of fathers wrest embraces from their sorrowing daughters."[126] Augustine contrasts the Roman lust for domination, embodied in their act of kidnapping and rape, with the intercession of the Sabine women for the sake of peace. During the battle, the women are the agents of the end of the war: "The evil day would not have ended even there, had not the ravished women dashed out with flying hair, and flinging themselves down before their fathers, stilled their just anger not by force of arms, but with pious supplication."[127] The women, forgetting their pride, their anger, and their desire to be reunited with their families, beg their fathers to bring peace. The fathers' love for their daughters allows them to put aside their righteous anger and desire for revenge in order to honor their daughters' request. Ultimately Romulus, who was so filled with the lust for domination that he had even killed his own brother so as not to share kingly rule, was put in the political position of accepting the king of the Sabines as joint ruler because the decisive action of the Sabine women.[128]

In this passage, the juxtaposition of Roman men and Sabine women can be interpreted to stand for a larger point. The ceaseless Roman desire for acquisition is halted by individuals who forget their most immediate concerns and outrages and plead for mercy. Imagine the interior courage it took these women to plead with their fathers to stop the fighting and to leave them with the men who carried them away against their will—the men who "with their hands stained with the father's blood . . . forced their embraces on luckless daughters." Augustine rightfully expresses the revulsion that the Sabine women must have felt toward their husband-conquerors, and he also notes their tragic emotional state. They cannot even weep for their fathers for fear of angering their new husbands, but they set this aside to intercede for an end to the battling that is destroying the sister communities, and produce a peace that benefits both cities.

Another example is found in the sister of the Horatii. The strength of this example is doubled because of Augustine's explicit and high praise for this unnamed woman. Augustine recounts the terrible fight between the two sets of three brothers, the Horatii and the Curiatii, citizens of mother-daughter cities embroiled in a war.[129] Their war is itself fundamentally an act of domination, given the association Augustine repeatedly makes between honoring the ties of family and friendship and the nature of justice itself.[130] The unnamed sister of the Horatii was engaged to one of the Curiatii, and she loved him as her future spouse; her brother returned victorious, carrying the shield of her betrothed, whom he had killed after an extended engagement that had left the other two Horiatii brothers dead. Understandably, on seeing the shield, the girl began to cry for the fiancé and the future she had lost. Enraged by her tears, her brother immediately killed her for weeping for the man who had killed her own brothers in war. Her tears are contrasted to the joy of her fellow citizens, who wrongly rejoice over Rome's slaughter of its kinsmen.

Augustine breaks with his angry and passionate characterization of Roman action to praise this lone woman, declaring, "[T]o my mind, this one woman who showed such affection had more humanity than the entire Roman people."[131] In spite of the loss of her own brothers, and in spite of the hostilities between her city and another, she is able to understand that tears are a fitting response to the death of another. The all-consuming nature of the Roman love of domination cannot accept this act of mercy, and the brother, moved by the rage of unjust war, destroys his own family bond by killing his sister.

Here Augustine again portrays a woman as a bridge of potential peace between warring factions and an agent of superlative virtue who is able to rise above the distractions inherent to the political situation and to identify what is truly just in a situation filled with injustice. She is contrasted to her fellow citizens, who wrongly rejoice over Rome's slaughter of its kinsmen. It is important to note that in both instances, tears are an important part of the virtue of the person in question—mourning is an act of mercy and compassion, a response to the needs of another, and an act of justice. A well-ordered soul is moved to weep at the sight of so much injustice and the destruction of the most intimate bonds. The rubric that Augustine offers in book 10 also helps us to understand more fully what he finds particularly brutal about the Romans. Like the Sabine women of book 3, the neighboring cities conquered by Rome are innocent victims who pay the highest cost. As Augustine notes in book 3, chapter 10, many approvingly attribute Rome's stature to continual wars. Augustine is quick to respond: "What a satisfying explanation! Why must an empire be deprived of peace, in order that it may be great?" He makes the comparison between a man of moderate stature and excellent health and a "giant" afflicted by endless problems. Augustine thus conveys the constant grasping of imperial Rome, which did not "rest when the stature is reached." He considers the war against Alba impious and credits the Roman victory to *libido dominandi*.[132] He also mourns the small kingdoms destroyed by the Punic Wars: "[H]ow many spacious and famous towns were razed, how many communities suffered disaster or utter ruin!"[133] He blames Regulus's desire for admiration and glory for the continuation of this destruction during the First Punic War. He cites the destruction of the city of Saguntum as the most devastating event of the Second Punic War. Finally, Augustine mourns the brutality of the civil wars of Roman against Roman.[134] The Romans destroy not only neighboring countries but one another. Their lust for power, which oppressed the "least of these" in their society, now turns against fellow citizens in the peace that follows the victory of Sulla. "The law of War was that the smitten should have the chance of smiting in return; the aim of peace was to make sure not that the survivor would live but that he should be killed."[135] He abhors the animal-like tortures that the losers are subjected to, and finally marvels that anyone can praise the accomplishments of the Romans: "You cannot show that men lived in happiness, as they passed their lives amid the horrors of war, amid the shedding of men's blood—whether the blood of enemies or fellow citizens—under the shadow of fear and amid the terror of ruthless ambition."[136] Such happiness is only fragile glass that can break at any moment; the joy of the Romans is coupled with anxiety and cannot be fully enjoyed for fear of its imminent end, whereas the tears of righteous women are well-ordered responses to the tragedy of their political world and bridges of peace to help heal broken political bonds. Augustine notes the way that the Roman desire for domination ultimately ends up dominating them; in ravaging the women and the countries around them, they ultimately despoil themselves and become subject to the vicious brutality of the culture which they have fostered. Whereas for the Sabine women their proper use of emotion may stem from humility, tremendous pride spurs on those who make war for the sake of acquisition and also moves those who pursue *apatheia*, understood as the absence of emotion.[137] Those who practice *apatheia* are as enthralled by the *libido dominandi* as the Roman rapists of the Sabine women; in seeking to dominate their emotion, they render themselves incapable of recognizing the emotional needs of others. Their lack of interest and sensitivity prevent them from acts of mercy because of cruel indifference, not because of the revolting, grasping lust that we find in the Roman abusers of the Sabines. All the same, Augustine considers their coldness ultimately just as destructive.

The contrast between the Roman rapists and warriors and the practitioners of *apatheia*, when compared to the Horatii woman and the Sabine women, embodies the distinction we witness in Augustine's conception of sacrifice. The former are enslaved by the lust for domination, the latter perform acts of mercy, which are the fitting sacrifice of God. The proper channeling of emotion and empathy for the plight of the downtrodden allows the women to act as they do. Similar attributes are found in the two post-Incarnation examples up for examination: St. Paul and Emperor Theodosius.

The more important model is found in St. Paul. According to Dodaro, Paul is the only person Augustine describes as an *optimus vir*, a best citizen and the foremost character in Augustine's reconfiguring of heroism.[138] Dodaro interprets Augustine as positing St. Paul in opposition to the noble yet hubristic Ciceronian statesman. In book 14 of *The City of God*, both St. Paul and Jesus are upheld as examples of the displaying of right emotion at the right time. Like Jesus, who weeps over Jerusalem and overturns the tables of the money changers, St. Paul showed proper emotions as a sign of his healthy soul. He experiences both joy and sadness; he feared for the souls of those he shepherds and he longs ardently for the conversion of Jews and gentiles alike. Jesus was angry at those with hard hearts, he wept for Lazurus, he longed for companionship, and he felt grief in the garden of Gethsemane.[139] Paul and Jesus exhibit great range of emotion, and the emotion is just because it is displayed at the right time and in the right way and for the right reason.[140]

Paul is depicted first and foremost as an acknowledger of his own sin, a man who performs the act of sacrifice of a contrite spirit, an admission of weakness that is the opposite of the behavior of the Roman hero. In fact, Augustine presents Paul's confession of sin as a prerequisite for justice in a person.[141] Augustine writes of the relationship between Paul's emotion and his performance of merciful deeds: he rejoices with those who rejoice and weeps for those who weep. He longs to be with Christ and experiences anxiety over internal and external turmoil in his life. He misses his friends in Rome; he fears for the Corinthians' purity with jealousy, and finally he suffers for the separation of his Jewish brothers and sisters from Christ.[142] Augustine says that Paul's "emotions and affections . . . come from love of the good and from holy charity," though his grief and fear are emotions possible for the redeemed only in earthly life. Still, if we experienced no emotions while on earth in the proper sense that Paul displays, we would be living unrighteous lives. It is his rightly ordered love that allows Paul to serve God and also to defy the tyrannical impulses of Rome when they seek to execute him for his acts of mercy.

Another example of a Christian actor that is significant for our inquiry is Emperor Theodosius, whom Augustine extols for offering sacrifices of merciful acts. After praising him for his mercy to the sons of his enemies and to the boy Valentinian, whom he reared as his own and restored to a throne that he could have instead stolen out of ambition, Augustine recounts that Theodosius went back on a promise of clemency out of human weakness.[143] The Thessalonians are guilty of revolt, though Theodosius is influenced by his faith to deal as leniently with them as is prudentially possible, and he promises the bishops that he will act with mercy. In spite of his promise, he is moved by the agitation of "the tumult of certain persons close to him" who desire vengeance rather than mercy, and he massacres the Thessalonians. Augustine is greatly displeased by this failure in mercy, the attribute Theodosius is primarily praised for in this text. However, Theodosius commits another "marvelous" act of sacrifice when he publicly repents for his failure in mercy before St. Ambrose, demonstrating the sacrifice of a contrite spirit, one of the greatest component parts of *latreia*.[144]

# Conclusion

Using the resources provided by Augustine's theory of sacrifice and *latreia*, we have analyzed how Augustine's account of emotions relates to his political theory and how pagans and Christians alike can approach true virtue on earth. Another way of explaining right worship is to describe it as a process: those who practice *latreia* cleave to God as their object (and hence perform an act of sacrifice); as they do so, God becomes the object of their will, or their love. Not only are the virtues born in a person's heart because of this cleaving, but his or her emotions will be purified as well, so that he or she may experience "compassion" or "fellow feeling" in their hearts for the plight of another. This compassion, in turn, plays a role in an individual's performance of acts of mercy, another essential component of the sacrifice truly desired by God. Finally, in the post-Incarnation world, participation in the Eucharist, the ultimate cleaving to God, conforms recipients to the person of Christ, so that they will what Christ wills. Given a broad understanding of the grace imparted by Christ's sacrifice, instantiated and participated in through the Catholic Mass, it is possible to imagine that all acts of true mercy, whether or not they are performed by those who assent to the doctrine of the Eucharist, find the source for their strength in the sacrifice of Christ.

Augustine's definition of sacrifice in conjunction with his explanation of and praise for compassion becomes the template for his political philosophy. I conclude by proposing two caveats. The first is that significant work needs to be done to examine the role that practical reason plays in this understanding of political action. The second is that the writings of Augustine are prolific, and this is only a starting point. It is my hope that through analyzing the role of sacrifice as compassion in Augustine, a positive model of political action emerges in Augustine that escapes accusations of abject passivity and otherworldly resignation but is also clearly grounded in an understanding of the virtues as Augustine understood them. Far from teaching Christians to be compliant witnesses of injustice, the Eucharist and the sacrifice of Christ inspire Christians to "prefer justice over power" and "recover [others'] birthright in the image of God."[145] They reveal that the true path to political action is to be found in the conjunction of the institution of sacrifice and the conforming of heroic acts to that sacrifice.

# Notes

1. Hannah Arendt, *Love and Saint Augustine* (Chicago: University of Chicago Press, 1996); Sheldon Wolin, *Politics and Vision: Continuity and Innovation in Western Political Thought* (Princeton, NJ: Princeton University Press, 2004).

2. Herbert Deane, *The Political and Social Ideas of Saint Augustine* (New York: Columbia University Press, 1975).

3. William E. Connolly, *The Augustinian Imperative: A Reflection on the Politics of Morality* (Lanham, MD: Rowman and Littlefield, 2002); R. A. Markus, *Christianity and the Secular* (Notre Dame, IN: University of Notre Dame Press, 2006); R. A. Markus, *Saeculum: History and Society in the Theology of St. Augustine* (Cambridge: Cambridge University Press, 1989); and Paul Weithman, "Augustine's Political Philosophy," in *The Cambridge Companion to Augustine*, ed. David Vincent Meconi (Cambridge: Cambridge University Press, 2014).

4. John Milbank, *Theology and Social Theory: Beyond Secular Reason.* (Oxford: Blackwell Publishers, 2006); Gilbert Meilander, *The Way That Leads There: Augustinian Reflections on the Christian Life* (Grand Rapids, MI: Eerdman's, 2006); and Jean Bethke Elshtain, *Augustine and the Limits of Politics* (Notre Dame, IN: University of Notre Dame Press, 1998).

5. Pierre Manent, *Metamorphoses of the City: On the Western Dynamic* (Boston: Harvard University Press, 2013), 217.

6. Manent, *Metamorphoses*, 257.

7. Manent, *Metamorphoses*, 288.

8. It is worth noting that Dodaro (2009), like Manent (*Metamorpheses*), also thinks that in Augustine's account it is fear of death that propels the Romans and that the tempering and alleviation of this fear is something that Augustine thinks Christianity can authentically accomplish. Robert Dodaro, "*Ecclesia* and *Res publica*: How Augustinian Are Neo-Augustinian Politics?" in *Augustine and Postmodern Thought: A New Alliance against Modernity?* ed. L. Boeve, M. Lamberigts, and M. Wisse (Leuven: Peeters, 2009), 257–71, at 245–46.

9. Augustine, *The City of God Against the Pagans*, trans. R. W. Dyson (Cambridge: Cambridge University Press, 1998), book 9.

10. Charles Norris Cochrane, *Christianity and Classic Culture: a Study of Thought and Action from Augustus to Augustine* (Indianapolis: Liberty Fund, 2003), 564.

11. *The City of God* 10.13, cited in Eric Gregory, *Politics and the Order of Love: An Augustinian Ethic of Democratic Citizenship* (Chicago: University of Chicago Press, 2008), 370.

12. *The City of God*, 1.35.

13. Sabine MacCormack, *The Shadows of Poetry: Vergil in the Mind of Augustine* (Berkeley: University of California Press, 1998), 206.

14. Dodaro, "*Ecclesia* and *Res Publica*," 245–46.

15. Dodaro, "*Ecclesia* and *Res Publica*," 238–39.

16. *The City of God*, 10.20.

17. John von Heyking, *Augustine and Politics as Longing in the World* (Columbia, MO: University of Missouri Press, 2001), 142 (emphasis added).

18. Von Heyking, *Politics as Longing*, 142.

19. Von Heyking, *Politics as Longing*, 185.

20. *The City of God*, 14.4.

21. Robert Dodaro, "Augustine on the Statesman and the Two Cities," in *A Companion to Augustine*, ed. Mark Vessey (Malden, UK: Blackwell, 2012), 239.

22. *The City of God*, book 17, cited in von Heyking, *Politics as Longing*, 185–87.

23. Ernest L. Fortin, "The Patristic Sense of Community," in *The Birth of Philosophic Christianity: Studies in Early Christian and Medieval Thought* (Lanham, MD: Rowman and Littlefield, 1996), 74.

24. Hayyim Angel, "'I Am a Hebrew!' Jonah's Conflict with God's Mercy Toward Even the Most Worthy of Pagans," *Jewish Bible Quarterly* 34, no. 1, 3–11, at 4.

25. Angel, "'I Am a Hebrew!'" 3; Alan Cooper, "In Praise of Divine Caprice: The Significance of the Book of Jonah" in *Among the Prophets: Language, Image and Structure in the Prophetic Writings*, ed. Philip R. Davies and David J. A. Clines (Sheffield, UK: Sheffield Academic Press, 1993), 144–63, at 148.

26. Angel, "'I Am a Hebrew!'"; Cooper, "Divine Caprice"; André and Pierre-Emmanuel-Lacocque, *The Jonah Complex* (Atlanta: John Knox Press, 1981); T. L. Wilt, "Jonah: A Battle of Shifting Alliances," in Davies and Clines, eds., *Among the Prophets*, 164–82.

27. In Uriel Simon, "Introduction," in *The JPS Bible Commentary: Jonah*, trans. Lenn J. Schramm (Philadelphia: Jewish Publication Society, 1999).

28. Angel, "'I Am a Hebrew!'" 5; Jonah 1:6, the *New American Bible*, rev. ed. (hereafter NABRE) (United States Conference of Catholic Bishops, 2011), United States Conference of Catholic Bishops website, accessed February 8, 2019, http://www.usccb.org/bible/jonah/1.

29. Angel, "'I Am a Hebrew!'" 7.

30. Cooper, "Divine Caprice," 154.

31. The NABRE commentary draws a parallel between Jonah 4:10–11 and Job 38.

32. Angel, "'I Am a Hebrew!'" 9.

33. Jonah 2:9–10.

34. Augustine, Letter 102, in *Augustine: Prologomena, Confessions, Letters*, Nicene and Post-Nicene Fathers, ed. Philip Schaff, first series, vol. 1 (Buffalo, NY: Christian Literature Publishing Co., 1887), 35.

35. Augustine, Letter 102, 35.

36. Augustine, Letter 102, 36.

37. Augustine, Letter 102, 37.

38. Joshua N. Moon, *Jeremiah's New Covenant: An Augustinian Reading*. Journal of Theological Interpretation Supplementary Series (Warsaw, IN: Eisenbrauns), 17.

39. Johannes van Oort, *Jerusalem and Babylon: A Study into Augustine's* City of God *and the Sources of His Docrine of the Two Cities* (Leiden: Brill, 1990), 100.

40. Augustine, "Exposition of Psalm 55," in *Augustine: Expositions on the Psalms*, Nicene and Post-Nicene Fathers, ed. Philip Schaff, first series, vol. 8 (Buffalo, NY: Christian Literature Publishing Co, 1888).

41. *The City of God*, 10.5–6.

42. *The City of God*, 18.47.

43. *The City of God*, 10.6.

44. Augustine, cited in Joseph McInerny, *The Greatness of Humility: St. Augustine on Moral Excellence* (Eugene, OR: Pickwick Publications, 2016), 93.

45. Johannes Brachtendorf, "Augustine on the Limits and Glory of Philosophy," in *Augustine and Philosophy*, ed. Philip Cary, John Doody, and Kim Paffenroth (Lanham, MD: Lexington Books, 2010), 3–22, at 22.

46. Augustine, *Confessions*, book 7, and *De trinitate* 11–12, cited in McInerny, *Greatness of Humility*, 100.

47. Brachtendorf, "Augustine on the Limits and Glory of Philosophy," 22.

48. Mary T. Clark, "De Trinitate," in *The Cambridge Companion to Augustine*, ed. Eleonore Stump and Norman Kretzmann (Cambridge: Cambridge University Press, 2006), 91–102, at 97.

49. Augustine, *De trinitate* 10.5.7; cited in Clark, "De Trinitate," 98.

50. Augustine, *De trinitate* 10.5.7; Mateusz Stróżyński, "There is No Searching for the Self: Self-Knowledge in Book Ten of Augustine's *De Trinitate*," *Phronesis* 58, no. 3 (2013): 280–300, at 292.

51. Jon. 2:4.

52. Josh. 2:9–12.

53. Gregory, *Politics and the Order of Love*, 269.

54. Gregory, *Politics and the Order of Love*, 175–76.

55. Gregory, *Politics and the Order of Love*, 379.

56. *The City of God*, 10.3.

57. *The City of God*, 10.3.

58. *The City of God*, 10.5.

59. *The City of God*, 10.3.

60. *The City of God*, 10.3.

61. Kevin Corrigan, "Love of God, Love of Self, and Love of Neighbor: Augustine's Critical Dialogue with Platonism," *Augustinian Studies* 34, no. 1 (2003): 97–106, at 105.

62. Raymond Canning, *The Unity of Love for God and Neighbor in St. Augustine* (Leuven: Augustinian Historical Institute, 1993), 64–65.

63. In a sermon, Augustine describes the Eucharist as bestowing *virtus*. See Pamela Jackson, "Eucharist," in *Augustine Through the Ages: An Encyclopedia*, ed. Allan D. Fitzgerald (New York: Eerdman's, 1999), 334.

64. Canning, *The Unity of Love*, 127–28.

65. *The City of God*, 10.3.

66. John Cavadini, "Jesus's Death Is Real: An Augustinian Spirituality of the Cross," in *The Cross in Christian Tradition: From Paul to Bonaventure*, ed. Elizabeth A. Dreyer (Mahwah, NJ: Paulist Press, 2000), 169–91, at 177.

67. *The City of God*, 10.6.

68. *The City of God*, 10.19.

69. *The City of God*, 10.6.

70. Cavadini, *Jesus's Death is Real*, 175.

71. Philippians 2:7, cited in *The City of God*, 10.6.

72. *The City of God*, 19.23.

73. *The City of God*, 10.20.

74. *The City of God*, 10.20.

75. Cited in William Cavanaugh, *Torture and the Eucharist* (Oxford: Blackwell, 1998), 12.

76. *The City of God*, 10.20.

77. *The City of God*, 10.5.

78. In this context, a term for receiving Communion.

79. *The City of God*, 10.6.

80. Jackson, "Eucharist," 331–32.

81. Cavadini, "Jesus's Death is Real," 185.

82. Dodaro, "*Ecclesia* and *Res publica*," 240.

83. Cavadini, "Jesus' Death Is Real," 186.

84. Cavadini, "Jesus' Death Is Real," 186.

85. Cavanaugh, *Torture and the Eucharist*, 9–10.

86. *The City of God*, 10.12; Gregory, *Politics and the Order of Love*, 247.

87. *The City of God*, 10.20–32.

88. *The City of God*, 10.21–22. The Chaldean theurgists practiced a type of ritual magic meant to purify the soul and lead it toward heaven. See Hans Lewy, *Chaldean Oracles and Theurgy: Mysticism, Magic, and Platonism in the Later Roman Empire* (Paris: Institut d'Études Augustiennes, 2011) 224. It is these rites that Augustine refers to in this part of book 10. Porphyry practiced theurgic rites, but it was Iamblichus "who moved theurgy from periphery to center" in the lives of the philosopher and the common person. See Gregory Shaw, *Theurgy and the Soul: The Neoplatonism of Iamblichus* (University Park: Pennsylvania State University Press, 1995), 10. Iamblichus's school introduced the rites to the Roman emperor Julian (Lewy, *Chaldean Oracles*, 68–69). The rites often included the attachment of a mediating "spirit" to a statuette meant to represent a divine image of some kind (Dodds, "Theurgy and its Relationship to Neoplatonism," *Journal of Roman Studies* 37 [1947]: 55–69, at 63). It is interesting to consider the relationship between the unity of the material and spiritual in the Eucharistic host according to book 10, and the unity of the material and spiritual in the theurgic rites, because both are rites of purification that involve physical modes of mediation that are more than representations.

89. *The City of God*, 10.23.

90. *The City of God*, 10.27.

91. *The City of God*, 10.24; 10.28.

92. *The City of God*, 10. 24.

93. Dodaro, "Augustine on the Statesman," 393, citing Plotinus, *Enneads* 1.2.1–2.

94. Dodaro, "Augustine on the Statesman," 394. MacCormack points out Augustine's esteem for Porphyry, because he held that human souls might at some point reach a definitive purification (*The Shadows of Poetry*, 120).

95. Dodaro, "Augustine on the Statesman," 394, citing *De mysteriis* 5.26.

96. *The City of God*, 14.8. Augustine both relies on and criticizes the Stoics. Book 14 of *The City of God* is extremely critical of Stoicism, though Wetzel convincingly argues that Augustine may be engaging in a rhetorical redescription of virtue's relationship to the passions in *The City of God* that is meant to emphasize certain aspects of their thought. See James Wetzel, *Augustine and the Limits of Virtue* (Cambridge: Cambridge University Press, 1992), 52. This redescription, on a cursory reading, belies the extent of what Sarah Byers has proven is the debt that Augustine's moral psychology owes to the Stoics. See Byers, "Augustine's Debt to Stoicism in the Confessions," in *The Routledge Handbook of the Stoic Tradition*, ed. John Sellars (New York: Routledge, 2016), 56–69; and Byers, "Augustine on the 'Divided Self': Platonist or Stoic," *Augustinian Studies* 38 (2007): 105–18.

97. *The City of God*, 14.8.

98. *The City of God*, 10.32. However, Augustine also admonishes Porphyry for causing those incapable of philosophy to turn to theurgists as their only path to salvation.

Because you wish to reward your teachers, however, you recommend such arts to others, who, not being philosophers, are seduced into using what you admit is useless to yourself, who are capable of higher things. Thus, those who are remote from the power of philosophy, which is too arduous for all save the few, may, with your encouragement, seek purification at the hands of the theurgists: purification not, indeed, of the intellectual, but of the spiritual part of the soul. Now since those incapable of philosophy form incomparably the greater part of the multitude of mankind, more may be compelled to resort to these secret and illicit teachers of yours than to the Platonic schools.

It is important to note that Augustine believes that the Chaldeans, not Plato, lead Porphyry down this erroneous path. It is Porphyry's pride that prevents him from seeing in Christ the way to universal salvation and causes him to turn to the Chaldean rites (*The City of God*, 10.27).

99. *The City of God*, 10.2.

100. Augustine also praises Plotinus for his discussion of Divine Providence (*The City of God*, 10.14).

101. *The City of God*, 14.9.

102. *The City of God*, 14.9. Contrast "Compassion" (in English etymology, literally "with passion") and *apatheia* (in Greek etymology, literally "not passion").

103. *The City of God*, 1.6.

104. Augustine, Letter 153, Augustine to Macedonius, in *Augustine: Political Writings*, ed. E. M. Atkins and Robert Dodaro (Cambridge: Cambridge University Press, 2007), 71–88, sect. 10.

105. Ernest L. Fortin, "Augustine and the Hermeneutics of Love: Some Preliminary Considerations," in *The Birth of Philosophic Christianity: Studies in Early Christian and Medieval Thought* (Lanham, MD: Rowman and Littlefield, 1996), 1–19, at 10.

106. Cochrane, *Christianity and Classical Culture*, 494.

107. *The City of God*, 9.5.

108. And hence right worship, as we learned in book 10.

109. *The City of God*, 9.5.

110. *The City of God*, 14.6.

111. *The City of God*, 14.6.

112. *The City of God*, 14.7.

113. *The City of God*, 14.6.

114. *The City of God*, 14.7.

115. *The City of God*, 14.6.

116. Recall *The City of God*, 10.4: "If a man loves himself, his one wish is to achieve blessedness. Now this end is to 'cling to God' (Psalm 73:28). Thus if a man knows how to love himself, the commandment to love his neighbor bids him to do all he can to bring his neighbor to love God."

117. Augustine, Letter 153, section 9. For an excellent treatment of this letter to Macedonius see Robert Dodaro's *Augustine on the Statesman*. In the introduction to their edited volume *Augustine: Political Writings*, Dodaro and Atkins point out that this letter was written after Augustine had finished the first three books of *The City of God*.

118. Augustine, Letter 153, section 8.

119. Augustine, Letter 153, section 4.

120. Augustine, Letter 153, section 15.

121. Dodaro and Atkins, "Introduction," in *Augustine: Political Writings*, xi–xxvii, at xxvii.

122. *The City of God*, 19.4.

123. Robert Dodaro, "Augustine's Revision of the Heroic Ideal," *Augustinian Studies* 36, no. 1 (2005): 141–57, at 142.

124. Brian Harding, "The Use of Alexander the Great in Augustine's *City of God*," *Augustinian Studies*, 39 (2008): 113–28, at 113.

125. *The City of God*, 3.18.

126. *The City of God*, 3.13.

127. *The City of God*, 3.13.

128. *The City of God*, 3.13.

129. *The City of God*, 3.14.

130. Mary M. Keys, "Augustinian Humility as Natural Right," in *Natural Right and Political Philosophy: Essays in Honor of Catherine Zuckert and Michael Zuckert*, ed. Ann Ward and Lee Ward (North Bend, IN: University of Notre Dame Press, 2013), 97–114, at 102.

131. *The City of God*, 3.14.

132. *The City of God*, 3.14.

133. *The City of God*, 3.18.

134. *The City of God*, 3.28.

135. *The City of God*, 3.28.

136. *The City of God*, 4.4.

137. *The City of God*, 14.9.

138. Dodaro, "Augustine's Revision of the Heroic Ideal," 148–49. Dodaro writes:

Yet although Augustine is certain that Christian rulers will find in Christ the supreme model of civic virtue and eloquence, he also recognizes that Christ's virtue cannot be fully imitated, because the source of his virtue, the unity between his divine and human natures, is unique to him. Moreover, Christ can never provide an example of contrition for sins or prayer for pardon. Instead, Augustine suggests that examples of this kind are given by the saints, whose struggle with the effects of original sin makes them fitting models of civic virtue in ways that Christ cannot be. For these reasons, Augustine contends in his political writings that many saints, both Old Testament figures such as Job and David, and those who follow Christ, such as Peter and Paul, offer statesmen of his own day an alternative model of civic virtue to that of Cicero's optimates.

139. *The City of God*, 14.9.

140. *The City of God*, 14.9; the citizens of the eternal city are untouched by either grief or fear.

141. Dodaro, "Augustine on the Statesman," 149.

142. *The City of God*, 14.9.

143. *The City of God*, 5.26.

144. *The City of God*, 5.26.

145. Cavadini, "Jesus's Death Is Real," 186.

Chapter Five

# The Investigation of Justice in Augustine's *Confessions*

## Adam Thomas

In this essay, I consider Augustine's account in the *Confessions* of his investigation of justice, especially his short discourse on "true, inner justice."[1] We are fortunate in the case of Augustine to have his autobiography to help us retrace the steps of his intellectual and spiritual career.[2] As I argue below, this discourse on justice has a unique place in the narrative of the *Confessions* and presents itself as a summary of Augustine's mature understanding of justice. It indicates the elements of that understanding and marks out for the reader the paths he took to arrive at it. In doing so it raises certain questions and points not only to the later books of the *Confessions* but also, through textual allusion, to Augustine's early dialogue *On Free Choice*, where he says the deeper reasoning behind the view sketched in the *Confessions* is to be found.[3] Considering the continued difficulties in ascertaining his moral and political philosophy,[4] this discourse and its context, which have not received much attention,[5] should be of interest to students of Augustine as a way of framing our consideration of his thought.

The discourse on justice occurs in the context of Augustine's recounting of his first association with the Manichaean sect, in which he mentions the difficulties that caused him to prefer that sect for nine years. In addition to the well-known difficulties regarding the origin of evil and God's spiritual nature, Augustine says that the morality of the Old Testament and the justice of the patriarchs were a stumbling block that he could not accept until he came to understand "true, inner justice."[6] There follows a discourse on the view of justice that Augustine would come to know and that enabled him to accept the Old Testament. Following Augustine's definition of justice, the discourse falls into two parts. Its first, introductory part[7] consists mostly of a series of analogies that shed light on the nature of Augustine's youthful error and on the true character of justice. Clarifying justice "from below," as it were, these analogies broaden our sense of what true justice is by appealing to certain everyday experiences of what is suitable, fitting, or proper. This comparison of justice with our sense of propriety encourages us to appreciate the complexities that legitimately attend the question of justice and to consider the diversity of laws and morals that may be permitted, and even demanded, by justice. It finally raises the question whether the unassisted human mind is capable of comprehending what is necessary to arrive at the true conception of justice.

The second, longer part of the discourse[8] marks a new beginning, as Augustine turns to what is always and everywhere just. He begins by deriving the demands of justice from the double commandment of the Gospels to love God and neighbor. These demands are mediated through the nature that God created in us and that we must maintain to continue in fellowship with him, the covenant or fundamental law that undergirds each particular human society, and the express commands of God, which take precedence over all human laws or customs. After considering some just rules from these three sources, Augustine turns to the question of God's concern for injustice, and from there to a more radical formulation of the rule of charity. He argues that our offenses against justice concern God not because he is corrupted or harmed by them, but because of the effect they have on us, and that the ultimate rule of our nature, and therefore of justice, is to subordinate all our goods and affairs to God. Finally, having articulated an uncompromising ideal of self-denial, Augustine insists that acts of distributive or retributive justice, which have the appearance of sins because they involve those lower goods that we are tempted to put in place of God, must be distinguished from genuine sins.

Augustine's discourse on justice is more a series of conclusions than an extended argument. As such, it raises several questions that it does not adequately answer. As we will see, the two major questions that Augustine's opening definition raises are first, whether Augustine considered true justice to be available to unassisted reason and, second, how he conceived of the unity of justice that simultaneously sanctions and limits moral diversity. In his discourse, Augustine does not come down clearly on one side of the first question, and his answer to the second question—that the core of justice is man's subordination of his whole self to God—leaves us with the further question of how this ordering occurs in practice. Augustine insists that ordinary acts of distributive and retributive justice are compatible with true piety, but he does not explain how this is so or give much detail regarding how those questions of political justice ought to be determined. It is here above all that Augustine's remarks indicate the necessity of turning to *On Free Choice*, in which he promises us a fuller answer to the question of justice. Within the limits of this essay, however, we can consider only what Augustine says about his mature view of justice in the *Confessions*, situating the discourse within his larger narrative, tracing the elements of that view and the questions they raise, and seeing the paths that we must take to make further progress.

## The Place of the Discourse on Justice in the *Confessions*

Augustine's discussion of "true, inner justice" occurs in the third book of the *Confessions*, where he recalls the time he spent in Carthage from the ages of seventeen to nineteen. The most important episode in this book is his experience with Cicero's *Hortensius*, which he says "changed my disposition [*affectus*]" and filled him with a great desire "that I might love and seek and pursue and hold and strongly embrace not this or that sect, but wisdom itself, whatever it was."[9] This moment, at which Augustine goes so far as to say that he "had begun to rise, in order that I might return to You,"[10] is a crucial point in the narrative of the *Confessions*. It interrupts the account of his youthful dissolution, begun in books 1 and 2, intensified in the experience of love and the theater that opens book 3, and resumed at the beginning of book 4. His account marks the beginning of his intellectual and spiritual struggle against that dissolution. This struggle would not be resolved for thirteen more years: at nineteen, his noble determination to pursue wisdom is quickly eclipsed by his association with the Manichaean sect, begun soon after this crucial moment and continued for nine years. It is in the course of explaining his initial association with the Manicheans that Augustine makes his remarks on "true, inner justice."

It is perhaps surprising that Augustine's desire for "wisdom itself," as opposed to the dogmas of any particular sect[11] is so quickly followed by his attachment to a heretical philosophic sect. Augustine gives two accounts of his turn to Manichaeism. In the first, general account, he emphasizes his simultaneous disappointment with Cicero and the Bible: he could not be wholly seized by Cicero's philosophy, since "the name of Christ was not there,"[12] but he found the Holy Scriptures impenetrable and unworthy when compared with what he calls "Ciceronian dignity."[13] The Manicheans, on the other hand, used the names of Christ and the Holy Spirit and insisted that they taught "the truth" about God and "the elements of this world."[14] A few paragraphs later, after describing some of their false doctrines, such as their deification of the sun and moon,[15] and deploring his former belief in them,[16] Augustine provides a second, more specific account of his turn from the Bible to Manichaeism. Here he lists specific theological difficulties that "sharply moved" him at that time and made him vulnerable to the Manichean arguments.[17] He lists three questions: first, the origin of evil; second, whether God was bound by a bodily form; and third, whether people in the Bible who had many wives, killed other people, and sacrificed animals were just.[18] Augustine says that these questions "perturbed" him while he was yet "ignorant of the matter" and knew "nothing else, that truly *is*" that he could oppose to the Manichean answers to these questions.[19]

Luckily for us, Augustine adds a summary of the mature answers that eventually resolved these difficulties for him. He attributes his difficulties concerning the origin of evil and God's form to his ignorance of two theoretical or metaphysical doctrines: "that evil is nothing but the privation of good" and "that God is spirit."[20] These are of course quite well known to readers of the *Confessions*, and Augustine's brief statement of them here is only the beginning of a treatment that ends in the decisive remarks of Book VII.[21] As for the justice of the Old Testament figures, he traces his difficulties to his ignorance of something he calls "true, inner justice."[22] It is only this third solution that Augustine elaborates here,[23] to which he barely alludes later in the *Confessions*. When Augustine announces the resolution of the question, "What is iniquity?" in book 7, he does so with reference to the origin of evil, not its practical definition: evil is not a substance, but rather a "perversity of the will."[24]

How do we explain this discrepancy? Was the definition of justice unimportant to Augustine, or not especially difficult?[25] James O'Donnell and Todd Breyfogle observe that the solutions to Augustine's three questions are given in reverse order later in the *Confessions*, with the discussions of Ambrose's preaching at the end of book 5 and beginning of book 6, resolving the difficulty of justice among the patriarchs, prior to the resolution of God's spiritual nature and the origin of evil in book 7.[26] It is perfectly reasonable to assume that Ambrose's figurative or spiritual interpretation[27] of the Old Testament, which led Augustine to accept the authority of scripture,[28] must have helped him overcome his moral objections, but it is striking that he makes no mention of this fact in those passages. He mentions no change in his understanding of justice, saying only that Ambrose corrected his misconception that patriarchs understood man's being made in God's image to mean that God had a bodily form.[29] Of course, it would be strange if Augustine finally accepted scripture without having some way of vindicating the justice of those praised in the Old Testament. In his retrospective later in book 6, he says Ambrose had inspired "a great hope" in him by showing that the church did not think of God carnally and blames himself for hesitating to "knock, that other things may be opened."[30] Among these other things, it would seem, was the truth about justice.

The passage that most clearly bears on Augustine's progress in investigating justice comes at the end of book 6, when he recalls discussing the definition of good and evil with Alypius and Nebridius.[31] Only belief in the soul's immortality and in final judgment prevented him from agreeing with Epicurus—that is, from identifying the good with pleasure—since he could not yet "ponder the light of honor and of beauty freely embraced, which the eye of the flesh does not see, but is seen deep within."[32] It seems that he thought that there was some divine law to which he would be held after death, but he did not yet see it as intrinsically binding. How did he then come to identify the good with honor and beauty, and thus happiness with obedience to divine law, in this world and the next? He tells us only that he had not considered the nature of friendship and its relation to happiness.[33]

Augustine returns to the subject of beauty at a crucial point in book 7, after narrating his "ascent" to knowledge of God's spiritual substance and the conclusion that evil is perversity and before turning to his embrace of the Mediator in order to enjoy God with stable faith.[34] He now relates that ascent to his questions about beauty and propriety (*debitum*): he had sought the source of his attraction to beauty and of his judgment of how things ought to be, from which he was led to an analysis of the human faculties until his reason "arrived at that which is, in the flash of a trembling glance."[35] It is difficult to conclude very much from this passage regarding a change in Augustine's particular conception of beauty and propriety, but considering the relations among beauty, propriety, honor, the supreme good, and justice, it is likely that Augustine did not resolve the question of "true, inner justice" much earlier or more easily than the questions of God's spiritual substance and the origin of evil.[36]

This brings us back to the discourse on justice. Considering the paucity of explicit statements about justice after book 3, we have no choice but to take up this long summary of Augustine's mature position. Having traced the basic problems that Augustine faced in settling the question of justice and having gained a provisional understanding of his doctrine, we will see how the argument points to the significant question of friendship running through books 4 through 6 of the *Confessions*, to which the question of the highest good, and thus justice, is linked. More important, we will see clearly the need to supplement this consideration of friendship and beauty with the analysis of law and politics found in *On Free Choice*.

## The Complexity of Justice

When we turn to Augustine's discourse on justice, we find first a lengthy definition:

> Nor did I know true, inner justice that [1] judges not according to human custom, but according to the most righteous law of Almighty God, [2] by which the morals[37] of the regions and times were formed for those regions and times, although it was itself everywhere and always, not one thing in one place and another in other places, [3] according to which Abraham, Isaac, Jacob, Moses and all those praised by the mouth of God were just.[38]

The third part of this definition is of course not surprising. The first two parts, however, are only superficially simple. The first rejects human custom as a criterion, consistent with our sense of the "objectivity" of justice. Yet the fact that Augustine links the independence of justice to its foundation in God's law raises the question of whether human reason can grasp this law, which therefore is transparently rational, or whether it is revealed by God as a matter of belief. These two senses of objectivity are not the same. What difference is there, then, between Augustine's doctrine of true justice and other doctrines that look explicitly to nature as something meant to be fully compassed by man's unassisted reason, such as those of Plato, Aristotle, or Cicero? The second part of the definition is obviously a paradox: since God's law itself is responsible for the differences between regions and ages, true justice is somehow one and the same, everywhere and always, and yet compatible with what Augustine later calls "the diversity of mores."[39] But what then is the unifying element that allows us to speak of justice as universally one and puts limits on our acceptance of diversity in mores, preventing this acceptance from overshadowing the denigration of human custom with which the definition of justice had begun?[40]

Augustine does not give immediate answers to these questions. Instead, he begins his exposition with a somewhat frustrating series of analogies that indicate what his error (condemning people praised by God in the Bible) was *like*. Augustine presents three absurd images, saying that to call these people wicked

> is as if [1] someone ignorant of armaments—what is suited for each member—should want his head to be covered with a greave and to be shod with a helmet and were muttering that it did not come together properly, or [2] someone should fume that it is not allowed him to set out anything for sale on an afternoon appointed as a public holiday, since it was allowed him in the morning, or [3] should see in one house that something is taken in hand by some slave that the minister of the cups is not allowed to do, or that something is done behind the stables that is prohibited before the table and should be indignant that the same thing is not assigned everywhere and to everyone, although it is one dwelling-place and one family.[41]

These analogies are obviously comic and therefore provocative in this context: to compare someone disturbed by certain aspects of Old Testament history with someone unable to dress himself, someone too boorish or greedy to enjoy a holiday, or someone incapable of grasping the idea of division of labor seems to be inappropriately dismissive of the difficulty. They are surely meant to be provocative, but Augustine clearly did not think his earlier objections were simply ridiculous. We should therefore look to see what is serious about them.

The absurdity of the images comes from a lack of awareness of some "whole" and the relation among its parts, or some absurd dullness to what is fitting. In the first analogy, there is an obvious, natural whole (the body) with obvious parts (a head and a leg), and a corresponding, intuitive understanding on our part of "what is suited for each member" (a helmet for the head and a leg covering for the leg) that is somehow absent in this man. In the second analogy there is another natural whole (one day),[42] with clear parts (the morning and the afternoon), but the comedy is not that someone fails to see this: it is rather that he is angry about a distinction made among the parts of that whole that is simply a human invention (i.e., that is purely conventional). There are some obvious relations between wholes and parts that are not "directly from nature," but are instead the product of human decision. This comic episode shows that humans' reliance on convention, however, does not necessarily reduce their dignity, since in fact we think it childish or boorish to fail to see their suitability in these situations.

The third analogy is the most complicated. It is obvious that a household forms some kind of natural unit or whole and that different parts of a house have different functions (the dining room and the stable, for instance) that are reflected in certain restrictions (no horses in the dining room) and some kind of division of labor among the members of the house (the person cleaning up after the horses does not prepare dinner). But these relations between the different tasks and the different members of the house are not equally spontaneous and intuitive. In the first place, although the children of the house are members by birth, their parents are probably present through a marriage covenant. Augustine also mentions slaves.[43] Some slaves may have been born there, but others may be a part of the house as the result of some transaction (or conquest). The power of nature and convention in establishing and maintaining these relationships among the members of a household is a matter of debate, but the fact that two particular people are married, or that one particular person is the master and another his slave, cannot be a matter of nature, if nature is taken to be some kind of spontaneous ordering, as we perceive in the case of the human body or a single day. To be clear, Augustine mentions here only the division of labor itself: the person in his analogy is not concerned that some people may be slaves to others within the house, but that any differentiation exists at all between the tasks and places of the household—which exists in any household, with or without slavery.

Augustine completes the series of analogies by drawing us back to the justice of the biblical figures and making its lesson explicit:

> Thus are those who are indignant when they hear that something was permitted to the just in that age that is not permitted them in this one, and that God commands one thing to those, [but] another to these for reasons of the times [*pro temporalibus causis*], although both serve the same justice, while they see in one human being and in one day and in one dwelling that one thing is suited to some member, that something was then permitted that is not permitted an hour later, and that a certain thing is permitted or commanded in that corner that in the one joined to it is forbidden and punished.[44]

The explicit lesson of the analogies is that those who are indignant at the situation of the Bible, in which something is permitted or commanded in one time and not at another, are like those who would be indignant at the three common, unobjectionable situations he has just described. The key to the argument is that Augustine relates the unobjectionable distinctions between the parts of one human body, one day, or one household to the distinctions between the old and new covenants ruling God's people, or the "household of God" whose history is recorded in the Bible. This identification gives force to his observation that those who object to the Bible accept in another form—even to the point of "commanding" and "punishing"[45]—the principle of diversity (that doing right does not always mean doing the same thing) that they reject in the case of the Bible. But is biblical history really a "whole" analogous to the situations Augustine has described? This would seem to mean that polygamy or animal sacrifice, to take earlier examples, was as obviously essential to the religion and society of the Old Testament as a helmet is to a head, a closed shop to a holiday, or a designated cook to a household, even if those practices are now the equivalent of putting a sock on your head or trying to set up a market during a Memorial Day parade or feeding your horses at the dinner table. It is hard to see how this can be more than a crude outline of Augustine's understanding of the matter.

Augustine follows up these apparently glib conclusions with a more explicit formulation about justice that indicates the barriers to our understanding:

> Surely justice is not various or changeable? But the times over which it presides do
> not proceed equally, since they are times. Human beings, however, whose life upon
> the earth is short, since their sense [*sensus*] is not strong enough to weave together the
> causes of prior ages and other peoples that they have not experienced with those that
> they have, but are able easily to see what fits with which member, which moments, and
> which parts in one body, one day, or one house, are offended by the former things,
> [but] obey the latter.[46]

On the one hand, although justice itself does not change, the conditions under
which it rules do, which means that what is just will change, depending on those
different conditions. On the other hand, we human beings are unable to weave
our history and experience together into a "whole" in the same way that we can
with an individual body, day, or household. Although we are certain about what is
fitting for the different parts of the body, the day, or the household, we are ignorant of the relations between prior ages and societies and our own, which causes
us to be offended at the diversity of morals and characters, either by disdaining
all other societies and morals but our own or by doubting the constancy and
firmness of justice itself.[47] We instinctively rebel at any rule of diversity among
human societies even as we unthinkingly adhere to some rule of diversity in our
own affairs.[48]

The more particular barriers to understanding have become apparent in the order
of the analogies Augustine has presented. The series of analogies moves from a natural, spontaneous whole with natural divisions (a human body) to a natural whole
with natural divisions that is conventionally divided (a holiday) to a composite natural and conventional whole with natural and conventional divisions (a household).
From the movement in these examples we can see what it would mean to rise not
only to a political community, a whole more conventional than a household, with
more moving parts whose relations are governed by laws and maintained by institutions, but to a community that stretches across many centuries, as does the City
of God, which according to Christian orthodoxy has comprised different political
communities. Can the human mind comprehend so broad a view unassisted? The
conclusion to this first part pushes toward this question.

The first part of the discourse closes with another analogy, this time comparing
justice with the art of poetry, which Augustine cultivated as a young man.[49] He
recalls his experience in composing poetry, which was governed by subtle rules corresponding to various meters or modes. However, the variability of these rules cast no
doubt on the unity of the poetic art itself, which "held all things at the same time."[50]
He says that the justice the patriarchs served was the same, possessing all rules or
commands at the same time without changing, but "assigning and commanding not
all things at the same time, but what is proper to the changing times."[51] The key

to this analogy is that a single poetic art governs an array of types of poetry, each of which is governed by a slightly different set of rules. In governing these various types, the poetic art sets formal limits to what is done in various situations. Our experience of the art of poetry shows that these limits are not always simple; good poetry neither simply repeats nor endlessly varies. The young Augustine failed to see that justice governs human action in the same way, itself containing every action that might be commanded, as something one and immutable, but assigning and commanding only what is proper to the changing times.

The analogy to poetry only deepens the paradox of the second part of the opening definition. Augustine introduces a new and important concept here in speaking of what is "proper" (*propria*),[52] which sums up the argument of this first part. Its meaning spans "particular" and "appropriate," the two senses of justice as giving to each his own and as doing in each case what is fitting. The unity of justice comes from its sovereignty over this notion of fittingness that simultaneously sanctions and limits moral diversity across different societies and ages, in the way that the arts sanction and limit diversity in action in their areas of competence. Augustine has argued that our desire for regularity makes us overlook how complicated true justice can be, which leads to either fanaticism or cynicism. According to the argument here, the first step toward understanding true justice is to see its connection to what is proper or fitting, a principle that we recognize quite easily (and even instinctually) in mundane situations but that grows more complicated as we ascend to matters of greater importance.

Of course, Augustine does not tell us how this argument led him to accept the Old Testament—he only gives us the kind of argument and investigation that he pursued. The effect of the argument is to lower our confidence in the face of the complexity of justice, tied as it is to what is fitting or proper in the wide variety of human circumstances. The analogy with poetry is interesting in this respect. Although subject to rational analysis and discipline, poetry was traditionally said to depend on the Muses—that is, on divine inspiration. Having unraveled some of the complexities involved in rising to an understanding of "true, inner justice," we seem to be left wondering whether our reason can comprehend it, and so whether we require divine instruction.

## Sure Points of Justice

The second part of Augustine's description of "true, inner justice" begins with an abrupt rhetorical question: "Surely it is not unjust anytime or anywhere to love God with your whole heart, soul, and mind and to love your neighbor as yourself?"[53] The adverbs "anytime" and "anywhere" emphasize that some things are just regardless of circumstances or are always proper. In this second part, Augustine mitigates the uncertainty of the first part by beginning from something that is certainly and universally just and drawing conclusions from it. It is not surprising that he starts from this famous verse, followed in one account by Jesus's statement that "on these two commandments hang the whole law and the prophets": it is not only a summary of Christian morality but also a crucial text for interpretation of the Old Testament.[54]

Augustine deduces three conclusions regarding the government of human passions from this double commandment, mediated by three sources of just rules: nature, human custom or covenant, and God's express commands. His example of a rule from nature concerns what is always unjust: "And thus outrages [*flagitia*][55] against nature must be hated and punished everywhere and always."[56] These actions, such as "those of the Sodomites," are held to be criminal "according to the divine law."[57] Augustine thus reminds us that the true measure of justice is God's law, which is independent of even unanimous human opinion.[58] As for this "accusation of crime" that results from lustful acts against nature, Augustine says it comes about because the divine law "did not make human beings so that they might use one another in that way."[59] The evil of such a transgression is made more explicit in the conclusion to this line of argument: "obviously the very fellowship [*societas*] that we ought to have with God is broken when the same nature of which he is the author is defiled by the perversity of lust."[60] Here the consideration guiding Augustine's deduction becomes a bit clearer. The fundamental commandment of justice is to love God, which results in fellowship with him. This fellowship, however, cannot be maintained by following just any rule of behavior. Augustine sees the origin of the rules that maintain this friendship in the divine law itself,[61] but their promulgation seems to be mediated by nature.

Augustine next deduces a second conclusion about what must not be done, this time apparently from the injunction to love your neighbor as yourself. His conclusion is that "outrages against the morals of human beings must be avoided for the sake of diversity of mores."[62] This marks what seems to be an abrupt turn back to the consideration of human opinion, which Augustine had just sharply contrasted with human nature.[63] As for why the general "diversity of mores" or a particular "covenant [*pactum*] of a city or nation among themselves" should be respected, Augustine says that "each part not fitting with its whole is base [*turpis*]."[64] This remark clearly recalls his earlier language of suitability, fittingness, and appropriateness: the argument is that our membership in a city or nation bound together by a given covenant, "strengthened by law and custom," obliges us to act in a way consistent with the activity of that whole, which (at a minimum) means not doing things that it considers shameful.[65]

Augustine's third conclusion immediately qualifies this obedience to human law and thus seems to undercut his statement about the baseness of each part not fitting with its whole. He says that "[b]ut when God commands anything contrary to the custom or covenant of any people whatsoever, even if it has never been done there before, it must be done, and if omitted, it must be resumed, and if it had not been established, it must be established."[66] His explanation for this, on its face, commonsensical statement takes the form of another simple analogy—this time between human kingship and God's rule:

> For if it is allowed that a king in the city that he rules commands something that no one before him, nor he himself had ever commanded, and it is not contrary to the fellowship of his city to obey him, but rather contrary to fellowship to disobey—it is of course a general covenant of human fellowship to obey its kings—how much more must there be ready submission to God, the Ruler of His whole creation, in those things that he has commanded. For just as a greater power is put before a lesser to be obeyed in the powers of human society, so God is before all.[67]

The explanation is superficially quite simple: we should follow God's commands regardless of human morals because whatever is owed to a human king, which includes the right to make new laws, is certainly owed to God (and more). The idea is that obedience to the king's commands defines the "fellowship" of his city, so that even wholly new commands are not inconsistent with the rules of society. Augustine then rises from this example of human prerogative to God's prerogative, implying that our more important "fellowship" with him is also defined by obedience to his commands.[68]

The analogy is clear but raises a question. Although the covenant to obey political authorities is a sine qua non of human society, it does not seem wholly to define its fellowship or good order. In a decent society, some broader notion of "fellowship," as embodied in a constitution, for example, would ultimately limit the king's right to introduce new legislation. It may well be "a *general* covenant of human society to obey its kings," taking "general" in the sense of sense of "most of the time" or "in most cases," if that obedience would ever be qualified by a notion of a higher law, whether a constitution, a moral law, or an idea of what constitutes genuine "fellowship."[69] The equivalent to this problem on the other side of the analogy is "ready" or "without doubt"—as in "God must be submitted to without doubt."[70] Is there any equivalent to the "fellowship" of the king's city that somehow limits what God would command? This question draws us back again to Augustine's remark that the "fellowship that ought to exist between us and God" is preserved by avoiding actions that defile our created nature.[71] Augustine's point here requires only the fact of God's superiority as grounds for obedience; however, in the next part of his discourse he elaborates on the claim that our nature suffers from separation from God.

Augustine says that this reasoning regarding sins of corruption applies also to "crimes" (*facinora*), which he refers to elsewhere as the second class of sins, fundamentally derivative of lustful passions but distinguished from them by always involving harm to others.[72] The fundamental definition of crime is given by the Ten Commandments,[73] which we transgress in order to satisfy one of the objects or passions that "spring out" of lust[74]—vengeance, gain, avoiding evil, envy, and pleasure at the suffering of others.[75]

Having outlined these sure points of justice, Augustine turns to a sudden question about God's concern for these matters: "But what are outrages to you, who are not corrupted? Or what are crimes against you, who cannot be harmed?"[76] Answering this question requires saying something more about the foundations of the precepts Augustine has outlined. He insists that God punishes "what human beings perpetrate in themselves, since even when they sin against you, they act impiously in their souls and 'iniquity lies to itself.'"[77] Augustine rejects the notion that punishment for sin is something entirely external to the sin itself, which would mean that we have no intrinsic reason for obeying God's commands.

The theme that "the punishment for sin is sin" is repeated many times in the *Confessions* and is one of its fundamental theses. For instance, in book 1, Augustine says that God was justly allowing him to be punished by his teachers "because you have commanded, and it is so, that each disordered spirit [*animus*] is its own punishment."[78] Here he stresses the self-deception that results from sin. He says that corruption of their nature and immoderation lead people to be "held" by their actions, remaining tied to them even to their detriment or to desire disorder in the vain hope of being able to satisfy their whims.[79]

At this point, Augustine's language reverts to the fervent, devotional style familiar to readers of the *Confessions*. In these next few lines Augustine presents a summary of many of the famous moral doctrines of the *Confessions* with Platonic overtones. He begins by saying that "these things [the effects of sin just described] happen when you are forsaken, the Fountain of Life, who are the One and True Creator and Ruler of the universe, and from private arrogance some false 'one' is loved in a part of creation."[80] This diagnosis, in which the one and true (*unus et verus*) creator is forsaken for love of some false "one" (*unum falsum*) under the influence of private arrogance, suggests the remedy for that sin: "And so there is a return to you from humble piety, and you cleanse us from evil habit [or custom][81] and are gracious to the sins of those confessing (them), and you hear the groans of prisoners and loosen the bonds that we have made for ourselves."[82] God is exchanged for whatever has been loved in place of him, and humble piety replaces the private arrogance that caused the initial exchange. This return to God is not simple, however, since our sin, as we have just seen, has the effect of corrupting our souls and establishing the force of habit, which must somehow be reversed. Augustine describes this change in terms of "cleansing" us and "loosening" our chains, but the warning that follows implies that this cure is far from a sure thing: "[I]f we should not raise up against you the horn of a false liberty, from greed for having more—at the penalty of losing all—by loving anything of ours [*proprium nostrum*] more than you, the Good of all."[83]

Augustine's formulations involve several characteristic paradoxes and antitheses. The "false liberty" that he warns against contrasts with the "chains" that hold the prisoners to sin, whose freedom is in fact hampered by their false sense of liberty. This false liberty evidently stems from "greed for having more," which reminds us of Augustine's earlier mention of the "private arrogance" that causes us to prefer anything else to God. His parenthetical remark here that, although this false liberty is pursued out of greed for having more, it comes "at the penalty of losing all," strengthens the paradox expressed in the phrase "false liberty": just as this false liberty leads us to slavery to sin, so the greed that propels it in fact leads to extreme poverty. Augustine's final definition of this false liberty—that it means loving anything that is "our own" more than God—further deepens the paradox, and brings us close to Jesus' own language in the Gospel insisting on the necessity of self-denial, such as the famous statement that "If any man would come after me, let him deny himself and take up his cross and follow me. For whoever would save his life will lose it, and whoever loses his life for my sake will find it. For what will it profit a man, if he gains the whole world and forfeits his life? Or what shall a man give in return for his life?"[84]

Augustine's use of the adjective *proprium* here, besides intensifying the meaning of *nostrum*, reminds us of the one previous use of this adjective in the conclusion of the introductory first part.[85] There the adjective is tied to art and the sense of what is fitting or appropriate. The clearest line of argument in this second part is that the love of God (and it alone) always falls under what is *proprium* in the sense that Augustine first used it. It turns out, however, that this love requires us to prevent anything that is ours, or particular to us[86] from impeding that love of God—an effort that Augustine, following Jesus, expresses in language of self-denial. Augustine's exclusive use of this adjective in two crucial sections of argument forces us to think about the relation between the as yet vague notion of "appropriateness" that is the province of true justice and the strict demands of the life of holiness, which subordinates every human concern to God.

The notions that sin is its own punishment and that the true rule of justice is to subordinate everything of ours to God are obviously related. They both seem to follow from the famous statement at the beginning of the *Confessions* that "you have made us for Yourself, and our hearts are restless until they rest in you."[87] Sin can be its own punishment only if it damages our nature, while the command to subordinate all that we have to God depends on the idea that our nature is made for God and finds its perfection in His fellowship.

Having articulated an ideal of radical detachment as the completion of our nature, Augustine turns to some conclusions about the practice of this life with God and what it means (or does not mean) to subordinate oneself and one's affairs wholly to him. He warns us that there are two classes of actions "among outrages and crimes and so many iniquities" that we must be careful not to misjudge.[88] First there are "the sins of those who are making progress," which good people will reproach insofar as they fall short of "the rule of perfection" but praise "in the hope of fruit."[89] The second class of actions, however, is much more puzzling, since is does not include sins but things "similar" to them:

> And there are certain things similar to lustful acts or crimes and are not sins, since they offend neither you nor social partnership [*sociale consortium*] when some things

are [1] procured for the use of life that are suited for[90] the time, and it is uncertain whether from a lust for possession; or [2] are punished out of a zeal for correction by an ordained power, and it is uncertain whether from a lust to harm.[91]

Augustine's vagueness is particularly frustrating here—in his use of "certain things" and "some things" rather than concrete examples and in his two strange parenthetical remarks about the uncertainty of lust. He divides these ambiguous actions into two groups, each of which has three characteristics.

The first group is distinguished as actions that "procure" some things "for the service of life."[92] We can imagine things such as growing food, building shelters, making clothing, and buying and selling goods, although Augustine offers us no examples. He only tells us that the things procured are "suited for the time."[93] They are susceptible to "lust for possession," and therefore must be things that we can call "our own."[94] It seems then that these actions have to do with the disposing of property of any sort and are similar to sins because they concern precisely the sort of things that we are tempted to put in place of God. The second subdivision, distinguished as actions that "punish" some things "with zeal for correction" is clearer, especially when we add the second criterion of these actions, that they are punished "by an ordained power."[95] Our primary experience of punishment is legal punishment, which is distinguished (and justified) by its being carried out by officers "ordained" by the community. The third criterion, that it is "uncertain" whether these actions come "from lust to harm,"[96] indicates how these actions are like sins: since legitimate acts of correction may involve seizing property or using aggressive (or even deadly) force, they may proceed from a desire to harm rather than a desire for justice. Identical actions could proceed from either intention.

Augustine's contention here is that acts of procurement and correction—that is, acts of distributive and retributive justice—are similar to sins insofar as they deal with things that are lower than God. They therefore at least give the appearance of elevating those goods to a higher place than they deserve, but are not in fact sins, since they do not necessarily grant to them a false status. This provides a basic answer to the question of how one orders all areas of human life "below" God according to a general rule of self-denial: that self-denial is evidently not incompatible with accumulating property or using force against others. However, it is not clear how these matters of distributive and retributive justice are legitimate. Besides the earlier standard of lust, which ultimately means only a desire that elevates anything in place of God, Augustine gives us two criteria for thinking about this problem: those goods should be arranged in a way that is "fitting for the use of life," and punishments that "correct" that arrangement should be carried out by an "ordained power."[97] Asking about what is fitting of course throws us back into the prior discussion, which emphasized first the variability of this notion, then its ultimate reference to God and his commands. As for the notion of "ordained power," what makes a power ordained seems to be only the law—police officers and judges are legally constituted authorities who carry out their tasks under established law. But their dependence on the law means that their actions are only as good as the laws that authorize them. As for good laws, they would seem to establish and preserve a way of life suited to the times or that order the society to God.[98] This discussion is obviously incomplete, giving us only Augustine's assurance that ordinary acts of political justice are compatible with the demands of piety. As we will see in the conclusion, to uncover the particulars of his reasoning we must turn to *On Free Choice*.

## Conclusion

The discourse on justice ends with two statements that sum up its general teaching. Augustine says that, on the one hand, it is not surprising that human judgment and God's judgment diverge, since "often the appearance of the deed is one way, and the mind of the one doing it and the crucial moment of the hidden time is something else"; on the other hand, we must obey God's commands, no matter how new or strange they seem.[99] As we have seen, the first part of the discourse expanded our notion of true justice by identifying it with the fitting. In doing so, Augustine made it seem very difficult to rise to a perfect understanding and perfect judgment. In the second part, then, he turned to some clearer statements about justice itself, rather than relying on analogies of lower arts. He began by identifying justice with charity, with love of God and neighbor. Charity demands that we maintain fellowship with others—with God by respecting the nature that He created and with other men by respecting the covenant that undergirds our political community. Where the words of God conflict with human custom, we must obey God rather than men, since our existence finds its perfection in complete devotion to him. This self-denial and detachment, however, are not incompatible with political justice and thus with deep involvement in procuring and fighting for lower goods.

If we revisit the two questions that we raised regarding Augustine's definition of justice, we see that they remain unresolved. The first question was whether Augustine understood true justice, rooted in God's law, to be fully accessible to reason. We have seen contradictory indications on this score. On the one hand, Augustine speaks of nature and the principle of the fitting or proper. He also speaks of the natural need we have for God and its corollary, that we suffer naturally from the effects of sin against His law. However, Augustine also insists at various points that our duty is to obey God's commands even when the reason for those commands is hidden from us. This suggests the necessity of acting based only on faith, rather than understanding; and yet Augustine gives us reasons to think this trust is not simply blind, since we stand in fundamental need of God. As for the second question, how we ought to maintain the unity of justice along with legitimate moral diversity, it did not become clear how the central point of true justice—our complete devotion to

God—is applied as a rule of life. We certainly must avoid gross violations of nature and transgressions of the Ten Commandments, and we know that justice does not require extreme asceticism or pacifism; it is therefore compatible with the elementary duties of human society. However, Augustine's discourse has stated only the most general principles of human laws and has not shown how he came to see our political duties and how they are compatible with piety.

Augustine's discourse points us in two directions. The centrality of charity and fellowship to the discourse points us directly to the account of beauty and friendship that takes up the bulk of books 4 through 6 of the *Confessions*. However, the discourse also points us back to Augustine's earlier dialogue *On Free Choice*. The guiding question of *On Free Choice* is the origin of evil, the first question that Augustine mentions in the *Confessions* as detaining him among the Manicheans. Near the beginning of *On Free Choice*, Augustine makes some autobiographical statements that echo his statements here about the difficulty he experienced with the question. When his interlocutor Evodius asks him "how it is that we do evil," Augustine says, "You move the question that vehemently exercised me as a youth and drove and threw me down fatigued among heretics. From which fall I was so afflicted and overwhelmed by such great piles of empty fables that, unless the love of discovering the truth had gained divine aid for me, I would not have been able to emerge from there and breathe in the very first liberty of seeking."[100] This passage certainly corresponds with the account Augustine gives in the *Confessions*. In *On Free Choice*, however, he not only advertises his prior difficulties with this question and the "freedom" he now enjoys from those difficulties but also promises to trace the question for Evodius in the very "order" that he followed in order to escape his doubt. As he says, "and since it was discussed assiduously with me, so that I was freed from this very question, I will discuss with you in that order by following which I escaped."[101]

A superficial comparison of the investigations in *Confessions* and *On Free Choice* shows that this "order" echoes but is not merely identical to the discussion in the *Confessions*, although there are some explicit parallels. In both cases there is a movement in the text that puts aside a theoretical question to take up a more obviously moral one. In *On Free Choice*, Augustine immediately refines their question from the origin of evil to the definition of evil, or to the question "what is wrongdoing?"[102] The equivalent of this movement in the *Confessions* is the fact that, of the three difficulties that Augustine says made him vulnerable to the Manicheans, only the third, moral question, is discussed at great length in book 3, with the others reserved for book 7. A second explicit point of similarity is in the particular moral examples that govern the respective discussions. When Augustine solicits Evodius in *On Free Choice* for examples of wrongdoing to discuss, Evodius mentions adultery, murder, and sacrilege; when Augustine introduces his doubt about the Old Testament in the *Confessions*, he mentions as examples of their injustice polygamy, murder, and animal sacrifice.[103]

The answer in *On Free Choice* to the question "what is wrongdoing," is given by the eternal law, which requires that we "turn our love away from temporal things and, having purified it, turn it toward eternal things."[104] The most pressing task of book 1 is to understand how ordinary acts of justice, such as self-defense or military service, are compatible with this devotion.[105] To answer this question, Augustine and his interlocutor Evodius must understand the difference between lust and (blameless) desire.[106] This brings us to a general difference between *On Free Choice* and the discourse on justice in the *Confessions*, which is the place of specifically political inquiry in their discussions. While Augustine alludes to the difficulties of political justice in the *Confessions*, in *On Free Choice* it becomes clear early on that Evodius' moral opinions, including his understanding of lust, are dependent in many ways on the law of his political community,[107] which is then made into a subject of investigation.[108] To my lights, this has no counterpart in the *Confessions* discussion, where concepts such as "nature," "lust," and the divine law carry most of the weight and where political law, where it is discussed, is treated only as something to be compared with the commands of God and obeyed or disobeyed depending on whether it conflicts those commands, rather than something to be taken up on its own terms.[109] The exception, of course, is the brief allusion to distributive and corrective justice that led us to brush up against the question of political laws. Augustine's statement in *On Free Choice* regarding the "order" by which he was freed from the problem of evil, combined with his silence about any such process of investigation in the *Confessions*, indicates that *On Free Choice* contains Augustine's more fundamental reflections on many of the questions about justice that we have been compelled to raise, and that it is the first place to turn to find a more satisfying account of this subject, whose importance at the beginning of his intellectual career Augustine singles out in the *Confessions*.

# Notes

1. I would like to thank the Tocqueville Program at Furman University, where I wrote this essay as the T. W. Smith Postdoctoral Fellow in Western and American Political Thought; my dissertation committee, Robert Bartlett, Robert Faulkner, Christopher Kelly, and Susan Shell, who commented on this first presentation of this argument; and my friend Daniel Burns, whose work on Augustine has been the constant inspiration for my own.

2. Augustine, *Confessions*, 3.7.13–.9.17. Citations of the text of *Confessions* will include book, chapter, and paragraph numbers, occasionally followed by line numbers, as found in *Confessionum Libri XIII*, ed. Lucas Verheijen, OSA, Corpus Christianorum Series Latina 27 (Turnhout: Brepols, 1981). All translations are my own.

3. *On Free Choice* is also linked by subject matter to the contemporaneous work *Against Faustus*, especially book 22, where Augustine adjudicates particular accusations of injustice against biblical figures. However, the eternal law to which Augustine appeals in that work is first and most adequately explained in *On Free Choice*.

4. For an introduction to those difficulties in modern times, see Michael J. S. Bruno, *Political Augustinianism: Modern Interpretations of Augustine's Political Thought* (Minneapolis: Fortress Press, 2014).

5. With the notable exception of John M. Quinn, OSA, "Anti-Manichean and Other Moral Precisions in *Confessions* 3.7.12–9.17," *Augustinian Studies* 19 (1988): 165–94, from which I have learned the most. My treatment differs most from his by situating Augustine's discourse more precisely in the context of the *Confessions*, by stressing the tensions among its various parts, and by indicating its connection with the earlier dialogue *On Free Choice* and the contemporaneous work *Against Faustus*.

6. Augustine, *Confessions*, 3.7.13.

7. *Confessions*, 3.7.13–14.

8. *Confessions*, 3.8.15–9.17.

9. *Confessions*, 3.4.7, 3–4, 6–7; 3.4.8, 28–31. Augustine considered the pursuit of wisdom as something requiring a reorientation of his entire life. In an earlier account of his experience with the *Hortensius*, he says, "I was inflamed by so great a love of philosophy that I immediately planned to transform myself for it" (*On the Happy Life*, 1.4). In Augustine, *Contra Academicos, De Beata Vita, De Ordine, De Magistro, De Libero Arbitrio*, ed. W. M. Green and Klaus-Detlef Daur, Corpus Christianorum Series Latina (hereafter CCSL) 29 (Turnhout: Brepols, 1970).

10. "Suddenly every vain hope became worthless to me and I greatly desired the immortality of wisdom with an incredible burning of the heart; and I had begun to rise, that I might return to You." *Confessions*, 3.4.7, 8–10.

11. *Confessions*, 3.4.8, 28–31; 18–21.

12. *Confessions*, 3.4.8, 32–33. He had introduced Cicero as someone "whose tongue nearly all wonder at, (but) not so his heart" (3.4.7, 4–5).

13. *Confessions*, 3.5.9, 1–7.

14. *Confessions*, 3.6.10, 1–4, 6–9. In an earlier work, Augustine recalls additional steps between his failure with the Bible and his attachment to Manichaeism, which promised a kind of "enlightened Christianity" involving no obedience to authority or demands of faith: "You know, Honoratus, that we fell in with such people for no other reason than their saying that, once separated from fearsome authority, they would introduce those who wanted to listen to them to God and free them from all error. For what else compelled me to follow those people for nearly nine years, having spurned the religion that was implanted in me as a young boy by my parents, except their saying that we were frightened by superstition and that faith was commanded to us before reason?" Augustine, *On the Benefit of Believing*, 1.2. In Augustine, *De Utilitate Credendi, De Duabus Animabus Contra Fortunatum, Contra Adimantum, Contra Epistulam Fundamenti, Contra Faustum*, ed. Joseph Zycha, Corpus Scriptorum Ecclesiasticorum Latinorum X (Milan: Hoepli, 1891).

15. *Confessions*, 3.6.10, 14–16.

16. Although Augustine laments that he ever believed the Manichean doctrines (*Confessions*, 3.6.11, 52), he also says that he was not feeding eagerly on them (3.6.10, 22–23). He seems to have hoped that the Manicheans had a secret teaching: he says elsewhere of the teaching about the sun's divinity that "I did not assent, but I thought that they hid some great thing under these coverings that they would sometime lay open" (*On the Happy Life*, 1.4).

17. Augustine, *Confessions*, 3.7.12, 1–2.

18. *Confessions*, 3.7.12, 3–6.

19. *Confessions*, 3.7.12, 6; 1 (my emphasis).

20. *Confessions*, 3.7.12, 7–16.

21. *Confessions*, 4.15.24–26; 5.10.18–20; 5.14.24–25; 6.3.4; 7.1.1–2; 7.3.4–5.7; 7.9.13–17.23.

22. *Confessions*, 3.7.13, 1 (*Vera iustitia interior*). I have chosen to translate the comparative adjective *interior* by the single term "inner," although it also may be translated (as seems to be required in previous places in the *Confessions*) as "deeper," "more intimate," "innate," "inward," "more profound," or even "hidden" (see, for example, 1.18.29, 27–29; 1.20.31, 3–7; 3.1.1, 5–6; 3.5.9, 7–9; 3.6.11, 57–58).

23. By my count, the discussion of justice is at least twelve times longer than the discussion of the first two doctrines combined. John M. Quinn suggests the discourses on memory (10.8.12–15.36) and time (11.14.17–29.39) as similar examples of "analytical excursus" (John M. Quinn, OSA, "Anti-Manichean and Other Moral Precisions in *Confessions* 3.7.12–9.17," *Augustinian Studies* 19 (1988): 165–94, at 166–67). However, these discourses do not break with the chronology of Augustine's narrative, since the subject of book 10 is the contemporary Augustine. The only other examples of elaborating a doctrine long before Augustine accepted it is the discourse on grief in book 4 (4.9.14–12.19). The discourse on justice therefore stands almost alone in the narrative books of the *Confessions*.

24. *Confessions*, 7.16.22.

25. John J. O'Meara concludes that Augustine's third question here "was of the least significance and cannot long have occupied his mind." John J. O'Meara, *The Young Augustine: The Growth of St. Augustine's Mind Up to His Conversion* (New York: Alba House, 2010), 69.

26. *Confessions*, 5.14.24, 6.3.3–5.8, 7.1.1–2.3, and 7.3.4–16.22. James J. O'Donnell, *Augustine* Confessions, vol. 2: *Commentary on Books 1–7* (Oxford: Oxford University Press, 2012), 184–85. Todd Breyfogle, "Book Three: 'No Changing Nor Shadow,'" in *A Reader's Companion to Augustine's* Confessions, ed. Kim Paffenroth and Robert Peter Kennedy (Louisville: Westminster John Knox Press, 2003), 35–52, n43.

27. Spiritual interpretation applies to the biblical text the rule that "the letter kills, but the spirit gives life." *Confessions*, 6.4.6, 21–27; see 2 Corinthians 3:4–6.

28. *Confessions*, 6.5.7–8.

29. *Confessions*, 6.3.4.

30. *Confessions*, 6.11.18.

31. *Confessions*, 6.16.26. The direct quotation of the title of Cicero's most important work of moral philosophy, *On the Definition of Good and Evil* (*De finibus bonorum et malorum*), connects this passage to book 3. Cicero says of *De finibus* that it treats "the foundation of philosophy." *On Divination*, 2.1, in Cicero, *On Old Age, On Friendship, On Divination*, trans. W. A. Falconer (Cambridge, MA: Harvard University Press, 1923).

32. "Lumen honestatis et gratis amplectendae pulchritudinis." *Confessions*, 6.16.26.

33. *Confessions*, 6.16.26, 16–20. Cf. 4.9.14.

34. *Confessions*, 7.17.23.

35. *Confessions*, 7.17.23, citing Romans 1:20. Most commentary takes this passage as "completing" Augustine's "Plotinian" ascent (O'Donnell, *Confessions*, 2:454–45). However, Augustine's use of the pluperfect tense (line 15: *inveneram*), the fact that its result is identical to that of the earlier ascent (cf. 7.10.16), and the fact that it is bookended by quotations of Romans 1:20 make it more likely to be a gloss on Paul and an elaboration of the earlier ascent. This gloss pulls us back not only to the end of book 7 but to the end of book 4 and the

discussions that led to Augustine's first work, *The Beautiful and the Fitting* (6.16.26; 4.13.20; 4.15.24–27).

36. It makes sense that these three questions would be related, since the conception of justice changes dramatically if evil is "natural" rather than a perversity of the will. Justice depends on the highest good, which Augustine saw in divine friendship, and it depends on seeing the honor and beauty arising in friendship and Augustine could not be friends with God before he knew him.

37. "Mores": I have chosen to translate this crucial word, which seems to mean variously "character," "customs," "sensibilities," or "manners," by the simple, if antiquated, English "morals."

38. *Confessions*, 3.7.13, 17–22.

39. *Confessions*, 3.8.15, 10.

40. *Confessions*, 3.7.13, 17–18.

41. *Confessions*, 3.7.13, 24–33.

42. There may be another natural whole here as well, if the holiday has some reference to the cycle of seasons in the year.

43. *Confessions*, 3.7.13, 30.

44. *Confessions*, 3.7.13, 33–40.

45. *Confessions*, 3.7.13, 39–40.

46. *Confessions*, 3.7.13, 40–47, reading *his* rather than *hic*, the reading in most manuscripts. The latter reading yields "are offended by those ages but obey here [in the present]." This would mean that human beings are offended by prior ages while being subservient to the prejudices of the present.

47. *Confessions*, 3.7.15, 23–24, 40–41.

48. Earlier, Augustine had said that the inexperienced people were "measuring the universal mores of the human race *from a part of their own*" (3.7.13, 23–24, emphasis added), which implies that they are overlooking the diversity of their own mores in condemning others, rather than simply condemning them for things totally foreign to their way of life.

49. *Confessions*, 3.7.14, 48–60.

50. *Confessions*, 3.7.14, 55.

51. *Confessions*, 3.7.14, 57–58.

52. Augustine applies this adjective once more at a critical point in the second part of the discourse on justice (3.8.16, 53).

53. *Confessions*, 3.8.15, 1–3. See Matthew 22:37–40, Mark 12:28–34, Luke 10:25–28; cf. Deuteronomy 6:4.

54. Matthew 22:40. Cf. O'Donnell, *Confessions*, 2:189–90.

55. For a discussion of this word's meaning, see note 72 below.

56. *Confessions*, 3.8.15, 3–4.

57. *Confessions*, 3.8.15, 5–6. As for the specific example of the Sodomites, Augustine's only concrete example in this section, see *The City of God*, 16.30 and Romans 1:26–27. See also O'Donnell's commentary on this sentence (*Confessions*, 2:190).

58. Cf. *Confessions*, 3.7.13, 18.

59. *Confessions*, 3.8.15, 6–7. His reference to the divine law here, as earlier (3.7.13, 18), is to a creative law rather than revealed law (either the Mosaic law or the Christian Gospel). It therefore appears to be equivalent to the "eternal law" of *On Free Choice* (1.6.48, 46–51) and *Against Faustus* (22.27).

60. *Confessions*, 3.8.15, 7–9.

61. *Confessions*, 3.8.15, 6–7, 8–9. Cf. 3.7.13, 18–19.

62. *Confessions*, 3.8.15, 9–10.

63. *Confessions*, 3.8.15, 5–6. Yet he says here only that things that offend human mores must be "avoided," rather than "hated and punished" (3.8.15, 4).

64. *Confessions*, 3.7.13–14; 3.8.15, 10–12, 12–13.

65. *Confessions*, 3.7.13, 25, 27, 38, 47.

66. *Confessions*, 3.8.15, 13–16.

67. *Confessions*, 3.8.15, 16–24.

68. *Confessions*, 3.8.15, 7–8.

69. *Confessions*, 3.8.15, 19–20 (emphasis added).

70. *Confessions*, 3.8.15, 22.

71. *Confessions*, 3.8.15, 7–8.

72. As for the contrast between *flagitia* and *facinora*, in the immediate context Augustine identifies *flagitia* with "corruption" and *facinora* with "harm" (3.8.16, 36–37). In book 4, he associates *facinora* with "anger" (*ira*) and motion, and attack and *flagitia* with "lust," an "immoderate disposition," and attachment to bodily pleasures (4.15.24, 17–15.25, 25). The most useful discussion of the two occurs in *On Christian Doctrine*: "I call charity the movement of the spirit to enjoying God for Himself alone and itself and neighbor for God. Desire, however, I call the movement of the spirit to enjoying itself and neighbor and anybody not for God's sake. What untamed desire does to corrupt the spirit and its body is called *flagitium*; what it does to harm another is called *facinus*. And these are the two kinds of all sins—but *flagitia* are first. When they empty out the spirit and bring it into a certain poverty, there is a rush into *facinora*, by which the impediments to *flagitia* may be removed or help sought for them" (3.10.16, in Augustine, *De doctrina christiana, De vera religione*, ed. K. D. Daur and J. Martin, Corpus Christianorum Series Latina 32 (Turnhout: Brepols, 1962).

73. *Confessions*, 3.8.16, 34–35.

74. Recall *Confessions*, 3.8.15, 9; 12.

75. *Confessions*, 3.8.16, 25–35.

76. *Confessions*, 3.8.16, 36–37.

77. *Confessions*, 3.8.16, 37–39, citing Psalm 26:12.

78. *Confessions*, 1.12.19, 14–15.

79. *Confessions*, 3.8.16, 38–46.

80. *Confessions*, 3.8.16, 46–48.

81. Cf. *Confessions*, 3.7.13, 17–18 and 3.8.15, 11.

82. *Confessions*, 3.8.16, 48–51.

83. *Confessions*, 3.8.16, 51–54.

84. Matthew 16:24–26; see also Mark 8:34–37 and Luke 9:23–25.

85. *Confessions*, 3.7.14.

86. Or "private," as at 3.8.16, 47.

87. *Confessions*, 1.1.1.

88. *Confessions*, 3.9.17, 1–9.

89. *Confessions*, 3.9.17, 2–4.

90. Reading *congrua* (an adjective modifying *aliqua*), as in most manuscripts, rather than the CCSL's conjectural *congrue*.

91. *Confessions*, 3.9.17, 4–9.
92. *Confessions*, 3.9.17, 6.
93. *Confessions*, 3.9.17, 6–7.
94. *Confessions*, 3.8.15, 8, 12; 3.8.16, 1, 33, 52.
95. *Confessions*, 3.9.17, 7–8.
96. *Confessions*, 3.9.17, 8–9; cf. 3.8.16, 25–32.
97. *Confessions*, 3.9.17, 6; 8.
98. See *Confessions*, 3.9.17, 12–27.
99. *Confessions*, 3.9.17, 9–18. This is the third time that he has followed up a series of complications with a simpler formulation (cf. the transitions at 3.8.15, 13 and 3.8.16, 46). The second part itself begins with a great simplification of the discussion, as Augustine throws us a lifeline by saying what actions are always just, plain, and simple (3.8.15, 1).
100. Augustine, *On Free Choice*, 1.4.10, 3–8, in *Contra Academicos, De Beata Vita, De Ordine, De Magistro, De Libero Arbitrio*, ed. W. M. Green and Klaus-Detlef Daur, Corpus Christianorum Series Latina 19 (Turnhout: Brepols, 1970).
101. *Confessions*, 1.4.11, 9–10.
102. *Confessions*, 1.6.14, 1–2.
103. *On Free Choice*, 1.6.14, 6–8; *Confessions*, 3.7.12, 4–6.
104. *On Free Choice*, 1.15.108, 42–43; cf. 1.16.115, 14–20.
105. *Confessions*, 1.5.32–33.
106. *Confessions*, 1.4.22.
107. *Confessions*, 1.3.18, 34–35; 1.4.25, 39.
108. As Daniel Burns has shown in his study of the dialogue, the first one I know that has done justice to its political aspects. Burns, "Augustine on the Moral Significance of Human Law," *Revue d'études augustiniennes et patristiques* 61 (2015), 273–98. My own contribution to the study of the dialogue is in my dissertation, "The Eternal Law in Augustine's Early Investigation of Justice" (PhD diss., Boston College, 2016).
109. *On Free Choice*, 3.8.15, 9–12; 22–24; 12–17.

*Part Two*

# St. Augustine and
# Ancient Political Philosophy

Chapter Six

# The Few, the Many, and the Universal Way of Salvation

## Augustine's Point of Engagement with Platonic Political Thought

### Thomas P. Harmon

As a part of one of the most penetrating and insightful analyses of St. Augustine's reflections on politics in recent years, the political philosopher Pierre Manent argues, "Christianity's point of impact is the separation between the few and the many. What Christianity attacks is not social or political inequality but the pertinence of the distinction between the few and the many, the philosopher and the non-philosopher, with regard to the capacity to attain or receive the truth."[1] It is precisely on the basis of the capacity of the non-philosopher to attain or receive the truth that St. Augustine provides a critique of Porphyry in book 10 of *The City of God*, saying that this eminent Platonist has not come across a universal way for the liberation of the soul (*liberandae animae uniuersalis uia*).[2] Instead, what Porphyry does provide are two separate ways of "purification" (*purgatio*) that liberate the soul: one affecting the higher or intellectual soul (*intellectualem animam*), the other affecting only the lower or "spiritual" soul (*ipsam spiritalem*) through theurgy.[3] The first way is for those few who are capable of philosophy; the second is for the multitude of men who for whatever reason are not capable of philosophy.

Through his critique of Porphyry on the basis of the concrete way of life lived by Christians, St. Augustine enters into a classic conversation,[4] the boundaries and stakes of which had already been charted out. The classical political problem of the division between the few and the many is that for a city to be properly ordered in justice, it must be ruled by the wise and according to wisdom; but the wise are few and outnumbered by the many, who are far too attached to their own opinions and customs to allow the wise to rule, even if they could (1) identify the wise; and (2) persuade or coerce them to rule—a doubtful proposition in either case. This lamentable situation requires the wise to cultivate ironic distance from the multitude—most famously in the figure of Plato's Socrates.[5] If the wise are to exert any influence on the city, it will have to be indirect and through the utilization of lies—the most famous instance of which is the noble lie in Plato's *Republic*.[6]

In the first part of this essay, I will chart out the argument between Augustine and Porphyry on the universal way of salvation, especially focusing on Augustine's theological argument that the resolution of the division of the few and the many rests on the mediation of the incarnate Word of God in Christ. But the Christian way of life, based on the mediation of Christ the incarnate Word of God, does not arrange matters so that "political power and philosophy coincide in the same place," as Socrates puts it in Plato's *Republic*.[7] What this means for Augustine, as I will show in the second part of this essay, is that Christianity is transpolitical: it issues forth in no laws or constitutions and demands the foundation—or abolition—of no particular regime or form of government. The good that Christians pursue transcends the good of the political order; nevertheless, Augustine is at pains to make clear that on the one hand, Christianity does not dissolve politics, and on the other hand, faithful Christians can contribute positively to the legitimate political goals of the city, although he does not deny that Christianity makes impossible the perfervid attachment to one's own city that political men may regard as indispensable for the welfare of the city. Augustine seems to think that, on balance and given the other positive contributions Christians make to civic welfare, sacrificing perfervid attachments to one's own city in the name of Christian, transpolitical moderation is a risk statesmen ought to be willing to embrace.

Remarkably few of Porphyry's writings have survived. Porphyry was the editor of the *Enneads* of his teacher Plotinus, yet as Frederick Van Fleteren argues, Poprhyry's thought differs from what we find in the *Enneads*, "at least in emphasis."[8] Van Fleteren has a discussion of the Poprhyrean texts we have compared with what Augustine had available to him.[9] Because of this limitation, I will not attempt here to give an interpretation of Porphyry himself. Our focus will be on Augustine. What is important for our discussion is not to understand Porphyry from his own writings but to understand the way in which Augustine understands Porphyry.

The first part of Augustine's *City of God*, which comprises books 1 through 10, is itself divided in two. Augustine dedicates books 1–5 to refuting those who worship false gods for the sake of temporal benefits; he dedicates books 6–10 to refuting those who worship false gods for the sake of "the future life after death."[10] The second part of *The City of God* is dedicated to an examination of the origin, progress, and end of the City of God. Fittingly, Christ the mediator provides the hinge between the two parts: book 10 ends with Augustine speaking of Christ the mediator, and book 11 begins with Augustine speaking of Christ the mediator. Porphyry occupies the pivotal place in the first part of *The City of God* by way of contrast, for Augustine, in his explication of Christ's mediation. The contrast is between the universal way of salvation provided through Christ's mediation and the bifurcated ways provided by Porphyry's recommendation of theurgy for the purgation of the "spiritual" soul to the non-philosopher on the one hand, and his recommendation of the purgation of the intellect to those capable of philosophy on the other.

Augustine's critique is deeper than appears at first. It is true that he laments Porphyry's exclusion of the multitude from a complete salvation, but his critique does not admit that the only defect in Porphyry's bifurcatory remedies is that the multitude is left out. If that were so, then Augustine would be admitting that the philosopher is capable of salvation without the mediation of Christ. Only the multitude would stand in need of Christ's mediation. That would leave things almost as they stand with Porphyry: the philosophers would take one way of salvation through their intellectual capabilities, whereas the multitude would take another way, which is opened up for them by Christ. The difference would be that, for Augustine and Christianity, both the few and the many could be saved; but *two* ways of salvation would remain, one of which depends on Christ and the other of which does not, rather than one, universal way. Augustine's critique is not only that Porphyry excludes the multitude from salvation but that his bifurcation of ways of salvation also excludes the philosopher from salvation.

Augustine's critique of Porphyry appears in an extended section where Augustine is refuting those who think that angels and demons ought to be worshiped. His basic argument is, "If [an angel] does not worship God, it is wretched, because deprived of God; if it worships God, it will not wish itself to be worshiped in the place of God."[11] Both angels and men ought to worship the one God who is the Creator of all else. If an angel truly worships this true God, then he will not want to be worshiped in God's place. Any angel that seems to want to be worshiped in God's place is evil. If an angel desires worship for himself in order to be a mediator between the human being offering worship and God, that angel is a deceiver. Mediation happens on the basis of commonality between both sides of the mediation. All the demon can claim is that it has a superior nature to man and, by virtue of that superior nature, stands between man and God and so can act as a proper mediator. But the angel or demon is not placed between men and God; on the contrary, demonic wickedness makes the demon inferior to the human being in a crucial respect.

Porphyry recommends commerce with demons, or theurgy, in his writings.[12] The purpose of Porphyry's recommendation of theurgy, according to Augustine, is so that "by means of certain 'theurgic consecrations,' which are called *teletae*, this spiritual element of the soul is put into a proper condition, capable of welcoming spirits and angels, and of seeing the gods."[13] These practices will result in "some sort of purification of the soul [*quasi purgationem animae*]."[14] Augustine says *quasi purgationem* because the purgation offered by Porphyry would only be partial, limited to the lower soul. Augustine counters that

[Porphyry] admits at the same time that those "theurgic rites" do not effect any purification of the intellectual soul which would fit it to see its God and to apprehend the
true realities. From this one can gather what kind of gods and what kind of vision he is
talking about in those "theurgic consecrations"; it is not a vision of the true realities. In
fact, he says that the rational soul (or, as he prefers, the "intellectual" soul) can escape
into its own sphere, even without any purification of the spiritual element by means
of the "theurgic art," and further, that the purification of the spiritual part by theurgy
does not go so far as to assure its attainment of immortality and eternity.[15]

Augustine's critique here is dense and requires a lot of unpacking. The full critique is presented in only a few lines. First, Porphyry's theurgy offers only a partial
purification of the spiritual or lower soul. The rational soul, on the other hand, is
capable of the contemplation of intelligible reality without any purification of the
spiritual soul. The lower soul seems to be the sensitive soul, the seat of the senses, the
imagination, the passions, and the emotions. The higher soul is the seat of the intellectual or rational power, by which the mind can understand the truth. The division
Augustine and Porphyry are talking about is the classic division that Plato expressed
in the image of the divided line[16] and the allegory of the cave.[17] The operations of
the lower soul take place below the divided line, and the operations of the intellectual soul take place above the divided line.

To see what Augustine is talking about in his own idiom, it may be helpful to
think back to his *Confessions*. The most significant event in the young Augustine's
time in Africa is his introduction to the pursuit of wisdom through Cicero's
*Hortensius*.[18] Using striking language, Augustine remarks that the *Hortensius*
"changed my affections. It turned my prayers to you, Lord, and caused me to have
different purposes and desires. All my vain hopes forthwith became worthless to me.
And with incredible ardor of heart I desired undying wisdom."[19] Augustine's change
of affections, however, did not result immediately in a life lived in philosophy. His
affections may have been turned toward wisdom, but his mind was crude. Because
of his intellectual crudity, he fell in with the Manicheans, a sect that posited a good
and an evil principle at war in the world. The Manicheans provided Augustine with
seeming wisdom in the form of a superficially satisfying answer to the problem of
evil and a way to exonerate God from responsibility for evil in the world: there is a
good god and an evil god. Good is the responsibility of the good god, and evil the
responsibility of the evil god. Augustine relates,

I did not know that other being, that which truly is (*nesciebam enim aliud, uere quod
est*), and I was as it were subtly moved to agree with those dull deceivers (*deceptoribus*)
when they put their questions to me: "Whence is evil?" "Is God confined within a corporeal form?" "Does he have hair and nails?" "Are those to be judged just men who had
many wives, killed other men, and offered sacrifices of animals?" Ignorant (*ignarus*) in
such matters, I was disturbed by these questions, and while actually receding from the
truth, I thought I was moving toward it. The reason was that I did not know that evil

is only the privation of a good, even to the point of complete nonentity. How could I do this, when with eyes I could see only bodies, and with my soul only phantasms?[20]

It was in working through his dissatisfaction with Manichaeism that Augustine was able, eventually, to determine the source of his intellectual problems. He laments, "By what steps was I led down into the depths of hell, struggling and burning for want of the truth! For then I sought for you, not according to intellectual understanding (*intellectum mentis*), by which you willed to raise me above brute beasts, but according to carnal sense (*sensum carnis*)."[21] We have no indication that Augustine himself undertook the Chaldean-inspired theurgical rites that Porphyry recommends, but the Manichean rites he participated in and his crude, sub-philosophic investigations as a young man seem to be similar to the theurgy Porphyry recommends: the search for God or gods to purify the lower soul to the neglect of the higher soul. Augustine's criticism of Porphyry is therefore grounded not only on philosophical and theological arguments but has an urgency and familiarity for Augustine based on his own personal experience.

Augustine not only had experience seeking purifications for his lower soul. By working through his intellectual problems, Augustine is eventually led to the point of intellectual conversion. His intellectual problem as he narrates it in the *Confessions* is his inability to conceive of spiritual substance, that is, the very thing that allows one to operate above the divided line by the powers of the intellectual soul. It is no accident that he does so, as he tells us himself, under the tutelage of the "books of the Platonists."[22] Which books and authors Augustine means is a vexed question among scholars. Frederick Van Fleteren sums up the *status quaestionis* by saying, "Not either Plotinus or Porphyry, but both Plotinus and Porphyry."[23] On the basis of Augustine's own writing in *The City of God*, it may be possible to tip the scales a little to the side of Porphyry. When trying to decide which philosophers with whom to engage on the highest matters, the matters of "natural theology,"[24] he looks for the philosophers whose conception of God is closest to that of Christian faith. These are the "Platonists, a name derived from their master Plato."[25] Augustine later calls the Platonists *nobilissimos*, "most noble."[26] He also calls Porphyry *pholosophos nobilis*, a "noble philosopher,"[27] and *doctissimus philosophorum*, "most learned of philosophers."[28] Augustine himself regards Porphyry as preeminent among philosophers. Porphyry's books were prominent among those books of the Platonists under whose tutelage Augustine experienced his intellectual conversion.[29] In other words, it seems likely that Augustine had personal experience with both of the ways of salvation that Porphyry holds out.

From the standpoint of the Platonic philosopher and Augustine, the drawbacks to theurgy and related pursuits are obvious: they do not accomplish what they promise. What is sought is the liberation of the soul; what is delivered is nothing of the kind. Until Augustine has his intellectual conversion, the various measures he takes in order to attain wisdom do not accomplish the task: he does not attain to God in truth, he only attains to a phantasm (*phantasma*) instead of God.[30] But phantasms have no power to save in truth, although those who cannot distinguish between a phantasm and the true God—such as Augustine before his intellectual conversion—might be deceived into thinking that they either are saved or are on the way to being saved. In fact, falsity or deception is one of the main concerns of Augustine in book 10: both the falsity of the philosopher who recommends theurgy and the falsity of the demons with whom the theurgist communicates.[31] Augustine's concern with the deception of the multitude by statesmen and philosophers in matters of religion is an ongoing concern throughout *The City of God*. It is on this basis that he also criticizes the civil theology of Rome. He says that the civil theology, which finds its home in the rites of the temples, hides the truth that the natural theology of the philosophers uncovers, thereby preventing its adherents from knowing the truth in religion and, therefore, barring access to any true deliverance or salvation. He says,

> What, however, are those doctrines which are harmful when placed before the multitude? Such statements, Scaevola says, as the following: "That Hercules, Aesculapius, Castor and Pollux are not gods; for it is asserted by the learned that these were men who had passed on from the human state." What else? "That cities do not possess the true images (*vera simulacra*) of the gods, because the true God (*verus Deus*) has neither sex nor age nor determinate bodily parts (*definita corporis membra*)." The pontiff [Scaevola] does not wish the people to know these things precisely because he does not think that such things are false (*falsa*). He considers it expedient, therefore, that cities should be deceived in matters of religion (*falli in religione*); nor does Varro himself hesitate to say the same thing in his books dealing with things divine. What a wonderful religion! He who is weak (*infirmus*) may go to it for refuge when he is in need of deliverance (*liberandus*); yet, when he seeks the truth (*ueritatem*) by which he may be delivered, it is pronounced expedient for him to be cheated (*fallitur*)![32]

These strategies are not new. In the *Phaedo*, which takes place dramatically in the shadow of Socrates' impending execution, Socrates' friends worry about what they will do in the absence of their wise friend. The dramatic movement of the dialogue makes it clear that Socrates' presence and teaching moderates their fear of death and hatred of argument, or *misologia*. Socrates's ministrations are described as incantations, which hold at bay the fear of death and the hatred of arguments. Only Socrates the philosopher, the dialogue implies, is able to face up to the radical uncertainty of the individual's personal destiny beyond death. The many nonphilosophers must be soothed by myths. Joseph Cropsey explains, "Philosophy, the musical art, speaking with the voice of the poet Socrates singing his swan song, thus relieves the pains of profoundest ignorance and of the fear of death."[33] Through his incantations, Socrates seeks to impart to his friends some of his own serenity in the face of death. But it is by no means clear that Socrates actually believes the content of the swan song. Cropsey, for instance, interprets two of Plato's signature teachings, the immortality of the soul and the intelligible forms, as poetic therapy for the many given by the Socrates who, after all, claims in the *Apology* that he is the city's greatest benefactor.

In Porphyry's hands, theurgy is the Socratic swan song in a Platonic key. The philosopher Socrates can lend his non-philosophic friends some of the serenity that he himself has in the face of death on the basis of his poetic-philosophic incantation. Porphyry can likewise lend his non-philosophic associates some of his own philosophic serenity by soothing their fears through the therapeutic ministrations of theurgy. Just like Socrates, Porphyry also seems to hold out hope that, through theurgy, the theurgist will have some kind of life after death. Augustine says, "[Porphyry] recommends us to cultivate the friendship of some demon, by whose assistance a man may be raised just a little above the earth after death."[34] But the strange way Augustine says Porphyry speaks of this existence after death ought to make us wonder about what he is saying. Later on, Augustine argues, "While you assert [theurgy] can purify the 'spiritual' soul—that is, the part of the soul inferior to reason—you confess that theurgic art cannot make it immortal [*immortalem*] and eternal [*aeternam*]."[35] In any case, needless to say, being raised a little above the earth after death falls far short of the philosophic achievement Porphyry says Plotinus achieved four times during his life and he himself once: merging with the One. Porphyry says, "There was shown to Plotinus the Term ever near: for the Term, the one end, of his life was to become Uniate, to approach to the God over all: and four times, during the period I passed with him, he achieved this Term, by no mere latent fitness but by the ineffable Act. To this God, I also declare, I Porphyry, that in my sixty-eighth year I too was once admitted and entered into Union."[36] There seems little doubt that Porphyry regards the true salvation of the soul to be in reach of the philosopher alone; the salvation of the soul able to be accomplished by theurgy is false. That is why Augustine says that the demons with whom the theurgists are encouraged to cultivate friendship are "either identical with that being who is called Deceiver, or else they are nothing but a figment of the human imagination."[37] Either the foolish theurgist is deceived by a demon or is saved only in his own imagination; in either case, he is not truly saved. His fear of death may be soothed, but not on the basis of truth. Augustine addresses Porphyry directly, saying, "You inveigle [*seducis*] those who are incapable of becoming philosophers to indulge in practices which, on your own showing, are of no use to you, because you are capable of higher things. Thus all those who cannot approach to philosophic virtue (a lofty ideal to which only a few attain) have your authority to seek out theurgists."[38]

But Augustine's criticism does not end at expressing concern for the deception of the multitude. In the *Confessions* he tells us that he himself was able to approach philosophic virtue, that "lofty ideal to which only a few attain," under the tutelage of the books of the Platonists. Here is how he describes that ascent:

> Thus I gradually passed from bodies to the soul, which perceives by means of the body, and thence to its interior power, to which the bodily senses present exterior things—beasts too are capable of doing this much—and thence to its interior power, to which

what is apprehended by the bodily senses is referred for judgment. When this power found itself to be in me a variable thing, it raised itself up to its own understanding. It removed its thought from the tyranny of habit, and withdrew itself from the throngs of contradictory phantasms. In this way it might find that light by which it was sprinkled, when it cried out, that beyond all doubt the immutable must be preferred to the mutable. Hence it might come to know this immutable being, for unless it could know it in some way, it could in no wise have set it with certainty above the mutable. Thus in a flash of its trembling sight it came to that which is.[39]

This is the achievement at which Augustine has been aiming ever since his affections were turned toward wisdom by Cicero's *Hortensius*. It is a great achievement and Augustine presents it as such. Even so, Augustine does not find the kind of satisfaction in it that he desired. He was incapable of sustaining the sight of *id, quod est*. His philosophic achievement turns out to be an anticlimax. Augustine explains himself, saying,

> I was not steadfast (*non stabam*) in enjoyment of my God: I was borne up to you by your beauty. But soon I was borne down from you by my own weight, and with groaning, I plunged into the midst of those lower things. This weight was carnal custom (*consuetudo carnalis*). Still there remained within me remembrance of you: I did not doubt in any way that there was one to cleave to, nor did I doubt that I was not yet one who would cleave to him. "For the corruptible body is a load upon the soul, and the earthly habitation presses down upon the mind that muses upon many things."[40]

Augustine has not found at all that his "rational soul (or, as [Porphyry] prefers, the 'intellectual' soul) can escape into its own sphere, even without any purification of the spiritual element."[41] The problem is that he cannot separate his mind from the rest of himself and that the rest of himself is no less truly himself than his highest part.

Salvation of the intellectual part that does not provide salvation to the whole man is doomed to be as unstable as Augustine's own abortive contemplation of *id, quod est* under the tutelage of the books of the Platonists. Peter Augustine Lawler argues, "The philosophical view of God is that our thoughts or minds alone are divine, and the mind detached from the whole human being is less a who than a what."[42] That is why, after Augustine's religious conversion, he and his mother, Monica, together ascend again "to touch eternal Wisdom which abides over all,"[43] but the experience is quite different than his abortive, Platonic ascent in book 7. Here is how he describes his ascent with Monica:

> And our conversation had brought us to this point, that any pleasure whatsoever of the bodily senses, in any brightness whatsoever of corporeal light, seemed to us not worthy of comparison with the pleasure of that eternal Light, not worthy even of mention. Rising as our love flamed upward toward that Selfsame, we passed in review the various levels of bodily things, up to the heavens themselves, whence sun and moon and stars

shine upon this earth. And higher still we soared, thinking in our minds and speaking
and marveling at your works: and so we came to our own souls, and went beyond them
to come at last to that region of richness unending, where you feed Israel forever with
the food of truth: and there life is that Wisdom by which all things are made, both
the things that have been and the things that are yet to be. But this Wisdom itself is
not made: it is as it has ever been, and so it shall be forever: indeed "has ever been"
and "shall be forever" have no place in it, but it simply is, for it is eternal: whereas "to
have been" and "to be going to be" are not eternal. And while we were thus talking of
His Wisdom and panting for it, with all the effort of our heart we did for one instant
attain to touch it; then sighing, and leaving the first fruits of our spirit bound to it, we
returned to the sound of our own tongue, in which a word has both beginning and
ending.[44]

The first difference between the two accounts is that the first ascent in book 7 is
undertaken by Augustine alone; the second, in book 9, is undertaken with another,
namely, his mother Monica. Monica's inclusion is significant both because the second ascent is made in conversation with another and because of the specific character of the other. Monica is unlettered—she has definitely not read the books of
the Platonists. The first, abortive ascent is like Porphyry's second way of salvation,
concerning the intellectual soul alone. The second ascent is accomplished in common between Monica and Augustine, who are the two types of person that Porphyry
thought needed two different ways of salvation. The second ascent in the *Confessions*
therefore exemplifies the universal way of salvation Augustine holds forth as possible on the basis of Christ's mediation. The most significant difference between the
two ascents is the goal. In both cases, God is the goal. But in the first ascent, God is
described as *id, quod est*—a true but entirely impersonal description, suitable for the
object of an ascent made purely on an intellectual plane. In the second ascent, God
is addressed directly, as "You." God is therefore drawn into Augustine and Monica's
conversation; or rather, Augustine and Monica's conversation is founded on a God
who can be addressed as a person. Third, in the first ascent, Augustine's senses are
relevant only as a beginning: he ascends beyond them to a flash of mental sight. But
in the second ascent, Augustine and Monica also attain to God, but the flash of the
mind allows them not just to see but to "touch" eternal wisdom.[45] Sensory descriptions abound as the final goal of their ascent is a region "where You feed Israel forever
with the food of truth,"[46] a reference to the sacrament of the Eucharist. Indeed,
Augustine makes sure to mention that all five senses are involved in the attainment
of the goal of ascent, a reference to the humility of the Word of God, who conde-
scends to subject himself to human senses in the Incarnation.[47]

At this point, it is possible to go back to Augustine's argument in *The City of
God*, book 10. Augustine does not simply argue against the philosophers' exclusion of the multitude from genuine salvation, he argues that the philosopher cannot achieve the salvation of the soul even through the operation of his intellect.
Augustine begins chapter 32 of book 10 by saying, "This is the religion which

contains the universal way for the liberation of the soul, since no soul can be freed by any other way."[48] Augustine's clear implication is that, while unbelieving philosophers may think that they are freed through philosophy, they are themselves deceived, because no soul is freed except by Christ. The key to Augustine's argument is the universality of the way of salvation in Christianity. The two ways that Porphyry mentions are based on a division of men into two classes: those who are capable of philosophy, who are few; and those who are not capable of philosophy, who are many. The philosopher is capable of living his life according to the higher soul, the intellectual soul, whereas the non-philosopher lives his life according to the lower, or spiritual, soul. The philosopher is capable of conceiving immaterial substance and therefore transcending the world of sense impressions and phantasms; the non-philosopher is not. The fact of the matter is, however, that even though the non-philosopher lives according to his lower soul, that does not mean that he has no intellect, only that he does not use it rightly. The fact that the philosopher is capable of using his intellect well and that he rightly regards it to be what is highest in him does not mean that his lower soul—or indeed even his body—is any less essentially constitutive of him as a human person. Augustine presses his case, saying, "For what is a universal way for the liberation of the soul, if it is not a way by which all souls are liberated, and therefore the only way for any soul?"[49] Christianity provides for the liberation of all souls, and is the only way of liberation for any soul, because it "purifies the *whole* man (*totum hominem*) and prepares his mortal being for immortality, in all the elements which constitute a man."[50] Theurgy claims to purify only part of a man, the spiritual soul, and therefore cannot claim really to liberate him in truth; Porphyry's philosophy claims to liberate the intellectual soul, which is also only part of a man, and therefore cannot claim to liberate him as a man in truth. The human person as human person involves body, lower soul, and higher soul. To neglect or excise one element is to be left with something that is not a man, not a human person.

Augustine's—and Christianity's—emphasis on the resurrection of the body is therefore a strong affirmation of the personal significance of each man as a man, as a person. The fear of death is so strong among men because they are right to fear it: it involves the sundering of man's constitutive elements, which is a great evil. The incantations of the philosophic swan song, either in its Socratic or in its Porphyrean, theurgic manifestations, are essentially deceptive. Death, as Augustine knows St. Paul says, is the wages of sin.[51] To die without the forgiveness of sin would be to die not only the death of separation of soul and body but to die what Augustine calls the second death, the eternal separation of the soul from God.[52] But St. Paul also says that "the free gift of God is eternal life in Christ Jesus our Lord."[53] Augustine therefore focuses on the gift of eternal life in Jesus Christ:

> The grace of God could not be commended in a way more likely to evoke a grateful response, than the way by which the only Son of God, while remaining unchangeably

in his own proper being, clothed himself in humanity and gave to men the spirit of his love by the mediation of a man, so that by this love men might come to him who formerly was so far away from them, far from mortals in his immortality, from the changeable in his changelessness, from the wicked in his righteousness, from the wretched in his blessedness. And because he has implanted in our nature the desire for blessedness and immortality he has now taken on himself mortality, while continuing in his blessedness, so that he might confer on us what our hearts desire; and by his sufferings he has taught us to make light of what we dread.[54]

For us to see how there can be a universal way of salvation that offers eternal life, it is necessary to examine the mediation of Christ more closely.

Augustine focuses on three aspects of Christ's mediation as the grounding of the universal way of salvation: first, who and what Christ is, namely the Incarnate Word who is true man and true God; second, what he does, namely, he assumes a whole human nature without abandoning his divinity and offers a fitting sacrifice to the Father that reconciles man to God; third, the manner in which he does these things, namely, in humility. The three are, of course, inseparable. Augustine insists that there is one, universal way of salvation for all men. He says, "We have not to seek one purification for that element which Porphyry calls the 'intellectual' soul, another for the 'spiritual,' and yet another for the body itself. It was to avoid such quests that our Purifier and Savior (*mundator atque saluator*), the true Purifier and the all-powerful Saviour, took upon himself the man in his entirety (*totum suscepit*)."[55] True purification and, therefore, true salvation is by the Incarnate Word. The principle of purification is the Word, not the flesh; but it was necessary for the Word to take on the entirety of the human nature, including the flesh, so as to offer up the atoning sacrifice: the entirety of himself, including his flesh.[56] All of these things are possible because of Christ's humility.

The universal way of salvation first depends on the Incarnation, which involves the Word's assumption of the whole of human nature. Augustine's argument for the universal way of the salvation of the soul therefore depends on Trinitarian and Christological orthodoxy. In chapter 24 of book 10—the chapter Augustine dedicates to his presentation of Christ as the true principle of purification—he begins by emphasizing that, unlike Porphyry's talk of "principles" that are separate, Christians speak only of one principle, that is, the Holy Trinity who is three Persons in one God.[57] Augustine's criticism of Porphyry is that Porphyry emphasizes the plurality of the "principles" such that they cannot be spoken of as being one principle in the final account. To provide a clarification of his own position by contrast, he also brings up and criticizes Sabellianism, which makes the opposite error. The Sabellians, Augustine says, "identify the Father with the Son, and the Holy Spirit with both Father and Son."[58] In contrast, Augustine holds to the orthodox doctrine of the Trinity, which preserves the distinction of persons of the Father, Son, and Holy Spirit, but does not divide the divine substance. He also preserves the orthodox teaching on Christology, which requires the union of divine and human in Christ to be in the Person of the Word.

The hypostatic union is vital to the understanding of the universal way of salvation because it allows God to assume a human nature whole and entire and yet not diminish or corrupt his divinity. It was because the Word had taken a whole and entire human nature that he was able to be, in Augustine's words, "both the priest, himself making the oblation, and the oblation."[59] Christ himself offers the sacrifice that is himself to the Father. As Augustine says in the *De libero arbitrio*, what the will has lost through misuse, it cannot replace through its own efforts.[60] Only God who created man can restore what he has lost through sin. But what God requires of man is himself. So it must be God who restores, and man that offers himself. Only the Incarnate Word is capable of doing both.

Nevertheless, it is not the flesh of Christ that is the principle of purification, Augustine is at pains to emphasize, nor the human soul of Christ, but the Word of God. Augustine says, therefore, "the flesh does not purify by itself, but through the Word by which it was assumed."[61] But the fact that the flesh, indeed the whole of human nature and every concrete man, which is purified, is purified through the Word, is the reason that Augustine can say that the church, as the Body of Christ, is purified eucharistically through the Word: "This is the reality, and he intended the daily sacrifice of the Church to be the sacramental symbol for this; for the Church, being the body of which he is the head, learns to offer itself through him. This is the true sacrifice."[62] It immediately follows from the wholeness and entirety of the human nature as perfected in Christ that Christ can assemble a whole and entire people composed of all manner of human beings, from the ranks of the wise or ignorant, as the Platonists judge, and from every nation and people. Augustine says, "What in fact is this universal way, unless it is one which is not the exclusive property of a particular nation but has been divinely imparted to be the common property of all nations?"[63] The universality Christ has in himself issues in the universality of the Church, which makes possible a sacrifice that offers universal salvation: "The whole redeemed community, that is to say, the congregation and fellowship of the saints, is offered to God as a universal sacrifice, through the great Priest who offered himself in his suffering for us—so that we might be the body of so great a head—under 'the form of a servant.' For it was in this form he offered, and in this form he was offered, because it is under this form that he is the Mediator, in this form he is the Priest, in this form he is the Sacrifice. . . . This is the sacrifice of Christians, who are 'many, making up one body in Christ.'"[64] The phrase "form of a servant," from St. Paul,[65] brings up the final aspect of Christ's mediation that Augustine regards as indispensable: his humility.

Although it has been a matter of speculation among Christian theologians for centuries about whether God would have become man if man had not sinned, the New Testament confines itself to saying that the reason for the Incarnation was so that men might be saved from sin. As David Vincent Meconi puts it, commenting on the role the Incarnation plays in Augustine's conversion in the *Confessions*, "The Divine, born of a woman, participates in our nature so that we might more fully participate in Him as brothers and sisters. Christ came to partake of our fallen humanity not out of His greatness but on account of our wretchedness."[66] This teaching brings to light the reason that it might be said that the Platonists are simultaneously the closest to and the furthest away from Christianity of all men. One condition, the metaphysical condition, of the Incarnation is the absolute transcendence of God over the creation. That is why, in *The City of God* 8.4, Augustine chooses to have his discussion about natural theology with the Platonists as his philosophic interlocutors because they do not regard the human soul as divine. The other condition, not shared with his Platonic interlocutors, is the divine condescension to save human beings from sin. But the recognition of human sinfulness requires the recognition that our current condition is miserable. Augustine therefore observes that the Incarnation "is rejected, as folly and weakness, by those who think themselves wise and strong by their own virtue. But this in fact is grace, which heals the weakness of those who do not proudly boast of their delusive happiness, but instead make a humble admission of their genuine misery."[67] Admission of *genuine* misery would include the truthful admission of fault for sin. But Augustine argues that Porphyry regards our condition to be evil because of the body, not because of sin, and so would despise Christ, who took on a body in part to show that "it is sin which is evil, not the substance or nature of flesh."[68] The humility of God in assuming human nature then ought to elicit the humility of man in confessing his responsibility for his own misery.

Instead, Augustine argues, Porphyry's pride makes him incapable of recognizing the principle of purification in Christ because of Christ's humility. Augustine says, "The fact is that he despised [*contempsit*] Christ as he appeared in flesh, in that very flesh which he assumed in order to effect the sacrifice of our purification. It was of course his pride which blinded [*non intellegens*] Porphyry to this great mystery [*sacramentum*], that pride which our true and gracious Mediator has overthrown by his humility, in showing himself to mortals in the condition of mortality."[69] Pride blinds Porphyry and presumably all philosophers who reject Christ. Augustine's general criticism of the pride of these philosophers is that "all these philosophers have wished, with amazing folly, to be happy here on earth and to achieve bliss by their own efforts."[70] The first part of book 19 of *The City of God* is dedicated to the argument that it is impossible to be happy in this life due to the vicissitudes of chance. The only happiness that is available in this life is a happiness in hope—that is, a happiness that depends on confidence in Christ's mediation of eternal life to his followers. In contrast, Augustine says, "These philosophers refuse to believe in this blessedness because they do not see it; and so they attempt to fabricate for themselves an utterly delusive happiness by means of a virtue whose falsity is in proportion to its arrogance."[71] Even setting aside Augustine's very strong polemics, he is making a deeply serious point: ultimately, human happiness must be received from God and depends on divine agency rather than human agency. Pride is the refusal to receive happiness from God and the concomitant insistence that, whatever happiness I attain to, I must attain to it based on my resources and my resources alone.[72] It is also the refusal to countenance the thought that the root problem for all human beings—whether philosopher or non-philosopher—is a common one, namely sin.[73]

Even if all of Augustine's arguments about the availability of a universal way of salvation based on the mediation of Christ are persuasive, there is still a question. What difference does it make? Classically, the division between the philosophers and the non-philosophers appears in political philosophy when it is admitted that the wise— or the comparatively wise—are the ones who ought to rule.[74] The classical problem of the rule of the wise is based on the fact that there are few who are philosophers, it is difficult for the non-philosophers to identify them, and it is an open question as to what would motivate the wise to want to rule, since that would presumably involve them in pursuits other than the pursuit of wisdom. But Augustine's argument about the universal way of salvation necessarily involves a different judgment about the availability of wisdom to the non-philosopher. The reason that, classically, there are few true philosophers is that the kind of rational independence required to live the philosophic life requires massive intellectual effort combined with rare natural intelligence along with a desire to know the truth above everything else. Wisdom is a very high goal whose achievement requires the rarest kinds of mental abilities. The number of potential philosophers is therefore already small; the number of actual philosophers would be vanishingly small. The Christian answer to the problem of the rarity of human beings capable of philosophy is the Incarnation. Instead of man needing to reach up to wisdom, eternal Wisdom reaches down by taking flesh. In principle, the Incarnation allows any human being to pursue wisdom even in the absence of the extraordinary personal resources required to live the philosophic life.

At least on the surface, that might lead us to believe that Augustine would regard the Christian, as a man who is apprenticed to Wisdom Incarnate, to be the natural ruler. If this were the case, we would expect to find a sustained treatment of the two most outstanding Christian emperors up to that point, Constantine and Theodosius, in *The City of God*. But that is far from what we find. As Ernest L. Fortin points out, "It is significant that the *City of God* devotes barely more than two short chapters to Constantine and Theodosius, the most renowned of the Christian emperors, and that, in reviewing their reigns, Augustine stresses their private virtues to the virtual exclusion of their political virtues."[75] The reason *The City of God* lacks a more substantial treatment of Constantine and Theodosius is that the wisdom that Christianity affords and the goal that the Christian seeks through the mediation of Christ is transpolitical. Fortin says elsewhere, "This does not mean that the city of God has done away with the need for civil society. Its purpose is not to replace civil society but to supplement it by providing, over and above the benefits conferred by it, the means of achieving a goal that is higher than any to which civil society can lead."[76] The goal of the Christian is not a this-worldly goal,[77] and so the wisdom of Christianity does not have direct and immediately applicable relevance for political life.

That Christianity is transpolitical does not mean that it has no relevance to political life. In light of transpolitical Christian faith, politics is able to appear in a different light: that is, in light of Christian faith, the limits of politics come into sight. The situation is similar to what happens with respect to politics in the light of classical political philosophy. As Leo Strauss points out, the political philosopher "is ultimately compelled to transcend not merely the dimension of common opinion, of political opinion, but the dimension of political life as such; for he is led to realize that the ultimate aim of political life cannot be reached by political life, but only by a life devoted to contemplation, to philosophy."[78] Although the goal of the transcendence of the classical political philosopher and the Christian, respectively, is different, what their respective transcendence of political life does to their apprehension of the limits of political life is similar, especially from the standpoint of politics. Regardless of the presentation of Christ and Socrates that their kingship or contemplative life were, as it were, not of this world, both were executed by the political authorities at least in part because of the limits they revealed about political life.

For Augustine, one of the clearest limitations of political life is that political life does not provide a final home—not only for the philosopher but for any human person. That judgment is what is behind his refusal to allow the earthly city to dictate to the City of God on matters of religion, especially about the worship of God,[79] and why he considered the witness of the martyrs against impiety to be so important.[80] That also provides a reason that he focuses on the private rather than political virtues of Theodosius and Constantine. Robert Dodaro points out, "Central to Augustine's conception of true piety as practiced by statesmen is their public acknowledgement of the limits of their virtue through prayer to God for forgiveness of their sins."[81] The emperor Theodosius's public exercise of the private act of repentance reveals the limitations not only of his own virtue but of political life itself through a clear acknowledgment of a standard that transcends the standards of ethics and politics that even an emperor must abide by, and the violation of which—even in the exercise of his political power—compels even the emperor to seek forgiveness of his sins.

Through its rejection of the worship of false gods, Christianity has the effect of secularizing political authority. But that raises another problem. The authority of the laws of the city was classically understood to flow from some divine source. As Leo Strauss puts it in his formulation of what he calls the theologico-political problem,

> Pre-philosophic life is characterized by the primeval identification of the good with the ancestral. . . . One cannot reasonably identify the good with the ancestral if one does not assume that the ancestors were absolutely superior to "us," and this means that they were superior to all ordinary mortals; one is driven to believe that the ancestors, or those who established the ancestral way, were gods or sons of gods or at least "dwelling near the gods."' The identification of the good with the ancestral leads to the view that the right way was established by gods or sons of gods or pupils of gods: the right way must be divine law.[82]

Along similar lines, Plato's *Laws* begins with the Athenian Stranger asking both of his interlocutors, "Is it a god or some human being, strangers, who is given the credit for laying down your laws?"[83] Both respond without hesitating that it is a god. It is far easier for a citizen to devote himself wholeheartedly to the good of a community whose source is divine than to one whose source is merely human.

There is a risk here when Christians make up a significant enough proportion of the populace that Christianity will detach the Christian from his city in the name of a transpolitical good such that the city will be unable to flourish.[84] That judgment or intuition is what initially provokes Augustine to write *The City of God*. As Fortin observes, Augustine's response to the patriotic, pagan critics of Christianity is that "Christianity does not destroy patriotism but reinforces it by making of it a religious duty,"[85] one grounded in Christ's commandment of love of neighbor. And although it is certainly true that Christianity reveals a transpolitical goal that is in principle accessible by all through grace, it is not true that Christianity detaches the members of the City of God from their duties in the earthly city. As Augustine points out, the New Testament in fact contains multiple exhortations to do one's civic duty.[86] But beyond that, even while claiming that the earthly city aims at an earthly peace based on what is merely a "compromise between human wills about the things relevant to mortal life," which he contrasts with the City of God's eternal goal, he still affirms that the City of God "must needs make use of this peace also, until this mortal state, for which this kind of peace is essential, passes away. And therefore it leads what we may call a life of captivity in this earthly city as in a foreign land, although it has already received the promise of redemption, and the gift of the Spirit as a kind of pledge of it; and yet it does not hesitate to obey the laws of the earthly city by which those things which are designed for the support of this mortal life are regulated."[87]

But the City of God does not engage in these actions half-heartedly. Because the City of God also depends on the earthly peace of the earthly city, the City of God positively "makes use of the earthly peace and defends and seeks the compromise between human wills in respect of provisions relevant to the mortal nature of man, so far as may be permitted without detriment to true religion and piety."[88] This risk is adequately compensated for by the commandment of love and the transforming power of grace available, if not guaranteed, within the City of God. Augustine could therefore say in one of his letters, "Therefore, let those who say that the teaching of Christ is opposed to the welfare of the state produce such provincial administrators, such husbands, such wives, such parents, such sons, such masters, such slaves, such kings, such judges, and finally such tax-payers and collectors of public revenue as Christian teaching requires them to be, and then let them dare to say that this teaching is opposed to the welfare of the state, or, rather, let them even hesitate to admit that it is the greatest safety of the state, if it is observed."[89] Obviously, the last phrase is key: *if* it is observed. There is no guarantee that members of the City of God live up to their membership. But it is a much likelier starting point for virtue than the Roman temple.

The similarity between Augustine and Porphyry regarding their attitude toward the city is best examined by reference to the transpolitical good that each characteristically pursues. But there is a difference between their attitudes, too, grounded in the distinctive objects they pursue: union with the One and loving knowledge of the Triune God, respectively. The former requires divestment by degrees of personal attachments to particular beings; the latter proceeds from and issues in a loving relationship with God and neighbor. The Porphyrian attitude toward the city must finally be one of indifference. The Augustinian attitude toward the city cannot be indifferent, because of those who live in it: human beings who are actual or potential members of the city of God, whose image in them elicits the Christian's love. *The City of God* 19.19 is the justly famous chapter where Augustine unveils this difference to its fullest degree.

*The City of God* 19.19 is about the universality of the City of God. Augustine begins by highlighting the universality of the City of God by stating that the City of God does not require or exclude any particular habit or custom of living [*habitu vel more uiuendi*].[90] In particular, he says that a Christian may be faithful in the living of any of the three classical candidates for the best way of life: the life of leisure, the life of action, and the life that combines leisure and action. There is, of course, no reason to believe that Augustine does not have an opinion about how to rank those candidates on a scale of human nobility. In fact, right after his conversion, Augustine indicates his own preference by retiring into a leisured retreat at Cassiciacum once he is freed of the duties of his chair in rhetoric at Milan.[91] But in living any of these three ways of life, even—or especially—the life of leisure, Augustine makes clear that the Christian faith imposes two obligations on the Christian: that he "loves the truth and performs the duties of charity."[92] Augustine explains: "For no one ought to live a life of leisure in such a way that he takes no thought in that leisure for the welfare of his neighbor; nor ought he to be so active as to feel no need for the contemplation of God. The delight offered by a life of leisure ought to consist not in idle inactivity, but in the opportunity to seek and find the truth, so that everyone may make progress in this regard, and not jealously withhold his discoveries from others."[93] Augustine is articulating a theoretical point that is well illustrated in his own life. As a lover of the truth, Augustine is drawn to the life of contemplation. But precisely because of his learning, he is called into an active life as a priest and then a bishop, which office he was exercising when he wrote *The City of God*. As he puts it, "It is on account of the life of truth that one seeks a holy leisure [*otium sanctum*]; it is on account of the necessity of charity that one takes up righteous work [*iustum negotium*]."[94] The bishop must both teach and rule. Unlike with the Platonic or Porphyrian philosopher, there is no open question as to what might make the Christian wise man want to rule.

Augustine and other Christian contemplatives are moved not by coercion or threats to take up these duties, but by love, grounded in their imitation of Christ the

Word made flesh and by graced insertion into the loving relations of the Trinitarian persons. Unlike the non-Christian multitude, the non-philosophic Christian seeks union with the same God by means of the same faith and the same sacraments as the Christian wise man.

# Notes

1. Pierre Manent, *Metamorphoses of the City*, trans. Marc LePain (Cambridge, MA: Harvard University Press, 2013), 272. Manent grants that Augustine owes an enormous debt to his philosophic teachers—indeed, Manent is almost unparalleled in his rigorous thought on precisely that subject. But his argument also entails a dialectical relationship between them, in which Augustine appears not only as a debtor to his Platonic interlocutors but also as a critic.

2. Augustine, *The City of God*, trans. Henry Bettenson (London: Penguin, 2003), 10.32. Unless otherwise indicated, all references to the English translation of *De ciuitate dei* (hereafter *Ciu*) will be from the Bettenson translation. The Latin text is from the Corpus Christianorum critical edition, either *De ciuitate dei Libri I–X*, ed. Bernardus Dombart and Alphonsus Kalb, Corpus Christianorum Series Latina 47 (Brepols: Turnhout, 1955), or *De ciuitate dei Libri XI–XXII*, ed. Bernardus Dombart and Alphonsus Kalb, Corpus Christianorum Series Latina 48 (Brepols: Turnhout, 1955).

3. *Ciu.*, 10.27.60–61.

4. There are many other places in the Augustinian corpus where Augustine addresses this division. Book 10 of the *City of God* provides Augustine's most direct and concentrated dialectical engagement with a specific philosopher who is operating in the tradition of Platonic political philosophy on the topic of the division between the few and the many.

5. There are plenty of indications that Augustine was aware of the esotericism of Platonic writing. In three texts in particular other than *The City of God* Augustine addresses philosophic esotericism: his *Epistula* 1, the first seven chapters of *De vera religione*, and *Contra academicos* 2.10.24. The dissembling of philosophers and statesmen, or lies about their true thoughts on the divine, is a main theme of *The City of God* and can be found in many, many places. For an excellent discussion of Augustine's relationship to esoteric writing, see Douglas Kries, "Augustine as Defender and Critic of Leo Strauss' Esotericism Thesis," *Proceedings of the American Catholic Philosophical Association* 83 (2009), 243–46. See also one chapter in particular from Ernest L. Fortin, "Augustine and the Problem of Christian Rhetoric," in *Collected Essays*, ed. J. Brian Benestad (Lanham, MD: Rowman and Littlefield, 1996), 1:79–93. Although Augustine himself did not engage in what could be called esoteric writing, as Fortin points out, "There is evidence that Augustine shared with his predecessors, both pagan and Christian, the view that the whole truth in matters of supreme moment can be safeguarded only if its investigation is accompanied by a prudent reserve in the expression of that truth." Fortin, "Augustine," in *History of Political Philosophy*, 3rd ed., ed. Leo Strauss and Joseph Cropsey (Chicago: University of Chicago Press, 1987), 176–205, at 178. For evidence, Fortin points to the following texts: *The City of God* 8.4; *Contra academicos* 2.4.10, 2.10.24, 3.7.14, 3.17.38, 3.20.43; *Epistula* 118.1, and *Epistula* 1. I would also add *De trinitate* 1.1.1 and *Contra mendacium* 10.23. Fortin also helpfully clarifies, saying, "It should be added that, whereas some of the earlier Church Fathers like Clement of Alexandria and Origen defended

the use of noble lies in the common interest, Augustine denounces all lies, salutary or otherwise, as intrinsically evil and, following a precedent he alleges to have been set by Christ, admits only of indirect forms of concealment, such as omissions and brevity of speech." Fortin, "Augustine," 179–80.

6. See Plato, *Republic*, trans. Allan Bloom (New York: Basic Books, 1991), 414b–e. Later on, Socrates says, "It's likely that our rulers will have to use a throng of lies and deceptions for the benefit of the ruled." *Republic*, 459c–d.

7. Plato, *Republic*, 473d.

8. Frederick Van Fleteren, "Porphyry," in *Augustine Through the Ages*, ed. Allan D. Fitzgerald, OSA (Grand Rapids, MI: Eerdmans, 1999), 661–63, at 661. Van Fleteren thinks that Augustine read and used in his own writing Porphyry's books *Kata Christianos*, *Zetemata*, *De regressu animae*, and *Philosophy from Oracles*.

9. See Van Fleteren, "Porphyry." Also see Van Fleteren, "Augustine and Philosophy: *Intellectus Fidei*," in *Augustine and Philosophy*, ed. Phillip Cary, John Doody, and Kim Paffenroth (Lanham, MD: Lexington Books, 2010), 26–28.

10. *Ciu.*, 10.32.

11. *Ciu.*, 10.3.

12. Robert Dodaro gives a concise explanation of theurgy: "The practice refers to the performance of ritual acts: prayers, hymns, and incantations, accompanied by meditation, which were intended to put the soul into contact with spirits and deities so that it would achieve moral purification and peace in an experience of spiritual ecstasy." Robert Dodaro, OSA, "Theurgy," in *Augustine Through the Ages*, 827–28.

13. *Ciu.*, 10.9.

14. *Ciu.*, 10.9.

15. *Ciu.*, 10.9.

16. Plato, *Republic*, 509d–511e.

17. Plato, *Republic*, 514a–517a.

18. Ernest L. Fortin comments on the influence of the *Hortensius* on the young Augustine:

> [*Hortensius*] held up the theoretical life as the highest human possibility and the philosopher as the highest human type. It thereby made a young and avid Augustine, who had more than his share of riot and high summer in the blood and for whom the familiar *cursus honorum* was the mandatory road to success, aware of the fact that one's whole life could be actuated, not by the love of pleasure, honor, or any of the other worldly goods to which the vast majority of human beings are drawn, but by that most unusual of all passions—a passion so rare that few people recognize it when they come face to face with it—the passion for the truth.

Fortin, "Augustine and the Hermeneutics of Love: Some Preliminary Considerations," in *Collected Essays*, 1:1–19, at 4.

19. "Mutavit affectum meum, et ad te ipsum, domine, mutavit preces meas, et vota ac desideria mea fecit alia. Veluit mihi repente omnis vana spes, et immortalitatem sapientiae concupiscebam aestu cordis incredibili." Augustine, *Confessiones*, 3.4.7. For the English text of Augustine's *Confessions*, I am using Augustine, *Confessions*, trans. Frank Sheed (Indianapolis: Hackett, 2006).

20. Augustine, *Confessiones*, 3.7.12.

21. *Confessiones*, 3.6.11. "Intellectual understanding" is better translated "understanding of the mind."

22. *Confessiones*. 7.9.13.

23. Van Fleteren, "Porphyry," 663.

24. As distinguished from the mythic and civil theology he discusses in early parts of *The City of God*.

25. "Platonicos appellatos a Platone doctore." *Ciu.* 8.1.

26. *Ciu.*, 10.1.

27. *Ciu.*, 7.25.

28. *Ciu.*, 19.22.

29. See Van Fleteren, "Porphyry," 661–63. Van Fleteren helpfully lays out the various opinions on which Platonists Augustine read leading up to his conversion.

30. *Conf.*, 7.17.23.

31. Some version of *fallo* occurs twenty-nine times, and some version of *decipio* occurs six times throughout book 10.

32. *Ciu.*, 4.27.8–19.

33. Joseph Cropsey, *Plato's World* (Chicago: University of Chicago Press, 1997), 192. For Socrates's reference to his "swan song," see Plato, *Phaedo* 84e–85b. Robert Dodaro astutely observes that theurgy serves as "therapy for fear of death." Dodaro, *Christ and the Just Society in the Thought of Augustine* (Cambridge: Cambridge University Press, 2008), 64.

34. "Admoneat utendum alicuius daemonis amicitia, quo subuectante uel paululum a terra possit eleuari quisque post mortem." *Ciu.*, 10.9.39–41.

35. *Ciu.*, 10.27.61–64.

36. Porphyry, "The Life of Plotinus," in Plotinus, *Enneads*, trans. Stephen MacKenna (London: Faber and Faber, 1966), 17.

37. *Ciu.*, 10.11. Augustine wonders later in *The City of God* whether Porphyry "falsely invented" the oracles he writes down in his book *Philosophy from Oracles*. *Ciu.*, 19.23.

38. *Ciu.*, 10.27.

39. "Ita gradatim a corporibus ad sentientem per corpus animam atque inde ad eius interiorem uim, cui sensus corporis exteriora nuntiaret, et quousque possunt bestiae, atque inde rursus ad ratiocinantem potentiam, ad quam refertur iudicandum, quod sumitur a sensibus corporis; quae se quoque in me comperiens mutabilem erexit se ad intellegentiam suam et abduxit cogitationem a consuetudine, subtrahens se contradicentibus turbis phantasmatum, ut inueniret quo lumine aspergeretur, cum sine ulla dubitatione clamaret incommutabile praeferendum esse mutabili, unde nosset ipsum incommutabile—quod nisi aliquo modo nosset, nullo modo illud mutabili certa praeponeret—et peruenit ad id, quod est in ictu trepidantis aspectus." Augustine, *Confessiones*, 7.17.23.

40. *Confessiones*, 7.17.23. Matthew L. Lamb remarks, "He immediately adds that this discovery was not yet habitual. For he could not live the theoretic or contemplative life demanded by discovery until Christ gave him the strength to do so." Lamb, *Eternity, Time, and the Life of Wisdom* (Naples, FL: Sapientia, 2007), 32.

41. *Ciu.*, 10.9.

42. Peter Augustine Lawler, "American Nominalism and a Science of Theology," in *Catholicism and America: Challenges and Prospects*, ed. Matthew L. Lamb (Naples, FL: Sapientia, 2012), 37–53, at 43.

43. *Conf.*, 9.10.25.

44. *Conf.*, 9.10.24.

45. Augustine repeats this twice: in attaining to God, Augustine and Monica "touch" eternal wisdom. He says this in *Conf.* 9.10.24 and 9.10.25.

46. *Conf.*, 9.10.24.

47. On the role of the senses and the body in the Christian ascent to God, see also, *inter alia*, Augustine, *Tractates on the Gospel of John*, 2.16.

48. *Ciu.*, 10.32.

49. *Ciu.*, 10.32.

50. *Ciu.*, 10.32 (emphasis added).

51. Romans 6:23.

52. See, *inter alia*, *Ciu.*, 10.6.

53. Romans 6:23.

54. *Ciu.*, 10.29. Pierre Manent comments, "The point of Christianity is not to propose a God pure of all human contamination—Greek philosophy had already done that—but to announce that this God is the friend of humans to the point of assuming their condition." Manent, *Metamorphoses*, 316.

55. *Ciu.*, 10.32.125–29.

56. Augustine is here faithful to the patristic soteriological principle that what is not assumed by Christ is not redeemed. If any part of a man is not assumed by Christ, then the whole man cannot be said to be redeemed. See, *inter alia*, Gregory of Nazianzen, Epistula 101.34.

57. Augustine does not seem entirely clear about the teaching of Porphyry or Plotinus on these principles, or at least his presentation of their positive teaching is not very clear. The sole point he wishes to make is that in some way or another, Porphyry's principles are plural, whereas the principle of purification for Christians is singular. See *Ciu.*, 10.23. See Van Fleteren, "Porphyry," for a summary of the scholarship about which works of Porphyry Augustine was able to access.

58. *Ciu.*, 10.24.

59. *Ciu.*, 10.20.

60. See *De libero arbitrio* 3.18.177–79.

61. *Ciu.*, 10.24.

62. *Ciu.*, 10.20.

63. *Ciu.*, 10.32.

64. *Ciu.*, 10.32.

65. Philippians 2:7.

66. David Vincent Meconi, "The Incarnation and Participation in St. Augustine's *Confessions*," *Augustinian Studies* 29:2 (1998), 61–75, at 71.

67. *Ciu.*, 10.28.

68. *Ciu.*, 10.24.

69. *Ciu.*, 10.24.15–19.

70. *Ciu.*, 19.4.

71. *Ciu.*, 19.4.

72. Ernest Fortin observes, "Aside from the fact that philosophers sometimes err in their teachings concerning God, however, there is still one crucial element which separates them from Christianity, and that is their refusal to accept Christ as mediator and redeemer. As a

seeker after independent knowledge, the philosopher is basically proud and refuses to owe his salvation to anyone but himself. His whole endeavor is motivated in the final accounting by self-praise and self-admiration." Fortin, "The Political Thought of St. Augustine," in *Collected Essays*, ed. J. Brian Benestad (Lanham, MD: Rowman and Littlefield, 1996), 2:1–29, at 18.

73. See Augustine's discussion of Victorinus in *Conf.*, 8.2.

74. Leo Strauss puts it succinctly:

> When attempting to guide the city, [the philosopher] knows then in advance that, in order to be useful or good for the city, the requirements of wisdom must be qualified or diluted. If these requirements are identical with natural right or with natural law, natural right or natural law must be diluted in order to become compatible with the requirements of the city. The city requires that wisdom be reconciled with consent. But to admit the necessity of consent, i.e., of the consent of the unwise, amounts to admitting a right of unwisdom, i.e., an irrational, if inevitable, right. Civil life requires a fundamental compromise between wisdom and folly, and this means a compromise between the natural right that is determined by reason or understanding and the right that is based on opinion alone. Civil life required the dilution of natural right by merely conventional right. Natural right would act as dynamite for civil society. In other words, the simply good, which is what is good by nature and which is radically distinct from the ancestral, must be transformed into the politically good, which is, as it were, the quotient of the simply good and the ancestral: the politically good is what "removes a vast mass of evil without shocking a vast mass of prejudice."

Strauss, *Natural Right and History* (Chicago: University of Chicago Press: 1965), 152–53.

75. Fortin, "Augustine's *City of God* and Modern Historical Consciousness," in *Collected Essays*, 2:117–36, at 128.

76. Fortin, "The Political Thought of St. Augustine," in *Collected Essays*, 2:1–29, at 20.

77. "My kingship is not of this world," Jesus says in John 18:36.

78. Leo Strauss, "On Classical Political Philosophy," in *An Introduction to Political Philosophy: Ten Essays by Leo Strauss*, ed. Hilail Gildin (Detroit: Wayne State University Press, 1989), 59–79, at 74.

79. See *Ciu.*, 19.17.

80. See, *inter alia*, *Ciu.*, 10.23.

81. Robert Dodaro, *Christ and the Just Society in the Thought of Augustine* (Cambridge: Cambridge University Press, 2008), 57, 192–93.

82. Leo Strauss, *Natural Right and History* (Chicago: University of Chicago Press: 1965), 83–84.

83. *The Laws of Plato*, trans. Thomas L. Pangle (Chicago: University of Chicago Press, 1988), 624a.

84. Ernest Fortin points out that one of Augustine's main purposes in writing *The City of God* was to depict how a universal way of salvation could be shown not to dissolve the particularities of political life. Christianity, Fortin says, "engendered a tendency to regard the natural differences and traditional boundaries that set men off as separate groups leading separate lives as politically irrelevant, and thus stripped the city of its status as an exclusive community, as

the all-embracing whole and unique expression of that common life which stands above its individual members and binds them together as fellow citizens." Fortin, "Political Idealism and Christianity in the Thought of St. Augustine," in *Collected Essays*, 2: 31–63, at 39.

85. Fortin, "The Political Thought of St. Augustine," 2:1–29, at 24. He says elsewhere, "Furthermore, any depreciation of the fatherland, if one can really speak of a depreciation, is amply compensated for by the fact that Christianity demands and very often obtains from its followers a higher degree of morality and virtue. It thus helps to counteract vice and corruption, which are the true causes of the weakness and decline of cities and nations." Fortin, "St. Augustine," in *History of Political Philosophy*, Chicago (University of Chicago Press: 1987), 201.

86. To mention just a few: Christ's command to "Render to the things that are Caesar's, and to God the things that are God's" in Mark 12:17, echoed in Matthew 22:21, admits that there are things that the members of the City of God owe to Caesar, in this instance, at least the paying of taxes. Jesus tells Pilate, "You would have no power over me unless it had been given you from above," in John 19:11, recognizing that Pilate's authority comes from God, even if he misuses it. Paul states in Romans 13:1–7 that Christians are to obey earthly authority, not just for expediency, but because political authority is "instituted by God" (Rom. 13:1).

87. *Ciu.*, 19.17.

88. *Ciu.*, 19.17.

89. Augustine, Letter 138, to Marcellinus, in *St. Augustine: Letters*, trans. Sr. Wilfrid Parsons, SND, Fathers of the Church (Washington, DC: Catholic University Press of America, 1953), 3:36–53, at 48.

90. *Ciu.*, 19.19.

91. See Peter Brown, *Augustine of Hippo* (Berkeley: University of California Press, 1975), 101–27. Augustine says in *Ciu.* 19.19, "If this latter burden [of righteous work] is not imposed on us, we should devote our freedom to the search for and contemplation of truth."

92. *Ciu.*, 19.19.

93. *Ciu.*, 19.19.

94. *Ciu.*, 19.19 (my translation).

Chapter Seven

# Echoes and Adaptations in Augustine's *Confessions* of Plato's Teaching on Art and Politics in the *Republic*

## Douglas Kries

In his *Republic*, Plato examines the political implications of art by means of an analysis of the nature and structure of the human soul. Because the soul has "parts" that usually exist in tension with each other, the soul usually finds itself in a disharmonious condition; in other words, the soul is usually bad or unjust. The artist, the *Republic* teaches, has the power to reproduce this injustice or discord within the souls of an audience by depicting it in a manner that the audience—antecedently inclined toward injustice anyway—finds attractive. The artist accomplishes this effect by presenting an imitation of a disharmonious soul to the audience; the audience then willingly imitates the imitation. Art thereby functions, as it were, as a photocopying machine for reproducing multiple unjust souls within a city. Because of this power it has to distort souls, poetic art is banned from the city being constructed in speech in the early books of the *Republic*; it is permitted back into the city, however, late in the work, when Plato seems to concede that art can be reformed under the influence of philosophy and even put in the service of justice or psychic concord. Indeed, the *Republic* concludes with an extended example of this reformed art—art in the service of the soul and the city—namely, the myth of Er.

This essay will argue that Augustine's *Confessions* echoes and adapts aspects of Plato's thought on art and politics as it is expressed in the *Republic*.[1] In its first and second sections, this essay will show how the initial book of the *Confessions* offers a criticism of art that proceeds along the same lines as the early books of the *Republic*, linking art and politics especially through the tripartite structure of the soul. Whereas Plato executes his critique primarily through an analysis of Homer, the first section of this essay will show how Augustine does this, especially through a critique of Terence and Virgil in *Confessions*, book 1. The second section will develop Augustine's criticism in book 1 by sifting evidence from books 3 and 4. In its third, fourth, and fifth sections, the essay will turn to book 1's "mirror image" in book 9 and show how, again echoing Plato, Augustine concedes that art can be reformed. The third section will show that Ambrose's new music is a prime example of using art to restore justice to the soul; the fourth section will argue that the "vision of Ostia" in book 9 relies heavily on "The Dream of Scipio," which is itself Cicero's rendition of the reformed art of Plato's myth of Er; and the fifth section will compare the approaches to politics broadly conceived of Monnica and the thumotic Juno.

Before proceeding, however, a note of clarification is needed regarding the nature of the influence of the *Republic* on Augustine's thought. For starters, there is no evidence that Augustine read any of Plato's dialogues in their original Greek; neither do we have evidence that he read them in Latin translation, except for Cicero's translation of a portion of the *Timaeus*. If Augustine did not learn the themes of Plato's *Republic* from the dialogue itself, however, where did he learn them? Summaries of Plato's doctrines in "doxographies," or handbooks of philosophy, seem to have been readily available in antiquity. In *The City of God*, Augustine himself refers to a book by Marcus Terentius Varro titled *On Philosophy* and perhaps also to one on *The Opinions of All the Philosophers*, perhaps written by a Celsus or Celsinus. Neither of these two works has come down to us, however, and we do not know whether the first one said much about Plato, anyway. Then there are followers of Plato from whom Augustine might have learned about the teachings contained in the *Republic*. Cicero's *Republic* would seem to be a place where we might anticipate that Augustine would have absorbed themes from Plato's *Republic*, but the former is modeled only very loosely on the latter and, of course, much of Cicero's dialogue remains lost to us anyway, so we cannot know what Augustine would have learned from those large portions of the work. Two ideas important to our essay—Plato's critique of poetry and his division of the human soul into three parts—were certainly available to Augustine through Cicero's *Tusculan Disputations*,[2] but we cannot assert that they were available *only* there. And then, of course, other Latin authors were influenced by Plato's political thought, such as Virgil and Sallust. Both were well known to Augustine, and so Augustine could have absorbed aspects of Plato's thoughts about art and politics through their mediation. In such cases, it is entirely possible that he was aware of certain teachings going back to Plato, even though he did not recognize that their ultimate source was Plato.

In a new treatment of the question of Augustine's knowledge of Plato, Gerd Van Riel goes farther than many scholars in emphasizing that Augustine possessed "a fairly good general knowledge of Plato's doctrines."[3] Moreover, Van Riel makes a plausible case that Augustine was familiar with the *De Platone et eius dogmata* of the famous African author Apuleius.[4] Particularly intriguing in this regard is a recent book by Justin Stover, which argues that an *epitome* of Plato's dialogues found in a Vatican manuscript from the thirteenth century is actually the lost third book of Apuleius's *De Platone*, and hence a text summarizing Plato's dialogues that Augustine would have had available to him.[5] So far, though, it has not been established with certainty that Augustine used this text of Apuleius or any other set of notes and summaries on the teachings of Plato.

Given the uncertainties of this situation, it would seem that Frederick Van Fleteren says about all that can be asserted confidently regarding Augustine's understanding of Plato:

> In antiquity Plato was *the* philosopher. He cast his shadow over the ancient world even more than Descartes over the modern. His dicta were constantly "in the air." A philosophical *koinē* existed, either derived from Plato himself or attributed to his genius. The term "Plato" and its cognates occur 252 times in Augustine's works. Nevertheless, . . . we conclude that Augustine knew Plato exclusively through secondary sources. Almost certainly he read Plato's *Timaeus* in Cicero's Latin translation. Likewise, he knew *Phaedo*, *Phaedrus*, and *Republic* through encyclopedias, doxographies, or other authors.[6]

This essay argues, then, not that the text of Plato's *Republic* can be set side by side with Augustine's so that sentences and word choices can be compared. Nor will it attempt to show the precise chain of texts reaching back to Plato and through which Augustine acquired his insights. Given the many lacunae in our knowledge of what Augustine was reading from the philosophers, such a study simply is not possible. Rather, what we will be showing is that there are thematic parallels between Plato's teaching on art in the *Republic* and Augustine's treatment of art in the *Confessions*. In the event, it will become clear that Augustine grasped the essence and importance of Plato's teaching quite well and thought it essential to adapt and thereby preserve it for his Christian readers. As a result of his passing on of the Platonic understanding of the relationship between art and political life, the *Confessions*, which would seem to be Augustine's most introspective and private work, turns out in the end to be a work with profound political implications.

## Twin Passages: Terence and Virgil in *Confessions*, Book 1

At the center of *Confessions*, book 1 stands Augustine's discussion of his parents' decision not to have him baptized as a child when his body was ill; following this discussion, the book turns to the corruption of soul the young Augustine then imbibed through the literature he learned in school. This tale of corruption reaches a high point in two passages that Augustine intends for us to read together.[7]

The first of these passages focuses on *The Eunuch* of Terence. In the crucial scene of this comedy, an unsuspecting noble virgin is left by her unsuspecting guardians in the care of a lustful young man, Chaerea, who has disguised himself as a eunuch and thereby passed himself off as a trustworthy family servant in order to be close to the young woman. His opportunity at hand, he is moved to violate the young woman by contemplating on a wall in the bedroom where she is preparing to nap a painting of the violation of Danaë by Jove. The vision of the desire of Jove for the beautiful young Danaë augments the desire of the faux eunuch and leads to his vile sin in imitation of the god. The crucial passage in the play is a recounting by Chaerea of his actions to his friend. In the prose translation of John Barsby, it reads thus:

> The girl sat in the room, looking up at a painting; it depicted the story of how Jupiter sent a shower of gold into Danaë's bosom. I began to look at it myself, and the fact that he had played a similar game long ago made me all the more excited: a god had turned himself into human shape, made his way by stealth on to another man's roof, and come through the skylight to play a trick on a woman. And what a god! The one who shakes the lofty vaults of heaven with his thunder! Was I, a mere mortal, not to do the same? I did just that—and gladly.[8]

This sin in turn places the familial politics of Athens, the city where it takes place, into disorder, but, as is often the case in comedies, everything turns out moderately well in the end, with the main obstacles being resolved through marriage.

What Terence himself wants us to think about his play is hard to know, especially because the play is thought to be based upon a lost Greek original by Menander; for Augustine, however, the scene clearly is a particularly apt example of the corrupting power that bad art—in this case visual art—holds over the soul and, from there, political life.[9] He quotes the last lines of the passage above and uses them to prove his point: even the artist Terence admits to the corrupting power of art. This reproductive power of art—its "photocopying" capacity—is possible because human beings, such as the faux eunuch, *imitate* the god and thereby incite themselves to wrongdoing through inordinate lust. The art on the wall is not a "play within a play" but a painting within a play—a form of "art within art." It leads not toward reform but toward reproducing the disharmony of injustice within a human soul already inclined to wrongdoing.

The second of the twin passages from book 1 of the *Confessions*, which immediately follows the treatment of Terence's play, reflects on an incident that occurred during Augustine's own schooling as a child.[10] He was, he says, given as an assignment the task of putting into prose the angry speech of Juno from the early part of the first book of the *Aeneid*. At the beginning of his epic poem, Virgil announces that he will sing of arms and a man, but this man, Aeneas, is hounded by the endless anger of Juno. The poet pleads,

> Muse, tell me the causes: how was godhead wronged,
> how injured the queen of heaven that she must force
> through many a fall of fate and many a toil
> that great, good man: can heaven hold such ill will [*ira*]?[11]

Virgil soon tells us that heaven can indeed hold such ill will, and he tells us the reasons for Juno's rage:

> She still recalled the anger [*ira*] and the pain
> that sent her there [to Troy]: deep in her heart lay stored
> the judgment of Paris, the insult to her beauty,
> a hated people, a Ganymede raped and honored.
> Her anger [*ira*] flared; she scattered all over the waves
> the Trojans Achilles and Greece had cast aside,
> and kept them far from Latium. (1.25–31)

Juno is angry because she has been dishonored both by the Trojan Paris and by Jove, her spouse and brother. She is angry, too, at a decree of fate that she has heard, according to which her dear city, Carthage, where she is particularly honored, will be destroyed by descendants of Troy. Plotting to herself, she declares that, despite fate, she will not drop her design of keeping Aeneas from Italy. She contemplates the example of Minerva, or Pallas Athena, who, because of anger, slew Ajax the lesser for dishonoring her priestess Cassandra. These are the words of Juno, spoken to herself, which the young Augustine was assigned to put into prose:

> What? Drop my design? Am I defeated,
> and can't keep a Trojan king from Italy?
> Fate forbids it? Pallas could burn the ships
> of Argos and drown their crewmen in the sea
> for Ajax' lone offense—that lawless fool!
> She threw Jove's shaft of lightning from the clouds,
> shattered the fleet, and blew calm waters wild.
> Through Ajax' heart she drove a hissing flame,
> whirled him away, and nailed him to a cliff.
> But I, who stand here queen of heaven, to Jove
> both wife and sister, year after year have fought
> one single people. Who'll worship Juno now,
> honor my altars, or come to me in prayer? (1.37–49)

From Virgil's telling of the story, it is not hard to recognize that Juno's flaw is excessive love of honor, which results in rage or anger when honor is not forthcoming. She may not require a divine exemplar to incite her anger, but she says in this speech that she has one, namely Minerva, or Pallas Athena. Just as Chaerea's lust is reinforced by the example of Jove, so is Juno's anger reinforced by the example of Minerva, who nailed the disrespectful Ajax to a cliff with "a hissing flame."

Lest there is any doubt that we are to see in Augustine's narrative about his school days the corrupting power of Virgil's art, Augustine notes that not only was he given the assignment of putting these angry words of Juno into prose but a competition was held to determine which of the young scholars could do this best. In the fashion of the *Aeneid* itself, he says that "there was the promise of glory if I won" this competition to portray the "rage" of Juno. And of course, Augustine won the competition, receiving the great reward of the honor-loving, "applause."[12]

## Echoes of the *Republic* in *Confessions*, Books 1, 3, and 4

There are two principal ways in which these twin passages from *Confessions* 1 echo the teaching of Plato's *Republic*. First, they both criticize art because its viewers or hearers *imitate* the bad desires and emotions portrayed in the art. The young man Chaerea experiences the desires of Jove because of the painting; the child Augustine experiences the emotions of Juno because of the poetry. Chaerea is moved by the art to commit rape. The child Augustine, we learn before the end of book 1, is willing to cheat in order to win athletic contests out of the "vain desire for first place" (1.19.30). And of course, the audiences of Terence and of Virgil are themselves moved in their souls toward disharmony and injustice through imitating the disordered souls of Chaerea and Juno, with the result that we are left with corrupted imitators of corrupted imitators of corrupted examples. These levels of imitation that convict art of "photocopying" corruption can be demonstrated by means of a simple chart:

| Author | Exemplar | Imitator within the Art | Second Level of Corrupted Imitators |
|--------|----------|-------------------------|--------------------------------------|
| Terence | Jove | Chaerea | applauding audience |
| Virgil | Minerva | Juno | Augustine, applauding audience |

Augustine's criticism of the imitative power of art occurs again in book 3 of the *Confessions*, wherein he states, in speaking of his student days in Carthage between ages sixteen and eighteen, "I developed a passion for stage plays, with the mirror [*imago*] they held up to my own miseries and the fuel they poured on my flame" (3.2.2). What was the subject of these plays? Apparently the young Augustine was particularly pleased with plays that featured love lost: "In those days when I went to the theatres I was glad with lovers when they sinfully enjoyed each other—although the whole thing was merely fictitious and part of a stage play—and when they lost each other I was sad for them" (3.2.3). He speaks repeatedly of the *miseria* of the characters of the plays that draws forth the *misercordia* of the audience; he says that the performances moved the audience to tears when they were well done, and he even refers to them as *tragica* (3.2.2). This imitative power of the theatre is particularly a problem because it is such a strong power:

> How is it that a man wants to be made sad by the sight of tragic sufferings that he could not bear in his own person? Yet the spectator does want to feel sorrow, and it is actually his feeling of sorrow that he enjoys. . . . The spectator is not moved to aid the sufferer but merely to be sorry for him; and the more the author of these fictions makes the audience grieve, the better they like him. If the tragic sorrows of the characters— whether historical or entirely fictitious—be so poorly represented that the spectator is not moved to tears, he leaves the theatre unsatisfied and full of complaints; if he is moved to tears, he stays to the end, fascinated and reveling in it. . . . In my wretchedness I loved to be made sad and sought for things to be sad about: and in the misery of others—though fictitious and only on the stage—the more my tears were set to flowing, the more pleasure did I get from the drama and the more powerfully did it hold me. (3.2.2, 4)

Plato, however, had already emphasized the power of imitative art in the *Republic*, and indeed, he thinks of this as precisely "the greatest accusation against imitation":

> When even the best of us hear Homer or any other of the tragic poets imitating one of the heroes in mourning and making quite an extended speech with lamentation, or, if you like, singing and beating his breast, you know that we enjoy it and that we give ourselves over to following the imitation; suffering along with the hero in all seriousness, we praise as a good poet this man who most puts us in this state.[13]

A second way in which Augustine's criticism of art in *Confessions*, book 1 echoes the *Republic* is that the lust of Jove and the anger of Juno that he depicts through the words of Terence and Virgil correspond to the two lower parts of the soul in Plato's famous tri-partition of soul. In book 4 of the *Republic*, Socrates first distinguishes the soul's rational and irrational parts. He then divides the irrational part into a desiring part and a spirited, or thymotic, part. The desiring part includes all irrational desires, but sexual desire, or lust, is one of the strongest of such desires. The spirited part seeks honor and glory, but if denied honor or glory it becomes angry or vengeful against those who have denied it honor or glory. When all three parts of the soul are working in proper harmony, the soul is said to the just, but if—as seems almost always to be the case—the parts clash and fight among themselves, the soul is said to be unjust. Of course, in the *Republic*, the principal conceit is that the interlocutors will study the soul by studying its reflection in the three parts of the city. Thus, in book 2 of the *Republic*, Socrates and Glaucon construct, in speech, a feverish city that is smitten by insatiable desires for sensorial pleasures; the inhabitants of such a feverish city are dominated by the desiring parts of their souls. In order to defend such a city, though, guardians will be needed who are driven by spiritedness rather than mere desire. Fortunately, they seek honor rather than pleasure; unfortunately, they tend to become ambitious and then angry if their ambition is frustrated. Honor comes from others, and thus, it would seem that Plato suggests that spiritedness is the major impetus behind political life. Echoing Plato, then, Augustine selects these two stories from Terence and Virgil because they correspond well to the two parts of irrational soul.

This pairing of stories with parts of the irrational soul gives rise to numerous parallel "couplets," as it were, in the *Confessions*. The first couplet already has been mentioned: the couplet of Jove and Juno corresponds to the couplet of desire and spiritedness. This couplet in turn gives rise to others: as Jove is to Juno and desire is to spiritedness, so is Chaerea to the child Augustine, for both Chaerea and the child Augustine are corrupted by desire and spiritedness, respectively. Moreover, whereas the first story features painting, the second features poetry. The first is therefore visual; the second audible. The first is exemplified by a male deity; the second by a female. The corruption of desire is lust; the corruption of spirit is wrath. Whereas desire seeks to embrace another, spiritedness seeks to glory over others. The former usually gives rise to private, intimate relationships; the latter to political ones.

We can expand this list of couplets by considering the young Augustine's experience with the Carthaginian theatre described in *Confessions*, book 3. There, as mentioned above, Augustine speaks of the ability of the imitative *miseria* of the actors to establish *misercordia* in the souls of the audience and refers to such theatre as "tragic" (3.2.2). But Augustine's description of the theatrical performances in Book 3 reminds one of what he had said about his childhood reading of the *Aeneid* in *Confessions*, book 1, where he speaks of how he was moved "to memorise the wanderings of Aeneas" and "to weep for the death of Dido" (1.8.20), as well as of how he came to know that "the Wooden Horse with its armed men, and Troy on fire, and Creusa's Ghost, were sheer delight" (1.8.22).[14] In both books 1 and 3, then, Augustine, first as a child and then as a young man, is moved by the theme of great lovers who are separated from each other, especially by death; since he calls such themes "tragic" in book 3, it would seem that he may well understand the *Aeneid* as tragic, also. If this is so, then it would seem that we can describe the twin Terence-Virgil passages of book 1 with yet another 'couplet': Terence's work is clearly comedic, ending as it does with "lovers" marrying; Virgil's must be tragic, featuring the theme of lovers parting, as in the suicide of Dido and the words of Creusa's ghost. In this, too, of course, Augustine is following the pattern of the *Republic*, for Socrates clearly calls Homer a poet of tragedy in book 10 (597e, 598d–e, 605c–d) and distinguishes tragedy's corrosive effects from those of comedy; comedy would thus seem to correspond more to the corruption of the desiring part of the soul, and tragedy more to spiritedness.

We find another important expansion of the list of couplets that correspond to aspects of the two irrational parts of the Platonic soul when we consider a passage in *Confessions*, book 4. At the center of this book, Augustine turns from addressing God directly to addressing his own soul directly. After telling his soul to turn from the transient world of sensation to the eternal world of God, for reasons that are not

immediately apparent he suddenly begins to tell his readers about a work he composed when he was twenty-six years old, the *De pulchro et apto*. We learn, ironically,
that the books that made up this work have been lost—they treated transient beauty
and were themselves transient. Augustine does not even remember whether there
were two books or three in that lost work. He does, however, remember something
of the contents of his book *On the Beautiful and the Fitting*:

> Loving the peace I saw in virtue and hating the discord in vice, I noted the unity of
> the one and the dividedness of the other; and it seemed to me that in the unity lay the
> rational mind and the nature of truth and the supreme Good: but in the dividedness I
> thought I saw some substance of irrational life, and the nature of a supreme Evil. This
> Evil I saw not only as substance but even as life: and yet, poor wretch, I held that it was
> not from You, my God, from whom all things are. I called the first a Monad seeing it
> as a mind without sex, and the other I called a Dyad—the anger I saw in deeds of vio-
> lence, the lust I saw in deeds of impurity ("iram in facinoribus, libidinem in flagitiis";
> 4.15.24).[15]

Of particular interest in this passage are Augustine's use of the words *Monad* and
*Dyad*. O'Donnell provides a list of three African Latin authors—Favonius Eulogius,
Macrobius, and Martianus Capella—who were writing about the Monad and the
Dyad around the same time as Augustine, or soon after him.[16] Augustine actually
taught Eulogius at Carthage, around or during the time he was writing *De pulchro
et apto*.[17] These three Africans, however, associate the Monad with Jupiter and the
Dyad with Juno;[18] Augustine does not mention Jupiter and Juno in speaking of
the Monad and the Dyad in this passage from *Confessions*, book 4 describing *De
pulchro et apto*, but in the Terence-Virgil twin passages in book 1 of the *Confessions*,
he associated Jupiter with lust and Juno with anger. We are not surprised, then, that
he departs from the African authors, including Eulogius, here in *Confessions*, book 4,
associating *both* lust and anger with the Dyad. Indeed, they are the two parts of the
Dyad: "the anger I saw in deeds of violence, the lust I saw in deeds of impurity." The
"mind without sex" is how he described the Monad, he says, but unlike his fellow
Africans, he does not associate the lustful Jupiter (Jove) with such a mind![19]

Augustine's youthful analysis of the Monad and the Dyad, then, reflects the tripartite structure of the human soul of Plato's *Republic*. As already mentioned, in
book 4 of the *Republic*, Socrates begins his search for justice within the soul by
distinguishing between the rational and the irrational "parts," or *meroi*. He then
divides the irrational part into two subdivisions, the desiring part and the spirited,
or thymotic, part. It seems clear that the term *Monad* in the description of the *De
pulchro* refers to the rational part of the soul described in the *Republic*—the *logis-
tikon*—whereas the Dyad divides into the spirited and desiring parts, characterized
by Augustine as anger, or *ira*, and lust, or *libido*.[20]

But how does this expand the list of couplets reflected in the twin passages from
Terence and Virgil? Augustine says at the end of his summary of the contents of

*De pulchro* that the Dyad concerns two sorts of wrongdoings, which he refers to as "the anger I saw in deeds of violence [*iram in facinoribus*], the lust I saw in deeds of impurity [*libidinem in flagitiis*]." In the lines that follow the quotation given above regarding the contents of *De pulchro*, Augustine explains himself further. Whereas much of what he had written about in the *De pulchro* he now understands to be inadequate, he apparently still thinks the distinction between the *facinora* and the *flagitia*, which are the misdeeds of anger and lust, respectively, to be legitimate: "Just as we have sins against others [*facinora*] if our emotion, in which lies the impetus to act, is vicious and thrusts forward arrogantly and without measure, and damage to self [*flagitia*] if that affection of the soul when carnal desires rise is ungoverned: similarly errors and false opinions contaminate life if the rational soul itself is corrupted (4.15.25)."[21] However, Augustine has already discussed at greater length his distinction between *facinora* and *flagitia* earlier in the *Confessions*, where he explains that *flagitia*, the sins that arise from desire or *libido*, are sins against the commandment to love God, for God is the author of our nature and sexual sins are ultimately an affront against our own nature. The *facinora*, the sins that arise from rage, or *ira*, are sins against the commandment to love the neighbor, for they involve a desire to harm others through things like revenge.[22] But of course, this distinction corresponds completely to the Terence-Vergil twin passages of *Confessions*, book 1. Jove is guilty of *flagitia*, harming himself through *libido*, and Juno of *facinora*, seeking to harm Aeneas and all other Trojans in her desire for revenge. Those guilty of practicing *facinora* are, not surprisingly, especially harmful to politics, Augustine says: "In complete contempt of the existing order of society they go their own insolent way with private agreements or private feuds according to their personal likes or dislikes" (3.8.16).

Our complete list, then, of couplets corresponding to the lower two parts of the tripartite soul includes the following:

| **Desiring Part** | **Spirited Part** |
|---|---|
| Jove (or Jupiter) | Juno (or Hera) |
| Masculine | Feminine |
| Visual | Audible |
| Depicted by Terence | Described by Virgil |
| Chaerea is corrupted | The boy Augustine is corrupted |
| *Libido* (lust) | *Ira* (anger) |
| Comedy | Tragedy |
| *Flagitia* | *Flacinora* |
| Violation of love of God, author of nature | Violation of love of neighbor |
| Harmful to ourselves | Harmful to politics |

What we observe, then, in book 1 of the *Confessions* is a striking thematic parallel between the criticism of art Plato offers, especially in the early books of the

*Republic*, and the criticism of art Augustine offers, especially in the first books of the *Confessions*. Both authors emphasize the imitative power of art; both emphasize the ability of art to produce souls with their three parts disordered.[23]

## Reading *Confessions*, book 9 as a Response to *Confessions*, book 1

If it has been established that book 1 of the *Confessions* contains a Platonic criticism of art, and especially of the art of Terence and Virgil, we have two reasons to antici-pate that in book 9 of the *Confessions* Augustine might communicate to his readers something about reformed or "good" art. The first of these reasons concerns the mir-roring or chiastic structure of the *Confessions*.

It is not hard to notice that the first nine books of the *Confessions* go together to form a narrative unit depicting Augustine's life until the eve of his return to Africa.[24] If these nine books are isolated from the four that follow, it is clear that Augustine intends for us to see the first set of books as observing a carefully structured, reflec-tive pattern. At the center of the central book stands Augustine's move from Africa to Rome, so that the first four and a half books describe events that took place in Africa, and the last four and a half books describe events in Italy; also, book 5 begins with the encounter with the Manichean "bishop" Faustus and concludes with the Christian bishop Ambrose. It also becomes clear that the books before and after book 5 are to be paired with one another in a mirrored or reflective structure. Thus, books 4 and 6 go together, as do 3 and 7, 2 and 8, and 1 and 9.[25]

This mirrored pairing is based predominantly around the tripartite structure of the soul. In book 2, Augustine explains how the desiring part of his soul was over-powered by sexual longings; he in effect offers a retelling of Genesis 3, emphasizing the incident involving seizing forbidden fruit from the pear tree. The correspond-ing book is *Confessions*, book 8, which features the healing of Augustine's excessive sexual desire at the foot of another fruit tree, this one a fig tree. Similarly, in book 3, Augustine is attracted to philosophy through Cicero but falls into the ontological materialism of the Manicheans; in book 7, his intellectual quandaries are resolved by reading the Platonic books that show him how to overcome Manichean materialism. Having treated desire and reason, Augustine does not surprise us when he turns to spiritedness in books 4 and 6. Augustine's approach to political or social life in these two books is especially through the theme of friendship. Book 4 is dominated by the discussion of Augustine's unnamed friend from his hometown of Thagaste, who grows sick and dies; book 6 is dominated by stories about the small circle of friends who are present with him in Milan, and especially by stories about Alypius.[26]

If the books of the *Confessions* mirror each other according to a chiastic structure as has been suggested, then we would anticipate that somehow the contents of book 9 would have something to tell us about the contents of book 1. Indeed, since the art discussed in book 1 has been shown to be corruptive or bad, we would anticipate a discussion of healing art or good art in book 9. To be even more precise, since the second half of book 1 is about the bad art of Terence and Virgil, we would anticipate that perhaps the first half of book 9 might say something about the antidote to such art. We would anticipate that Augustine might say something about an art that purifies as opposed to an art that corrupts.

Our hopes are not disappointed. Augustine opens book 9 by explaining how and why he quit Milan and spent the fall of 386 and the subsequent early winter at Cassiciacum, returning to Milan for baptism at Easter 387. This first half of book 9 is dominated by a discussion of two forms of music: the psalms of David, especially Psalm 4, and the Ambrosian hymns of the Milanese church. The art of Cassiciacum and Milan is no longer the poetry of Terence and Virgil but a new, reformed music that moves Augustine not to lust or anger but to God. In speaking of his time at Cassiciacum, he exclaims, "What cries did I utter to You in those psalms and how was I inflamed toward You by them, and on fire to set them sounding through all the world" (9.4.8). Despite the illness he was experiencing in his lungs, he was chanting or singing them. He calls them "songs," or *cantica*, and says that they are being "sung" (*cantare*) through all the world. He gives an especially lengthy exegesis of Psalm 4 (the longest treatment of any literary work in *Confessions*, books 1–9), emphasizing how that psalm has inflamed his soul.[27]

After recounting the events of Cassiciacum, Augustine explains that he returned to Milan to prepare for baptism with Alypius and Adeodatus. At Milan, however, Ambrose has started the Christians singing, and not just the Psalms. Augustine was moved by the results: "I wept at the beauty of Your hymns and canticles, and was powerfully moved at the sweet sound of Your Church's singing. Those sounds flowed into my ears, and the truth streamed into my heart: so that my feeling of devotion overflowed, and the tears ran from my eyes, and I was happy in them" (9.6.14; cf. 9.7.16). He goes on to explain how Ambrose had introduced singing hymns into the Christian churches in Milan at the time of the crisis with Justina and the Arians (9.7.15), when the Christians of the city, including Monnica, had staged a sort of sit-in to prevent Christian basilicas from being turned over to the Arians. "It was at this time," he says, "that the practice was instituted of singing hymns and psalms after the manner of the Eastern churches. . . . The custom has been retained from that day to this and has been imitated by many, indeed in almost all congregations throughout the world" (9.7.15).

We can supplement Augustine's remarks on music as "good" art by considering some related texts in which he discusses music. In the *Confessions* themselves, in book 10, Augustine the mature bishop also reflects upon the nature of music. He says, however, that he is no longer certain whether music can be completely reformed. Sounding like Socrates in the *Republic*, he asserts, "I observe that all the varying emotions of my spirit have modes proper to them in voice and song, whereby, by some secret affinity, they are made more alive" (10.33.49); however, since audible music still clings to the world of sensation, its utility is ambiguous.

When he remembers the advantageous effect music had on him at the time of his conversion, as described in *Confessions*, book 9, Augustine the bishop is inclined to be indulgent toward it, but at other times he is tempted to be overly severe toward music—as Athanasius is said to have been (10.33.50). He concludes with a provisional endorsement of the practice of singing hymns in church, which Ambrose had brought to the Latin Church from the East, but he still thinks that it can become a temptation to sensuality and even sin. It is best, he thinks, if those singing or listening to music in church are focused more on the words—the rational element—in the songs and hymns rather than the sounds themselves.[28]

Augustine's lengthiest statement on music, though, is his work *De musica*. Shortly after his baptism and subsequent return to Africa, Augustine began an entire series of books on the liberal arts, intending, in the manner of *Republic*, book 7, to demonstrate how they could be used to turn the mind from the temporal and spatial toward the eternal and infinite. The most extensive surviving fruit of this plan is his *De musica*, consisting of six books dealing primarily with rhythm. Augustine says that this work was based on his experience with music in Milan, but that it was not actually written until 389, after he returned to Africa.[29] In a letter from 409, he seems to downplay the significance of the first five books, but he does still recommend a newly revised book 6.[30] At the beginning of that sixth book, he states the purpose of the entire effort: "We thought it ought to be undertaken so adolescents, or men of any age God has endowed with a good natural capacity, might with reason guiding be torn away, not quickly but gradually, from the fleshly senses and letters it is difficult for them not to stick to, and adhere with the love of unchangeable truth to one God and Master of all things."[31] In executing this purpose, the sixth book of *De musica* soon turns to numbers and virtues, with the result that the numbers of rhythm are correlated to the proportions that result in the same cardinal virtues discussed by Socrates in the *Republic*. Music, mathematics, and morals are ultimately all tied together through God.[32]

The example that Augustine uses to accomplish such a lofty task in *De musica*, book 6 is the first line of Ambrose's most famous hymn, *Deus creator omnium*. Augustine introduces this line at the beginning of book 6, asking his student about its syllables and scansion—its numbers.[33] By the conclusion of this book he asserts to his student that it was appropriate that they began with this line, because all numbers are based on the unity that is God, the creator of all things. The hymn's opening line thus "sounds with the harmony of number not only to the ears" but is also "most pleasing in truth" because all numbers have their origin in the creator, and numbers extend throughout creation. Augustine also says in the *De beata vita*, written from Cassiciacum just prior to his baptism at Milan, that Monnica had introduced *Deus creator omnium* into their country conversations.[34] He himself quotes eight lines from the hymn in *Confessions* 9.12.32, referring to them as "true verses," because he was comforted by the *Deus creator omnium* after Monnica's burial. The threads of Monnica, Ambrose, Milan, and music all seem to be linked in Augustine's memory through *Deus creator omnium*. Indeed, it seems to be *the* example of good or reformed art in Augustine's view—the proper antidote to the art of Terence and Virgil.[35]

## The Myth of Er; The Dream of Scipio; The Vision at Ostia

In addition to the reflective or chiastic structure of the *Confessions*, a second reason for anticipating that book 9 of this work might tell us something about reformed or salvific art concerns the final poetic narrative in the *Republic*, in which Plato addresses the question of art. As noted in the introduction, although Socrates severely criticized art in the early books of the *Republic*, he himself turns artist at the end of the book and gives Plato's readers an example of art put in the service of truth and justice rather than vulgar passions. Since Socrates concludes the *Republic* with the salutary, reformed art of the myth of Er, we now have a second reason to expect Augustine to speak of good art in book 9 of the *Confessions*. One does not recognize *clear* allusions to the myth of Er in Augustine's ninth book, however, but we remember that Plato's *Republic* received a Latin retelling in Cicero's book of the same name. Favonius Eulogius, mentioned above as a Carthaginian rhetor and student of Augustine, notes at the beginning of his commentary on Cicero's "Dream of Scipio" that Cicero's myth about Scipio is clearly meant to parallel Plato's myth about Er,[36] and it would seem that we *do* indeed find quite a number of allusions to "The Dream of Scipio in Augustine's ninth book.

In calling to mind briefly some of the features of Scipio's dream, we remember that Scipio falls into a deep sleep and ascends to the heavens, where he meets his deceased adoptive father, called there simply "Africanus." His father shows him the nine spheres of the universe and predicts his son's death when he is seven times eight—or fifty-six—years of age. In the heavens, Scipio also meets his biological father, Paullus, and asks him, "Why do I delay on the earth? Why don't I hasten to come here to you?"[37] Paullus tells him that indeed he should turn his attention from earth to heaven and view his work on earth as a relatively unimportant situation, but that he should still act nobly in the earthly political realm until the proper time for his transition to the heavens. Scipio also hears the most beautiful music in his dream; he is told that he does not hear it always because "Human ears, filled with this ringing, have become deaf to it. . . . Indeed this ringing from the very rapid revolution of the entire universe is so great that human ears cannot take it in."[38] This sound comes from the nine spheres, which constitute eight orbits that produce seven intervals of sound, or notes. Each of these three numbers is in some sense perfect, and eight times seven is said to be the key or "knot of almost everything."[39]

The parallels between Scipio's dream and an event at Ostia in that part of *Confessions*, book 9 that may be referred to as "Monnica's story" are unmistakable. Augustine says that only a few days before his mother died, he was with his mother when a strange experience occurred: "Rising as our love flamed upwards toward that Selfsame, we passed in review the various levels of bodily things, up to the heavens themselves, whence sun and moon and stars shine upon this earth. And higher still we soared, thinking in our minds and speaking and marveling at Your works" (9.10.24). Paralleling Scipio's question of Paullus, Monnica asks, "Son, for my own part I no longer find joy in anything in this world. What I am still to do here and why I am here I know not. . . . What then am I doing here?" (9.10.26; cf. 9.11.28). Augustine later tells us, as if it is for some reason important for us to know, that it was "on the ninth day of her illness, in the fifty-sixth year of her life" that Monnica died (9.11.28). But of course, fifty-six is seven times eight, and the number nine corresponds to the number of the spheres. With respect to Scipio's music of the spheres, Augustine and Monnica, immediately after their ecstasy at Ostia, speak of how their vision had shown them the possibility of a moment of supreme silence, in which all human tumult and dreams and images and visions grow silent, and the heavens themselves become silent, so that in a moment of silent understanding human beings should hear God's word speaking (9.10.25).[40] The music of the spheres from Scipio's dream thus becomes in the ecstasy of Augustine and Monnica the very word of God.

Even from this summary of the two texts, some rather clear parallels stand out: Among the most obvious are that Scipio and Monnica are both in some sense "Africans" and were both fifty-six when they died.[41] Each passage also includes a question about why the dreamer and the visionary are delayed on earth rather than rushing to heaven. They both also include the presence of a biological parent (Paullus and Monnica), and then each contains the important numbers seven, eight, and nine. Surely Augustine wants us to read this part of "Monnica's story," which has come to be known as "The Vision at Ostia,"[42] as a retelling of Cicero's "Dream of Scipio." In fact, Augustine probably knew in addition his student Eulogius's commentary on the dream as he was writing the *Confessions*, and perhaps also that of Macrobius.[43] If so, he would know that the numbers 7, 8, and 9 belong to the Pythagorean decade, and that each was thought to be perfect in some way, for 7 is prime, 8 is the first even cube (and sometimes associated with justice), and 9 is the first odd square (since 1 is not actually a number according to the ancient Pythagorean decade).[44] Most of all, of course, both Scipio's dream and the vision at Ostia—and for that matter Plato's myth of Er—all include a description of how the spheres appear to the eyes as well as to how they seem to the ears. They all thus allude to the liberal arts of both astronomy and music as somehow supreme in the process of the mind's ascent to the greatest truths.[45]

The differences between Scipio's dream and Monnica's vision are of course themselves significant. The most obvious difference is that Monnica's vision is *not* a dream—something that cannot be shared—but a vision that she shares with Augustine. If Augustine indeed knew the commentary of Eulogius and even that of Macrobius, he would have known that the reputed reason that Cicero changed his story from an account of a man returning from a funeral pyre to an account of a dream is that Plato's story was just not believable. And therefore we can surmise that one reason that Augustine retold the dream as a vision that he could share in is that Augustine can serve as an independent witness. The vision at Ostia, then, is that much *more* believable than Cicero's account. What is key for our thesis, though, is that just as the *Republic*s of Plato and Cicero each offer examples of reformed, salvific narratives at the end of their works, so does Augustine include such an example of a salvific narrative almost at the end of the unit of the *Confessions* that comprises books 1 through 9. Thus the "vision of Ostia" is a Christian retelling of those poetic narratives.

## The Politics of Juno and the Politics of Monnica

One final way to bring home the point about a destructive art that harms political life and a reformed art that sustains it is to consider Augustine's statement on the remarkable political life that Monnica practiced in Africa. In the first section of this essay, we argued that *Confessions*, book 1, by using the art of Terence and Virgil, presents Jupiter and Juno as an unharmonious pair whose souls are dominated by lustful desire and wrathful spiritedness, respectively. It was also suggested that, in accord with the teaching of Plato's *Republic*, spiritedness is at the root of politics or society because spiritedness seeks the glory and honor that can come only from others, and that, within the *Confessions*, Augustine discusses spiritedness in terms of smaller human relationships such as friendship. In this last section of this essay, we return to that dyad of distorted souls and suggest that Augustine himself concludes the first nine books of his *Confessions* by bringing to the attention of his readers a Christian pair who were tempted by but ultimately were able to avoid the unfortunate situation of Jupiter and Juno. Just as book 1 presents to the reader "art within art" in the stories from Terence and Virgil, book 9 presents its own "art within art," or "narrative within narrative" in the form of "Monnica's story." And just as in book 1 Juno practices a destructive form of politics, so in book 9 Monnica practices a constructive form.

In Monnica's narrative, the first thing we read regarding her husband, Patricius, is that he was, like Jove, unfaithful:

> When she [Monnica] reached the age for marriage, and was bestowed upon a husband, she served him as her lord. She used all her effort to win him to You, preaching You to him by her character, by which You made her beautiful to her husband, respected and loved by him and admirable in his sight. For she bore his acts of unfaithfulness quietly, and never had any jealous scene with her husband about them. She awaited Your mercy upon him, that he might grow chaste through faith in You. (9.9.19)

Thus, rather that becoming wrathful with Patricius for his infidelity—and thereby imitating Juno—Monnica responded patiently to her husband. Augustine goes on to explain that Patricius, though generous, was hot tempered. Nevertheless, through her continued and unyielding patience, Monnica was eventually able to appeal to his reason. Indeed, Augustine describes Monnica as though she were the anti-Juno, for instead of brooding on her disgrace and dishonor like Juno, Monnica had the ability to avoid anger in her own soul.

However, Monnica extended her ability to avoid becoming wrathful from herself to others through a prudent and effective political strategy. Not only did she make every attempt to calm her own temptations to wrath but she also worked to control the harmful effects of disproportionate anger through her interactions with her neighbors, becoming thereby a peacemaker:

> This great gift also, O my God, my Mercy, You gave to Your good servant, in whose womb You created me, that she showed herself, wherever possible, a peacemaker between people quarreling and minds at discord. For swelling and undigested discord often belches forth bitter words when in the venom of intimate conversation with a present friend hatred at its rawest is breathed out upon an absent enemy. But when my mother heard bitter things said by each of the other, she never said anything to either about the other save what would help to reconcile them. This might seem a small virtue, if I had not had the sorrow of seeing for myself so many people who—as if by some horrible wide-spreading infection of sin—not only tell angry people the things their enemies said in anger, but even add things that were never said at all. Whereas, on the contrary, ordinary humanity would seem to require not merely that we refrain from exciting or increasing wrath among men by evil speaking, but that we strive to extinguish wrath by kind speaking. (9.9.21)

This passages describes a Christian kind of politics, one that seeks to control and confine the temptation to excessive spiritedness. It seeks to deescalate feelings of dishonor and hatred in order to avoid their destructive effects. Monnica is thus the antidote to Juno, whose tendency was always to magnify anger into wrath. Monnica had, at least in Augustine's telling of it, every commonsensical reason to be angry with her lusty, unchaste, unfaithful husband. Rather than permit her feelings of disrespect to dominate her, however, she imitated Christ and endured wrongdoing with patience. She is Virgil's Juno reformed, and she was able, through mastery of anger, to reform her Jove. Moreover, unlike Juno, whose wrath spread from herself to others, Monnica used her social abilities to limit and even temper the spread of wrath.

This Christian politics of Monnica presumably transcends, in Augustine's eyes, even the rule of the philosopher in Plato's *Republic*. In describing Christian politics as transcending ancient political philosophy, though, Augustine preserves many of the latter's insights. In this essay we have tried to show how he repurposed some ideas of the *Republic* on art and politics so that the old was not lost while being lifted into the new. To be sure, we have consistently juxtaposed "bad" and "good" art according to whether art is harmful or beneficial to political society, and we have repeatedly suggested that there are echoes or parallels in Plato's *Republic* for treating art in this way. In closing, though, it is necessary to qualify such a stark juxtaposition. Augustine did not simply reject Virgil and Terence; indeed, oddly enough, he helped preserve their work by discussing it within his own. Such a situation is reminiscent of Plato's treatment of Homer in the *Republic*. Just as Plato did not simply reject Homer but attempted by the end of the dialogue to rehabilitate and repurpose his art, even so did Augustine not simply reject Virgil or Terence but repurposed their artistic impulses to new and higher ends. In his view, there is a truth in what the earlier thinkers had said, and such truth needs to be preserved in the new art that is the *Confessions*, even as the *Confessions* transcends it.

# Notes

1. Michael P. Foley has shown how Augustine's Cassiciacum dialogues reflect the *Republic*'s teaching on art in "The Quarrel Between Poetry and Philosophy in the Early Dialogues of St. Augustine," *Philosophy and Literature* 39, no. 1 (2015): 15–31.

2. Compare *Tusculans* 2.27 with *City of God* 2.14 and 8.13 (on the banishment of the poets) and *Tusculans* 1.20 with *City* 14.19 (on the tripartite soul).

3. Gerd Van Riel, "Augustine's Plato," in *Brill's Companion to the Reception of Plato in Antiquity*, ed. Harold Tarrant, Danielle A. Layne, Dirk Baltzly, and François Renaud (Leiden: Brill, 2018), 448–68, at 448, 449.

4. Van Riel, "Augustine's Plato," 455–59.

5. Justin A. Stover, *A New Work by Apuleius: The Lost Third Book of the* De Platone (Oxford: Oxford University Press, 2016), 68–69. It is most unfortunate that the manuscript Stover studies is missing its initial section; this means that its summary of the *Republic* begins only after the treatment of art and poetry in the third book.

6. Frederick Van Fleteren, "Plato, Platonism," in *Augustine through the Ages: An Encyclopedia*, ed. Allan D. Fitzgerald, OSA (Grand Rapids, MI: Eerdmans, 1999), 651. Regarding the general topic of this paragraph, see also Gerard O'Daly, *Augustine's* City of God*: A Reader's Guide* (Oxford: Clarendon Press, 1999), 255–60; G. Bardy, note to *Bibliothèque augustinienne*: Oeuvres de Saint Augustin 34 (Paris: Desclée de Brouwer, 1959), 593–94n51; Harald Hagendahl, *Augustine and the Latin Classics* (Göteborg: Almquist and Wiksell, 1967) 2:586–87; Aimé Solignac, SJ, "Doxographies et manuels dans la formation philosophique de Saint Augustin," *Recherches Augustiniennes et Patristiques* 1 (1958): 113–48; Pierre Courcelle, *Late Latin Writers and Their Greek Sources*, trans. Harry E. Wedeck (Cambridge, MA: Harvard University Press, 1969), 165–96.

7. One clue that the two passages (1.16.25–26 and 1.17.27) are to be read together is derived from their structural parallels. The first passage begins with "O torrent of established custom" ("Sed uae tibi, flumen moris humani"); the vocative is repeated in the middle of the second passage: "O torrent from hell" ("o flumen tartareum"). The second begins with "O my God" ("Sine me, deus meus"); the vocative is repeated within the passage: "O my true life, my God" ("o vera vita, deus meus"). The translation of the *Confessions* used throughout this essay will be that of F. J.

Sheed, 2nd ed., ed. Michael P. Foley (Indianapolis: Hackett, 2006). The Latin text used throughout will be that of the Corpus Christianorum Series Latina 27 by Lucas Verheijen, OSA (Turnhout: Brepols, 1981). Further references to the *Confessions* will be given in parentheses in the text itself.

8. Terence, *The Eunuch*, trans. John Barsby (Cambridge, MA: Harvard University Press, 2001), 583–91.

9. Augustine goes on to cite the passage in contexts where he is discussing politics, such as three times in *The City of God* (2.7–8, 4.26, and 18.13) and in Letter 91.4–5.

10. See also the treatment of this event in Augustine's education in Sabine MacCormack, *The Shadows of Poetry: Vergil in the Mind of Augustine* (Berkeley: University of California Press, 1998), 132–37.

11. Virgil, *Aeneid*, trans. Frank O. Copley, 2nd ed. (Indianapolis: Bobbs-Merrill, 1975), 1.8–11. Copley's translation of the *Aeneid* will be used throughout.

12. "Mihi recitanti acclamabatur prae multi coaetaneis et conlectoribus meis." Since acclaim comes from others and places one over others, Augustine appropriately puts the passage in the passive and uses the prefixes "co-" and "con-." James J. O'Donnell reports that this is the first use of the rare word *conlectoribus* in surviving literature, which would suggest that Augustine probably chose it carefully. O'Donnell, *Augustine: Confessions*, vol. 2, *Commentary on Books 1–7* (Oxford: Clarendon Press, 1992), 91.

13. Plato, *Republic*, trans. Allan Bloom, 2nd ed. (New York: Basic Books, 1991), 10:605c–d. Bloom's translation will be used throughout this essay.

14. On Augustine's use of the mournful in Virgil, consider Camille Bennett, "The Conversion of Vergil: The *Aeneid* in Augustine's *Confessions*," *Revue des études augustiniennes* 34 (1988): 47–69.

15. Working from this brief description of the contents of the lost work, a number of commentators during the twentieth century attempted to discern the philosophical influences on the book. A summary of these efforts is offered by Takeshi Katô, "Melodia interior: Sur le traité *De pulchro et apto*," *Revue des études augustiniennes* 12 (1966): 229–40. See also Solignac, "Doxographies et manuels," 129–37.

16. O'Donnell, *Confessions*, 2:257–58.

17. See Augustine, *De cura pro mortuis gerenda* ("On the care of the dead"), 13.

18. Favonius Eulogius, *Favonii Eulogii: Disputatio de Somnio Scipionis*, 6; ed. with French trans. by Roger Van Weddingen (Brussels: Peeters, 1957); Macrobius, *In Somnium Scipionis*, trans. William Harris Stahl (New York: Columbia University Press, 1952), 1.17.12–15; Martianus Capella, *The Marriage of Philology and Mercury*, 7:731–32, trans. William Harris Stahl and Richard Johnson, Martianus Capella and the Seven Liberal Arts (New York: Columbia University Press, 1977), 2:276–77.

19. Verheijen does list *sensu* as a variant for *sexu* in eight of the surviving manuscripts (p. 53). In other places, however, Augustine is quite clear that sexual differentiation does not extend to mind, except in a metaphorical sense; see, e.g., *De genesi ad litteram* 3.22.

20. Of course, the presence of the *Republic*'s teaching on the tripartite soul in the *Confessions*'s description of the contents of the *De pulchro* does not exclude the possibility of other influences on the *De pulchro* in addition. From Augustine's description, it seems rather obvious, for example, that Manichean ideas were also included in the *De pulchro*.

21. For all its merits, Sheed's translation here imports the phrases "against others" and "to self," presumably from *Confessions*, 3.8.15–16, where Augustine also refers to the *facinora* and the *flagitia*. Augustine also mentions this pair in *De doctrina Christiana* 3.10.14.

22. See *Confessions*, 3.8.15–16, which provides an entire overview of ethics in that it attempts to link the two charity commandments, the ten commandments, the distinction between *facinora* and *flagitia*, the distinction between what is right by nature and what is right by convention, and the tripartite division of soul—and all in a few hundred words.

23. It is not the intent of this essay to explain how Augustine learned of these aspects of the *Republic*, but we note that he composed the *De pulchro* prior to reading the *Libri platonicorum* in Milan in 386. This suggests that someone other than Plotinus or Porphyry was the link between the two. Perhaps this someone was Cicero, but, oddly, Cicero's *De republica* does not much discuss the tripartite soul, which is so crucial to Plato's *Republic*. Did Cicero treat it in those portions of his *De republica* that do not survive? Cicero does refer to the tripartition in a few other places: see especially *Tusculans* 1.10.20, 4.5.10; also *Academica* 2.124 (*Lucullus*). Cicero's reference to the tripartition at *Tusculans*, book 4 is intriguing because it states that the tripartition was also employed by Pythagoras, who may have been the first to use the term "Dyad." So perhaps Pythagoreans were Augustine's immediate source.

24. The *Confessions* were at least begun and probably finished in 397; the first nine books depict the years 354 to 387.

25. Michael P. Foley has published a useful chart depicting this mirroring or chiastic structure of the first nine books of the *Confessions* in "St. Augustine: *The Confessions*," in *Finding a Common Thread: Reading Great Texts from Homer to O'Connor*, ed. Robert C. Roberts, Scott H. Moore, and Donald D. Schmeltekopf (South Bend, Ind.: St. Augustine's Press, 2013), 81–97. See also William A. Stephany, "Thematic Structure in Augustine's *Confessions*," *Augustinian Studies* 20 (1989): 129–42; and Frederick Crosson, "Structure and Meaning in St. Augustine's *Confessions*," *Proceedings of the American Catholic Philosophical Association* 73 (1990): 86–97, as well as his "Book Five: The Disclosure of Hidden Providence," in *A Reader's Companion to Augustine's* Confessions, ed. Kim Paffenroth and Robert P. Kennedy (Louisville: Westminster John Knox, 2003), 73–84.

26. That Augustine uses friendship in books 4 and 6 as the basis for discussing what Plato had called *thumos* in the *Republic* is perhaps harder to grasp than that he pairs books 2 and 8 to discuss desire and books 3 and 7 to discuss reason. The matter is clarified by considering the *De vera religione*, a striking work that Augustine had composed in 391, prior to writing the *Confessions*. In the *De vera religione*, he treats each part of the tripartition in the order a Plato scholar might expect: desire, spiritedness, and then reason; there he also clarifies, as he does in the *Confessions*, how the three parts are distorted by the sins of sensuality, ambition, and curiosity, respectively, and links each of these sins to the three phrases of 1 John 2:16. (The order of the *Confessions* corresponds instead to the order of 1 John 2:16 itself: "lust of the flesh" or sensuality, the distortion of desire [book 2], "lust of the eyes" or curiosity, the distortion of reason [book 3], and then "pride of life" or ambition, the distortion of spiritedness [book 4].) Like the *Confessions*, the *De vera religione* treats ambition, or the lust for domination, in terms of family or friends rather than in terms of tyranny or the city as a whole. Indeed, in the *De vera religione*, Augustine refers in the section on spiritedness to "the foul and detestable vice of not loving a human being as a human being ought to be loved" (46.87) and to the man who "is not seriously upset by the death of anybody, because one who loves God with his whole being knows that he himself does not lose what God does not lose" (47.91). These phrases have clear correlates in the story of the death of the unnamed friend from Thagaste in *Confessions*, book 4. *De vera religione* is translated by Edmund Hill, OP in *On Christian Belief*, The Works of Saint Augustine, vol. 8 (Hyde Park, NY: New City Press, 2005).

27. Carl Johann Perl notes especially how the Alleluia or Jubilation in the Christian liturgy was an heir to the music of the synagogue and how this form of music especially moved Augustine to write about it in his *Ennarationes in psalmos*, especially Psalms 32, 94, and 56. See Perl, "Augustine and Music: On the Occasion of the 1600th Anniversary of the Saint," *Musical Quarterly* 41, no. 4 (1955): 498–500.

28. This remark perhaps provides a rationale for Augustine's lengthy exegesis of Psalm 4 in book 9.

29. *Retractions*, 1.6.

30. Letter 101.3.

31. *De musica*, trans. Robert Catesby Taliaferro, in Fathers of the Church, vol. 4 (Washington, DC: Catholic University of America Press, 1947), 6.1.

32. *De ordine* 2.14.41, written from Cassiciacum in late 386 or early 387, includes a description of the discipline of music similar to that of *De musica*.

33. Augustine repeats the exercise of scanning the first line of the hymn in *Confessions*, 11.17.35.

34. *De beata vita*, 35.

35. In addition to the provocative article on Augustine and music by Perl (see note 22), see Brian Brennan, "Augustine's *De musica*," *Vigiliae Christianae* 42, no. 3 (1988): 267–81; Nancy van Deusen, "Music, Rhythm," and "*Musica, De*," in *Augustine through the Ages*, 572–76; and MacCormack, *The Shadow of Poetry*, 59–63.

36. Favonius Eulogius, *Disputatio de Somnio Scipionis*, 1. Eulogius says that Cicero writes his story in the form of a dream because Plato's story of a man dying and returning from the netherworld was just too implausible! Macrobius makes the same point at the beginning of his own *Commentary* at 1.1.8–2.5.

37. Cicero, *Republic*, trans. David Fott (Ithaca: Cornell University Press, 2014), 6.18 (Z:15).

38. Cicero, *Republic*, (Z:19).

39. Cicero, *Republic*, 6.18 (Z:23).

40. In the important sixth book of *De musica*, Augustine also speaks of the importance of silence to music. Beginning with the sense in which unity extends through "earth," he moves through the unity that extends more purely through "water"; from water he moves through the unity of "the supreme circuit of the heavens." However, "Now all these things we've enumerated with the help of the carnal senses, and all things in them, can only receive and hold local numbers seemingly in a kind of rest, if temporal numbers, in motion, precede within and in silence" (6.17.58).

41. Augustine actually says that Monnica was "in her fifty-sixth year" when she died. In other words, she was fifty-five, but Augustine states her age in such a manner that he is able to use the number 56, which corresponds to the "knot" of Scipio's dream.

42. The scholarship on "The Vision of Ostia" is enormous but organized helpfully by O'Donnell, *Augustine* Confessions, vol. 3: *Commentary on Books 8–13* (Oxford: Oxford University Press, 2012), 3:122–37.

43. Since there are difficulties in dating the two commentaries, this cannot be stated with certitude.

44. See Favonius and especially Macrobius for more complete treatments of the Decade.

45. See Augustine's description of these two liberal arts in *De ordine*, 2.14.39–2.15.42.

Chapter Eight

# Truth, Lies, Deception, Esotericism

## The Case of St. Augustine

### Ryan K. Balot

Seneca was a hypocrite. Varro was a liar. Conquered by pride, Porphyry denied truths that he understood well. The classical philosophers disseminated lies and deceived ordinary citizens, largely out of cowardice, but also in order to create a specious civic unity and to further projects of imperial domination. It was for these reasons, among others, that Augustine lambasted their writings in the first ten books of *The City of God*. Augustine's denunciations of lying in works such as *Against Lying* and *On Lying* are well known; at the end of his career, in his *Retractationes* (2.26, 2.86), Augustine again reinforced his repudiation of lying. In *The City of God*, he explained the wider human context that made sense of these ideas. His chief point was that lies, deception, and falsehood significantly detract from human happiness: "Nor will the soul be truly happy, no matter how long its happiness may last, if, in order to be happy, it must be deceived" (10.31).[1] The implication is that human beings are unlikely ever to be happy, because of our inclination to resist the clear truth (10.31). Ignoring the truth is an inescapable human tendency because of our fallen condition.

It is this tendency that alone explains why those who think clearly, like Augustine, must expound and clarify their ideas at such length and, of course, honestly (2.1), and in a spirit of openness and candor (5.26).[2] Out of care for his fellow human beings (e.g., 1.9, 5.19), Augustine devoted the ground-clearing part of *The City of God*, books 1 through 10, to laying bare the deceptions of pagan statesmen and philosophers, to criticizing those deceptions as the work of demons, and to exposing the role of deception in furthering projects of self-destructive pride. In short, through emphasizing honesty and truthfulness, Augustine sought to subvert the entire classical Greek and Roman order founded on "civil religion," falsehoods, and deceit. That is why he began his long work by shining a light on the pervasiveness of such practices at Rome: "Away, then, with concealments and deceitful whitewashings! Let these things be examined openly" (3.14). We cannot help sympathizing with his attachment to investigating the truth and to speaking openly about it.

However, Arthur M. Melzer's recent examination of esoteric writing argues strikingly that Augustine supported the cause of esotericism and held complex and ambiguous views on this topic.[3] In making that argument, Melzer builds on Ernest L. Fortin's observation that Augustine endorsed concealment of the truth in highly circumscribed contexts; but unlike Fortin, Melzer fails to pay close enough attention to Augustine's strict denunciation of all lies of any sort. In Fortin's words, "Augustine denounces all lies, salutary or otherwise, as intrinsically evil and, following a precedent he alleges to have been set by Christ, admits only of indirect forms of concealment, such as omissions and brevity of speech."[4] More important, though, in *The City of God*, Augustine speaks clearly on truth, lies, deception, and esoteric communication in ways that his readers, or at least many political theorists, have not adequately appreciated.[5] In fact, Augustine's perspective on esotericism is much less complex than Melzer leads his readers to believe. Augustine aspired to create a culture of truth, honesty, inclusiveness, and understanding. It may be unusual to insist, at the beginning of an essay, that the topic is *less* complex than others have stated. Yet what is needed, however surprising it may sound, is an effort to reconstitute Augustine's position in all its clarity. Paradoxically, this effort will deepen, rather than undermine, Melzer's presentation of esotericism and the Leo Strauss–inspired narrative of European thought with which it is linked.[6]

Clarifying Augustine's position will reveal the inadequacies of this narrative specifically in relation to Christian interpretations of truth, lies, deception, and esotericism. It is useful to discuss the narrower topic of esoteric writing in the context of truth and lies altogether. Central to Augustine's purposes was the effort to overthrow what he viewed as the Roman regime of deception. He wanted to establish a new culture of respect for the truth—that is, the truth of Christianity. To be sure, regarding "truth," Augustine did not refer only, or even primarily, to those truths that can be grasped by unassisted human rationality, much less by science; he was referring to the revealed truth of a specific form of Christianity, which he understood both on the basis of scriptural revelation and human reason. It was against that background, as we will see, that he discussed the esoteric strategies of writers such as Varro, Plato, Apuleius, and Porphyry. Equally, it was in relation to truth and lies in general that he condemned the hypocrisy of figures such as the pontiff Scaevola, the Ciceronian character Balbus, and Seneca. The specifically Christian color of Augustine's understanding of the truth, however, did nothing to detract from one of his most important legacies in European thought and culture—namely, an unwavering dedication to the truth, altogether.

The evaluation, *pro* or *con*, so to speak, of esotericism depends upon the nature of esotericism itself. Any inquiry into esoteric communication is necessarily connected to certain traditional puzzles concerning lying, dishonesty, deception, concealment, and rhetorical persuasion. Is concealing the truth—for purposes of social tact or national defense or pedagogical enticement—equivalent to lying, and should it be ethically evaluated as such? Addressing this type of question will often enable us to sort out what is essential from what is inessential in the discussion of esotericism.

Most citizens of liberal democracies accept the necessity of secrecy, confidentiality, and privacy in a variety of contexts, including national security, medical records, and intimate or personal details. Few would deny that national security agencies should hide computer codes from public view; few would object to the practice of granting certain information a special, or "classified," status. In truth, there is a lively, and far from esoteric, public debate over the finer-grained questions of what should be classified and why, and over what we now call "freedom of information." Similarly, in the ordinary social world, few would reject the customs of social tact or diplomacy among friends, which often require contextual judgments about when and how to say what to whom. In pedagogical domains, finally, no liberal democrat would be outraged to learn that a celebrated cosmologist often recasts his complex, theory-laden account of the universe in such a way as to help students deepen their rudimentary understandings, even if he is aware that his pedagogical vocabulary will simplify and even distort the truth (as he grasps it).

An acceptance of necessary secrets, personal confidentiality, and pedagogical simplification is compatible with a generalized belief in equality, with revulsion at elitism, with an attraction to sincerity, and with a commitment to the basic norms of respect and honest cooperation that characterize liberal democratic society. Hence, what liberal democrats find objectionable is not "esotericism" in the wider sense (a sense to which Arthur Melzer, for example, often has recourse, when he refers to the "esotericism" of John Rawls, or when he broadens the concept to include what is normally considered to be nothing more than rhetoric, literary playfulness, or poetic allusion).[7] Instead, liberals are understandably hostile to the view that only members of a privileged and elite philosophical corps can or should understand the most profound truths about humanity and the world. The suggestion is that ordinary people are too stupid, undisciplined, or cowardly to face "truths" such as the nonexistence of God. It is worth noticing two points about this suggestion. First, finding the suggestion offensive is hardly incompatible with our willingness to employ thoughtful strategies of conveying meaning, and with our everyday awareness that a decent respect for others, not to mention political prudence, will sometimes require concealing certain truths, not "saying everything" to everyone at all times. Second, we can acknowledge the existence of the "offensive" kind of esotericism, in the past or the present, without affirming or endorsing it. We can still evaluate it in a critical or negative spirit.

Melzer is correct to characterize the contemporary outlook as follows: "The idea of esotericism would seem to systematically violate every cherished moral and intellectual ideal of our time"—through its promotion of practices such as elitism, secrecy, dishonesty, caution, obscurity, and the "effort to cloister knowledge."[8] Yet my contention is that this outlook is not limited to the contemporary world. Augustine, too, was offended by the pagan authors' elitist suggestions and devoted the better part of some of his most important political writings to showing them to be unpersuasive and destructive. While recognizing the existence of esotericism, he expressed great hostility to the elitism, contemptuous attitudes, pride, and hypocrisy that characterized the esoteric philosophical writings of classical antiquity. Like all Christians, Augustine held to an unwavering belief in basic human equality. This belief carried with it a transformative consequence: that the distinction between intellectually "elite" and "ordinary" individuals was far less significant than their spiritual and psychological similarities. This belief, needless to say, did nothing to deter Augustine from addressing others in a way that manifested care, sensitivity, and tact; in fact, it implied the necessity of doing so.[9]

Augustine's ideas are significant not only because of Christianity's long-term success as a world religion, both now and since the Roman era, but also because modern European political philosophy is "post-Christian" in the sense that many of its guiding themes and unquestioned presuppositions derive from, and are continuous with, the foundational beliefs of Christianity.[10] In addition, political theorists should never lose sight of not only Christianity's saliency in pre-modernity but also its unbroken persistence as a major presence right up to the present day. Christianity is a religion that bridges the divide between the premodern and modern worlds. Hence, the status of esotericism within Christianity has far-reaching consequences for our understanding of culturally prominent political and ethical ideals from antiquity to the present. Augustine's thought represents a turning point in the evaluation of deception and esotericism, on the one hand, and in the promotion of ideals of honesty, popular enlightenment, and equality, on the other. Once his line of thinking is fully laid bare, it will become clear that we have incorporated Augustinian ideals in our own political thought and life—in novel and distinctively modern, secular forms, to be sure, but also in ways that remain traceable to this formative stage in Christian thought.

## Rome, City of Lies

In Augustine's presentation, the philosophers' esoteric strategies were embedded in a much wider framework—one that merited particularly fine-grained excavation, because Augustine's larger target was the entire culture of elitism and dishonesty at Rome. He located philosophical deception within a careful psychological and political analysis of Roman society. This analysis led him to investigate the larger theological or metaphysical framework that made philosophical deception possible and even predictable. He introduced these questions phenomenologically, beginning with the appearances and contradictions of political life and religious ritual, and only then moving on to his interpretation of the underlying causes and meaning of deception at Rome. To Augustine, pagan Rome exhibited a deep-seated failure to respect the truth.

The Romans' self-justifying ideology of virtue served as an obvious preliminary target. In the early part of *The City of God*, Augustine examined the Romans' self-proclaimed virtues and compared their ideology with their military and political activities. In the course of their imperial ventures, as Augustine details at length, the Romans sacrificed their ideals of clemency, trustworthiness, and justice for the sake of expanding power without limit. Augustine criticized precisely the Romans whom Machiavelli admired. Poets such as Virgil, who presented the Romans as ready to "spare the humble and subdue the proud" (*City of God* 1.Pref.; *Aeneid* 6.853), were shown to be spreading obvious falsehoods: the Romans revealed themselves to be hypocrites every time they bloodied the altars and temples of other peoples (e.g., 1.6). Christians, by contrast, were courageous enough to undergo torture in order to confess the truth—that is, Christ—in Whom their goodness and happiness could be found (1.10). Christian martyrs were witnesses to the truth about the world and about themselves. No form of cowardice or hypocrisy (not to mention any attachment to worldly goods) could prevent them from bearing witness to their faith or abiding by its ideals.

The Romans may or may not have deceived foreign peoples through spreading their imperial propaganda. On the other hand, they were certainly parties to and victims of deception within the city itself. Augustine centered his critique on the Romans' religious deception and manipulation. Rome's statesmen used religious deception to exploit their fellow citizens and to further their own political goals. Augustine introduced this topic, however, not in a directly political way, but rather by focusing on the Roman gods themselves, who were exceptional, in his telling, for their disreputable and immoral demands. To Augustine, these gods were nothing more than demons who had somehow deceived, and thereby corrupted, Rome's statesmen. The consequence was that Romans lived lives characterized by absurd lies—lives that could never be called good, lives that could never be adequate to the human capacity to flourish. According to Augustine, human flourishing requires living in the truth. Hence, Rome could never constitute the good society, because the good society is one in which lies are unnecessary and suspect.

On Augustine's showing, the Romans were, at best, confused about the gods' role in their lives. They were somehow ignorant of their gods' identities, intentions, and capacities. The Romans worshiped their gods in order to guarantee earthly security and prosperity, but the gods were too weak to provide these things (*City of God* 2.17, 3.7, 3.9, 3.11, etc.). Despite appearances, the gods did not instruct the Romans in living flourishing human lives (2.4, 2.6, 2.14, 2.24, etc.). Instead, they demanded expensive theatrical performances and civic rites that brought shame on the city (2.13). The Romans' gods were actually parasites rather than benefactors, corrupting examples rather than exemplars (cf. 2.25). This inner corruption, according to Augustine, made the city susceptible to eventual failure (e.g., 1.33, 1.36; cf. by contrast 5.15), since the Romans imitated shameless, lustful, self-indulgent gods (2.7, 2.25). To drive home this point, Augustine gave a memorable example: the Romans carried out sacred rites to the goddess Cybele, the "Great Mother," that offended against decency by demanding that eunuchs disgrace the city's public and religious spaces. Absurdly enough, the Great Mother was supposed to add to Rome's strength by castrating her men, as Augustine remarked in astonishment (7.26, cf. 2.4–5, 7.24).

The Romans' gods were disreputable, immoral, and weak. As Augustine pointed out, for example, the Romans' entire cultural system was degraded to such an extent that the gods themselves were happy to be insulted in the theater (2.9–10). He expressed outrage at the idea that the defamation of the gods could be defended by the argument that these theatrical stories were nothing more than fables or false inventions. This defense of this practice was even worse than the practice itself. Hence, he replied with an adamant rejection of lying about the goodness of God: "When some opprobrium is hurled at a good and beneficent governor of the fatherland, is this not unworthy in proportion as it is remote from the truth and foreign to the true facts of his life? What punishments will suffice, then, when such wicked and manifest injury is done to a god?" (2.10; cf. 4.27). Augustine's critique of Roman religion was closely linked to his absolute respect for and attachment to the truth.[11]

It was precisely with respect to the gods' own character and motivations, in fact, that Augustine shifted the ground of his critique of deception to a different and more expansive level. Why would the gods themselves tolerate being ridiculed in the Roman theater by human beings whose duty was to worship them? And why didn't the Romans grasp the absurdity of their own religious practices, which conflicted in obvious ways with their pursuit of virtue? How, in other words, could the Romans have been unaware of these contradictions between their commitments to virtue, their desires for worldly success, and their loathsome religious practices? Why did the Romans worship such gods as these, if they offered so few benefits, if they brought shame on the city, and if their worship required the expenditure of so many resources (cf. 2.11)?

What the Romans should have known, according to Augustine, is *not* that their gods were nonexistent. Contrary to our initial impressions, perhaps, Augustine does not say that the Roman gods were figments of the pagan imagination. Rather, he held that the pagan gods were actually harmful demons (1.31). He develops and deepens his case, over the course of the first five books of *The City of God*, that even the most powerful Romans at the city's height were nothing more than the dupes of evil demons who manipulated their activities for the sake of their own self-aggrandizement and malicious delight (2.4, 2.22), and for the sake of enjoying company in their eventual punishment (2.10). The demons' successful deception of humanity is compatible with their incapacity to bring about anything else in the world, at least directly, including the material success for which they were worshiped in the first place (2.23, 2.29, 2.7, etc.). Their chief power lay in preventing the Romans from grasping "the immutable and eternal truth" (6.4)—a reference point that reappears persistently throughout Augustine's condemnation of Roman religion.

Strikingly, though, Augustine acknowledged that the Romans' gods, or rather these demons, grasped the universally recognized importance of virtues such as honesty and chastity (2.26). It was precisely for that reason that they, in their cunning, practiced their own form of esotericism. While cultivating shameful and pernicious behavior among most citizens, they taught the honorable few to respect probity through an array of secret teachings: "The secret teaching is intended to ensnare honest men, who are scarce, and the public exhibition of wickedness to keep the many, who are wholly base, from improvement" (2.26). The evil gods (or demons) practiced a form of "pedagogical esotericism," to refashion Melzer's phrase, that was designed to further the corruption of the city by deceiving even the best individuals and keeping them out of sight, thereby diverting them from their proper roles as leaders and ethical examples. Where would this type of activity happen? "Where," Augustine asks, "save in the dwelling-place of lies?"—that is, the temples of the pagan gods (2.26; cf. 2.27).

Understanding the theological foundations of deception, lies, and esoteric teaching enables us to return to politics, because Augustine's theological views had important implications for his analysis of Roman class relations. He observed a close connection between the city's traditional religion and the power dynamics that characterized relations among rich and poor. Contrary to Roman traditions of justice and civic virtue, he argues, the evidence of the Roman historians, above all, shows that even at the birth of the Roman Republic, the patricians "treated the common people as their slaves, and dealt with their lives and bodies after the fashion of the kings" (2.18, quoting Sallust's *Histories*, a work that is no longer extant; cf. 5.12). Religious deception played a prominent role in this hierarchical relationship.

To be specific, Augustine says, the ancient Romans believed many fabulous stories about the gods because their allegedly prudent leaders worked hard to deceive them (4.32). The Romans' political leaders—and the philosophers who, as we will see, conspired with them—wanted to "bind men more tightly, as it were, in civil society, so that they might likewise possess them as subjects" (4.32). They persuaded the people to believe obvious falsehoods through manipulating their religious sensibilities (4.32). For example, the Senate once calmed the angry people by bribing a certain Julius Proculus to pretend that the divine Romulus had appeared to him, which, combined with a solar eclipse, calmed the people (3.15). At another time, when the otherwise unknown Terentius had unearthed the secret notebooks of Numa Pompilius, the Roman Senate ordered those notebooks to be burned immediately, so as to obscure permanently the ideas on which Rome's religious institutions were founded (7.34). In the first case the Senate actively lied to the people, whereas in the second it concealed an obviously comprehensible truth in order to maintain its own grip on power. That distinction is worth keeping in mind as we proceed, though it is equally worth keeping in mind that the motivation in each case—that is, untrammeled exploitation—was the same. In deceiving their fellow citizens for their own gain, the city's leaders imitated the demons, who were intent on deception themselves (4.32). They were under the false and harmful impression that their own positions of dominance were possessions of great significance.

Augustine elaborated the parallels between demons and statesmen by tracing their deceptiveness to their efforts to dominate others. Imitating the demons themselves in both deception and imperialism, both inside and outside the city, Rome's manipulative leaders were the victims of their own aggressive passions (e.g., 5.12; cf. 3.10). This ethic extended to the city itself: ever bent on the conquest of its neighbors, Rome was itself conquered by its own lust for domination (*libido dominandi*, 1.Pref.). Hence, in thrall to these unwholesome lusts, the Romans failed to know themselves as cruel-hearted brigands or to see that unjust kingdoms closely resemble "bands of robbers" (4.4). Contrary to Cicero, Augustine held that Rome was not even a *res publica*, because a true commonwealth requires justice, and justice was never present in Rome (2.21). That is why Augustine could imagine a worshiper of Rome's gods explaining that the city's highest ideal is that the strong should rule the weak, and that Rome's provincial subjects should cater to their Roman overlords out of a sense of fear and craven humility (2.20). The lust to dominate, whether internally or externally, whether in the upper orders or in the lower classes, was given strength by a plague-ridden haze of religious deception and falsehood.

Augustine wanted to discredit the Romans in these ways, no doubt, but his chief purpose was to enable his followers to embrace God's truth. This purpose led him to discern admirable elements of pagan Rome alongside those he found objectionable. As an opening gambit, he had to undermine the *au courant*, celebratory interpretation of the Romans' imperial success. In order to do so, he reminded his readers of the biblical principle that God distributes kingdoms to good and bad rulers alike, so that his followers, "who are still no more advanced in mind than little children, may not value these gifts from Him as though they were something great" (4.33). Having defused any admiration for Rome's awe-inspiring greatness, Augustine was free to acknowledge that the Roman experience shed light on certain praiseworthy human qualities, and that his Christian followers might accordingly learn important lessons from contemplating the Romans. For all its limitations and deficiencies, in particular, the Roman experience showed that the human capacity to strive and even to transcend humanity's apparent limitations is wondrous and honorable. If the Romans could make such progress in human excellence when motivated only by a desire for earthly goods, Augustine asks, then how much further could Christians go if they were to base their aspirations on the acknowledgment that humanity's goodness lies in union with God (5.15–16, 5.18)? Everyone should now acknowledge, according to Augustine, that the Romans' success, such as it was, resulted from God's mysterious providence, which allowed the Romans to flourish materially in order to teach human beings that material things are neither good nor evil in themselves and should never be loved for their own sakes (1.8–9, 2.23). It is prudent, he says, to pay attention to this important truth about God's providence (2.23). Augustine's cardinal desire was that every reader of his book should understand such truths as these. He saw no reason to hide the truth. On the contrary, his book was designed to explain the truth to all who were open to listening, precisely in order to enable them to fulfill their vocations as human beings.

## The Christian Regime of Truth

In order to explain his vision of a new "regime of truth,"[12] Augustine suggests that the corrupt city will one day be replaced by another city, "a City founded not upon the plaudits of vanity, but on the judgment of truth" (2.18). If lies and manipulation enabled Rome's leaders to control the people, then this future city will have no need of deception: it will encompass a wide and strikingly inclusive diversity of people who strive to live in trust, friendship, and solidarity. This city will be one in which people of every age, race, and profession, and both men and women, will understand and cherish Christian ethical virtue (2.19). This heterogeneous group will know itself as a unity defined by solidarity and friendship, without any distinction or hierarchy, because all these diverse individuals exist in order to serve Christ (2.19). Christ's servants might be "kings or princes or judges, soldiers or provincials, rich men or poor, free or slaves, of whichever sex" (2.19). What is intriguing is that such an inclusive and robustly egalitarian ethos has come, first in theory and then eventually in practice, to displace Rome's sociopolitical hierarchies and, as a result, its internecine quarrels and "necessary" lies. Augustine imagines results that are as affirmative as they are novel. By contrast with the Romans, specifically, citizens of the Christian commonwealth would never experience shame or disgrace in their temples; rather, they would hear the scripture and receive moral instruction, which would be proclaimed openly, for all to see and hear (2.28). In the Christian City, "victory is truth" (2.29), and victory is open to all.

These ideas help us to grasp the Augustinian polarities between hierarchy, elitism, and injustice, on the one hand, and inclusiveness, respect, and equality, on the other. In concluding his critique of the Romans' religious deceptions and his attack on the lies and hypocrisy that supported Roman imperialism, Augustine might have asked: Why are so many lies necessary, if not to perpetrate injustice against ordinary people, or foreign peoples, who deserve better? Because they were possessed by demons, though, the dominating members of the Roman elite were as corrupted and destroyed as those plebeians whom they exploited—or even more so, since they were more deeply entrenched in the lies of Roman culture than anyone else, except perhaps the classical philosophers. On the other hand, it is particularly telling, for reasons that we will explore, that Augustine expressed respect for the sound moral compass of even the ordinary citizens of pagan Rome, who could at least approach the most important truths when they were not entirely misled by the educated classes (3.16).

Opponents might retort that an inclusive or thoroughgoing regime of truth, a full-scale culture of enlightenment, is impossible. To be more precise, philosophers from Plato to Seneca to Porphyry might have argued that, although disseminating the truth widely sounds attractive in theory, most human beings are incapable of grasping the highest truths. The inclusive, egalitarian City of God, imagined in its imperfect form on earth (not to mention its perfect form in heaven), is therefore impossible. As a result, it is necessary to conceal, to dissimulate, and even to lie in order to create a healthy and well-functioning social order. Philosophers who take this position do not necessarily embrace injustice, exploitation, or imperialism; they might simply want to promote political stability while also preserving a space for free philosophical thought, independent of custom or tradition. It is critical to grasp how Augustine would respond to such objections, since they are so closely linked to the classical philosophers' esotericism—a characteristic of their writing that he took for granted.

At a practical level, Augustine provided examples of honest and honorable Christian societies from recent history—namely, those governed by Christian emperors such as Constantine and Theodosius (5.24–26; cf. 5.19). The just ruler, Augustine says, uses his power without any self-aggrandizement, in order to disseminate Christian worship as widely as possible (5.24). That is why Augustine states so confidently that it is beneficial for good men to rule to the greatest extent, spreading worship of the true God (4.3). One of the benefits of a just regime is that philosophers like Augustine could disseminate the truth as widely as possible in their books, so that both educated and uneducated members of society could understand it.

Augustine's philosophical rather than practical response is that all human beings are equal, and they are equally capable of understanding the most important truths. Specifically, Augustine anticipated that a highly inclusive body of people would form the commonwealth of Christians. They would, as a Christian fellowship, strive to attain to virtue, that is, a rightly ordered love of God. The gates to this commonwealth are open to all, because all human beings were made in God's image (12.24; cf. 11.28). In that fundamental way, we are all equal. That equality persists even amidst the diversity of inessential or accidental characteristics such as social standing, gender, profession, and so on. As Augustine points out, God began to create humanity by focusing on a single man, Adam, "in order to show mankind how highly He prizes unity in a multitude" (12.23; cf. 12.22). The unity underlying our human diversity derives from humanity's shared reflection, by nature, of God's goodness. We can recognize in ourselves, Augustine argues, the trinitarian image of God (11.26). With regard to this vital point, Augustine says, we will not be troubled by any falsehoods or half-truths, because we know our trinitarian nature more clearly than we know anything else, such as what we might learn from our sensory impressions.

It stands to reason, on the basis of these considerations, that for Augustine the human community is not permanently divided into an admirable philosophical elite and a wretchedly non-philosophical class. Instead, as he goes on to explain, God arranged the world in such a way as to make the most important truths comprehensible to all human beings. In writing *The City of God*, Augustine saw himself as uprooting error and all opinions opposed to the truth (7.1); and he requested that those of superior intellect bear with his explanations patiently while he conducted his teaching of others (7.1). Augustine would never have denied the obvious point that some human beings are intellectually superior to others. Some ideas, such as the origins of evil, are highly abstract and difficult, and they are the appropriate objects of philosophical thought—explicable, if they are explicable, to ordinary people only by those with exceptional intellectual gifts. Other truths, however, the most important ones, can be understood by even the plainest of Christian men: "And even if the Christian who is ignorant of their [the Platonists'] writings does not use in disputation words which he has not learned . . . he nonetheless knows that it is from the one true and supremely good God that we receive the nature with which we are made in His image" (8.10). Special benefits, such as eternal life, are available for those who seek the truth in the right way, through the Christian faith—not those who are merely intelligent or philosophical (7.31). That is why Augustine explains, "For it is not he who knows what is good who is justly called a good man, but he who loves it" (11.28). For these reasons, in fact, Augustine constantly admonishes his readers to avoid the intellectual pride that had always tarnished the accomplishments of the classical philosophers.

Hence, although it remains true that philosophers may command an impressive knowledge of abstruse subjects, as Augustine himself did, and although that knowledge is important and worth pursuing, Augustine argued vigorously that all of God's children can gain access to the most important truths.[13] With respect to the comprehension of truth, we cannot compare even Plato to a "prophet of truth, or to any apostle, or to any of Christ's martyrs, or to any Christian man" (2.14). Any Christian man! In criticizing Porphyry, Augustine similarly quips snidely, "It was difficult, forsooth, for so distinguished a philosopher to understand or firmly to refute the whole fellowship of demons, when any little old Christian woman would not hesitate to acknowledge their existence and heartily detest them!" (10.11). In light of this view of human rationality and the courage and clarity required to recognize the truth, it was reasonable for the just ruler (and for Christian philosophers) to disseminate the truth widely, because even the humblest Christians are capable of understanding the most important truths and holding fast to them despite social pressures or temptations.

This account of the citizen-subjects of the Christian regime of truth enables us to recognize, by contrast, the characteristic vice of those trained in classical philosophy.

Although the classical philosophers made strides in understanding the hidden facts of nature's order, God resisted their efforts when they began to display pride instead of humility (2.7). As Augustine later explains in detail, in fact, their telltale vice was pride, which Augustine interprets as "an appetite for a perverse kind of elevation" (14.13). The idea of a natural hierarchy of the few over the many is a falsehood motivated by the attempt to rationalize and rehabilitate a perverse desire for status. The source of pride, according to Augustine, is thinking of oneself as one's own ground or foundation, when in fact only God can be humanity's foundation (14.4). Acknowledging God as the ground of our existence is the key to appreciating our fundamental human equality. Before God, all human beings are equal in rank and dignity, even if they are separated by differences in natural ability. They are all equally members of Christ's fellowship, capable of appreciating the core elements of devotion to God.

To drive these points home, Augustine quotes John 8:44, a passage in which the evangelist calls the devil the "father of lies" (14.3). The devil is the primordial liar who lives according to himself, instead of appreciating God as the ground of his existence. His pride led him to reject the truth, so that "the lie he told was his own, and not God's" (14.3). Human beings who lie and live according to lies imitate the devil in this critical respect. They misunderstand the genuine vocation of humanity, which is to live according to God's intention in creating human beings: "falsehood consists in not living in the way for which he [the human being] was created" (14.4).

For all these reasons, the late Platonist Porphyry could never have joined the Christian republic of truth. Porphyry held even Christ in contempt because he had assumed mortal form out of humility, in order to sacrifice Himself and to purify humanity (10.25). As a result, he is Augustine's cardinal representative of the vicious pride of the classical philosophers. Porphyry distinguished sharply between the philosophical elite and the non-philosophical many, who required theurgy in order to make spiritual progress (10.28). His great mistake, in fact, was to think that only the few were talented and intelligent enough to reach God (10.29). Yet the fact is, Augustine says, that Christ taught even a fisherman to compose such miraculous and powerful lines as "In the beginning was the Word" (10.29). On the basis of the reasoning articulated throughout this section, then, Augustine disparaged Porphyry's grandiose self-conception and above all his denigration of plain people: "Your exalted wisdom rejects such lowly and abject things [i.e., Christ on the cross], and looks to higher regions. But He fulfills what the holy prophets truly foretold of Him: 'I will destroy the wisdom of the wise, and bring to naught the prudence of the prudent.' [quoting Is. 29:14]. He does not, however, destroy and bring to naught His own gift in them, but only what they arrogate to themselves, and do not attribute to Him" (10.28).

This important passage refines a common, and unfortunately blunt, idea found among many modern interpreters of Christianity's intellectual legacy. Specifically, the so-called humbling of the intellect sometimes attributed to Christianity is actually a humbling of intellectual *pride*, a "humbling" that preserves intact an appropriate and proportionate respect for intellectual gifts, as for all other gifts of God, without any special adulation or exaltation. On the other hand, as Christ came in humility, all human beings should acknowledge their equal dependency on God and forgo pride in developing and exercising their intellectual (and other) gifts. Augustine is suggesting, after all, that esoteric communication typically turns out to be a self-destructive strategy of the proud. Rather than responding to God's abundant gifts with humility and gratitude, and rather than appreciating humanity's fundamental equality before God, those who envision hierarchies between the philosophical elite and the untutored many ignore their own dependence on God, immerse themselves in delusion, and ultimately isolate themselves from the Christian fellowship of truth.

## Lying Classical Philosophers

In Augustine's presentation, the classical philosophers not only suffered from pride, but also proved to be hypocrites and cowards in practice. They may have spoken the truth as they understood it in private, but they would never have publicized their rejection of the traditional gods or the civil religion.[14] Augustine's analysis of the philosophers' hypocrisy takes different forms throughout *The City of God*, but at the center of his understanding is the idea that a Christian society is superior to any other precisely because it enables all human beings, whether sophisticated or humble, to pursue the truth sincerely, honestly, and openly.

In the early books of *The City of God*, Augustine presents Roman statesmen, pontiffs, and philosophers as allies in the project of deceiving the people for civic advantage (as they thought). Scaevola, probably as he appears in Varro's writings, is reported to have distinguished between the gods of the poets, those of the philosophers, and those of the statesmen (4.27).[15] Without commenting on the gods of the statesmen, Scaevola dismissed the first as shameful and found the second to be mostly "superfluous" but occasionally harmful. Particularly harmful, for example, was the idea that Hercules was not a god but an exceptional man who had made a transition from his human form. Also harmful was the philosophical tendency to criticize the city's images of the gods as embodied, on the grounds that the gods have no age or sex and no specific body. The pontiff, Augustine argued, wanted to prevent the dissemination of these ideas, precisely because he held them to be true—but injurious to the city's civil religion (4.27). In other words, he wanted ordinary citizens to immerse themselves unknowingly in a framework of religious lies. Augustine remarks: "What a wonderful religion! He who is weak may go to it for refuge when he is in need of deliverance, yet, when he seeks the truth by which he may be delivered, it is pronounced expedient for him to be cheated!" (4.27). Both Varro and the pontiff agree, he says, that ordinary citizens should be deceived in their religious beliefs (4.27).

Before turning to Varro in greater detail, Augustine commented on the hypocrisy and cowardice of Quintus Lucilius Balbus, a character in Cicero's *De natura deorum* (4.30). Augustine quotes Balbus, a Stoic, as decrying the popular understanding of the gods, according to which they are subject to passions such as grief and anger. Although Augustine praises Balbus for rejecting that popular myth, he finds it reprehensible that Balbus would never publicly proclaim his criticisms. More precisely, he says, Balbus was constrained, against his better judgment, to worship the traditional gods and their images in public (4.30).

Constrained by what, or in what sense? Did those constraints extenuate the gravity of his outward practices or somehow render Balbus less blameworthy? (Note that the question of possible extenuation is the only one raised by Augustine's account; there is no indication that Augustine could endorse or approve of Balbus' behavior, or even find it blameless.) According to Augustine, Balbus was afraid to disregard the city's customs (4.30). In that case, is Augustine charging Balbus with cowardice? If so, then we might counter that Balbus' fear was justified, on the grounds that he chose his only reasonable option in the circumstances. That possibility, however, is one that Augustine intends to rule out. In his presentation, Balbus was nothing more than a self-interested intellectual acrobat, a thinker who quixotically tried to show respect for his city's disgraceful traditions and to disentangle the Romans' ancestral religion from blatant superstition, and yet also to free himself, as an individual, so as to be able to live in the truth. But this project of balancing the claims of truth against those of the city's needs and traditions proved to be impossible, harmful to Balbus, and disrespectful of the truth. Truth is not a proper subject of negotiation; rather, it constitutes the basis of any practical deliberation and, accordingly, deserves the greatest respect, whatever the consequences.

Balbus seems to express his criticisms openly, at least in a private conversation; Augustine does not say that he wrote esoterically, but rather that through his behavior he knowingly encouraged others to live a lie. Because of his failure to respect the truth, in that sense, Balbus implicated himself in the very superstitions that he railed against in Cicero's dialogue:

> When he finds fault with these things [traditional images of the gods as having spouses, families, and so on] as superstitious, he implicates in that fault (*implicat ista culpa*) the ancestors who set up and worshipped such images; he implicates also himself (*implicat et ipsum*), for, although he tries with all his eloquence to extricate himself from their toils, he regarded it as necessary to worship these things (*necesse habebat ista venerari*). And the things which he, as a learned man, loudly proclaims in this treatise he would not dare to whisper in the popular assembly. (4.30)[16]

Because Balbus judged it crucial to worship superstitious gods, it was impossible for him to live with integrity. It is important, though, that Augustine objected not so much to Balbus as an individual, whatever his cowardice and lack of sincerity, as to the political context that constrained him, in some sense or other, to practice the city's religion without integrity and to obscure the truth that he understood.

Christianity improves on both the traditional individual and the traditional society by cultivating genuinely truthful heroes and a social climate favorable to the truth.

Augustine follows his discussion of Balbus by saying that, by contrast, and fortunately, through Christ's humility, through the preaching of the apostles, and through "the faith of the martyrs who have died for the truth and now live with the Truth," the superstitious gods that Balbus both criticized and worshiped have been eradicated (4.30). The martyrs appear again and again in books 6 through 10, and beyond, as Christian heroes who were more dedicated to the truth than to their own lives. As "martyrs," that is, "witnesses to the truth," the Christian heroes exemplified a courageous dedication to the faith and to the truth, one that enabled them to overcome extraordinary physical suffering (10.32). They were transitional figures whose courage and outspokenness were necessary in transforming the Roman culture of deception into the Christian regime of truth. Even so, as we have seen, Augustine's ideal society requires teachers who are encouraged to disseminate the truth freely and openly, rather than martyrs who are forced to sacrifice themselves in order to express the truth (8.27).

Augustine mounted a similar attack on Varro's hypocrisy and lack of integrity—an attack that brings out more clearly the Roman philosopher's esoteric strategies of communication, as well as his endorsement of deceptive myths, told, allegedly, for the sake of the city's welfare. Unquestionably, Augustine attributes esoteric purposes to Varro's lengthy tomes, inferring from the order of Varro's treatment of things human and things divine that his treatment of the divine was esoteric: he explained the divine as a human institution, without offering a full or honest account of the pre-human, pre-conventional nature of divinity (6.4). Hence, like Balbus, but perhaps more discreetly, Varro followed the traditional religion against his judgment (4.31) and was even "in thrall" to it (4.9). Despite his commendation of Rome's traditional religion, Varro understood the gods along naturalistic lines, as was common among non-Christian philosophers, and he criticized the Roman gods when he could do so with impunity (6.5). But at least on the surface of his texts, he encouraged ordinary people to continue to revere the traditional gods, for pragmatic social reasons. He also worshiped the people's gods and considered himself to be performing a significant service to the fatherland in encouraging the people to continue to practice their traditional religion, which he himself despised (6.2):

> I should be suspected of conjecture here had he himself, speaking of religious observances in another place, not plainly said that there are many truths which it is not useful for the common people to know, and, moreover, that there are many false views which it is expedient that the people should take to be true. This, he says, is why the Greeks held their initiations and mysteries in secret and behind closed doors. Here, beyond doubt, he discloses the whole policy of the supposedly wise men by whom cities and peoples are ruled. But malignant demons are wonderfully delighted by such deceit, for, by it, they possess deceivers and deceived alike. (4.31; cf. 6.2)

In this passage, Augustine indicates that Varro not only "discloses" the policy of the "wise and prudent men" who govern (here and at 4.32) but also approves of that policy. Yet elsewhere Varro goes even further in demanding that even the elite should be deceived by the gods, because, as he asserts, it is useful for states if their leaders and heroes believe (falsely, of course) that they are descended from the gods (3.4). The reason is that they would thereby carry out "great enterprises (*res magnas*) more boldly (*audacius*) and act more vehemently (*vehementius*)" (3.4). In context Augustine takes himself to be expounding Varro's understanding of successful imperial leadership. Wouldn't the leaders' false beliefs, though, inevitably compromise the quality or goodness of their courage, prudence, and other virtues? If so, then Varro was less concerned about their cultivation of virtue than about the instrumental use of brave citizens for the sake of the city's welfare, understood in a narrow, materialistic sense.

Although Augustine praises Varro for approaching the truth about God in his own philosophical reflections, he argues that this philosopher was pressured by custom and tradition into keeping his judgments hidden from public view. Varro knowingly conspired with the city's leaders to further traditional religious falsehoods, supposedly for the sake of the city's welfare. Augustine does not hold back from criticizing Varro as an individual on this score, even if the Roman cultural context was so resistant to the truth. In part, as we have seen, his criticism had teeth because Christianity could provide examples of men and women who stood up for the truth in the face of hatred and suffering—above all, the martyrs, who witnessed to the truth, no matter how lowly or despised a truth in the minds of the people (5.14). They embodied the love of truth, as opposed to the love of praise (5.14). They were models of "true godliness" for other, less celebrated Christians, who nonetheless despise human praise in their search for genuine virtue (5.20). At the same time, however, he sympathizes with Varro and even "grieves" (7.5) to think that such an erudite and intelligent man found himself in such deeply unfulfilling circumstances—although he also "grieves" over Varro's vanity in quixotically defending the Romans' traditional rites by offering naturalistic interpretations of them (7.18–7.19, cf. 7.22).

Augustine no doubt respected the classical philosophers for attempting to move beyond the absurd "vanities and lying follies" of popular religion (6.1). These philosophers typically expressed their criticisms of the people's rituals and beliefs quietly or obscurely (6.1). As we have seen, Varro communicated esoterically that he did not subscribe to the city's religion, but rather considered it a human invention; and if he had been able to refound the city, he says, he would have done so on more naturalistic lines. He showed outward respect to the traditional religion only because his own city was so old and conservative (6.4). Varro recognized that respecting the traditional religion was a lamentable necessity because of his own time and place, though, according to Augustine, Varro did believe that the natural theology that he himself endorsed was too difficult for ordinary citizens to grasp (6.6).[17]

In interpreting Varro as he does, Augustine illustrated one of his own chief quandaries. Although he insisted that philosophers should speak the truth, and that esoteric communication was cowardly by comparison with the self-sacrificial frankness of the martyrs (6.6; with respect to Apuleius: 8.19), he also wished to claim for Christianity the authority of pre-Christian philosophers, who manifested a dim awareness of the monotheism that Christianity had shown to be true (4.31). That is why, for all his criticisms of Varro and others, he understands Varro as rejecting the Romans' civil religion, on the grounds that it is just as worthy of criticism as the poets' myths (6.8, 6.9). Varro understood, and indicated through the order of the books he wrote, that the civil religion was a lie propagated by particular human beings (6.5; cf. 7.17). God himself led Varro to make such implicit arguments, even unknowing (4.31), precisely in order to prepare the ground for the eventual disclosure of religious truth—the truth of Christian monotheism.

By contrast with his moderately sympathetic treatment of Varro, Augustine reserved particular venom for Seneca's hypocrisy. In Augustine's presentation, Seneca is an outspoken critique of both poetic and civic religion, which he "hacks to pieces" (6.10). Seneca did not write esoterically. But he did contribute to the Roman culture of lies and deception. As a Roman senator, Augustine says, he felt obligated to worship the city's gods in public. He thereby robbed the people of his leadership and example, while teaching them through his lies and hypocrisy to persist in their degrading rituals:

> But though Seneca was, as it were, made free by philosophy, yet, because he was a distinguished senator of the Roman people, he nonetheless worshipped what he condemned, did what he deplored, and adored what he blamed. Philosophy, clearly, had taught him something great: not to be superstitious in the world, but to do in the temple what he certainly would not do in the theatre. It had taught him to imitate the part of an actor for the sake of the laws of cities and the customs of mankind. This was all the more damnable (*eo damnabilius*) in that he acted out his lying part in such a way that the people deemed him to be acting truthfully. An actor, at least, would rather amuse the people by playing than deceive them by cheating. (6.10)

To the charge of lacking integrity, then, Augustine added that of the overt deception of the people through highly public, hypocritical behavior. It is striking that even though the systemic conditions of Roman society put pressure on Seneca, Augustine still blames him personally for acting out a role that he knew to be both false and harmful. Augustine repudiates any philosophy that would license hypocrisy. He does not explicitly say why he blames Seneca so much more vehemently than Varro, but the answer appears to lie in Seneca's active promotion of falsehoods through his public behavior as a senator. Elsewhere, he seemingly indicts both the hypocrite and the people when quoting the well-known passage from the book of Job in which God says that He makes "the man who is a hypocrite to reign by reason of the people's wickedness" (5.19).

## Socrates, Plato, and the Platonists

Socrates and Plato, according to Augustine, adhered to the well-known practice of "concealing" their "knowledge or opinions," which makes it difficult to grasp their own genuine views (8.4). In Plato's dialogues, on the other hand, Augustine found ideas that were "favourable to the true religion," and he tended to ascribe them to Socrates or to Plato himself (8.4). Specifically, those ideas were that "the true God is the author of all things, the illuminator of truth, and the giver of happiness," an immaterial God who was the first cause of things *ex nihilo*. Thus Plato was remote from and hostile to philosophers who sought cosmological explanations in matter because of their enslavement to the body (8.5). Augustine's chief argument in books 8 and 9 is that Plato is the greatest predecessor of Christianity, which, conversely, is the culmination and fully adequate completion of Platonism (cf. especially 8.5, 8.9). As a result, he removes himself as far as possible from any implication that Socrates or Plato actively lied or deceived anyone, even though he would confess that he cannot grasp their ultimate teachings with regard to the human end.

Still, in light of the Academic turn to skepticism, Augustine was hardly in a position to argue that the later Platonists had taken an explicit and forthright stand in favor of the immaterial realities. The Skeptics rejected the dogmas of other philosophical systems, particularly Epicureanism and Stoicism, but they did not directly promote an "enlightened" belief in Platonic forms or other immaterial existents. How, then, are we to understand Augustine's interpretation of Plato and the Academic Skeptics? It turns out that most of his direct commentary on the Platonists' esotericism is found in other texts, such as his letters and his texts *De vera religione* ("On true religion") and *Contra Academicos* ("Against the Skeptics").[18]

Having paid particular attention to passages in these texts, Melzer offers the following quotation as "Augustine's view of esoteric writing": according to Augustine's Letter 1, "The pure stream of philosophy" should be "guided through shady and thorny thickets, for the possession of the few, rather than allowed to wander through open spaces where cattle [i.e., the 'common herd'] break through, and where it is impossible for it to be kept clear and pure. . . . I think that that method or art of concealing the truth is a useful invention."[19]

Arthur Melzer comments on this passage as follows: "To say it again, we may find this view offensive, immoral, and even dangerous, especially in the contemporary world. But precisely if we value truthfulness, we must not allow our own moral sentiments or the new imperatives of our democratic and technological age to obscure the plain fact that, among philosophers of the past, the legitimacy of salutary lying or concealment was very widely accepted."[20] In light of the preceding discussion, however, it is impossible to accept that Augustine endorsed the legitimacy of lying or that he found it salutary in any serious way. He stood for the creation of a culture of honesty and truthfulness. What, then, can we make of Augustine's statement about the Skeptics' concealment of the truth?

In the fuller context of Letter 1, Augustine is arguing that for the philosophers of the Skeptical Academy full transparency was inadvisable because the "vulgar herd"— that is, the materialist philosophers, above all, who believed that soul was a material thing—would immediately subject their supposedly pure views about immaterial souls to withering attack. They would, in turn, cause others to form the misguided impression that soul is material and therefore mortal. That result was so abhorrent, the Academic Skeptics judged, that their best option was to go on the offensive for a time. They attacked the materialists' "brutish" views through skeptical questioning, which prevented their impressionable audiences from falling into grave error. The Academic Skeptics thereby destroyed false doctrine without deterring anyone from pursuing the truth; at the same time, they did not proclaim their own views forthrightly. They adopted this strategy specifically in order to eradicate deep errors, because only such a more limited contribution (rather than a full dissemination of the truth) was possible at the time, given the rhetorical and philosophical context. As Augustine admits, however, they may have been unwittingly too successful in carrying out their project. In their eagerness to combat false, though zealously held, doctrines, they eventually convinced their audiences that the human mind is incapable of grasping the truth. Fortunately, he says, times have changed, and no philosophical sectarians are now disputatiously fighting over the truth. As a result, the Christian philosopher's task is to encourage his audience to believe in the human capacity to grasp the truth as it really is.

Three features of this discussion are notable for our purposes. First, Augustine's chief concern in this passage is to express admiration for the Platonists' attempt to extinguish errors of the gravest sort and to encourage his contemporaries to search for the truth. He is speaking throughout primarily of philosophers, though he does not specify any particular distinction between philosophers and non-philosophers. Second, Augustine conveys a strongly contextual sense of what is rhetorically appropriate and what is not. In certain times and places, attacking falsehood—which, in his view, is different from concealment and far different from active lying or deception—is the most appropriate option. It might at least help people to avoid error, an admittedly less ambitious goal than Augustine generally embraces. In the Christian era, however, such caution is not only unnecessary, but also dangerously counterproductive. It might lead readers of the Skeptics to adopt false judgments about God, the nature of the world, and the intelligibility of the most important truths. In either case, Augustine manifests great care for the spiritual well-being of these audiences. He holds that their spiritual well-being is best served by their understanding the truth, or, failing that, by avoiding the noxious errors derived from materialism.

Finally, given Augustine's devotion to the truth and his concern (rather than contempt) for all these audiences (except the misleading materialist philosophers, for whom he does express a certain disdain), it is hard to see why anyone in our own time would, as Melzer proposes, find these ideas offensive or unsettling. Not everything can be spoken to everyone, everywhere; sometimes, tact and sensitivity require those who care for others and embrace the truth to conceal their true beliefs, albeit without lying, until the time is right. No liberal finds that idea offensive. What's offensive is the idea that because of their natural deficiencies, plain citizens cannot in principle understand or accept the truth, and hence that they should be lied to for their own good. For modern and contemporary liberals, as for Augustine, that idea is deeply problematic. That is why, in his conclusion, Augustine contradicts that idea by encouraging philosophers to disseminate the truth and to teach their audiences to have faith in the truths that they understand.

Full consistency, all the same, would demand that Augustine should criticize the Platonists for refusing to be martyrs to the cause of truth (cf. 8.27), as he criticized Balbus and Varro. In *De vera religione*, in fact, he criticized Plato and Socrates for their lack of persuasiveness, for their incomplete efforts to institute ethical and political reform, and for their fearful unwillingness to dare to communicate to ordinary people the need to seek spiritual growth (1–7 ). The logic of his arguments suggests that the Academic Skeptics, like Cicero's Balbus, "negotiated" strategically with the truth, rather than suffering and sacrificing their own blood, like the Christian martyrs, in order to change the world permanently (5).

In Letter 1, Augustine referred to his previous work *Contra Academicos* ("Against the Academics"), and it is worth pursuing his criticisms there in order to deepen our grasp of his account of the later Academics. In *Contra Academicos*, too, at 3.38, Augustine refers to Arcesilaus decision to hide the ineffable Platonic doctrines from the view of other philosophers, in particular Zeno, who had begun to embrace the doctrine of the soul's mortality. Augustine argues that Arcesilaus took this decision out of a humane concern for others (3.38), which is reminiscent of Augustine's own concern for his contemporaries in Letter 1. Carneades completed the effort, he says, by extinguishing the plausibility of the Stoic doctrine entirely (*Contra Academicos*, 3.39). In the course of doing so, Carneades preserved a staunch and unqualified orientation toward the truth, by referring to whatever is "like the truth" as "probable." Augustine comments approvingly on Carneades' innovations. In fact, he credits Carneades with adjusting his representation of the truth appropriately in the circumstances, a feat that he could accomplish correctly only because of his understanding of the actual truth: "A man, indeed, can rightly 'approve' of a representation when he looks upon its exemplar" (3.40).[21] Despite his defense of the Academics' strategies, though, Augustine offered only a qualified endorsement of the Platonists' methods of spiritual and intellectual warfare. They manifested only a severely restricted ability to disseminate the truth for the welfare of humanity. At the same time, he appreciated their commitment to the truth and built upon their desire to spread the truth widely among human beings. Hence, he expressed relief when he mentioned the emergence of the brilliant truth-teller Plotinus, after the Stoics had, he says, been routed (3.41).

From all these reflections on the issue, Augustine concluded that skeptical attack, rather than frank expression of Platonic idealism, was useful for a restricted period; yet it was also, at best, a lamentable necessity in a particular time and place. It was not a permanent necessity, and hardly a practice worth admiring or embracing in all times and places. Would it have been better for Plato and his followers to have become martyrs to the truth, like the Christian martyrs? Augustine's answer seems to be yes, despite his discussion in Letter 1. His admiration for Plato had clear limits:

he faulted Socrates and Plato, and all the Platonists, for being unable to convince ordinary people that beauty and truth are immaterial entities, which must be comprehended by a purified mind and spirit (*De vera religione*, 3.3). He also faulted Plato for his fear of, and excessive sensitivity to, the misguided opinions of his contemporaries, who were antagonistic to his decision not to marry (*De vera religione*, 3.5). Above all, he argued that, if Socrates and Plato could be resurrected during Christian times and see the people worshipping in Christian churches, they would have to say, with regret: "All this is what we never dared to put across to the common herd, and we gave in to what they were accustomed to, instead of attempting to bring them across to the object of our faith and will" (*De vera religione*, 4.6).[22]

By contrast, through the emergence of Christianity, God brought it about that "one system of really true philosophy" could emerge and be announced openly (*Against the Academics*, 3.42). In fact, Augustine says, God's divine intellect, "out of a certain compassion for the masses," helped to lift humanity out of its material cage and its numerous errors: "By the precepts as well as deeds of that intellect souls have been awakened, and are able, without the strife of disputation, to return to themselves and see once again their fatherland" (*Against the Academics*, 3.42). As he says in *The City of God*, using vocabulary that echoes the language of this passage, God's excellent commandments are straightforward, not like "the noisy disputes of the philosophers" (2.19). In short, Augustine encouraged his readers to embrace fully the Christian era in which the truth could be proclaimed openly, because people were nowadays open to the possibility of immaterial realities, having been instructed by God through miracles and other divine gestures, and then by the work of forthright and honest Christian philosophers. In the Christian era, there was no question of concealing the truth for elitist or manipulative purposes; there were no noble lies; there was no lack of sincerity or authenticity. Unlike the disputatious philosophers of the past, ordinary Christians can grasp the immaterial realities that Plato outlined in only the dimmest and sketchiest way. In so doing they reveal all over again that distinctions between the few and the many might pertain to philosophical accomplishments, but not to an understanding of the truths that contribute most substantially to human flourishing.

## Conclusion: The Modern Appropriation of Augustine's Regime of Truth

Augustine rejected the pride, hypocrisy, and deceptiveness of both Roman statesman and classical philosophers. His case against those figures grew out of his belief that they were fundamentally similar to the demons, who deceived human beings for their own gratification. Both the philosophers and the demons were, in turn, similar to the devil, whose pride led him away from the true ground of his being—that is, God. Augustine substituted important and enduring ideas for those he found in the classical tradition: first, that truthfulness and honesty are necessary to good societies and good human lives; second, that a new regime of truth was possible because of the rise of Christianity; and, third, that the most important truths can be understood clearly by ordinary people. Contrary to the impression conveyed by modern students of esotericism, Augustine did not simply report on the esotericism of previous philosophers, much less embrace it as his own strategy. Instead, he observed it, interpreted it, condemned it, and tried to subvert the conditions that made it so misguidedly and destructively appealing.

Augustine's fundamental belief on the subject is that lying is always wrong, because it leads human beings away from the possibility of communion with God, who is Truth. Since that point is unequivocally clear, everything else—such as concealing the truth for fear of being misunderstood or posing obscure problems to students in order to exercise their minds—is a matter of detail and of judgment about particular, and perhaps regrettable, circumstances. Even in the case of the Platonists who helpfully turned to skepticism in their context, truth, honesty, and truthfulness provided Augustine's starting point and ending point. Augustine would never say that "noble lies" help to create good societies or that plain citizens cannot understand the truths that enable them to live flourishing lives. Any form of concealment (not to mention the even more extreme activity of lying) is both lamentable and immediately suspect; concealment should be remedied by further explanation or by the attempt to transform social circumstances in order to make popular dissemination of the truth both possible and effective. Even though Augustine acknowledges obvious differences among human beings with respect to their diverse intellectual gifts, those differences do not compromise the basic equality that pertains to all human beings by virtue of their status as creatures formed in the image of God.

These issues are not merely footnotes in a dusty, antiquarian research program. They affect not only how we see ourselves, but also how we do philosophy and history. This point becomes clear in light of Arthur Melzer's account of our contemporary ignorance of, and hostility toward, the very idea of esotericism. His "theory of error" proposes that the liberal democratic emphasis on transparency, honesty, sincerity, and, above all, equality makes contemporary scholars antagonistic toward the possibility that philosophers of the past were somehow deceptive, particularly if that deceptiveness implies a contemptuous attitude toward the majority of people of all times and places. To reinsert Augustine's ideas into the picture would not show that other authors, of other times and places, in general, did or did not read and write esoterically. That is an empirical question that still deserves fine-grained historical investigation. However, doing justice to Augustine's contribution will encourage us to recognize that our own attitudes, too, have deep, premodern, and remarkably persistent historical sources. One turning point in the history of debates over truth, lies, honesty, and deception is the political thought of Augustine, who provided an intellectual vocabulary for addressing these issues in a new and lasting way.

To grasp fully the persistence of these ideals in modernity would, of course, go well beyond the scope of this essay. Nonetheless, it is illuminating to hold in our minds the reflections of the prototypical modern exponent of such ideals, Immanuel Kant. Kant left a heavily freighted imprint on subsequent discussions and practices of honesty, publicity, and transparency. Kant's transcendental formula of public right adopts a characteristically adamant stance: "All actions affecting the rights of other human beings are wrong if their maxim is not compatible with their being made public."[23] Shortly after making this pronouncement, Kant vigorously defends honesty as, not only the best policy, but also as "better than any policy."[24] Kant held it to be an essential feature of just governance that philosophers should be allowed, or even invited, to speak publicly on the question of the "conditions under which public peace is possible."[25] Ideas or maxims that cannot be disseminated will inevitably fail the test of publicity and thereby show themselves to be unjust. Even more important, lying manifests a fundamental disrespect for others, a failure to appreciate their "end status" as human beings, because it treats them as instruments or (at most) as objects of paternalistic care, rather than as intrinsically dignified, mature, and autonomous rational agents. Above all, this Kantian spirit—along with, to be sure, the Rousseauian emphasis on sincerity or authenticity, and the egalitarian impulses of modernity more generally, which have their roots in figures such as Thomas Hobbes—tends to govern our own norms of political and philosophical communication.

A more concrete connection with Augustine emerges when we recall that Kant emphasizes the simplicity of the moral norms that result from his conception of autonomy. Gone, he says, are the abstruse calculations of prudent, strategic individuals trying to predict the future or to cultivate their own "happiness." Anyone can understand straightforward ideas such as "tell the truth" or "do not steal," the maxims that satisfy the categorical imperative. As Kant wrote in *Theory and Practice*, "The concept of duty in its complete purity is incomparably simpler, clearer and more natural and easily comprehensible to everyone than any motive derived from, combined with, or influenced by happiness, for motives involving happiness always require a great deal of resourcefulness and deliberation."[26] Yet the straightforwardness of these maxims hardly discredits them: on the contrary, they alone provide practical guidance for those striving to develop purity of will, which is the greatest perfection of a rational agent's highest faculty.

In emphasizing the plainness of moral maxims, to be sure, Kant goes further than Augustine. Despite stressing that moral understanding is available to all human beings, Augustine also acknowledges the mysteriousness of reality, including the truths unfolded by biblical revelation. Only such a sensibility could explain his persistent recourse to symbolic and allegorical interpretation. Even so, by subverting the classical understanding of truth as open only to the few, and by showing that even uneducated Christians could grasp the most important truths, Augustine provided the deep inspiration for the ideals of publicity, honesty, and truthfulness that we find in modern philosophers from Immanuel Kant to Bernard Williams. Christianity's persistence in modernity is, at least in these restricted and redefined ways, both striking and worthy of our endorsement and respect.

A final question, which is necessarily left unanswered by this discussion, is how, precisely, to understand the moral and political equality presupposed by the modern tradition of European political philosophy. In rejecting the theological framework that had once made human equality readily intelligible, modern political philosophers have created a substantial theoretical quandary for themselves. Somehow philosophers such as Hobbes, Locke, and Rousseau could preach the gospel of human equality while also themselves showing, through their intellectual ascendancy and influence, that in many ethically and politically salient ways human beings are *not* equal. That they did so through obscuring their own role, or even through obscuring the philosophical life as such, is one of the hallmarks of Leo Strauss's overarching narrative.[27] Equally, the stability, or lack thereof, of modernity's presumptively secular basis for our entrenched norms of equality has been recognized as a major question in the study of early modernity and beyond.[28]

Rousseau's shorter writings bring out these tensions in such a way as to isolate this major fault line and to indicate directions of future inquiry. Most vividly, in his reply ("Observations") to Stanislas Leszinski, the former king of Poland, Rousseau utilized precisely the Augustinian ideas that we have analyzed in order to shield his *First Discourse* from the charge of irreligiosity. Supposedly relying on his reading of the New Testament, Rousseau argued that Jesus avoided placing learned doctors and philosophers in charge of Christianity's proselytizing mission: "And in his instruction of his disciples, there is not a single learned or scientific word to be found, lest it be to indicate his contempt for everything of that kind."[29] The philosophers, he says, found "a Religion that preached humility unrewarding."[30] The Bible, according to Rousseau, is the only book a Christian needs; all by itself, it will encourage the love of God and the will to carry out his commands. "Never did virtue speak in such gentle terms; never did the deepest wisdom express itself with such energy and simplicity," Rousseau says. In short, the first Christians repudiated philosophical learning and abided by the simple yet powerful prescriptions of the Gospel: "That is how the Gospel should be practiced and preached, and how its first defenders made it triumph in all the Nations, *not in the manner of Aristotle, the Church Fathers used to say, but in the Fisherman's.*"[31]

To be sure, it seems likely that Rousseau himself has two audiences in mind.[32] He presents himself as a virtue-oriented champion of the plain citizen, who strives against the corrupting incursions of the sophistical *philosophes*; he also relentlessly, though obscurely perhaps, furthers the philosophical projects initiated by Hobbes, Spinoza, and Locke. However that question of interpretation may stand, his rhetorical posture benefited dramatically from the Christian discourses on truthfulness and simplicity that we have excavated in Augustine's *City of God*. Even if (as seems plausible) Rousseau himself maintained a critical distance from Christian doctrine, he recognized that Christianity's affirmation of the plain individual, and its critique of the pride, deceptiveness, and hypocrisy of the learned, constituted a highly useful rhetorical strategy for his own purposes. It has been our contention that Augustine represented as true the Christian ideals that Rousseau regarded as merely rhetorically useful. That difference can hardly be overestimated.

# Notes

1. Unless otherwise indicated, translations of *The City of God* are from R. W. Dyson, *Augustine. The City of God against the Pagans* (Cambridge: Cambridge University Press, 1998).

2. Note that Augustine criticizes those "foolish women" whom the apostle Paul targets when he says that they are always learning things but never arriving at "knowledge of the truth" (2.1).

3. Arthur M. Melzer, *Philosophy between the Lines: The Lost History of Esoteric Writing* (Chicago: University of Chicago Press, 2014).

4. Ernest Fortin, "Augustine," in *History of Political Philosophy*, 3rd ed., ed. Leo Strauss and Joseph Cropsey (Chicago: University of Chicago Press, 1987), 179–80; Fortin, "Saint Augustine and the Problem of Christian Rhetoric," *Augustinian Studies* 5 (1974): 85–100, at 97–98.

5. In addition to discussing esotericism in *The City of God*, Augustine also wrote three important homilies on the Gospel of John (16:12–13) that address Jesus's potentially troubling statement to his disciples that he has many things to tell them still, but they are unable to bear them now. Augustine's reflections are not central to my purpose in this paper, because they are arguably concerned with Manichaeism rather than classical Greek and Roman philosophy. I do, however, hope to provide an analysis of them in the future. For an excellent investigation of those sermons, see Guy G. Stroumsa, "Milk and Meat: Augustine and the End of Ancient Esotericism," *Schleier und Schwelle: Geheimnis und Öffentlichkeit*, ed. Aleida Assmann and Jan Assmann, 1:251–62 (Paderborn: Fink Verlag, 1997). Stroumsa's brief article on these sermons reaches conclusions that are strongly complementary to my own.

6. This essay builds on the illuminating treatment of Augustine, esotericism, and Leo Strauss provided by Douglas Kries: see Kries, "Augustine as Defender and Critic of Leo Strauss's Esotericism Thesis," *Proceedings of the American Catholic Philosophical Association* 83 (2009): 241–52. An interesting and related discussion of Augustine on mendacity and esotericism was published after I had completed work on this essay: see Jeremiah Russell and Michael Promisel, "Truth, Lies, and Concealment: St. Augustine on Mendacious Political Thought," *Review of Politics* 79 (2017): 451–73. Although Russell and Promisel address esotericism in Augustine and in the modern secondary literature, they are more concerned with distinguishing between truthful and misleading esoteric writing than with a close investigation of Augustine's rejection of the esotericism practiced by classical Greek and Roman philosophers. To the extent that they are relevant, however, their conclusions are mostly consistent with the conclusions of this essay.

7. See, for example, Melzer, *Philosophy between the Lines*, 135.

8. This list comes from Melzer, *Philosophy between the Lines*, 105–6.

9. I say the "necessity" of doing so, because through paying attention to our basic similarities, we develop sympathy with others and thereby appreciate more fully the desirability of treating others with honesty, respect, and tact. One should compare Fortin's comments on

Augustine's recognition of the importance of varying his rhetorical registers depending on his audience: Ernest L. Fortin, "Augustine and the Problem of Christian Rhetoric," *Augustinian Studies* 5 (1974), 85–100, at 95–96.

10. One useful explication of the meaning of "post-Christian" can be found in Stephen Salkever, "Aristotelian *Phronêsis*, the Discourse on Human Rights, and Contemporary Practice," *Polis* 33 (2016), 7–31. For helpful remarks on the "continuity thesis," the "secularization thesis," and the ameliorative critique of those theses offered by Hans Blumenberg, see Ernest L. Fortin, "Otherworldliness and Secularization in Early Christian Thought: A Note on Blumenberg," in *Human Rights, Virtue, and the Common Good: Untimely Meditations on Religion and Politics*, ed., J. Brian Benestad (Lanham, MD: Rowman and Littlefield, 1996), 135–43.

11. In light of these passages and many others, it is difficult to credit Ernest L. Fortin's statements that "even as he pokes fun at the pagan gods in general, Augustine is careful to avoid any direct assault on the last remnants of the old civil religion" or that he was led by a "profound attachment to Rome . . . to temper the radicalness of his own critique by couching it in terms that remain somewhat cautious." Ernest L. Fortin, "Augustine and Roman Civil Religion: Some Critical Reflections," in *Classical Christianity and the Political Order: Reflections on the Theologico-Political Problem*, ed. J. Brian Benestad (Lanham, MD: Rowman and Littlefield, 1996), 85–105, at 95, 97. Despite Fortin's welcome acknowledgment that Augustine was firmly condemnatory of lies of any sort, his effort to assimilate Augustine's treatment of Roman civil religion to that of writers such as Varro and others (cf. Fortin "Augustine and Roman Civil Religion," 97–98) is implausible.

12. Although the associations may be inescapable at this time, I do not mean to call to mind Foucault's use of this concept.

13. Cf. Strousma, "Milk and Meat," 251: in Christianity "the same redemption was offered to everyone."

14. Compare the slightly different treatment of this theme in *De vera religione* (composed ca. AD 390), trans. Edmund Hill, in Boniface Ramsey, *Augustine: On Christian Belief* (Hyde Park, NY: New City Press, 2005), at 1.1.

15. For a searching discussion of the relationship between the stances of Scaevola and Varro that also comments on earlier scholarship, see Fortin, "Augustine and Roman Civil Religion"; for an illuminating treatment of Augustine's appropriation of Varro and an attempt to see behind it, see P. Van Nuffelen, "Varro's *Divine Antiquities*: Roman Religion as an Image of Truth," *Classical Philology* 105 (2010), 162–88.

16. This translation is adapted from that of William M. Green, *Augustine: City of God* (Cambridge, MA: Harvard University Press, 1963), 2:15.

17. For a different account—one that interprets Augustine as more sympathetic to Varro—see Fortin, "Augustine and Roman Civil Religion," 92–93. According to Fortin, Varro's case illustrates "accurately the possibilities as well as the limits of the political activity of the philosopher" (93). My reading of Augustine shows that Augustine's criticisms are more decisive and "rejectionist" than Fortin's interpretation would suggest.

18. Compare the treatment of these texts found in Kries, "Augustine as Defender," 244–45.

19. See Melzer, *Philosophy between the Lines*, 123–24, citing part of Letter 1.3.

20. See Melzer, *Philosophy between the Lines*, 124.

21. This translation, along with subsequent translations of *Against the Academics*, is from John J. O'Meara, *St. Augustine: Against the Academics* (Westminster, MD: Newman Press, 1950).

22. This translation is from Edmund Hill's version of *De vera religione*, in Boniface Ramsey, *Augustine: On Christian Belief* (Hyde Park, NY: New City Press, 2005).

23. For a discussion of these topics in Kant and Plato, see Ryan K. Balot, "Politics, Philosophy, and Likelihood in Three Platonic Dialogues," in *Probabilities, Hypotheticals, and Counterfactuals in Ancient Greek Thought*, ed. Victoria Wohl (Cambridge: Cambridge University Press, 2014), 65–83. All translations of Kant in the following pages are from H. S. Riess, ed., *Kant: Political Writings*, trans. H. B. Nisbett (Cambridge: Cambridge University Press, 1970).

24. Kant, "On the Disagreement between Morals and Politics in Relation to Perpetual Peace," *Kant: Political Writings*, 116–25, at 116.

25. Kant, "Perpetual Peace: A Philosophic Sketch," *Kant: Political Writings*, 114–15.

26. Kant, "On the Relationship of Theory to Practice in Morality in General," *Kant: Political Writings*, 70.

27. A helpful treatment of Rousseau along these lines can be found in Clifford Orwin, "Rousseau's Socratism," *Journal of Politics* 60 (1998), 174–87.

28. See, most notably, Jeremy Waldron, *God, Locke, and Equality: Christian Foundations of Locke's Political Thought* (Cambridge: Cambridge University Press, 2002).

29. The translations of Rousseau in the following paragraph are from Jean-Jacques Rousseau, *Rousseau: The Discourses and Other Early Political Writings*, trans. Victor Gourevitch (Cambridge: Cambridge University Press, 1997), 41–44.

30. As a result, Rousseau adopts an ostentatiously Christian stance of hostility toward the ancient philosophical practice of esotericism, along with the pride that motivated it and the hypocrisy to which it inevitably led (cf. Rousseau's note on this discussion, at Rousseau, *Discourses*, 41–42).

31. Rousseau, *Discourses*, 44.

32. Orwin, "Rousseau's Socratism." This essay is dedicated to Dr. Laura Rabinowitz.

Chapter Nine

# Augustine's Ciceronian Response to the Ciceronian Patriot

## Veronica Roberts Ogle

### Reading Augustine as *Rhetor*

Reading Augustine's *City of God* is like walking into an auditorium where a skilled orator is passionately addressing a diverse crowd.[1] One finds oneself quite aware one is not the intended audience, but with the sense his message is still somehow relevant. At times, one is drawn in, seeing elements of one's own concerns in those of his audience and feeling his prose stir the heart. At others, one finds his arguments elusive and his rhetoric jarring. One wishes one could better understand their context in order to grasp his message more fully.

Because Augustine is a true rhetorician—a careful student of his audience's loves, longings, and very soul—it can be difficult to interpret his thought, particularly his political thought. It is not surprising, then, that there is much debate about what Augustine's political teaching is or whether he even has one. Some scholars, such as Ernest Fortin, Michael Foley, and Mary Keys, read Augustine to be developing the tradition begun by classical political philosophy.[2] Others, such as Herbert Deane, Reinhold Niebuhr, and R. A. Markus, read Augustine as breaking with this tradition, offering instead a proto-modern analysis of political life.[3] Finally, some, such as Peter Brown and John Milbank, find Augustine to be too pessimistic about politics to have formulated a political theory independent of his ecclesiology.[4]

Accordingly, with a view to understanding Augustine's political thought, I approach his *City of God* with the premise that Augustine's writings become more accessible when we pay as much attention to his audience as he did.[5] Though the

*City of God* masterfully addresses multiple audiences at the same time, here I focus on one: the virtuous Roman patriot.

Moreover, I study this patriot as a Ciceronian, not because Cicero was his only influence, but in recognition of the "extraordinary grip" that Cicero "had upon the imagination of posterity."[6] Even in Augustine's day, Cicero's writings remained influential, forming an integral part of Augustine's own education.[7] Yet, more than this, as Rome's preeminent philosopher-statesman, Cicero inspired Romans, even in the imperial age, to pursue the *beata vita* of noble citizenship.[8]

It is clear that Augustine recognizes those who pursue this life as serious and respectable interlocutors. In his exchange with Nectarius, an elderly patriot who had written regarding the prosecution of an anti-Christian mob, this respect is palpable.[9] In his reply, written only a year before he began *The City of God*, Augustine exclaims, "I do not find it odd but praiseworthy that your heart burns with love of your country even as your limbs grow colder with age. I also admit, not unwillingly but wholeheartedly, that you not only call to mind but also demonstrate through your life and morals that there is no boundary or limit to the good of caring for our country."[10] Although Augustine will persuade officials not to resort to capital punishment, he cannot ask them to drop the fines, he explains, because this would not contribute to the public good. Significantly, Augustine tells Nectarius to reflect on Cicero's *De re publica*, whence he "drank in that disposition of a most devoted citizen" in order to understand this decision. In this, Augustine highlights his own civic-mindedness as well as Cicero's importance in the formation of the patriotic imagination.

An important benefit of focusing on Augustine's engagement with the civic-minded in *The City of God* is that it allows us to interpret his stance toward Cicero's political vision more precisely. The question of Augustine's relationship to Cicero has been well studied in the literature.[11] Michael Foley has emphasized the strength of Cicero's influence on Augustine's early thought; others, such as Sabine MacCormack, have noted that Augustine began to distance himself from Cicero after this early period.[12] She writes that although Cicero's ideas about "human relations, the virtue, passions and emotions" remained throughout Augustine's writings, they were increasingly reshaped by Christianity.[13]

Nevertheless, although MacCormack is right that Christianity is more fundamental to Augustine's framework than the ideas he shares with Cicero, it remains to be seen precisely what Augustine thinks of Cicero's political vision by 410, and how this relates to the message he conveys to the civic-minded in *The City of God*.[14] As I will argue, Augustine's message to these readers is clear: although Cicero's patriotic vision has many merits, it is too bound up with glory. Glory, even what Cicero calls true glory, should not be relied on to bind citizens to the city. It has negative political effects and is not virtue's reward. It cannot make man happy.

It would be wrong, however, to conclude from this that Augustine blames Cicero for ignoring an alternative not yet revealed—what else was there for him to love other than glory?[15] As Pierre Manent has remarked, the aspiration for glory is a response to the "ontological constitution of humanity" which is to say, it is a response to our mortality.[16] In reality, Augustine's harsh treatment of Cicero is for the sake of his Ciceronian readers: he wants to impress on them that a new *beata vita* has been made manifest.[17] This intention, I argue, shapes Augustine's entire approach to Cicero in his text.

In categorizing Augustine's response to the Ciceronian, we face a decision. We can either say that Augustine breaks with Cicero's vision or that he fulfills it. As Manent has noted, the Christian synthesis can seem "to weaken or blur what is most proper, most sharp, most "interesting"" in the traditions it subsumes.[18] Thus, to someone like Nectarius, Augustine's adaptation of the Ciceronian vision could look like a denial of its fundamental character: it interferes with that sacrosanct relationship between citizen and *patria*. Augustine's challenge is to convince this reader that heart of Cicero's project is not his glorification of patriotic devotion *per se* but the aspiration behind it—the aspiration to present an effective and fulfilling motive for caring for the common good.

Indeed, by "purging and perfecting" Cicero's noble patriotic vision, Augustine sees himself as fulfilling the aspirations of the Ciceronian project.[19] For Augustine, this is more like fulfilling the dying wishes of an old friend than an act of betrayal. Cicero was an old friend, and when his *Hortensius* stirred up the love of truth in Augustine's young soul, it was not for this or that articulation of truth, but truth *itself*.[20] Building on Cicero's own anthropology, in which man must grow to understand the purpose of his natural inclinations, Augustine argues that these inclinations point beyond the purposes that Cicero could discover by his own lights.[21] The result is a new way of looking at political life that claims better to serve the goals for which the old was undertaken.

## Rome as *Patria*

Before we turn to Augustine, it is fitting to sketch out Cicero's political thought with a view to understanding the patriotic vision it cultivated. Although there is much worthy of note in his writings pertaining to civic education, here my intention is to draw on his corpus only insofar as it lends insight into our inquiry regarding Augustine. With this in mind, it is fitting to begin with *De re publica*, whence men like Nectarius drank in the disposition of a devoted citizen.

As Cicero explains in its preface, in writing *De re publica*, he strove to "remove all grounds for hesitation" that good men might have "about taking part in public affairs."[22] Indeed, our first encounter with Cicero in its extant pages finds him singing the praises of patriotism.[23] Without this virtue, he writes, the great Roman heroes would never have defended Rome against Carthage, nor would the great Cato have left the quiet life (*otium*). Patriotism is a truly vital civic virtue.

Moreover, Cicero argues, the desire "to make human life safer and richer by our thought and action" is natural.[24] Writing to an audience eager to be virtuous but attracted to the quiet life of contemplation, Cicero invokes nature's authority as an indication of the right (*honestum*). He, too, was attracted to the life of *otium*, he writes, and would have flourished in it more than most. Yet he could not help but "secure, at the cost of his own personal danger, a quiet life for all the rest."[25] Will his readers respond to the same call?

Cicero complements this rousing introduction with a conversation among the "most eminent and wise" Romans of a bygone age.[26] Willing to spend even their holidays making themselves useful to their *res publica*, Laelius and Scipio are patriotic models, not only to their young interlocutors, but also to their readers.[27] Considering them men "whose authority and reputation stand highest among learned men," Cicero makes his case for patriotism through them.[28]

Cicero teaches his fellow Romans that essentially, their primary duty is to preserve Rome in gratitude and filial piety (*pietas*).[29] Rome does not gratuitously give its citizens birth, education and leisure, he writes in the preface.[30] Rather, Rome expects "to appropriate to her own use the greater and most important part of our courage, our talents and our wisdom, leaving to us for our own private use only so much as may be left after her needs have been satisfied."[31] This expectation, moreover, is justified: the *civitas* is *the* necessary prerequisite for a good life, and Scipio spends much of the dialogue explaining why. After identifying the attributes of the Roman constitution that shaped its success, examining justice and the variety of constitutions, and discussing education and the qualities of a good citizen, Scipio concludes, "It is impossible to live well except in a good commonwealth, and nothing can produce greater happiness than a well-constituted state (city, *civitate*)."[32]

Yet, because little of these books remains for our study and a parallel argument runs through *De officiis*, it is fitting to divert our attention there.[33] In teaching his son why the happy life is the noble life, Cicero gives an account of human nature that, again, justifies patriotic duty. Nature, he writes, has implanted intelligible, harmonious, and beneficial inclinations in the human heart to propel man toward his fulfillment.[34] However, these inclinations must be attended to, properly interpreted, and rightly directed.

Listing man's natural appetites, Cicero starts with the inclination toward self-preservation and reproduction common to all living things; identifies the special affection for family, shared with some animals; and ends with the inclinations particular to man, for truth, independence, order, and propriety, for example.[35] The most noteworthy of these, indeed, the "deepest feeling in our nature," is the desire for society (*communitas*).[36]

The *civitas*, Cicero argues, is the rational response to these inclinations. It is the *locus* of their fulfillment. His argument is as follows: of all the things necessary for life, many, such as medicine, navigation, and agriculture, are produced by human labor.[37] Yet only through human cooperation do they become beneficial to all. The *civitas* is the greatest product of human ingenuity because it fosters this cooperation. By virtue of its institutions, laws and customs, the *civitas* cultivates a "humane spirit" in its citizens, allowing civilized life to form such that it becomes the forum for "giving and receiving" *par excellence*.[38] Through this "mutual exchange of commodities and conveniences," man's wants and needs are met in a way otherwise impossible.

For Cicero, human cooperation either makes possible or improves every human good. Even the greatest men cannot accomplish greatest deeds without others' help.[39] Foreshadowing Augustine's famous insight that man is the most social creature by nature but the most quarrelsome by perversion, Cicero writes that "man is the source of both the greatest help and the greatest harm to man," and observes that "injustice is fatal to social life and fellowship between man and man."[40] Because the city's laws, customs, and leaders foster virtue and discourage vice, they protect and nurture man's social inclinations and make the happy life possible.

Turning to book 5 of *De re publica*, we find Cicero's Scipio echoing this message.[41] The Roman Republic is "the greatest and best possible [achievement] among men" because of the quality of customs and institutions its patriotic citizens have contributed.[42] To be sure, Cicero's Scipio speaks of an idealized Rome—what Augustine later calls a colored picture—and this is to some degree indicated in the dialogue.[43] Yet in this beautiful picture, Cicero gives his readers a lens through which they can look at Rome without despairing. It becomes the true Rome—the Rome the reader must recover.

Thus, in filling his readers with nostalgia for a lost *res publica*—a golden age when leaders like Scipio had "a happy life" for their fellow citizens as their aim, one "fortified by wealth, rich in material resources, great in glory, and honored for virtue"—Cicero aims to motivate his readers to dedicate themselves to Rome's improvement.[44] For, Cicero's Scipio makes clear, Rome's prosperity depends upon virtuous citizens to preserve the customs and institutions that make Rome great.[45]

## Virtue's Reward

So far, we have outlined Cicero's *apologia* for patriotism as a noble way of life that renders the *patria* the service it is due, to the benefit of all. Yet not all of Cicero's readers came to his texts enamored with the virtuous life. While some would not dare ask about virtue's reward, lest they seem ignoble, for others, it was a pressing question.[46] In *De Officiis*, Cicero tackles it head on, recognizing that, whether in their secret thoughts or open doubts his readers wonder whether virtue really is expedient [*utile*], he must bolster their commitment to the life of duty by showing that it is.[47]

Throughout the text, Cicero warns that false understandings of the *beata vita*, the happy life, can lead one to subordinate what is right to what seems beneficial. For Cicero, the fulfillment of our moral duties directs us toward our personal good, which is in harmony with the common good.[48] The pursuit of happiness by treachery, selfishness and deceit, on the other hand, is evidenced by its personal and political ill-effects.[49]

Taking a step back, we see that Cicero's rhetorical approach, which Augustine adopts, is based on a particular understanding of the human condition.[50] Both believe that, although man's natural inclinations are harmoniously and intelligibly ordered to a common good, people easily misinterpret them and become attached to false ideas about the *beata vita*. Both also recognize that when these inclinations are misinterpreted, they seem to conflict with one another, and that often, people choose the lower, stronger inclinations to the detriment of themselves and others.[51] Rhetoric, for both, cuts through their readers' disordered attachments and strengthens their noble inclinations.[52]

In *De officiis*, Cicero challenges his readers' misconceptions about the *beata vita* through the strategic use of praise and shame.[53] Writing in a world steeped in excessive love of military glory, Cicero counsels his son not to covet honorable military posts, explaining that they sometimes ought to be declined or resigned.[54] The desire for glory (*gloriae cupiditas*) that drives so many, he warns, "robs us of liberty, and in defense of liberty, a high-souled man (*magnanimis viris*) should stake everything."[55] When one is bound to this glory, one is no longer free, but compelled to do whatever it takes to win it.

Accordingly, he explains, this "passion for victory," quickly leads to injustice and an "excessive lust for power (*nimia cupiditas principatus*)."[56] As it is for Augustine, this desire is excessive to Cicero because it overpowers love of virtue, compelling one to forsake the *honestum* for the so-called *utile*. Cicero attributes the Romans' degrading treatment of the conquered to this *cupiditas*, reminding them of their behavior at Corinth, Carthage, and Numantia. If Rome had followed a more humane foreign policy, he suggests, it would still have a constitutional government. "As it is," he laments, "we have none at all."[57] Driving the point home, he repeats, it is because the Romans "have preferred to be the object of fear rather than love and affection" that they have lost their Republic ("rem vero publicam penitus amisimus").

Although Rome's lust for domination, its *cupiditas principatus*, had begun to warp its foreign policy long ago, Cicero emphasizes how individual actors in influential positions can affect the whole trajectory of society. Sulla, Cicero explains, exacerbated Rome's moral decline by providing his fellow Romans with an example of cunning and injustice that seemed to go unpunished, even gaining him fame and power.[58] Sulla's influence cost the Romans their greatest treasure, glorified injustice and tyranny, and inspired many atrocities. If his readers have any social feeling, they should be ashamed to imitate him.

Not only that, they would be foolish to imitate him. Cicero's message in *De officiis* is clear: if one abandons the path of virtue, it is to the community's detriment as well as one's own. Whereas Machiavelli exalts the lion and the fox, Cicero exalts virtue as the best path to winning over "the hearts of men" ("consiliare animos hominum"), arguing that love produces more loyalty than fear from the good and the bad alike, albeit for different reasons.[59] True glory, like all good things, is achieved with others' help, and depends particularly on the affection and esteem of the people.[60]

Thus, Cicero never challenges his readers' ambition for true glory—"the command of means and wealth," "influence" and "power by which they may be able to help themselves and their friends."[61] Rather, he constructively reroutes their pursuit of it. Although many "have sought occasions for war from the mere ambition for fame," he writes, "if we face the facts, we shall find that there have been many instances of achievement in peace more important and no less renowned than in war."[62] Indeed, he tells his readers, civil service requires "even greater energy and greater devotion" than military service.[63]

In sum, as long as Cicero's virtuous man does the right for its own sake, in doing so, he receives the reward he desires: "the enhancement of personal honour and glory."[64] This is the narrative we will later see Augustine scrutinize. Here, it is enough to observe that it is necessary for Cicero to maintain that virtue is intrinsically lovable and that it is the way to true glory, despite any tensions this might leave unresolved. For Cicero, the *honestum* and the *utile* can only be held together by refusing to think of the *honestum* merely as a means to the *utile*; if virtue is not loved for its own sake, it will be forsaken in difficult circumstances—the very ones in which patriotism is most needed. Yet, nature also goads man on to his fulfillment through the desire for happiness, and so must Cicero.

## The Epicurean Temptation

Before turning to Augustine, it is important to point out one final aspect of Cicero's public-spirited philosophy that Augustine takes up in *The City of God*. As we have seen, Cicero believed that if he could teach the Romans the nature of "the good and happy life" ("bene beateque vivendum"), he could provide a firm foundation for the life of good citizenship and help to reverse the degeneration of Roman morality.[65] Although we have seen evidence of this project in *De officiis* and *De re publica*, and there is much more to be found elsewhere, for our purposes, it is enough to focus on his engagement with Epicureanism in *De finibus*, on which Augustine later builds.[66]

In *De finibus*, Cicero exchanges speeches with an Epicurean named Torquatus, a descendant of the Titus Manlius Imperiosus Torquatus who, in an astonishing act of patriotism, executed his own son for disobedience while serving as general.[67] In his speech, the Epicurean Torquatus argues that the motive of "heroic men," including his famous ancestor, "was not a love of virtue in and for itself" but for the sake of "honor and esteem."[68] Augustine will later agree.

Yet because Cicero aims to exhort young Romans to lives of great patriotism, he uses his discussion with Torquatus to problematize the Epicurean position.[69] Epicureanism is a threat to Cicero's project because it deflates his ability to inflame the hearts of its adherents for anything beyond their own gratification. Whereas the Epicurean school holds that virtue makes for the most pleasant life, Cicero protests, "How can a man be at once a sensualist and keep his desire within bounds?"[70]

By subordinating virtue to pleasure, Cicero tells Torquatus, he leaves "no form of desire whose possessor could not be morally approved. He will be a miser—within limits; an adulterer—in moderation; and a sensualist—to the same extent."[71] In order to avoid this dangerous outcome, Cicero trains his followers to disdain Epicureanism, depicting it as a corrupting influence that can lead potential statesmen into hedonism. He writes, "[T]he better and more noble . . . the character with which a man is endowed, the more does he prefer the life of service to the life of pleasure."[72]

## From Cicero to Augustine

We have seen that Cicero's fundamental teaching is that the common good and the individual good converge in and through virtue. Happiness does not consist in pleasure, fame, or power, but in true glory, which is achieved by fulfilling one's patriotic duty. It "ought to be the chief end of all men," Cicero writes, "to make the interest of each individual and of the whole body politic identical. For, if the individual appropriates to selfish ends what should be devoted to the common good, all human fellowship will be destroyed."[73] Augustine's Ciceronian readers will have taken this message to heart.

It is easy to be sympathetic to the idea that virtue should be cultivated so that citizens will want to work for the common good. Augustine agrees. In many ways a Ciceronian, Augustine endorses the judgment of Cato about how much better it was when the Romans had a "diligence at home, a just rule abroad, and a free spirit in counsel, devoted neither to crime nor to lust."[74] Before, Augustine recalls, when there was a shortage of money in the public treasury, citizens sold their private property and each contributed what he had; even the senators "left themselves no gold beyond one ring and one seal, the miserable insignia of their rank."[75] That the great Romans of the past were highly patriotic went a long way in saving Rome from the evils afflicting other nations.[76]

From Augustine's analysis, it is clear that he thinks concern for the common good is important; civic-mindedness is good. What, then, is his dispute with the Ciceronian project of cultivating civic virtue? Augustine agrees that it is better for citizens to seek honor, glory and power by virtuous means than by deceitful intrigue. Not only is it better for the citizens themselves but for the community as well: these citizens, he writes, are "more useful to the earthly city when they have even that imperfect kind of virtue than they would be if they did not have it."[77] Yet to stop here betrays Augustine's intention; his point is to make the Ciceronians, who already want to be virtuous, amenable to a better option. In the second part of this article, I will unpack this claim, focusing on Augustine's attack on political glory insofar as it is crafted for the sake of the Ciceronian, and ending with a look at how he presents the Christian vision as a fulfillment of Ciceronian longing.

## An Invitation

As Pierre Manent has said, "The Christian critique is concerned to reveal a noble error," and "the accent can fall either on the nobility of the error or the erroneous character of the noble movement."[78] For Augustine, the patriot's noble error is excessive devotion to Rome. It is excessive, Augustine thinks, because it leaves no room for devotion to anything greater than Rome. Wherever the accent falls in any given passage of *The City of God*, Augustine is single minded in his effort to draw his readers beyond this error and into the pilgrim city: "O admirable Roman character—O offspring of the Reguli, Scaevolae, Scipios, Fabricii," he exclaims, why do you settle for Rome? "Incomparably fairer is that Supernatural City where victory is truth, where dignity is holiness, where peace is happiness and where life is eternity."[79] The mythical Rome that motivates the noble Ciceronian was a placeholder, serving so long as "the true religion" was "withheld from . . . choice." Now, it threatens to obscure what it anticipated. "Awake," Augustine tells the patriot, "it is day!" The night of anticipation is over, and the Just City that Cicero surmised from afar has been unveiled.[80]

## The Benevolent *Patria* Reconsidered

Because Augustine thinks his readers' vision has been clouded by their excessive devotion, he makes it his mission to desacralize Rome. Whereas Cicero depicts the *patria* as a benevolent and provident mother, Augustine unmasks "her," revealing Rome to be nothing more than a reflection of its members' collective interests.[81] Whereas the Romans celebrate the virtue and "blessedness" of someone like the noble Regulus, this does not mean that they actually value virtue above security. In reality, Augustine argues, Rome celebrates its noble citizens because they are useful: they protect its worldly glory.[82] Augustine wants his readers to see that this dynamic has always been at play in Rome.

Having claimed that the Romans have a collective interest in cultivating noble citizens, Augustine prepares to argue that the public service Rome demands and the reward it offers actually undermine the good and happy life to which the Ciceronian rightly aspires. He does this by spelling out what happens when Rome appropriates its noble citizens' service to selfish ends, flipping the Ciceronian narrative by introducing a new possibility it does not consider. In retelling how Rome earned its empire in book 5 of *The City of God*, Augustine works hard to show Ciceronians that the Roman arrangement is unsatisfactory.

Book 5 begins with Augustine defining felicity as "the full attainment of all desirable things" and insisting that no power should be worshiped for anything less than such felicity.[83] Here, he sets a standard, insinuating to the Ciceronian that he should cease serving Rome as if she could bestow this kind of felicity. Even the blessings that Rome does seem to bestow, blessings "received even by men who are not good, and . . . therefore do not have felicity," he writes, ultimately come from God. In this, Augustine sets up his inquiry into why God gave the Romans their empire in light of, but severed from, felicity.

Although Augustine's subsequent digression into the existence of fate seems of little relevance to our present inquiry, he is a master of crafting arguments that speak to different audiences for different reasons. For the Ciceronian, he showcases the character and limits of Cicero's reasoning. Drawing on *De natura deorum*, *De divinatione*, and *De fato*, he explains that Cicero "feared" fate because if it exists, "then nothing is in our power and there is no free choice of the will; and if we concede that, he says, then the whole of human life is undermined. It is in vain that laws are given; it is in vain that reproaches, praises, denunciations and exhortations are used; nor is there any justice in the appointment of rewards for good men and punishment for bad."[84] Fearing these "absurd and pernicious" consequences, and believing that divination, or any kind of foreknowledge, necessarily implied fate's existence, Cicero wished (*vult*) "to say that there is no foreknowledge of things to come."[85]

Augustine chooses his words carefully. Cicero *wished* to argue against the Stoic belief in fate because it threatened the political order. He *wished* (*vult*) "to make man free" because freedom is the basis of political life.[86] Acting on these wishes, Cicero proceeded "with all his might" to demolish any argument supporting foreknowledge, but to the point of making "vain arguments" even when "the truth" was "clearer than day."

Seeing, for example, that the denial of divine foreknowledge implied the denial of God's existence, Augustine's Cicero did not withdraw or rethink his protreptic against divination. Rather, knowing "how hateful and offensive such an opinion would be found, he "makes" (*fecit*) the character Cotta take the atheistic position in *De natura deorum*, and "chooses" (*maluit*) to side with Lucilius Balbus in defense of Stoic theology.[87] In the end, Augustine suggests, Cicero preferred to obscure the implications of his position than to reconsider it, for, "in his attempt to refute" the Stoic view on fate, Augustine explains, "Cicero considers himself helpless against [the Stoics] unless he can dispose of divination."[88]

It is significant that here, Augustine expresses sympathy for Cicero, affirming that he was a "great and learned man" who was "wisely instructed in matters pertaining to human life."[89] Cicero knew the importance of free will for human life, just as he knew the importance of virtue. Augustine claims that yet he lacked an understanding of the divine things that could solve the antinomy that compelled him to make "abominable" arguments. Staging a conversation with Cicero, Augustine communicates to the Ciceronian that what Cicero feared to lose is not lost with Christianity.

God, he tells Cicero, preordained that man should have free will as part of his divine plan: "laws, reprimands, exhortations, praise and denunciations," are indeed "of great efficacy," as God knew they would be.[90]

In casting Cicero as genuinely baffled about how he can admit foreknowledge while preserving free will, Augustine aims to cast doubt on Cicero's teachings without maligning his character. By showing that in this case, Cicero "restricts the mind of the religious man" to a false choice, Augustine wants the Ciceronian to wonder what other strategic decisions Cicero made out of a false sense of necessity.[91] He signals that it is possible to separate what Cicero argues from why he argues it, retaining and honoring the Ciceronian concern for the human things ("rebus humanis"), while discarding the "pernicious" arguments Cicero thought he must make to defend them.

In the seeming digression of 5.9–10, then, we actually find Augustine preparing his Ciceronian readers for the larger argument in store for them. Thus, in 5.11, Augustine begins again, dividing felicity from emptiness, and promising to explain why the Romans deserved their empire. Because he highlights the "great things" the Romans "despised," "subdued," and "endured" for the sake of glory in this explanation, Manent has argued that Augustine "shows esteem" for the "pagan order of glory" as it was "deployed in life and action."[92] However, I argue, Augustine's primary goal is to cut through the allure this order, which he sees as a stumbling block to the Ciceronians and an obstacle to their happiness.

To see this, we must look more closely at Augustine's analysis of true glory. Quoting Sallust's observation that "glory, honour and power are sought by good and base men alike," Augustine concludes that in the Roman mind, the good and the base do not differ in what they seek, but how they seek it.[93] True glory, he writes, is just human praise pursued by good arts, and these good arts are what the Romans call virtue.

Thus, whereas Cicero taught that the noble man seeks virtue for its own sake, in Augustine's analysis, Torquatus was right: the Roman heroes did their "many wonderful and famous deeds" *for the sake* of glory.[94] Enflamed with this love, they "did not hesitate" to place Rome's safety before their own, performing deeds "praiseworthy and glorious in the estimations of men."[95] Again, Augustine choses his words carefully, adding that those who see more clearly understand that "even love of praise is a vice."[96]

What Augustine claims next strikes the Ciceronian vision at its core. Even Cicero, he charges, "was not able to conceal" ["dissimulare non potuit"] this fact.[97] Worse, he still recommended that statesmen should be "nourished on glory" ("alendum esse gloria"), observing that the ancient Romans did great deeds "because of their desire" for it. So although Cicero knew that true happiness was not to be found in human praise, distinguishing the "true good" from the "fickle praise of men" in his philosophical works, he judged it necessary to rouse love of glory for the sake of the great deeds it motivated.

Once again, we find Augustine attributing a "pestilential opinion" to Cicero that he ascribes to his excessive patriotic devotion.[98] Yet as before, Cicero is guilty of a failure of imagination for which he cannot entirely be blamed. Augustine's Cicero thinks "men always neglect" what is "held in low esteem" because he has no experience of anything else; in his world, "all men" really are "fired in their endeavors by the prospect of glory." The desire to be thought well of, Augustine charges, is so ingrained in Roman culture that it might as well be a fact, unquestioned and unquestionable.[99] Augustine's Cicero supposes he must rely on glory to rouse citizens because he has been formed in a *patria* where it is almost impossible to imagine man being motivated by anything else. As we will see, Augustine soon indicates that this is because Rome has nothing better to offer.

Before doing so, however, Augustine turns to the apostles. These men, he writes, "preached the name of Christ . . . where it was held in low esteem," and even where it was "held in the utmost detestation."[100] Amid curses, revilement, and persecution, the apostles conquered hard hearts, doing what Cicero thought impossible. Even when glory began to follow them in the church, Augustine recalls, they refused to rest in it "as if it were the virtue which they sought as their end." Instead, they referred it to God, "by Whose grace they were what they were": they were something new, and lived for something new.

Here, Augustine invites the Ciceronians to compare themselves with the apostles: whereas the Ciceronians cling to what they heard from Cicero, the apostles "held fast to what they heard from the good teacher who is also the Physician of minds."[101] Whereas Cicero taught his followers to think they sought virtue for its own sake while secretly enflaming their love of human praise, Christ teaches his followers how to avoid doing good in order to be seen by others, while not being so afraid of pleasing others that they conceal their goodness. Whereas Cicero taught his followers to be zealous and noble citizens for the sake of human glory, Christ teaches his followers to be good for the "glory which is from God alone" (Jn 5.44).

True Glory Reconsidered

By now, Augustine expects his Ciceronian readers to be either intrigued, irked, or incredulous, and proceeds by assuming they are still unsure whether the love of political glory really is a vice. Augustine has already established that virtues are only truly such when they direct man "toward that end in which man's good—the good than which nothing better exists—is found."[102] This, in a teleological world, was common sense. His job now is to show the Ciceronians their own dissatisfaction at the hero's reward.

He does this by juxtaposing the service the hero and the saint give and the reward they receive from their respective cities or, in keeping with his earlier claim, from God. He presents what at first seems like a satisfactory resolution for the patriot: the

Romans who "held their private interests in low esteem" for the common good ("re communi"), or, he clarifies, "the commonwealth" ("re publica"), have received the reward they desired.[103] They are honored by the whole world, remembered "to this day, in literature and history." Yet, his tone shifting, he adds, these are the ones of whom Christ spoke when he said that some had "received their reward" (Matt 6.2): they "seemed to do good . . . that they may be glorified by men," and so they are: they "have no reason to complain" of God's justice.

They do, however, have reason to complain of Rome's justice. The Roman heroes died protecting their city, and before that, lived directing all their efforts toward its security: Rome needed them, and they admirably protected her, but why? In glory, Augustine explains, these Romans sought a kind of life after death "in the mouths of those who praised them." In a realm "where the dead pass away and are succeeded by the dying," Augustine asks, what else were they to love?[104] By casting eternal life as the true goal of man's natural inclinations, Augustine suggests that Rome unfairly binds its citizens to itself by offering them political glory as a shadowy counterfeit of their true end.

Adding to his readers' dissatisfaction, Augustine juxtaposes this to the reward of those serving the city of God. Through their trials in this life, he writes, these men and women gain membership in an eternal city where God will protect them. There they will have to devote "no great industry" to maintaining the common good—God's fellowship—and by participating in it, they will be fully happy.[105]

Having presented the heavenly *patria*, Augustine changes course, speaking as if his only audience were those already committed to journeying toward it. This allows the Ciceronian to feel the weight of choosing Rome over and against it and allows Augustine to presuppose the leap of faith in its existence that his Ciceronian readers have probably not yet taken. The Ciceronian now stands on the outside, peering in as if through a window to watch Augustine use the Roman heroes to counsel his flock against pride.

Thus, it is for a twofold purpose that Augustine asks the Christians how they can be proud of their sacrifices when Brutus executed his own sons for the sake of Rome. Writing that it is "more difficult to slay one's sons" than to "give to the poor those things heaped up and preserved to be given to one's own sons" as Christians must, Augustine challenges the Ciceronian esteem for difficult service *per se*, drawing it back to a measure prior to itself: a genuinely common good.[106] Observing that "neither we nor our sons are made happy by earthly riches" but by God, Augustine indicates that the City of God sets a standard Rome fails to meet. It asks its pilgrim members for a service (*latreia*) that prepares them for happiness: the sacrifices of love, though difficult, are what enable man to participate in God's fellowship.[107] Rome, however, encourages its citizens to make sacrifices that destroy their happiness. It squanders their lives for its own imperial ends.

Augustine continues, casting Brutus's once glorious sacrifice in an increasingly tragic light. Even Virgil, he says, could not help but shudder as he praised Brutus, exclaiming, "But what an unhappy man this is, no matter how much his deed may be celebrated in days to come!"[108] Yet, "as if to console this unhappy man," Virgil adds, "But love of country drove him, and the immense love of praise." In quoting Virgil's conflicted response, Augustine holds up a mirror to the Ciceronian, challenging him to find consolation in Virgil's words while chipping away at his ability to do so.

Putting the final nail in the coffin, Augustine retells the stories of other Roman heroes driven by the twin loves of *patria* and glory. Highlighting the trajectory of these loves, he tells how Curtius and the Decii did not just suffer death at enemy hands but actively launched themselves into their own destruction, and how Mucius thrust his right hand into a fire to show a foreign king the kind of people he had made an enemy of in the Romans. Augustine does not intend that these stories should impress the Ciceronian. Rather, he uses them to elaborate on an earlier aside, in which he claimed that the martyrs surpassed the heroes in virtue because their sufferings were not self-inflicted.[109] He also builds on Cicero's own distinction between the noble motivations of those willing to defend their *patria* and the disordered motives of those who pray for a war, that they might gain glory.

In clarifying, for example, that Torquatus did not execute his son for treason, but for violating his father's command in his zeal to slay Rome's enemies, Augustine wants Torquatus's decision to strike the Ciceronian as excessive. Glory, he implies, distorted Torquatus's judgment: it made him willing to making an example of his son. In telling how Marcus Pulvillus ordered his son's body to be thrown out without burial in order to avoid being interrupted during a prestigious ceremony, Augustine wants Marcus Pulvillus to strike the Ciceronian as callous. Glory, he writes, had entirely overcome his heart: there was no room left for paternal love. In their pursuit of glory, Augustine shows how these too passed beyond admirable self-sacrifice and into tragic self-mutilation. Although they did not physically harm themselves, they did violence to their humanity.

This, however, is not surprising. Glory, Augustine reveals, acts as a competitive mechanism in Rome, encouraging citizens to distinguish themselves by demonstrating the lengths to which they will go to serve their *patria*. In this environment, it actually becomes desirable to sacrifice everything to the *patria*, oneself and one's own, precisely because it is difficult to do so. In the end, self-mutilation is the pathological outcome of the Roman order of glory. Indeed, Augustine submits, absolute devotion to an unjust city could yield nothing other else. Rome is not benevolent enough to discourage the harmful behavior from which it benefits. Having shown how and why the allure of glory has become unmoored from man's deepest natural inclinations—the very inclinations that the Ciceronian believes are meant to guide man toward happiness—Augustine hopes to have made a convincing case as to why love of political glory is a vice. Although shame for ignobility and praise for nobility is, in the short term, an efficacious way to cultivate *useful* citizens, glory cannot hold together the good of man and the greatness of Rome without subordinating one to the other. Ultimately, the Roman reliance on love of glory, even after Cicero has recast it, is based on a misleading portrayal of the link between glory and happiness that is born out of a political, rather than a philosophical consideration.[110]

Although Cicero saw problems with love of praise, and at times distinguished true glory from human praise, at other times, he did not. In the end, Augustine does not think he had the tools to do so. For Augustine, Cicero's limitation reflects the limits of politics. On its own, the political is incapable of harmonizing the good of the human person with the good of the *civitas*; the most the *civitas* can offer is an immortal name, a mere shadow of the immortal happiness man truly desires.[111]

## The Just City

Thus, having challenged the Ciceronian's noble error, Augustine presents the City of God as the interpretive key that renders the Ciceronian paradigm coherent. He affirms Cicero's claim that man is naturally inclined to sociability, truth, order, peace, and virtue and that these direct him toward life in a just society.[112] Yet, he says, if they are honest, his Ciceronian readers will admit that Rome cannot be this society—they want something more than it can offer. As we have seen, Augustine claims that man's sociability is actually ordered to an eternal fellowship with God and with one another in God—the fellowship that constitutes the City of God.[113] By taking the inclinations that his readers recognize in themselves and making the case that he understands them better than they do, Augustine is able to present this city as the true object of their longing.[114]

That said, Augustine also recognizes and affirms the Ciceronian's desire to do what he can to make human life better here and now. Accordingly, he tells the Ciceronian, "nothing could be more fortunate for human affairs" than that political actors combine love of God with a good life and a knowledge of the art of governing.[115] Not only are the morals taught in the churches the morals that Cicero would have wanted but *latreia* fosters the common good more than glory does.[116] Whereas glory pits citizens against each other—for in a world where everyone is honored, no one is honored—*latreia* directs man toward an intrinsically social end by demanding a thoroughly social activity. Whereas the pursuit of glory by the true way is often thwarted or distorted in a world limited by opinion and appearance, the pursuit of God's fellowship through authentic *latreia* is guaranteed by God's omniscience and benevolence.[117] Cicero sought an effective and fulfilling way to motivate his readers to serve the common good, and, Augustine suggests, Christ offers it.[118]

What is more, Augustine presents the city of God itself as an important check on Rome. As we have seen, Cicero surmised that the *res publica* ought to be a community guided by justice, and defined it as such. Yet, as we have also seen, Augustine has made it clear that the idea of a just Rome provides an airbrushed facade behind which the real Rome can hide.[119] Having presented this problem to his Ciceronian readers, when he redefines the *res publica* in book 19, he signals to them that with the help of revelation, he can modify the Ciceronian paradigm without losing its merits.

At first, Augustine's redefinition of a people as an assemblage of "a multitude of rational creatures bound together," not by justice but "a common agreement as to the objects of their love" seems to forsake Ciceronian vision, which roots politics in justice.[120] Yet because the City of God is marked by rightly ordered loves, it stands as the eternally just city.[121] It alone de-divinizes and unmasks all earthly commonwealths while still managing to hold them to itself as a standard.

Thus, Augustine's definition not only preserves the good in Cicero's definition but also adds to it: it draws the standard of the Just City beyond the realm that Rome or any political regime can claim. In asking what a city loves, Augustine points his readers toward the most pressing question any citizen must ask.[122] Rome, Augustine has argued, loves glory and fosters a love of glory in its citizens in order to bind them to it. Augustine has warned the Ciceronian to resist this; the love Rome exalts is not right.[123] For Augustine, if one loves something contingent *as if* it were worthy of all devotion, one loses perspective, turning a secondary good into an idol and gaining an empty reward.[124]

Although it may seem that Rome would do better by having citizens who understand their goals in light of its own goal, Augustine argues this is not the case. If citizens allow Rome to masquerade as the locus of their greatest good, they allow the fundamental threat to political life to fester.[125] Augustine argues that the core of the dynamic of the earthly city, which has plagued Rome since its beginning, is actually the desire to be worshiped by its citizens.[126] It is a desire, literally, to dominate, use, and control them. It is always destructive, even when dressed up in noble language.[127] Augustine thinks that any regime, through its handling of power, is tempted by this dynamic, and argues that it is therefore the role of the good citizen to temper this tendency. Although political life provides important human goods, it is not the locus of man's *summmum bonum*. Rome does not merit absolute dedication because it cannot bestow felicity. Augustine suggests that ultimately, a new attitude must be taken toward the political: one of respect, but not of idolatry. The Ciceronian needs to take a certain distance for clarity and critical thinking, particularly about questions of justice. Only if political life is understood within its proper context can citizens properly assess what actions are appropriate to serve the common good. Augustine demotes Rome, but promises that in subordinating it to the City of God, Rome will be better served.

## Evaluating Augustine's Response

In reading *The City of God* as a response to the Ciceronian patriot, we encounter Augustine's political teaching: although it is good to want Rome to truly prosper, idolizing Rome does not achieve this. Paradoxically, by allowing the hearts of its citizens to be drawn beyond it, Rome will be better served. In order to transform the Ciceronian patriot into a citizen with such a heart, Augustine acts with the skill of a surgeon. He separates the longing for the Just City and the desire for happiness from concern for Rome's prosperity, then reunites them in the city of God.

For Augustine, the Christian promise renders intelligible what was falsely resolved in Cicero's account. To him, Cicero knew that the public and private good had to come into harmony in a Just City, but, not knowing where to find this city, he blurred it with Rome. Because only the City of God can offer a *beata vita* in which there is no tension between public and private good—the eternal enjoyment of God and one another in God is truly a common good—Cicero was compelled to motivate citizens to public-spiritedness by human praise, a second best for the citizen and thus, for the *civitas*.[128]

Cicero sought to form citizens who were dedicated to their public duties, enamored of justice, and concerned for the common good. Augustine echoes these concerns but sees himself as liberating the Ciceronians from political idolatry. This is primarily for their sake, but also for Rome's: by offering them an effective and fulfilling reason to serve the common good, Augustine does the citizen and the *civitas* a service.

# Notes

1. As Peter Brown writes, *The City of God* "is all movement, ducking and weaving . . . [engaging] nothing less than the whole of the pagan literary culture available to him." Brown, "Saint Augustine and Political Society," in *City of God: A Collection of Critical Essays*, ed. Dorothy Donnelly (New York: PLang, 1995), 17–35, at 17.

2. See, *inter alia*, Harold Hagendahl, *Augustine and the Latin Classics* (Goteborg: Acta Universitatis Gothoburgensis, 1967); Maurice Testard, *Saint Augustin et Cicéron*, 2 vols. (Paris: Études augustiniennes, 1958); Ernest L. Fortin, "The Political Thought of St. Augustine," in *Classical Christianity and the Political Order*, ed. Brian J. Benestad (Lanham, MD: Rowman & Littlefield, 1996), 1–30; John M. Rist, *Augustine : Ancient Thought Baptized* (Cambridge: Cambridge University Press, 1996); John von Heyking, *Augustine and Politics as Longing in the World* (Columbia: University of Missouri Press, 2001); Michael P. Foley, "The Other Happy Life: The Political Dimensions to St. Augustine's Cassiciacum Dialogues," *Review of Politics* 65, no. 2 (March 2003): 165–83; Robert Dodaro, *Christ and the Just Society in the Thought of Augustine* (Cambridge: Cambridge University Press, 2004); Mary Keys, "Augustinian Humility as Natural Right," in *Natural Right and Political Philosophy: Essays in Honor of Catherine Zuckert and Michael Zuckert*, ed. Ann Ward and Lee Ward (Notre Dame, IN: University of Notre Dame Press, 2013), 97–116.

3. Herbert Deane, *The Political and Social Ideas of St. Augustine* (New York: Columbia University Press, 1963); Reinhold Niebuhr, "Augustine's Political Realism," in *City of God: A Collection of Critical Essays*, 119–34; R. A. Markus, *Saeculum: History and Society in the Theology of St. Augustine* (Cambridge: Cambridge University Press, 1970). It is worth noting, however, that Markus moderates his position in *Christianity and the Secular* (Notre Dame, IN: University of Notre Dame Press, 2006). For an extensive and rich review of realist

and protoliberal readings of Augustine, see Eric Gregory, *Politics and the Order of Love: An Augustinian Ethic of Democratic Citizenship* (Chicago: University of Chicago Press, 2008), and Michael Bruno, *Political Augustinianism: Modern Interpretations of Augustine's Political Thought* (Minneapolis: Fortress Press, 2014).

4. Peter Brown, "Saint Augustine and Political Society," in *City of God: A Collection of Critical Essays*, 17–36; John Milbank, *Theology and Social Theory: Beyond Secular Reason*, 2nd ed. (Oxford: Wiley-Blackwell, 2006). Cf. Michael J. S. Bruno, *Political Augustinianism: Modern Interpretations of Augustine's Political Thought* (Minneapolis: Fortress Press, 2014), 140–47; Gregory, *Politics and the Order of Love*, 125–48; Robert Dodaro, "*Ecclesia* and *Res publica*: How Augustinian Are Neo-Augustinian Politics?" in *Augustine and Postmodern Thought: A New Alliance Against Modernity?* ed. L. Boeve, M. Lamberigts, and M. Wisse (Leuven: Peeters, 2009), 257–71.

5. Cf. Robert Dodaro, OSA, "Language Matters: Augustine's Use of Literary Decorum in Theological Argument," *Augustinian Studies* 45, no. 1 (2014): 1–28, at 3. Dodaro helpfully notes that according to classical literary decorum, rhetoric must be appropriate to the author himself, the audience, and the circumstance.

6. Charles Norris Cochrane, *Christianity and Classical Culture: A Study of Thought and Action from Augustus to Augustine* (Indianapolis: Liberty Fund, 2003), 43–4. Cf. Testard, *Saint Augustin et Cicéron*; Sabine MacCormack, "Cicero in Late Antiquity," in *The Cambridge Companion to Cicero*, ed. Catherine Steel (Cambridge University Press, 2013), 251–305.

7. Cf. Augustine, *The Confessions*, trans. Maria Boulding (Hyde Park, NY: New City Press, 1997), 2.3.5, 3.4.7; Hagendahl, *Augustine and the Latin Classics*, 384, 479, 692–93; MacCormack, "Cicero in Late Antiquity," 282; Dorothy H. Donnelly, "Augustine and Romanitas" (PhD diss., University of California Berkeley, 1973), 67; Johannes van Oort, *Jerusalem and Babylon: A Study into Augustine's* City of God *and the Sources of His Doctrine of the Two Cities*, Supplements to Vigiliae Christianae, v. 14 (Leiden: Brill, 1991), 22.

8. As we will see, the overarching aim of Cicero's political philosophical project was to restore the health of Rome by cultivating good citizens. Cf. Peter Brown, *Through the Eye of a Needle: Wealth, the Fall of Rome, and the Making of Christianity in the West, 350–550 AD* (Princeton, NJ: Princeton University Press, 2014), 68–70.

9. Robert Dodaro has made an excellent case that Augustine's letters ought to be taken seriously as windows into his understanding of politics and offers important historical background for the exchange between Nectarius and Augustine. Dodaro, *Christ and the Just Society*, 196–99; Dodaro, "Augustine's Secular City," *Augustine and His Critics: Essays in Honor of Gerald Bonner*, ed. Robert Dodaro and George Lawless (Abingdon, UK: Routledge, 2000), 231–50; Dodaro, "*Ecclesia* and *Res publica*," at 254–55.

10. Augustine, Letter 91 to Nectarius, in Augustine, *Political Writings*, trans. Michael W. Tkacz and Douglas Kries (Indianapolis: Hackett, 1994), 203.

11. See Ernest L. Fortin's comparison of *De oratore* and *De doctrina christiana* in "Augustine and the Problem of Christian Rhetoric," *Augustinian Studies* 5 (1974): 85–100. Robert Dodaro has also done excellent work on Augustine's transformation of Ciceronian ideas in *Christ and the Just Society*, 6–26, 182–214 and in "Augustine's Revision of the Heroic Ideal," *Augustinian Studies* 36, no. 1 (2005): 141–57.

12. Michael P. Foley argues that Augustine's Cassiciacum dialogues are "specific responses to Cicero's philosophical dialogues" in "The Other Happy Life," 169; MacCormack, "Cicero in Late Antiquity," 274.

13. MacCormack, "Cicero in Late Antiquity," 275.

14. John M. Warner and John T. Scott have argued that Augustine finds Cicero naive for endorsing the "'true way" of virtue and civic republicanism, However, in my reading, following James Holton's reading of Cicero, I find Augustine to be critical not of Cicero's naiveté but of his esotericism. Warner and Scott, "Sin City: Augustine and Machiavelli's Reordering of Rome," *Journal of Politics* 73, no. 3 (July 2011): 857–71, at 863; James Holton, "Marcus Tullius Cicero," in *History of Political Philosophy*, ed. Leo Strauss and Joseph Cropsey (Chicago: University of Chicago Press, 1987), 155–75.

15. Augustine, *The City of God against the Pagans*, trans. Robert Dyson (Cambridge: Cambridge University Press, 1998), 5.14 (hereafter *Ciu.*). I use the Dyson translation, but compare it with *De ciuitate dei Libri I–X*, ed. Bernardus Dombart and Alphonsus Kalb, Corpus Christianorum Series Latina 47 (Brepols: Turnhout, 1955), or *De ciuitate dei Libri XI–XXII*, ed. Bernardus Dombart and Alphonsus Kalb, Corpus Christianorum Series Latina 48 (Brepols: Turnhout, 1955), quoting the Latin text or augmenting Dyson's translation in parentheses where necessary.

16. Pierre Manent, *Metamorphoses of the City: On the Western Dynamic*, trans. Marc LePain (Cambridge, MA: Harvard University Press, 2013), 261.

17. As Augustine makes explicit in *Ciu.* 10.29, when he speaks to dead men, he is really speaking to their living disciples.

18. Manent, *Metamorphoses of the City*, 294.

19. That is, by taking what is good in it, which is quite a lot, and resting it on a new foundation. Augustine *Ciu.*, 2.29.

20. Augustine, *Confessions*, 3.4.7. Cf. van Oort, *Jerusalem and Babylon*, 30–33.

21. For a wonderful passage in which Cicero's Piso explains the process of discovering the purpose of one's inclinations, see Marcus Tullius Cicero, *De finibus*, trans. H. Rackham (Cambridge, MA: Harvard University Press, 1914), 5:24.

22. Marcus Tullius Cicero, *De re publica; De legibus*, trans. Clinton Walker Keyes (Cambridge, MA: Harvard University Press, 2006), 1:12. For all of Cicero's texts, I quote the Loeb translation, but have compared it with the Latin text, and include the Latin or my own translation in parentheses if I judge it illuminative.

23. Notably, Cicero's ode to patriotism ends with the Scipio whom we are soon to meet. *De re publica*, 1:1.

24. *De re publica*, 1:3.

25. *De re publica*, 1:7–8.

26. *De re publica*, 1:13.

27. *De re publica*, 1:20.

28. *De re publica*, 1:12.

29. Cf. Marcus Tullius Cicero, *De officiis*, trans. Walter Miller (Cambridge, MA: Harvard University Press, 1954), 1:58.

30. Cicero, *De re publica*, 1:8.

31. *De re publica*, 1:8.

32. *De re publica*, 5:7. J. Jackson Barlow perceptively describes Scipio as the "statesman who is capable of teaching legislators" in Cicero's *De re publica* in "The Education of Statesmen in Cicero's 'De Republica,'" *Polity* 19, no. 3 (1987): 353–74, at 353.

33. Cf. *De re publica*, 356.

34. Cicero, *De officiis*, 3:21–22.

35. *De officiis*, 1:11–14.

36. *De officiis*, 1:159.

37. *De officiis*, 2:12.

38. *De officiis*, 2:15.

39. *De officiis*, 3:21.

40. *De officiis*, 2:21; Augustine, *Ciu.*, 12.28.

41. Barlow describes Scipio as the "statesman who is capable of teaching legislators" in "The Education of Statesmen," 353.

42. Cicero, *De re publica*, 5:8.

43. *De re publica*, 1:14; Augustine, *Ciu.*, 2.21.

44. Cicero, *De re publica*, 5:8.

45. *De re publica*, 5:1.

46. Cicero, *De re publica*, 3:18.

47. *De re publica*, 1:5, 3:36, *inter alia*.

48. *De re publica* 3:11, 3:28. Cf. Walter Nicgorski, "Cicero's Paradoxes and His Idea of Utility," *Political Theory* 12, no. 4 (November 1, 1984): 557–78, at 563.

49. Cicero, *De officiis*, 3:35, 3:28.

50. Accordingly, Michael Foley has been right to argue that Augustine's indebtedness to Cicero reveals "much more than an interest in style or format"; "The Other Happy Life," 169. In this he follows Testard, who writes that Augustine values Cicero's spirit ("la qualité d'une âme, le caractère, ce qui fait l'homme") in *Saint Augustin et Cicéron*, 1:I.

51. Cf. Nicgorski, "Cicero's Paradoxes," 564.

52. Cf. MacCormack, "Cicero in Late Antiquity," 281; Cicero, *Tusculan Disputations*, trans. J. E. King (Cambridge, MA: Harvard University Press, 1927), 3:2–4.

53. Cf. Cicero, *Tusculan Disputations*, 3:3–4.

54. Cicero, *De officiis*, 1:61.

55. *De officiis*, 1:68.

56. *De officiis*, 1:64.

57. *De officiis*, 1:35.

58. *De officiis*, 2:28–29: "cupiditatum ad multos improbos venit hereditas" (an inheritance of his lusts descended to many wicked men).

59. *De officiis*, 2:17, 2:21–26, 2:44.

60. *De officiis*, 2:31–32.

61. *De officiis*, 1:99.

62. *De officiis*, 1:74; cf. Augustine, *Ciu.*, 5.12.

63. *De officiis*, 1:78.

64. *De officiis*, 2:42.

65. Cicero, *De re publica*, 1:9–12, Augustine, *The City of God*, 4.12. Cf. Cicero, *On Divination*, in *Cicero: On Old Age; On Friendship; On Divination*, trans. W. A. Falconer (Cambridge, MA: Harvard University Press, 1923), 2:1–7.

66. Cf. Walter Nicgorski, "Cicero, Citizenship and the Epicurean Temptation,'" in *Cultivating Citizens: Soulcraft and Citizenship in Contemporary America*, ed. Dwight Allman and Michael Beatty (Lanham, MD: Lexington Books, 2002), 3–28.

67. Cf. Livy, *Rome and Italy: Books VI–X of The History of Rome from Its Foundation*, trans. Betty Radice (New York: Penguin, 1982), 7:7; Augustine, *Ciu.*, 5.18.

68. Marcus Tullius Cicero, *De finibus bonorum et malorum*, trans. Harris Rackham (Cambridge, MA: Harvard University Press, 1977), I.x.34–5 (hereafter *De finibus*).

69. Michael Foley also notes the Epicureans' "bemused contempt for the civic life" in "Cicero, Augustine, and the Philosophical Roots of the Cassiciacum Dialogues," *Revue des Études augustiniennes* 45 (1999): 51–77, at 59.

70. Cicero, *De finibus*, 2:22.

71. *De finibus*, 2:27.

72. Cicero, *De officiis*, 3:25.

73. *De officiis*, 3:26.

74. Augustine, *Ciu.*, 5.12.

75. *Ciu.*, 3.19.

76. *Ciu.*, 5.13.

77. *Ciu.*, 5.19.

78. Manent, *Metamorphoses of the City*, 265.

79. Augustine, *Ciu.*, 2.29.

80. *Ciu.*, 10.29.

81. Cf. *Ciu.*, 19.17.

82. *Ciu.*, 1.15.

83. *Ciu.*, 5.Preface.

84. Cf. Cicero, "De Fato," *Cicero: On the Orator: Book 3; On Fate; Stoic Paradoxes; Divisions of Oratory*, trans. Harris Rackham (Cambridge, MA: Harvard University Press, 1942), 17:40.

85. Augustine, *Ciu.*, 5.9.

86. *Ciu.*, 5.9.

87. Cf. Cicero, *On the Nature of the Gods; Academics*, trans. Harris Rackham (Cambridge, MA: Harvard University Press, 1933), 3:95.

88. Augustine, *Ciu.*, 5.9.

89. *Ciu.*, 5.9.

90. *Ciu.*, 5.10.

91. *Ciu.*, 5.9.

92. *Ciu.*, 5.17; Manent, *Metamorphoses of the City*, 266.

93. Augustine, *Ciu.*, 5.12.

94. *Ciu.*, 5.13.

95. *Ciu.*, 5.12.

96. *Ciu.*, 5.13.

97. *Ciu.*, 5.13.

98. *Ciu.*, 5.13.

99. Cf. *Ciu.*, 5.12, 19.24.

100. *Ciu.*, 5.14. In the middle of this sentence, Augustine repeats Cicero's claim that all are roused by glory to show the newness of the apostles.

101. *Ciu.*, 5.14.

102. *Ciu.*, 5.12.

103. *Ciu.*, 5.15.

104. *Ciu.*, 5.14.

105. *Ciu.*, 5.16.

106. *Ciu.*, 5.18.

107. Cf. *Ciu.*, 10.3.

108. *Ciu.*, 5.18.

109. *Ciu.*, 5.14.

110. Augustine's goal is to emphasize a problematic aspect of Cicero's thought for his Ciceronian readers, not to make them reject his thought entirely, but to highlight a tension in it that Christianity overcomes.

111. Augustine, *Ciu.*, 5.14.

112. Cf. von Heyking, *Augustine and Politics as Longing in the World*, 558–60.

113. Augustine, *Ciu.*, 19.13.

114. Cf. Cicero, *De finibus*, 5:24.

115. Augustine, *Ciu.*, 5.19.

116. Augustine, Letter 138 to Marcellinus, in Augustine, *Political Writings*, 206–11. Cf. Dodaro, "*Ecclesia* and *Res publica*," 242–44.

117. Augustine, *Ciu.*, 5.14, 19.14.

118. The challenges of living out *latreia* present us with another issue, bound up with the effects of the Fall on the human soul. Here, my only intention is to show the reasons why it would be acceptable to the Ciceronian, on his own terms, to convert.

119. Augustine, *Ciu.*, 2.21.

120. For this argument, see R. A. Markus, *Saeculum*, 65.

121. Augustine, *Ciu.*, 19.24. Cf. Dodaro, *Christ and the Just Society*, 69; Rowan Williams, "Politics and the Soul: A Reading of the City of God," *Milltown Studies* 19, no. 20 (1987): 55–72.

122. Markus writes that Christian hope "deflates all ideologies and utopias" and "resists political programmes which seem to make an ultimate claim on men." *Saeculum*, 171–72.

123. Augustine, *Ciu.*, 5.14–15.

124. Cf. *Ciu.*, 11.16, 12.1, 14.16, *inter alia*.

125. Cf. *Ciu.*, 3.4, 4.27–32, 6.5–7, *inter alia*.

126. Cf. *Ciu.*, 5.18, 7.26, 15.4, 19.12, *inter alia*. Cf. Markus, *Saeculum*, 172; John M. Rist, *Augustine: Ancient Thought Baptized* (Cambridge: Cambridge University Press, 1996), 217.

127. Cf. Augustine, *Ciu.*, 1.31, 3.14, 15.4, 16.28.

128. *Ciu.*, 19.13.

Chapter Ten

# Augustine's *City of God* and Roman Sacral Politics

## Daniel Strand

Books 1 through 10 of *The City of God* are an extended polemic against Roman civic religion and Neoplatonism. When it comes to contemporary scholarship on Augustine's political thought, these concerns tend to play only a peripheral and supporting role if they are mentioned at all. The argument of this essay is that books 1–10 are a critique of the various ways that Roman religion influenced Roman political thought and practice. Roman religion is the primary resource that informs Roman politics. Despite the recent tendency of discussions of political thought to be centered around themes and passages in book 19, books 1 through 10 give us a rather capacious window into Augustine's criticisms of Rome and his own political thought. This essay will seek to clarify Augustine's understanding of Roman religion and his critique of Roman sacral politics in *The City of God*. Roman religion is not something peripheral to Augustine's description and critique of Roman politics in *City*; rather, it lies at the very heart of Augustine's formulation of the two cities and his critique of Rome. When we see the connections between the Roman religion and Roman politics and society in the Roman mind more clearly, the criticisms developed in *City* will become more transparent and their relevance amplified.

Politics and religion are intertwined phenomena in the ancient world, so it is not surprising that Augustine treats the two together. I use the term "sacral politics" to name this combination of politics and religion as practiced in Rome. Augustine will name different forms of religion in Roman history, but he thinks that one way or the other they all serve the same purpose—to deceive the Romans into serving false gods who only seek to harm them. Roman religion and sacral politics are two distinct things, even as they are intimately bound together. Religion did not have purely political purposes, but the two were linked together across Roman public life in a variety of different ways, including rites and festivals that did not have overt political purposes.

Sacral politics as practiced in Rome was rooted in three assumptions. First, the Romans believed there were gods and that these gods were powerful. The religious world of the ancients was filled with demons, gods, and a host of other spiritual beings. Gods were the greatest and most powerful of these spiritual beings. Second, the Romans believed that these gods should be offered sacrifices to promote the welfare of the *res publica*. Ancient religion as a whole, and Roman religion in particular, was unabashedly *quid pro quo* in nature. Sacrifices to the civic deities were performed for the purpose of receiving blessings and benefits from these divine beings. If a sacrifice was pleasing and performed well, then it was believed the gods would reciprocate with blessing. Something akin to a contract existed between the gods and their worshipers. If the Romans held up their end of the bargain, then the gods would hold up theirs. The third assumption was that if Rome prospered it was because the Romans had succeeded at the second assumption—properly honoring the gods—which is what the Romans believed of themselves. More than most people of the ancient world, the Romans were particularly scrupulous in their observance of religious and cultic rites. They believed it was their *pietas* that had secured the growth and prosperity of their empire *sine fine*.

Sacral politics is a major problem for Christians, according to Augustine, because it essentially treats the relationship between human persons and the divine as a patron-client relationship—which is exactly what Christianity is not. The goal of the Christian faith is not to receive blessings in this life but to receive the one blessing beyond this life: uninterrupted enjoyment of God in the heavenly city with the angels and other citizens of heaven. Roman religion, despite its claims, not only distorts the view of the relationship between humanity and the divine, it encourages vice, licentiousness, and violence, and brings harm to humanity rather than blessing. Augustine seeks to demonstrate the falsity and harmfulness of Roman religion and how its dangers lie at the source of Rome's misguided and destructive political ambitions.

Augustine will spend a great amount of time criticizing various facets of Roman religion, but the core problem that Roman religion presents for Roman politics is less apparent. In fact, understanding that problem requires a great act of discernment that Rome's most impressive figures—Cicero, Seneca, and others—had been unable to undertake. What Augustine discerns on the basis of reason and revelation through the grace of Christ (*gratia Christi*) is that behind the civic cult lie sinister spiritual forces that have taken Rome captive. As Augustine surveys Roman history, he seeks to make the character of these forces visible. Roman religion and sacral politics provide the means for these sinister spiritual powers to exercise their dominion over the Romans without Rome's awareness. Romans are deceived about the nature of the gods they worship and the gods' ability to fulfill their promises of blessing. In reality, the Romans are captive to the power of these seemingly angelic overlords, but they cannot see it. The burden of Augustine's argument is to reveal the demonic nature of these powers and Rome's domination by them. Roman religion is the vehicle for accomplishing these purposes; sacral politics further feeds into Rome's captivity and deception.

## Roman Religion and Augustine's Political Thought

With the growth of scholarship on the specific topic of Augustine's political thought, I will begin with a brief review of recent literature. What is the understanding in current scholarship on the relationship between Roman religion and Roman political thought in *City*? A second question I will examine in the current literature is how Augustine's criticisms of Roman religion in books 1 through 10 figure within the broader interpretation of his project in *City*. The overall general trend has been to view Roman religion as peripheral to Rome and Augustine's analysis, or as an epiphenomenon that was not a part of Augustine's primary concern in *City*.

Not everything that flies under the banner of Augustinian political theology engages the text of *City* extensively and historically,[1] so I will limit myself to examining a couple of representative positions within recent scholarship. In most twentieth-century scholarship on Augustine's political thought, Roman religion is a peripheral issue, if it is mentioned at all. A good example of this is R. A. Markus' *Saeculum*, which has dominated discussions of Augustine's political thought for the last fifty years. It was both the virtue and the limitation of Markus' work to stress the inner dimensions of the *civitas terrenae* and the *civitas dei*. "The distinction between the two cities," Markus writes in characteristic fashion, "lies in the dimension of men's wills, in their inner response to their world and their experience."[2] It is love that generates these two cities.[3] However, this advancement in understanding Augustine's theology has brought with it an overemphasis on "love" to the detriment of other foci in *City*. In terms of Roman religion, Markus has little to say on the matter. His summary of the first ten books of *City* is terse: "His diatribe against Roman idolatry and corruption of manners, against the addiction to the dissipations of the theatre, are too constant a feature of these books to require special mention. What is striking about them is Augustine's determination to use them in denunciation of a contemporary moral decline."[4] No doubt Augustine is moralizing, to a certain extent, but his polemics against Roman religion, and, specifically, civic religion, are much more substantive and important than Markus realizes.

A few factors may help account for Markus's blind spot. First and foremost is a methodological blind spot. Markus subscribes to the trend, which was begun before him, of overemphasizing book 19 as *the* source of Augustine's political thought, in part because he is looking for something like ancient political philosophy and cannot find it.[5] In book 19 Augustine takes up some themes that approach a resemblance to political thought, and so Markus and many others have started their work from there. This may reveal a deeper distinction between religion and politics that is more modern than ancient, when politics and religion walked together quite natu-rally. Most revealing is that Markus talks about Augustine's corpus and "political theory" proper, that is, "questions about human society and its institutions in gen-eral, and especially in relation to the ultimate purposes of human life; questions about political authority and obedience, about law and social order."[6] On questions such as these Augustine's corpus constitutes "no clear body of political thought"; and only by way of "implications drawn from what he has to say on other, though related matters" can we formulate a basis for Augustine's political thought.[7] In the background of Markus's reading one detects an inability to see Roman religion, quite contrary to Augustine's insightfulness, as having direct and indirect connections to Roman political thought.

Current interpretations of Augustine's political thought make similar mistakes in seeing Roman religion as epiphenomenal. John Milbank's influential constructive proposal advanced in *Theology and Social Theory* reduces all discussion of the Roman gods to a faulty ontology, "ontological antagonism," as opposed to the Christian "ontology of peace."[8] Roman religion and myth inscribed violence within public belief and practice in Roman society at a fundamental level, which could be altered only by a new myth. The violent founding myth of Romulus and Remus is exem-plary of this deeper view of violence as necessary to counter violence. Milbank writes, "Mythical beginnings of the legal order are therefore traced back to the arbitrary lim-itation of violence by violence, to victory over rivals, and to the usurpation of fathers by sons."[9] In this view it is not important whether the gods are real or not, which surely it was for Augustine and the Christians of his time, but what is important is how these myths and practices constitute "the vestigial remains of an entire pagan mode of practice, stretching back to Babylon."[10] Rome's pagan worship reinforces the ontological violence that encouraged seeking *dominium* over others as an end in itself. In this way, Rome, which manifests its violence in its practice of *imperium*, is the perfect embodiment of the earthly city in its lust for power and domination. In contrast to Rome's *imperium*, the church is a communion of love and forgive-ness that, "as the realized heavenly city, is the *telos* of the salvific process."[11] Milbank reduces Augustine's talk of Roman religion to a "practice" that is concrete and linked to the actual and visible political communities.

Other contemporary accounts of Augustine's political thought have taken his critique of Roman religion more seriously, even as they reaffirm Milbank's predi-lection for aligning the earthly and the Roman Empire in Augustine's thought. John Cavadini and Oliver O'Donovan both acknowledge the role of spiritual entities in varying degrees in Augustine's thought, and have linked Augustine's criticisms of Roman religion in part to Roman politics. Cavadini links Roman religious practice and myth to the project of imperial expansion and domina-tion that bears similarities to Milbank's account, though he recognizes that the spiritual forces Augustine is describing are real and have an effect on human soci-ety.[12] Oliver O'Donovan, along similar lines, is able at times to bring Augustine's critique of Roman religion into closer proximity to his political thinking.[13] In a very interesting discussion of sin, O'Donovan turns to Augustine's account of the fall of Satan and Adam to open up deeper motivational categories for understanding the motivation of Rome. "Polytheism," he writes, "a deception practiced on Rome by demons and willingly acquiesced in, is the natural accompaniment of empire, and enslavement to the sensual is its natural corollary."[14] Though, at times, both O'Donovan and Cavadini display an awareness of Augustine's more apocalyptic side, they do not make direct connections between his criticisms of Roman religion and his political thought.[15]

No contemporary scholar comes closer to seeing Augustine's criticisms of Roman religion connected to his political thought than Robert Dodaro. In fact, Dodaro devotes a sizable section in one of his longest chapters in *Christ and the Just Society in the Thought of Augustine* to Roman religion, and civic religion in particular.[16] Dodaro has a real appreciation for how Roman religion and the "demons" corrupt Roman politics and society. Whether it is the theater, athletic games, festivals, cultic performances, sacrifice, or other forms of religious ritual or practice, there is deep sense that Roman religion has a profoundly negative impact on Roman mores and society. Dodaro even spends a good amount of time exploring the comprehensive role that Augustine assigns to demons in Roman society and politics.[17]

Dodaro spells out, in great detail, Augustine's view of the all-encompassing nature of Roman religion as a means of mediating lies and immorality. Emphasis is primarily placed in Dodaro's account on the soul and virtue. The first ten books of *City* are focused on "the soul's efforts to overcome obstacles to the true knowledge and worship of God are crucial to his understanding of the creation and preservation of a just society."[18] But the human soul is weak and ignorant, unable to break through its own self-imposed and society-imposed obstacles without grace mediating truth and righteousness to the soul. Still, although Dodaro comes close to appreciating Augustine's critique of Roman religion in its apocalyptic dimensions, he never puts all the pieces together. Books 1 through 10, by Dodaro's lights, are about illustrating "the failure of ancient religions and philosophies to help their adherents to live justly."[19] Is Augustine concerned with virtue? Yes, it is a prominent theme to be sure, but as I will argue below that concern is couched in a larger concern about the true nature of Roman religion and its dangerous effects.

## *Pax Deorum* and Roots of Sacral Politics

The entirety of the first half of *The City of God* is devoted to a critique of Roman religion. Roman religion is a complicated phenomenon to comprehend because it stands in stark contrast to the Judeo-Christian religions that have dominated Western civilization. No Romans or Greeks or Egyptians talked about having "faith" in the gods, because the gods were always there.[20] *Religio* is a set of cultic practices and ritual obligations to be performed that are handed down by the ancestors and have to do with human and divine relations. But *religio* is not private and extends into all areas of life (family, city, and so on), and cannot be isolated as a specific phenomenon called "religion."[21]

The roots of Roman sacral politics have a long history that extends beyond their own particular cultural and religious milieu. Though the uniqueness of Roman republicanism or Greek democracy is more often stressed, Rome's religious and political ideas were deeply traditional and had their origins in the pre-classical world. Francis Oakley, with a growing number of historians, has highlighted the deep roots of sacral politics in the ancient Near Eastern view of kingship.[22] Kings were the special representatives of the people before the gods; they wielded divine authority and played an important role in securing the harmonious and orderly relationship among the gods, spiritual entities, nature, and society. Drawing on the work of Henri Frankfort, Oakley notes that the cultic and priestly roles of Egyptian and Mesopotamian kings made them the mediators between the people and the gods to ensure a good harvest and favorable weather, victory in battle, and good fortune in the affairs of state.[23] The cultic duties of the king maintained the cosmic or sacral order through complex and highly elaborate sacrificial systems and symbolic ceremonies, designed to preserve and protect the delicate balance of harmony among the spiritual forces that could potentially burst forth and bring chaos into all areas of life. The family, tribe, and king were all subservient to this one great concern for the "harmonious integration" of the community with the divine and nature over against the primeval forces of chaos. The tradition of sacral kingship was the dominant and unrivaled political ideology in the ancient world until the early church began to contest its basic suppositions.

Looking from the vantage point out of which Roman culture and politics grew, we see many continuities between the sacral politics of Rome and its ancient forebears. "The object of early cult," writes H. H. Scullard of early Roman religion, "had been to secure the goodwill of the spirits or deities by certain rituals which if correctly performed were thought to guarantee the 'peace of the gods' (*pax deorum*)."[24] Thus the misfortunes that were inflicted on the people of Rome—as was believed by most people in the ancient world—could be traced to a failure to appease the gods in some way.[25] Scullard describes this relationship as "semi-legal" and "contractual," because the Romans practiced *religio* in the expectation that if they performed cultic ritual appropriately, the deities would grant material benefits ranging from an abundant harvest to victory over enemies.[26] The *pax* that was the goal of their cultic rituals was more than just the absence of violence, though that is part of it, but constituted a much fuller sense of both basic goods for survival and material abundance and military victories and security. The growth and expansion of Rome was largely attributed to the beneficence of the gods and the *pietas* of the Roman people.[27]

Aeneas, that most Roman of heroes, was praised for his piety: *pius Aeneas*. In fact, the *Aeneid* is perhaps *the* exemplary text of Roman sacral politics. When read against the long backdrop of sacral politics in the ancient world, Virgil's great epic displays the very working out of the logic of sacral politics in the journey, struggles, and triumph of Aeneas precisely because he is faithful to the gods. It is the famous words of the gods to Aeneas and the Roman people—"parcere subiectis et debellare superbos" ("to spare the submissive and war down the proud")[28]—that typify the ethos of Roman pride that Augustine will oppose in the preface of *City*, but these words also exemplify the sacral character of Rome's mission from the gods as the conqueror and ruler of the nations.

Mary Beard and colleagues explain the relationship between the gods and the Greco-Roman city-state succinctly:

> [T]he gods and goddesses of an ancient city, as we have seen, were members of the city's community in much the same sense as were the human citizens. The city's activities required the involvement of humans and deities alike, the performance of rituals playing a critical role in maintaining communication and good faith between them. It follows that a great sequence of victories for the city implied both a triumph for the gods and goddesses and also a vindication of the religious system operated by the human members of the community. Rome's success was the gods' success.[29]

This basic conviction about the relationship of the gods to Rome and the meaning of Roman success and growth as achieved by the *providentia* of the gods[30]—preeminently Jupiter Optimus Maximus—is a stable feature of Roman sacral politics throughout the republican and imperial periods.[31]

One of the clearest examples of Roman sacral politics in action is recorded by Livy during the Hannibalic threat to Rome in the Second Punic War. In response to both Hannibal and a series of prodigies reported to the Senate from across Italy, the Romans undertook a number of religious activities, such as the institution of games at the dedications of temples to specific gods and festivals held in the honor of certain gods.[32] The most unprecedented of their responses was a solemn vow by the consul, Q. Fabius Maximus, dubbed "Sacred Spring" (*ver sacrorum*), that promised to sacrifice to Jupiter the offspring of all pigs, sheep, goats, and cattle born within a set period of time in exchange for safety through the next five years. The formula for the offering is most precise and exacting in its detail, specifying conditions and stipulations in a legal fashion. If Rome fulfills its end of the vow, Jupiter should be expected to protect Rome from Hannibal's army. Aside from the baldly *quid pro quo* nature of the vow, what is most revealing in this event is the reason for undertaking this series of responses and what the Romans believed the root cause of the crisis to be. Rome was not in this predicament, the consul assured the senators, because of bad generalship or foolhardiness but because they failed in their cultic duties—*neglegentia caerimoniarum*. It is for this reason that they consulted the Sybilline Books and drew up drastic new measures to appease the anger of the gods against them.

The implication of these events and the response to them is that the gods had brought this state of affairs on the Romans, but with a reassessment of the situation they could appease the anger of the gods by fulfilling their vow, and with games, dedications, and temples. Ritual performance does not require the gods to respond, but the assumption that undergirds the ritual is that the honor and worship offered through the sacrifice or other cultic ritual is of equal benefit to the divine benevolence being petitioned. Roman gods were not all-powerful, nor were they weak and willing to be controlled. They could be negotiated with because "they were bound to the human community by a network of obligations, traditions, rules, within which the skill of the priests, magistrates and senate could keep them on the side of the city."[33]

Bookending this period toward the end of the war in 204 BC, the Romans brought the statue of Magna Mater (Cybele) from Phrygia, believing this would aid them in their struggle with Carthage. The Romans came to this conclusion through an examination of the Sybilline Books, sacrifices at the Oracle of Delphi, responses from the Oracle, and other omens and prodigies.[34] P. Cornelius Scipio, voted the best man by the Senate, traveled to Ostia to welcome the statue and transport it to a Roman temple that had been built for it. How exactly the statue and the cult of Magna Mater, with its castrated, ecstatic priests in tow, was meant to give Rome an advantage is not completely clear. What is clear is that the Romans believed the power of this eastern goddess would in some way aid them in their epic contest with Hannibal. Augustine himself recounts this event as evidence of the extent to which the Romans were blinded and enthralled to sacral politics.[35]

The measures taken during the Punic Wars are out of the norm, but they do highlight the logic of sacral politics more sharply than the everyday activities of Roman political administration. Sacral politics was part of the mundane functioning of Roman politics, but it achieved a special prominence in times of crisis. And for that reason it is especially telling, because when crisis hits we see where people place their trust.

## *Religio, Superstitio,* and the Altar of Victory

From the very earliest confrontations between Christians and Roman imperial authorities during the first and second centuries, it becomes quite clear that the primary point of contention has to do with Christians refusing to participate in the Roman civic cult, thus offending fundamental Roman sacral political convictions. The term that the Romans deploy to describe this is *superstitio.*[36] It has an evolving meaning over time and covers a multitude of sins, but the basic sense in Rome's engagement with Christians and other non-Roman cults is foreign religious practice that threatens to undermine Rome's relationship to the gods, and thereby, disrupts the safety and prosperity of Rome.[37] The *pax romana* required the *pax deorum.*

Christopher Bryan likens the situation to the way we might view terrorists or suicide bombers as security threats, though in a different sense.[38] Christians never advocated overthrowing the Roman government or taking up arms in the ways that the

Jewish zealots did. In fact, Christians were adamant in their claim that they prayed *for* the emperor.[39] Christians, Druids, and other foreign cults failed to show *religio*—proper respect and honor—to the gods of Rome and were, therefore, *impius* and a threat to the *res publica*. It was not the beliefs, *per se*, of Christians that were threatening but their outright refusal to participate in the public cult. It was the proper performance of this public cultic ritual, so the Romans believed, that secured the right relationship with the gods and the security and prosperity of the *res publica*.[40] Actual belief mattered little. Performance of ritual was essential and the failure to sacrifice to the gods of Rome was tantamount to denying their existence, thereby risking their anger and the loss of peace and blessings for the political community.

In Augustine's own time, the tensions between Christianity and Roman sacral politics continued, though the tables had been turned on the pagans and now the Christians accused the pagans of *superstitio*.[41] The Altar of Victory affair presents us with an important link to Augustine's own thinking on Roman religion and politics. Not only was Augustine present in Rome and Milan as the scuffle played out but the two adversaries in the public contest over the altar standing in the Senate were men with whom Augustine had some direct connection. Symmachus, appointed prefect of Rome in 384, was responsible for Augustine's appointment that same year as orator of the city of Milan, though it does not appear that Augustine knew him personally.[42] During that same year, Augustine first encountered the formidable and influential bishop of Milan, Ambrose, who was instrumental in Augustine's own conversion to Christianity. It was also in that year that the Altar of Victory contest reached its dramatic height with both Symmachus and Ambrose submitting petitions to the young emperor, Valentinian II. Augustine's recollections of this time leave out any mention of the affair, and he does not mention it specifically by name, but we can see the impression it left on him in *The City of God*.

The Altar of Victory was dedicated to celebrate Augustus's victory over Marc Antony at the battle of Actium, a victory that Virgil depicts as the battle of Roman gods triumphing over the foreign gods of Egypt: "Monstrous gods of every form and barking Anubis wield weapons against Neptune and Venus and against Minerva. . . . Actian Apollo from above was bending his bow; in terror at this all Egypt and India, all Arabians, all Sabaeans, turned to flee."[43] Symmachus' original appeal to Emperor Valentinian is filled with the common tropes invoked by the advocates of sacral politics: imperial expansion, prosperity, and the *pax deorum* due to the gods' favor; the traditions of the ancestors (*mos maiorum*) as the repository of the sacred rites whose observance is necessary and responsible for the *res publica*'s endurance; the fact that natural and political disasters are traced to divine animosity that has its origins in human failure to honor the gods appropriately. For example, in the mouth of a personified Rome, Symmachus attributes Rome's military victories to Roman cult: "[Rome's] cultus subdued the world to my laws, these sacred rites repelled Hannibal from the walls of Rome and the Senones from the Capitoline Hill."[44] Though Symmachus is writing some 450 years after the Punic Wars, his belief in the efficacy of Rome's sacral politics is remarkably similar to that held by the Romans fighting Hannibal. Echoing the conviction mouthed by Fabius Maximus, Symmachus makes the blanket claim that it is through the offense of the gods that "all the disasters to the Roman race have arisen."[45] Vestal Virgins and pagan priests had traditionally received support from the state on account of their service to the gods and the dividends it brought to the public welfare. When those funds were seized, temple properties confiscated, and privileges (*munera*) revoked, Symmachus argues that the famine of 383 arose not from natural causes but from divine ones: "It was blasphemy that dried up the year's yield; and it was bound to follow that all would perish, for religion was being denied its proper support."[46]

In Ambrose's detailed reply to Symmachus (Epistula 73) he rejects the central logic of sacral politics that Symmachus straightforwardly advocates. Reminiscent of early Christian apologists, Ambrose argues that the Roman cult was ineffective and delusional. The gods of Rome are not the great gods whose providential care has maintained the empire from its inception; rather, "the gods of the nations are demons."[47] It must be noted that Augustine himself will draw on this same proof text in his polemics against Roman civic religion.[48] Taking up Symmachus's claim that the gods were fighting against Hannibal on behalf of Rome because of Roman cultic worship, Ambrose retorts that "though the gods were fighting against him, he advanced victorious right up to the walls of Rome."[49] The persuasiveness of sacral politics relied on a direct causal link between the performance of the cultic ritual and the intervention of the gods. If Rome had been performing the sacred rites, why were the gods not able to stop Hannibal?

Responding to Symmachus's literary device of a personified Rome pleading for a return to her past ways, Ambrose places his argument in the mouth of a personified Rome as well. However, Ambrose's Rome repents of her ignorance and disowns her past cult by bringing up counterexamples that prove the cult did not always bring victory. Rome interrupts the pagans putting words into her mouth with a spirited rebuke:

> Why do you stain me every day with the useless blood of harmless herds? Trophies of victory derive not from entrails of cattle but from the strength of warriors. It was with quite other disciplines that I subjugated the world. . . . Africanus won his triumph fighting amid the battle-lines of Hannibal, not among the altars on the Capital. . . . And what about those two emperors one of who was taken captive, setting a wretched and novel precedent, while in the reign of the other the whole world was taken prisoner? Did they not demonstrate that their rituals, which promised victory, deceived them?[50]

As to whether famine is a punishment by the gods for the proscription of certain pagan rites, Ambrose notices that these rites were abolished many years ago. He wryly quips, "Has it only just now occurred to the gods of the pagans to avenge the wrong done to them?"[51] But if that argument doesn't satisfy, he follows up by asking why this year's harvest is so plentiful. Did the gods ignore the wrongs done this year? Ambrose will deal with other aspects of Symmachus's plea, but at the heart of his response is a rejection of the logic that undergirds traditional Roman civic religion.

## Augustine's Critique of Roman Religion and Sacral Politics

The preparatory work done in the previous sections is intended to show how Augustine's critique of Roman civic religion addressed a political phenomenon (sacral politics) that was prominent and pervasive throughout Roman history. In examining the Altar of Victory affair, we can see how Ambrose, a contemporary and influential figure in Augustine's own intellectual development, deploys arguments that foreshadow Augustine's critiques in *City of God*. A more foundational purpose for the preparatory work is to frame Augustine's critique of Roman religion properly, as in continuity with the tradition of criticism of Roman sacral politics. The critique of Roman religion is a political critique.

In *The City of God*, Augustine focuses primarily on civic religion and develops a consistent, and consistently harsh, unrelenting critique of this religion as the root of Rome's problems.[52] As we have seen from our earlier survey of contemporary Augustinian political thought, scholars generally downplay or misconstrue Augustine's overarching claim of an essential link between Roman religion and politics.

In outlining the road map for the first half of the book, Augustine sets out to offer a counterargument against Rome's sacral politics, which have, in part, been Christianized by Augustine's fellow coreligionists. He claims he is going to offer an argument, based on Roman sources, as to why the Christian God deigned to extend the Roman Empire and, conversely, why the gods who were believed to have extended it did not. However, Augustine's argument consists of more than disproving that the Roman gods were able to do what they claimed to do. Books 1 through 10 are a comprehensive argument for the interconnectedness of all Roman religion as a single phenomenon deployed to deceive and harm the Roman people. The project of these early books is to reveal the reality that is already operating and has been operating since the very founding of Rome.

It is clear that Augustine understands the basic claim of sacral politics: that the gods are powerful and able to bless those who honor them appropriately. The Romans, for their part, believed their piety far surpassed that of all other peoples in honoring the gods of Rome, which thus accounted for the growth and victory of Rome. Augustine writes, "Let us then see on what grounds our opponents have the boldness to ascribe the immense expansion and the long duration of the Roman Empire to the credit of the gods to whom, so they claim, they offered honorable worship in the dutiful performance of degrading spectacles by the agency of degraded performers."[53] It was Jupiter Optimus Maximus, the patron god of Rome, who was believed to be "king of the gods, and giver of their Empire."[54] The relationship among Jupiter and other deities of the civic cult and the Romans was one of patron to client. From the beginning, Christian apologists had railed against the civic gods, but Augustine goes deeper and farther in his criticisms than anyone before him by attempting to not merely critique the civic cult but to get at its basic assumptions and then completely undermine it.

Rome's civic religion (and Neoplatonism to a lesser extent) is a disease on the body politic.[55] It is both harmful and false. The Romans no doubt believed the gods that were the objects of the civic cult were real and did possess the powers that the Romans attributed to them. Augustine argues that the civic religion preys on the masses even as it deludes the elites. It encourages vicious and licentious behavior by shrouding vice with the patina of piety. Whether it was the founding myths, the epic poetry of Virgil, the public cult, the theater, games, or other forms of religious and cultic practices, all of these fed into a warped view of the gods and encouraged behavior that was both vicious and self-defeating.

Although it is easy to get lost in Augustine's rhetorical artistry, a single core argument holds together the rest of the arguments he makes against Roman religion. In 1.29 and at other points in *The City of God* he will return to Psalm 96:4 (Vulg. 95:4) as a guiding proof text for his main thesis, "the gods of the nations are demons,"[56] the same passage that Ambrose invoked in his polemics against Symmachus. It is a simple text, but it captures well Augustine's primary objective to argue not only for the falsity and harmfulness of Roman religion and sacral politics but that "the gods of the nations" are in fact demons who are wicked, weak, and exercise a tyrannical dominion over Rome through the various aspects of Roman religion.

These pseudo-gods are a real spiritual force. They are demons. They exercise real power, and the civic religion has been its primary vehicle, though all of their power is allowed by the "fixed rule of divine providence."[57] Roman religion has been tailor made by the rebellious and wicked spirits to keep the Romans under their dominion. All the various cultic forms, practices, and myths serve the purpose of maintaining their rule. Roman religion has a unity to it, but that unity can be discerned only beyond the visible forms of worship to the invisible entities that maintain the system. In step with Ambrose's apocalyptic interpretation of the Altar of Victory, Augustine follows his mentor in a similar fashion, asserting "the gods of the nations are demons" and that the Roman alliance to these spiritual powers is the core reason for Rome's suffering and misery. Christianity does not present a panacea on this front, since it does not magically transform the fallen nature of humans or human community. But it does offer liberation from the delusion that Roman civic religion is responsible for Rome's power and glory.

Augustine will not reveal until books 11 and 12 the real identity of these demons. In those books he offers a biblical account of the rebellion of the angels, led by the devil, which forms the basis for the earthly city. The real story that Augustine is telling about the Roman Empire and Roman religion is not that the fundamental problem lay in the *cupiditas* of Rome but in the *cupiditas* of the demons. All of the criticisms of Rome are designed to push our view back beyond the merely visible manifestations of the lust for domination to the rulers of the earthly city. In this way, the polemics have the aim of making the true nature of these fallen angelic powers apparent.

Those engaged in the civic cult or in Platonic theurgy are alike ruled by the domination (*dominatio*) of the angelic powers. Throughout the first ten books of *The City of God*, Augustine will often resort to a formula that restates his primary thesis: "And it is only the grace of God through Jesus Christ our Lord, that frees [*liberat*] us from [the demons'] domination."[58] This formulation reveals much about Augustine's thinking. First, fallen humanity prior to the advent of Christ and even afterward is in a state of demonic domination (*daemonia dominatio*). Rome itself lives under this domination, as is evidenced by its various cults and depraved religious practices that, in fact, stand at odds with austere Roman morals.[59] Second, it is only the grace of Christ that frees one from this state of domination. Humans are as helpless against these demons as they are of earning their salvation through their own righteousness. It is the Lord who frees them from their bondage. And even after liberation, humans do not completely escape the demons' temptations nor their influence.

A couple of examples will help to illustrate the power of this domination. Scipio Nasica Corculum, voted the best man in the Senate, had successfully convinced the Romans to abandon the building of a theater in Rome that would "allow Greek corruption to infiltrate into the virile morality of Rome," and "undermine and weaken the Roman moral character."[60] But Augustine faults him for opposing the morally repugnant theatrical spectacles while failing to reject the gods who commanded them. Even this Scipio, this man of great virtue and principle, was unable to "take a stand against the authority of those whom he supposed to be gods." Without "the revelation from heaven of the teaching which can cleanse the heart by faith," Scipio was unable to oppose "the oppressive domination of demonic powers."[61] Similarly, the great Platonist Porphyry, as learned and close to Christianity as he was in his understanding of "the one true God," was unable to oppose the "envious powers" that he was subjected to.[62] He acted out of shame and fear, unwilling and unable to object to the angelic powers that lorded over him. All the great men of Rome were unable to see the true nature of these demons. Even when Roman morals stood in opposition to certain aspects of Roman religion (e.g., the theater) the Romans, on account of their piety, refused to see the gods as wicked or perverse.[63]

For these spirits, domination is not an end in itself. The psychology of evil angels is more sinister and subtle. Their deep-seated desire is to be like God: to be worshiped by the creatures whom God created for fellowship with himself. Roman religion is the tool whereby they achieve this end. Their deep and fundamental motive does not concern the exercise of power over someone, but aims at denying God the worship and recognition that is due to God alone and receiving that worship and recognition in God's place. Filled with envy and pride, they have rebelled against the fellowship of holy angels and sought to establish their own city, with the worship of themselves as its guiding principle. The devil stands out as the angel who most supremely embodies envy and pride in his motivation and action.[64]

*Latreia* (worship) is the inner act of clinging to an object as the fundamental source of one's happiness. The language of sacrifice is used as a synonym for worship. A "true sacrifice" is "offered in every act which is designed to unite us with God in a holy fellowship, every act, that is, which is directed to that final Good which makes possible our true felicity."[65] True sacrifices are not offered to a deity in order to receive something, whether it be the blessings of empire or material wealth, because this will not bring true happiness. Our greatest good, or "true good," is to "cling to God."[66] The good angels seek only for us to offer our sacrifices to God, whereas the devil and his angels seek sacrifices to be offered to themselves.

What makes these spiritual powers so effective is not merely the persuasiveness of their ideas or the attractiveness of the cults, important as they are. They are intelligent and powerful spirits who are motivated to shape reality and the human experience of that reality. We may think that the world we experience is merely passive, but Augustine says it is active and pulls people in a certain direction. A spiritual reality beyond your perception desires to possess and shape you. It has the power to shape that reality and influence people who are ignorant and prone to deception. Roman religion wields its power not only as a set of social practices, or as a set of ideas, but as an actual spiritual, apocalyptic reality that becomes identifiable in political and social life to those who can discern it.

Books 1 through 10 are Augustine's discernment of the spirits within Roman history and social life. As he looks back on Roman history and its glorious feats he sees an inverse image of the reality that is presented. Virgil's prophetic proclamation in the prologue that Rome's mission is to "subdue the defeated and war down the proud" (*parcere subiectis et debellare superbos*) stands as the epitome of the earthly spirit.[67] Rome is dominated by a spiritual tyranny even as it seeks to tyrannize others. The gods whip the Romans onward to ever greater deeds in the name of glory, which has an altogether self-defeating quality. But to the Romans and everyone else, these deeds appear to be a sign of divine favor. Roman rule has spread far and wide; how could Romans imagine this was not an act of divine providence? Only an act of discernment that has a completely different reference point from outside of Roman religion can criticize this paradigm. In books 2 and 3 Augustine offers a reading of Roman history that shows how it admits of a radically different interpretation. In Oliver O'Donovan's words, Roman history in Augustine's hands "turns into a kind of photographic negative of Vergil." By that he means that on a more discerning reading, the history of glory that Vergil's *Aeneid* comes to represent "turns out in fact to have been a demonic history, which expresses the divine purpose only as providence."[68]

For instance, book 3 culminates in chapter 17, when Augustine recounts a series of horrors in Roman history followed by the rhetorical question, "Where were the gods?" The answer of course is that they were present but unable and unwilling to stop the atrocities. In rough chronological fashion, he reveals highlights of Roman history as tragedies over which the gods preside with sadistic pleasure, "like spectators in the amphitheatre." Events such as the Punic Wars, which would have been considered unassailable evidence of the efficacy of Roman civic religion and their gods' power, are revealed to be self-defeating, tragic events encouraged by malicious demons. Recounting the renewed Secular Games during the First Punic war in order to win the gods' favor, Augustine writes, "No doubt when those games were restored the infernal gods were delighted to join in the celebrations, at a time when they were enriched with such a supply of dying men. For there were certainly splendid games being put on for the demons, and lavish banquets provided for the infernal gods by wretched men in their crazy wars and bloody hatreds, and in the tragic victories on either side."[69] The Roman gods are jealous to have worshipers of their own, but they do not care for those worshipers and in fact enjoy watching them suffer and die. This is because their concern is to deny God the worship of human beings. The Romans, in fact, suffer immensely under the tutelage of their deities, but have infused their suffering with a meaning and value that it does not in reality possess.

The extended interpretation of Rome in the first half of *City* aims to reveal the true nature of the gods of Rome. Augustine seeks to show how they operate at present by demonstrating how they have operated in the past. He will turn, primarily, to the kingdom and republican periods of Roman history to show the gods at work.[70] Scripture plays an important role in discerning the nature of these spirits, even though Augustine does not make scripture the basis of his analysis.[71] On the basis of reason one might be able to come to some understanding of the gods but, on Augustine's reading, our rational capabilities are unable to come to a true account of the gods and their effects. Given the forces the Romans are up against, reason is too weak. Only the gracious activity of God will allow us overcome our own weakness and ignorance in order to understand the nature of these so-called gods.[72]

The domination of Rome by these spiritual powers could not occur except by means of deception (*deceptio*) and seduction (*seduco*).[73] The two are linked in Augustine's mind because they rely on each other for their efficacy. Deception is a form of seduction; seduction is a form of deception. Deception happens because someone is seduced by evil spirits to love and cling to oneself and not the one true God. From this self-love (*amor sui*) arises all deception. In turning to the self as our object of love, we reject the truth. We refuse to see and love the world as it is and the God who is the source of all that is. Even those who practice deception are themselves deceived.[74] The devil is paradoxically the most deceived even as he deceives, because he does not "stand fast in the truth," but rather "in his arrogance supposed that he wielded power as his own private possession and rejoiced in that power. And thus, he was both deceived and deceiving. . . . He refused to accept reality and in his arrogant pride presumes to counterfeit an unreality."[75]

The deception that Augustine has in mind is both cognitive and affective, though the sources of the deception lie within the human will and desire. We are blinded, in the first case, by our disordered love (*cupiditas*). Rome is deceived as to the true identity and power of these false deities and thereby led astray as to the true sources of happiness and rule. Conversely, the Romans are seduced by the promises and practices of Roman religion, which further enslaves them: "The Romans thought they ought to worship their gods, to ensure the insignificant and deceptive happiness of this world. But where were the gods when the Romans, whose worship they canvassed with their cunning lies, were vexed by such calamities?"[76] Deception is brought about and maintained through an inversion of the proper order of use (*uti*) and enjoyment (*frui*). Roman religion invites its worshipers to use the gods in order to enjoy worldly honors, glory, and material comfort.[77]

The Romans have been deceived on a number of fronts, beginning with the nature of their gods and then cascading in to all areas of life, society and history. They believe gods are morally praiseworthy and the primary cause of Roman military success and material wealth. On all these points, the general populace is deluded. Augustine does not deny that Rome has in fact achieved visible success, but he will show how the expansion cannot be due to the will of the gods, nor indeed are these victories in fact glorious and morally praiseworthy. In book 3, chapters 2–17, Augustine examines Rome from its founding to the end of the kingdom period and finds only tragedy. Certainly the dominion of Rome was expanded and "great victories" were had, but "All those victories, won at the price of so much blood and such heavy calamities, had scarcely extended the Roman dominion to twenty miles from the city."[78] Rome's expansion was in reality a pyrrhic one. If we remove the rosy shades of the Virgilian glory narrative, we could defend the purpose of the gods in Rome only as "simply to be able to punish the Romans, rather than to benefit them with their favours, by seducing to them with hollow victories and exhausting them with terrible wars."[79]

What is particularly striking about Augustine's account of deception by these malicious spiritual powers is how he understands the deception working through various cultural, social, and political forms. He does not account for deception merely on the level of will or intellect but also through social and political forms, where it is an integral part of creating a false understanding of the gods and their power. Not only do Romans have to fight their own propensity to reject the truth but they are confronted with countless familial customs, mores, patterns of life, civic entities and celebrations, political and social institutions, and religious practices and beliefs that form an interlocking web that reinforces the foundational convictions of sacral politics.

Whether it is civic religion, cults and cultic practices, theater, religious festivals, games, literature, or myth (e.g. Varro, Livy, Virgil, Sallust), historical exemplars (Regulus), or Platonic theurgy (Porphyry and Apuleius), what gives these dimensions of social life their power is the authoritative status that they are accorded within Roman society. Augustine does not use the language of "system," but this modern term would be an apt description of the comprehensive way in which legal, social, civil, familial, and religious institutions and traditions form an interlocking "iron cage," to borrow Max Weber's term, that appears impossible to escape on the basis of one's own will power. In order to escape this world one would have to create a completely different world with a completely different plausibility structure to challenge and undermine it, which is what happens with Christianity.

Augustine will invoke the concept of *auctoritas* ("authority") to explain, in part, why the Romans remain ensnared in the false reality mediated by their civic religion. The mere existence of different institutions and tradition is not enough to explain their power. They must possess an authoritative status that causes people to relate to them differently than something that lacks that authority. They are accepted as true and, therefore, trustworthy accounts of reality, as the way things work. Virgil's *Aeneid*, for instance, is granted canonical status within the broader Roman culture, which gives it power as a mediator of truth. In turn, it shapes those who interact with it. Augustine's deep affective responses to the death of Dido, which he describes in the *Confessions*, puts the power of this *auctoritas* on display.[80] This is the same in *City* but with one important difference: whereas *Confessions* focused on the effects of the play itself, in *City* the emphasis is on the relationship between theatrical displays and the spiritual entities who use these displays for insidious ends.

Although Roman religion has no scripture or authoritative revelation, it still possesses and exercises authority over Romans and their society as a whole.[81] Even setbacks can be processed through this overall explanatory framework because it offers an account of why bad things are happening. It is not that the framework is persuasive *per se*, since it is the framework that provides the very basis for plausibility of those who subscribe to it. How Roman religion in fact achieves this status is an altogether different question and one that Augustine answers only partially. Earlier sections of this essay sought to go some way toward clarifying that the assumptions of Roman religion and sacral politics were part of a broader shared set of assumptions with other Mediterranean societies about the interrelationship between politics (kingship) and the gods.

The role of authority helps to explain how the Romans developed a host of religious and civic practices that were at deep odds with their own moral code. In fact, Augustine points out how the very logic of the civic cult and the sacral political system invites an inversion of virtue. The Romans seem oblivious to it or unable to grasp the extent of the corruption that this system promotes. For Augustine everything is to be used only with reference to enjoying God, who is the greatest good for all humans, whereas the civic cult invites using the deities in order to enjoy worldly benefits. Thus the logic of Roman religion itself is perverse. Not only does it produce vice in practice but the very rationale undergirding the system also promotes vice by offering a distorted and self-serving reason for engaging in religious activity. The effect of this system is to inculcate beliefs that will so harm the soul that it will be "less and less able to adjust itself and attach itself to eternal truth."[82]

Augustine's account of the theater demonstrates the power that Roman civic religion exercises. The theatre is a religious institution, since "the gods themselves sternly commanded, indeed almost extorted, the production of such shows, demanding that they should be consecrated in their honor."[83] The content of the performances were often sexual as they portrayed the gods in all sorts of lewd behaviors, in contrast to the prohibition placed on poetic license in slandering people in the performances. Thus, poets were restricted from dishonoring men but praised for slandering the gods. Augustine points out that this inconsistency is due solely to the authority granted to Roman religion. Roman morals refuse to denounce the sort of immoral and shameful behavior presented in the theaters; gross and immoral sexual behavior receives divine sanction. "How then could such gods prevent, by their commands and laws, the corruption of character and conduct which threatened from outside, or effect a cure of corruption already implanted, since those gods were anxious that such behavior should be made familiar to people through theatrical displays. . . . The result was automatically to kindle the most depraved desires in human hearts by giving them a kind of divine authority."[84]

The lust for domination, that vice which Augustine credits as most fully embodied by the Romans, is not just the manifestation of vice within Roman society but also the display of the character of their gods. Rome's vices, which Augustine catalogues extensively, are a symptom of the deeper source of the disorder that Roman political problems, chaos, violence, and *libido dominandi* are manifesting the spiritual disorder within and without Rome. Rome's lust for power is not just a vice but a "yoke of slavery" that has control over the Roman imagination. The slave masters, the *domini*, are none other than Rome's own gods. Augustine seeks to hold up a mirror to Rome so that it can see how it has become enslaved. Roman history is the best argument Rome has going for it, which is why Augustine works his way methodically through it, showing how its glory was in fact suffering and domination.

## Unmasking the Civic Deities

Augustine's critique of Roman religion in books 1 through 10 of *The City of God* amounts to an extended polemic against Roman religion, but that religion takes shape primarily within the social and political sphere. He seeks to display the various ways that civic religion functions within Roman society and politics and how it works against Rome and its flourishing. And yet, it is not merely that the system of sacral politics or the ideology itself is flawed, though that is the case on Augustine's reading. In addition, he demonstrates how the gods themselves, who are evil spirits, originated and sustain this system, which effectively enslaves the Romans. With painstaking detail he reveals the truth of Roman history and its political life, such that rather than glory it is a tragedy of epic proportions. Augustine's goal in all of this is liberation, though *true liberation* and not merely liberation of a political sort. Here we can see how the theological and the political overlap and inform one another. For Augustine, ultimately, there can be no complete separation of the two.

What sets Augustine's *City of God* apart from other Christian apologetic works is the scope and depth of the synthesis he is undertaking. The themes that he uses are not necessarily unique and many of the apologetic moves that he makes are part of the tradition that he is no doubt familiar with. The great achievement of Augustine's "magnum opus et arduum" is not only in his ability to work through a bewildering array of material but especially how he effortlessly brings these materials together into a single, intelligible account. Whether or not we grant Augustine's arguments, we can only be impressed at the scope of his ambition and the sophistication of his project.

# Notes

1. Two recent examples, Charles Mathewes, *A Theology of Public Life* (Cambridge: Cambridge University Press, 2007), and Eric Gregory, *Politics and the Order of Love: An Augustinian Ethic of Democratic Citizenship* (Chicago: University of Chicago Press, 2008), present accounts of Augustinian thought that prescind from exegetical and historical scholarship on the question.

2. R. A. Markus, *Saeculum: History and Society in the Theology of St. Augustine* (Cambridge: Cambridge University Press, 1970), 63.

3. See *The City of God* (hereafter *City*) 14.28, for Augustine's most widely quoted, pithiest formulation of the two loves and the two cities: "The two cities, then, have been created by two loves; that is, the earthly city by love of self extending even to contempt for God, and the heavenly by love of God extending to contempt for self." Augustine, *The City of God against the Pagans*, trans. and ed. R. W. Dyson (Cambridge: Cambridge University Press, 1998).

4. Markus, *Saeculum*, 56–57.

5. Markus repeats this claim throughout his writing on Augustine. Some of his views in *Saeculum* were modified over time, but he held firm on this point. See *Christianity and the Secular* (Notre Dame, IN: University of Notre Dame Press, 2006), 41.

6. Markus, *Saeculum*, 72.

7. Markus, *Saeculum*, 73.

8. John Milbank, *Theology and Social Theory: Beyond Secular Reason* (Oxford: Basil Blackwell, 1990), 390.

9. Milbank, *Theology*, 391.

10. Milbank, *Theology*, 406.

11. Milbank, *Theology*, 403.

12. See John Cavadini, "Ideology and Solidarity in Augustine's *City of God*," in *Augustine's "City of God": A Critical Guide*, ed. James Wetzel (Cambridge: Cambridge University Press, 2012), 93–110.

13. Oliver O'Donovan's magisterial essay "The Political Thought of *City of God* 19," in Oliver O'Donovan and Joan Lockwood O'Donovan, *Bonds of Imperfection: Christian Politics,*

*Past and Present* (Grand Rapids, MI: Eerdmans, 2004), comes very close to seeing Augustine's analysis of Rome as a "demonic history" (69) without making the leap.

14. Oliver O'Donovan, *The Ways of Judgment* (Grand Rapids, MI: Eerdmans, 2005), 79.

15. O'Donovan seems to lapse back into a more constructivist interpretation of Augustine here.

16. Robert Dodaro, *Christ and the Just Society in the Thought of Augustine* (Cambridge: Cambridge University Press, 2004), 43–53.

17. Dodaro, *Christ and the Just Society*, 43–50.

18. Dodaro, *Christ and the Just Society*, 31.

19. Dodaro, *Christ and the Just Society*, 32.

20. See A. D. Nock, *Conversion: The Old and the New in Religion from Alexander the Great to Augustine of Hippo* (Oxford: Oxford University Press, 1933), 18–19: "Just as in describing a strange people you spoke of *chresthai nomois* (using or having customs), so you spoke of *chresthai theois* (having gods). The gods of the people were one of its attributes."

21. John North points out that "religious rituals and practices were integral to all civic, local, or family activities; and religious roles, sometimes overlapping with political ones, were ubiquitous. . . . [I]n some sense all groups in the pagan world were religious, since they all involved some degree of cultic and ritual activity, some orientation toward the gods." North, "The Development of Religious Pluralism," in *The Jews Among Pagans and Christians in the Roman Empire*( London: Routledge, 1992), 177.

22. See Francis Oakley, *Kingship: The Politics of Enchantment* (Malden, MA: Wiley-Blackwell, 2006) and Oakley, *Empty Bottles of Gentilism: Kingship and the Divine in Late Antiquity and the Early Middle Ages (to 1050)* (New Haven: Yale University Press, 2010). See also Robert Bellah, *Religion in Human Evolution: From the Paleolithic to the Axial Age* (Cambridge, MA: Belknap Press, 2011) for a similar account, though Bellah's concerns have to do primarily with the "Axial Age" and the changes that came about in religion, society, and politics in that period.

23. See Henri Frankfort, *Kingship and the Gods: A Study in Near Eastern Religion as the Integration of Society and Nature* (Chicago: University of Chicago Press, 1948), and Frankfort, *Ancient Egyptian Religion: An Interpretation* (New York: Harper & Row, 1948).

24. H. H. Scullard, *Festivals and Ceremonies of the Roman Republic* (Ithaca, NY: Cornell University Press, 1981), 19.

25. See Robin Lane Fox, *Pagans and Christians* (New York: Alfred A Knopf, 1987), 95ff.

26. See also Mary Beard, John North, and Simon Price, *Religions of Rome*, vol. 1, *A History* (Cambridge: Cambridge University Press, 1998), 34.

27. Cicero is adamant on this point in *De natura deorum*, 2.8: "Religio id est cultu deorum multo superiores."

28. Virgil, *Aeneid*, 6.853. Cf. *City*, 1.pref.

29. Beard et al., *Religions of Rome*, 74.

30. Robert Louis Wilken, *Christians as the Romans Saw Them* (New Haven: Yale University Press, 2003), 59, notes that the language of *providentia* ("providence") of the gods is one of the prominent features of the literature and coins of the late Republic.

31. L. F. Janssen writes, "As long as Rome's citizens would not fail in showing *pietas* to the gods and displaying *virtus* in the defense of their city, Rome would stand forever. Whereas during the regal period the patron-gods of Rome had their homestead in or near the Regia, after the foundation of the republic they had their stronghold in the Capitolium,

where Jupiter O[ptimus] M[aximus] was thought to represent the supreme sovereignty of the *imperium p[opuli] R[omani]*; it was here that Rome had its deepest roots of life and the preservation of the Roman *civitas* ultimately depended on the defense of this holy site." Janssen, "'Superstitio' and the Persecution of the Christians," *Vigiliae Christianae* 33, no. 2 (1979): 131–59, at 141.

32. See Livy, *Ab urbe condita*, 22.9–10.

33. Beard et al., *Religions of Rome*, 34.

34. See Livy, *Ab urbe condita*, 29.10.

35. See *City* 1.30 and 2.5 for Augustine's discussion of the cult of Cybele, or Magna Mater.

36. See Tacitus, *Annals*, 15.44.5; Suetonius *Nero*, 16.2; Pliny, *Letters*, 10.96.8.

37. For a particularly lucid study on this point see Janssen, "Superstitio." See also Beard et al., *Religions of Rome*, 211–44 and Dale Martin, *Inventing Superstition* (Cambridge, MA: Harvard University Press, 2007), 125–39.

38. Christopher Bryan, *Render to Caesar: Jesus, the Early Church, and the Roman Superpower* (Oxford: Oxford University Press, 2005), 114–19.

39. See, for instance, 1 Clement 60.4–61.3; Tertullian, *Apology*, 30.1.4–5; Origen, *Against Celsus* 8.73. In *Render to Caesar* (115–16), Bryan notes that even Tatian, intensely critical of Greco-Roman culture as he is, pays his taxes and honors the emperor (Tatian, *Oration against the Greeks* 4).

40. See Ittai Gradel, *Emperor Religion and Roman Worship* (Oxford: Clarendon Press, 2002), 1–4. Although the evidence demonstrates that it was the refusal to participate in the cultic sacrifice that earned Christianity the label of *superstitio* by implication, it is also accurate to say that it was the Christians' beliefs about God that were the primary motivation for their refusal. ·

41. See Martin, *Inventing Superstition*, 207–25; and Michelle R. Salzman, "'Superstitio' in the Codex Theodosianus and the Persecution of Pagans," *Vigiliae Christianae* 41 no. 2 (1987): 172–88.

42. See *Confessions*, 5.13.23.

43. Virgil, *Aeneid*, 8.698–700, 704–6, in *Aeneid VII–XII*, trans. H. Rushton Fairclough, rev. G. P. Goold (Boston: Harvard University Press, 2000).

44. Symmachus, *Relatio*, 3.9, in *Prefect and Emperor: The Relations of Symmachus, A.D. 384*, trans. and ed. R. H. Borrow (Oxford: Clarendon Press, 1973).

45. Symmachus, *Rel.* 3.15.

46. Symmachus, *Rel.* 3.15.

47. In Epistula 72.1, in *Ambrose of Milan: Political Letters and Speeches*, trans. and ed. J. H. W. G. Liebeschuetz (Liverpool: Liverpool University Press, 2005). Ambrose is using Psalm 95:5 (Vulg. 96.5) as a proof text here. Ambrose wrote this first reply before he had seen the contents of Symmachus's letter to Valentinian, though he had a good idea of its basic argument.

48. For example, see *City*, 1.29.

49. Ambrose, Epistle 73.4.

50. Ambrose, Epistle 73.7.

51. Ambrose, Epistle 73.19.

52. Augustine's views on Roman religion and pagan literature changed greatly over time. His earlier writings have a much more conciliatory tone and engagement with Roman

literature and religion, whereas *Confessions* marks a turning point where he begins to take a more critical and polemical stance against Roman religion and culture. *The City of God* introduces the most critical stance that comes to mark his later writings. See Sabine MacCormack, *The Shadows of Poetry: Vergil in the Mind of Augustine* (Berkeley: University of California Press, 1998), for a perceptive study on his change of mind.

53. *City*, 4.3.

54. *City*, 4.29. John Scheid, *The Gods, the State, and the Individual: Reflections on Civic Religion in Rome* (Philadelphia: University of Pennsylvania Press, 2016), 139, clarifies this client-patron relationship: "Until the Christian era, the Romans regarded the gods as earthly partners maintaining relations with mortals with an eye toward reciprocal earthly benefits: the necessities of life for the humans, and honor and recognition of their superiority for the gods. In no case did they regard their gods as absolute masters requiring from mortals a complete and perpetual submission. Roman gods were seen as *patroni*, as powerful persons who protected and helped their *clientes*, according to a model of social relations shared by all Romans. The contradiction with the Christian way of seeing things is total."

55. Although Augustine professes to be interested in giving equal weight to civic religion and Neoplatonism, he does not get away from civic religion until book 8. The Neoplatonist he is most intent on engaging with is Porphyry, but he devotes only a portion of book 10 to refuting Porphyry and theurgy.

56. See also *City*, 9.23.

57. *City*, 10.16.

58. *City*, 4.31. For similar formulations see *City*, 1.31, 2.24, 2.29, 4.26, 4.31, 5.18, 7.33, 8.23, 8.24, 9.15, 10.27, 19.23.

59. Book 5 praises certain Roman figures, but book 2 continually raises the tension between Rome's morals and the theater.

60. *City*, 1.31. Most commentators note that Augustine makes the mistake of confusing Scipio Nasica Corculum with his father, Scipio Nasica, in this passage.

61. *City*, 1.31.

62. See *City*, 10.24.

63. In *City*, 2.12, Augustine points to the deep contradiction in the poets' and playwrights' being prohibited by law from insulting citizens in their work and in the theatrical performances, whereas they have complete freedom to insult the gods.

64. See *City*, 10.10.

65. *City*, 10.6.

66. Augustine will often quote Psalm 73:28 as his proof text, "As for me, my true good is to cling to God." For example, see *City* 10.6.

67. *City*, 1.prol.

68. Oliver O'Donovan, "The Political Thought of *City of God* 19," in Oliver O'Donovan and Joan Lockwood O'Donovan, *Bonds of Imperfection: Christian Politics, Past and Present* (Grand Rapids, MI: Eerdmans, 2004), 20.

69. *City*, 3.18.

70. Augustine chooses the republican period for two reasons: (1) it was before the advent of Christ and therefore provides a necessary point of comparison. If bad things happened back then when the Roman gods were ostensibly worshiped piously then the bad things happening now cannot be blamed on Christians; and (2) the republican period is extolled as a period of virtue and piety.

71. This methodology stands in stark contrast to the second half of *City*, which is framed completely by scripture.

72. See *City*, 2.1 for a good example of the inability of reason to overcome human ignorance, pride, and resistance to the truth.

73. Augustine calls the devil himself the "Deceiver" (e.g. *City* 10.11). The fall of Adam and Eve (*City*, 14.11) came about through the serpent's "deceitful conversation" with Eve, "who was seduced."

74. In *City*, 4.31, Augustine notes that even those intellectuals and political leaders who considered civil religion as merely useful to bind the city or political community together fall into the same trap as those who worship the civic deities: "The malign demons rejoice exceedingly in this deceit, since they control the deluders and deluded alike. And it is only the grace of God through Jesus Christ our Lord, that frees us from their domination."

75. *City*, 11.13.

76. *City*, 3.17.

77. E.g. see *City*, 3.20. This distinction between "use" and "enjoyment" is basic to how Augustine conceives ofvthe citizens of the two cities: "And this is the characteristic of the earthly city—to worship a god or gods so that with their assistance it may reign in victories and an earthly peace, not with a loving concern for others, but with lust for domination over them. For the good make use of this world in order to enjoy God, whereas the evil want to make use of God in order to enjoy the world" (*City*, 15.7).

78. *City*, 3.15.

79. *City*, 3.15. See also 3.17: "Rome's expansion did not bring the substantial joys of happiness, but only the empty consolations of misery, specious allurements to tempt restless spirits to submit to more and more hardships, all of them unproductive."

80. See *Conf.*, 1.13.20–21.

81. The closest that Rome comes to possessing an authoritative scripture is the Sibylline Books. In *City*, 3.18 Augustine points out how the Romans responded to major losses in the First Punic War by consulting the Sibylline Books. "On the authority of the Sibylline Books the Secular Games were renewed" in a desperate act to gain the favor of the gods for help in overcoming the Carthaginians.

82. *City*, 6.4.

83. *City*, 2.8.

84. *City*, 2.14.

Chapter Eleven

# Augustine and Platonic Political Philosophy

## The Contribution of Joseph Ratzinger

### Daniel E. Burns

Long before his election as Pope Benedict XVI, the young Joseph Ratzinger was known among Augustine scholars for his path-breaking studies of Augustine's ecclesiology. Later, as Cardinal Ratzinger, he was known widely for speaking out on political issues and controversies of our day, particularly those related to the future of Europe and the place of Christianity within it.[1] Rarely has anyone connected his interest in politics with his early writings on Augustine. In the past sixty years of scholarship on Augustine's political thought, Ratzinger has received barely a mention, and as far as I am aware, Michael Bruno's valuable 2014 monograph on the past century's interpretations of Augustine's political thought was the first ever to classify Ratzinger as even having offered such an interpretation.[2] But perhaps it would be more accurate to say that Bruno is the second, the first being Ratzinger himself. In a 1990 public lecture titled "Europe: Chances and Dangers," he made a number of bold claims about the historical importance of the "decisive interpretation" that Augustine had given to the "Platonic tradition . . . [of] political philosophy" and supported those claims with a footnote to a monograph chapter he wrote in 1961 on Augustine's debate with Roman "political theology."[3] Drawing on that chapter, Ratzinger now made a series of claims about Augustine (in relation to controversies over the meaning of Europe today) that must be striking to any scholar of Augustine's political thought and are worth quoting at length.

> What can and ought Europe really to be, for itself and for the world? We open the
> path to answering this question when we look somewhat more closely into . . . the

claim that a state without justice is nothing but a robber band grown immeasurably large. . . . [In its pre-Augustinian form,] this claim took concrete shape on the basis of real experiences of rulers who were in point of fact robbers. But its philosophical presuppositions lie deeper. To examine them, we are led into the heart of Greek and Roman political philosophy, in which the spiritual roots of Europe lie. . . . [Plato's basic political teaching, which Ratzinger here spends a page summarizing] means that a state that is basically agnostic with respect to God, one that builds justice only on majority opinions, declines in and of itself into a robber band. In this respect one must simply acknowledge the correctness of Augustine's decisive interpretation of the Platonic tradition: where God is excluded, the principle "robber band" has already been laid down (in either a more blatant or a more mild form). . . . Here it would be of interest to consider how Augustine, after the sack of Rome by the Visigoths in 410 and under the threatening signs of impending decline, integrated the Platonic and the Roman traditions [of political thought] into a synthesis within the new framework of Christian faith. . . . He corrected the one-sidedness of both those traditions and so formed the spiritual foundations on which Europe could be built. Certainly, his work too is not free from one-sidedness: it allowed for misunderstandings that could be quite misleading. But in its essential core, his work showed itself to be strong enough to build up history anew after the collapse of the Roman Empire. It offered a new beginning—one broad and open enough that it could be developed and deepened, yet still great and pure enough that we remain on the right path when we follow its guidance. But this is not the place to enter into historical research.[4]

I am not aware of any postwar interpretation of Augustine's political thought that precisely corresponds to the one that, admittedly in a very preliminary and popular format, Ratzinger sketches here. I do however believe that considered simply as an interpretation of Augustine—and therefore as separated from the even thornier "historical" question of Augustine's later influence on Europe—Ratzinger's view is fundamentally accurate. It even captures aspects of Augustine that are crucial for an authentic understanding of him, aspects unfortunately neglected by most contemporary scholarship on him.

In defense of the neglect of Ratzinger by students of Augustine's political thought, it must be admitted that Ratzinger never did offer a detailed interpretation of Augustine's views on politics. The closest he came to doing so was in the 1961 chapter mentioned above, which lays out what he emphasizes is an inadequate and preliminary summary of some main points of Augustine's political thought.[5] That summary builds on Ratzinger's earlier scholarship, especially on Augustine's ecclesiology; and Ratzinger's later essays and speeches also occasionally refer in passing to Augustine in the manner of the 1990 lecture quoted above. But these various works, when put together, do actually make a valuable contribution to scholarship on Augustine's political thought. They establish, as no other scholarship in the past century has established, the centrality of political thought—in particular of critical engagement with Platonic political philosophy—to the body of Augustine's theological thought as a whole. They also indicate some of the most important questions that must be asked if Augustine's political thought is to be understood more thoroughly. They do not, however, provide us with any direct suggestion as to how we should go about answering those questions. I will therefore spend most of this chapter summarizing what Ratzinger does teach us about Augustine, and will conclude with some suggestions as to the kind of study that his work points us to. My argument is a defense of Ratzinger, not so much as a scholar of Augustine's political thought proper, but rather as a source of valuable and perhaps even indispensable guidance for us who do seek to be scholars of that thought.

## The Place of Platonic Politics in Augustine's Thought

In the long quotation above, Ratzinger sketched a case for the importance of Augustine's political thought to those wishing to understand the situation of Europe today. Augustine scholars are of course always delighted when we see any chance of persuading others that he is as perpetually relevant as we are convinced he is, and it may well be that the connection Ratzinger draws here offers such a chance. But the desire for relevance, especially immediate relevance, can easily lead into a scholarly temptation against which Ratzinger's earliest work on Augustine warns us in no uncertain terms. Ratzinger observes there how "surprising" it is that one major lifelong concern of Augustine's, to which we will return shortly, has "barely been observed" by Augustine scholars.[6] Such a serious gap in the literature can "probably" be blamed, he says, on "a certain unhistorical type of examination" that, seeking to find only the "timelessly valid ideas" in Augustine, tries to ignore as much as possible those aspects of his thought that have proven themselves to be "temporally conditioned" and hence irrelevant to us today. By doing this, he says, one misses "essential" aspects of Augustine's thought, which cannot be understood if one tries to sever it from the living historical context in which it developed.[7] This warning applies not only to the analysis of Augustine's texts but to the very questions that one brings to that analysis: Ratzinger criticizes scholars who "essentially ignore the way these questions are posed within Augustine's own thought, who ask him (so to speak) about something foreign to him rather than about himself."[8] Forty years later, he even blames this "still regnant incapacity" of "the nineteenth- and twentieth-century academy" "even to perceive" Augustine's own "basic categories" of thought as distinct from their own—for example, their insistence on asking whether some aspect of his thought is "idealistic" or "empirical" in the "modern" senses of these terms—for the fact that his own dissertation on Augustine has been "almost constantly misunderstood" since it was published in 1954.[9] These are serious warnings for all Augustine scholars to take to heart, and they apply *a fortiori* to any attempt to read Augustine under the guidance of Ratzinger himself.

How, then, can we pose to Augustine what we take to be major questions of political philosophy without committing this cardinal interpretive sin, "asking him about something foreign to him rather than about himself"? Evidently we must begin by determining why Augustine himself cared about what we would call political philosophy or political thought, and what sort of questions he himself brought to the study of it. This preliminary investigation has not received much attention in the past century's scholarship on Augustine's political thought. But as it happens, a great deal of material on this topic can be found in Ratzinger's own early writings on Augustine and especially in his doctoral dissertation, *Volk und Haus Gottes in Augustins Lehre von der Kirche*. His arguments there are supported by meticulous and on the whole powerful textual evidence from Augustine's writings. An engagement with the hundreds of passages Ratzinger cites is well beyond the scope of this chapter, so I will for the most part simply summarize his arguments, mentioning only when he makes a point that seems to me not as well or clearly supported by his textual evidence.

Ratzinger's dissertation is devoted to the theme of the church in Augustine's writings, a theme whose centrality to Augustine's theology as a whole is well known. Already in his earliest and (in Ratzinger's view) still immature post-conversion writings, Augustine recognizes faith in the authority of the church as the single and decisive new step that has saved him from the unsatisfactory results of his previous attempts to philosophize.[10] During his subsequent ecclesial career, three major polemics are generally recognized as having absorbed most of his literary energy—namely against Manichaeism, Donatism, and Pelagianism. Of these, the first was intimately tied to, and the second entirely concerned with, the question of the nature and authority of the Church.[11] And more generally, the "true center of [Augustine's] teaching, at which all the paths of his thought find their unity," is the concept of the "body of Christ," a term that Augustine uses throughout his writings to refer to the church.[12] The question that Ratzinger's dissertation seeks to answer is therefore fundamental to the understanding of Augustine's thought: what does Augustine mean by this "church"? Is it the "invisible church" of true believers, scattered throughout the world and identifiable with no concrete human community—according to the "idealistic" interpretation suggested by Luther and then developed into its "classic form" by late-nineteenth-century liberal theologians in the school of Harnack?[13] Or can the body of Christ be identified with some visible human community, such as the Roman Catholic Church or the Christianized Roman Empire, which as such ought to govern all the kingdoms of the world as Christ deserves to—according to the "theocratic" interpretation that was already arising in Augustine's time, and that became more dominant during the period from Charlemagne until the Reformation?[14] For Augustine this question has to be answered in light of sacred scripture and hence in light of the relationship between the Old Testament and the New. Clearly the Old Testament describes a religious community that we today would call theocratic, in which "the people of God" is identified with a concrete political community. Equally clearly, the New Testament invites the Gentiles to join a new and broader "people of God." Precisely to what extent, then, does this new people of God, the Church, adhere to or depart from the Old Testament model of a political "people" united into a visible community by their worship of him?[15]

This question not only is central to our understanding of Augustine but also vice versa: no small part of Augustine's stature as "the greatest Church teacher of the West" is attributable to his place as the first theologian to give a satisfactory answer to this question about the relation between the two Testaments, a question that obviously goes to the very heart of Jesus's own message and to the self-understanding of Christians in all times, including our own.[16] Yet despite or even because of the enduring relevance of this question, if one still wishes to avoid the pitfall of misunderstanding Augustine through asking him "timeless" questions that divorce him from his own historical context, one must bear in mind that "the treatment of the Old Testament achieved its full stature above all in Augustine's critical engagement with paganism."[17] Precisely this "critical engagement with a paganism that was at the time still very much alive" is the major lifelong concern of Augustine's mentioned above that "surprisingly" had "barely been observed" by scholars prior to 1954[18]—and one must now add, has received too little attention since then as well. Although it was "perhaps the most fertile intellectual engagement of [Augustine's] entire life," scholarship has "hardly appreciated" the equal if not greater place that his engagement with paganism merits alongside the better-known controversies with Manichaeism, Donatism, and Pelagianism; Ratzinger devotes nearly half his dissertation to what he modestly calls the "attempt" to accord it that rightful place.[19] And the core of this engagement with paganism turns out to consist of Augustine's argument with a certain form of ancient political philosophy.

For "paganism" here Ratzinger means not so much the "common paganism" still widely practiced in Augustine's day, but rather especially the "late-classical philosophy" that had undertaken a more intellectually weighty defense of that "vulgar paganism" and thereby become related to it as "theology is related to religion."[20] More precisely, late antiquity had seen two different philosophic attempts to defend the pagan religion that was slowly losing its grip on the educated classes,[21] attempts that were characteristic of two respective forms of Platonism. On the one hand, Neoplatonists sought to "justify" pagan religion by arguing that it could provide to the common man a lesser form of that spiritual "purification," or ascent in the cosmic scale of being, which the elite could receive more fully through philosophy.[22] This conception of "purification" left a significant mark on the younger Augustine, and important elements of it remain present in his thought to the end, even if Ratzinger (like most contemporary scholars) finds it "astonishing" that Augustine never saw any contradiction between some of those elements and his own mature understanding of the Christian faith.[23] On the other hand, other Roman Platonists such as Marcus Terentius Varro defended religion on the basis of its utility for the community rather than for the individual as individual: "Varro's grounding of religion is fundamentally different from that of Neoplatonism. While the latter is concerned purely with the metaphysical and attempts a cosmic definition of the gods, Varro begins from the *civitas* and places the realm of the gods there."[24] This difference is traceable to the difference between "the political attitude of Platonic and of Neoplatonic philosophy: in [Neoplatonism], the concept of the *polis* is really abandoned."[25] While critical engagement with Neoplatonic philosophy also remained a lifelong interest of Augustine's,[26] it is his engagement with the latter Roman-Platonic philosophy (whose roots in Plato we will examine below) that Ratzinger shows to have been crucial for Augustine's working out of the relationship between the Old and New Testaments. For the "people of God" in the Old Testament, in contrast to the Christian Church, was a *populus* in the "natural" or "ordinary sense of the word."[27] Augustine's interpretation of the significance of the Old Testament, or more precisely of its "literal" meaning, is therefore based on his understanding of what a "people" in this ordinary sense means.[28] And as Ratzinger shows through both philological and substantive considerations, Augustine's usage of the term *populus* reflects and presupposes the "classical Roman teaching on the *civitas*" as articulated by Platonic philosophers such as Cicero and Varro, whose "sociological" understanding of earthly human communities Augustine largely appropriated.[29] Already at Cassiciacum Augustine had said, "populus una civitas est": the literal meaning of "people" is thoroughly political and nearly interchangeable with *civitas*, which (particularly when it refers to Rome) is the closest Latin equivalent to the Greek *polis* and so means "city" and "state" at once.[30]

Why should the Platonic-Roman understanding of the *civitas* or *polis* be so important to Augustine's understanding of the church? The answer becomes visible when we remember the immediate context in which Augustine wrote what was both his "greatest work" and the one most clearly devoted to his "critical engagement with paganism," the *De civitate dei*.[31] The pagan Romans had blamed the sack of Rome by the Visigoths in 410 on the Christianization of Rome and so had brought to the foreground "the question concerning what use religion should or should not serve within history, what its meaning should be for life in this world. . . . Against this background, Augustine undertook a comprehensive critical engagement with the non-Christian philosophies of his time. . . . The question about worship was not an intra-theological but a central political and philosophic problem."[32] The new threat to the very existence of the city of Rome had caused a sudden "flaring up of *polis* consciousness, which was directed against the Christianity that it blamed for the collapse of the *polis*." Ratzinger explains here that the *polis*, as experienced by "classical antiquity" in general and analyzed by Platonic political philosophy in particular, is "essentially" characterized by "a proper and unbroken unity of the political and the religious. The *civitas-polis* is the locus not only of man's social-political existence but also of his religious existence."[33] "The ancient *polis* is the church of her religion, and her *populus* is a *cultor populus*."[34] Christian monotheism—as distinguished from (for example) Platonic monotheism, which had not sought to make the true god an object of religious worship and so had been fully compatible with cultic polytheism—had been compelled from the beginning to openly deny the gods of the *polis* and hence its right to exist as a *polis*, as an authoritative human religious community.[35] Christian monotheism was thus "a program of decisive political meaning": "it was forced to claim public legal validity in at least a negative sense, i.e., it had to claim the right to deny the religious character of the public law then considered valid."[36] Christianity had thereby "called into question the spiritual foundations of life in antiquity," "negated the self-understanding of the state and thereby also its spiritual foundations, at any rate as these had existed up to that point," and so produced "a fight over the basic form of the public life of antiquity."[37] It was this fight that Augustine entered self-consciously in his *De civitate dei*, defending Christianity against the demand for such a "reestablishment of the religious status of the *polis*" as would require Christians in effect to abandon their own biblical-monotheistic faith.[38] *De civitate dei*, Augustine's "apologetic against the idolatrous *civitas deorum*," must therefore reply, perhaps above all, to those opponents of Christianity whose critique of it is not based on any serious theology of the Roman gods so much as on a certain "conception of the *polis*": a critique based not on metaphysics but on political philosophy.[39] For this reason, "the chief point of his anti-pagan polemic," which is to say of that "fertile intellectual engagement" that in turn allowed him to resolve the question of the relation of the two Testaments, "lies principally in the critical engagement with the conception of the *polis*" or with classical political philosophy.[40]

## The Critique of Political Theology

"Augustine's task at this moment [i.e., after 410] was to clarify the Christian standpoint and, in opposition to the pagans, to prove its legitimacy."[41] He was then obviously not satisfied to point out that from the Christian point of view, if it were indeed true that Rome needed the worship of idols in order to survive, then that would just be too bad for Rome.[42] Instead he responded to the pagans on their own terms, explaining how human considerations alone militate against our accepting the sort of "political" or "civil theology" that Platonists and other philosophically sophisticated representatives of paganism—Varro above all—had defended in the name of the classical *polis*.[43] Ratzinger summarizes two such considerations, both familiar to any reader of *De civitate dei*, but highlighting in each a universal political significance that is not as obvious from Augustine's text alone.

The first of these is that political theology is not true. It "rests on a canonization of custom over against truth." The Roman gods do not exist, and this has long been known to the most prominent defenders of Roman religion, such as Scaevola, Varro, Seneca, and Cicero.[44] The philosophy that defends "political theology" subordinates truth to political utility, since it "believes that the well-being of the state is bound up with the perdurance of its old [religious] forms." Christianity's attack on political theology, by contrast, liberates us from slavery to custom and allows us instead to ground our religious observance on the truth as we understand it.[45] From any human point of view, this is a liberation, and it is one that Seneca, Varro, and their educated compatriots ought to have welcomed. After all, Varro himself had admitted that he would have preferred to institute a different and more philosophically sound religion for Rome had its old customs not prevented him from doing so.[46]

The second consideration militating against political theology is that although the gods it worships do not exist as such, the worship of them delivers us into the hands of terrible powers that are all too real. "Behind the unreal gods stands the very real power of demons, and behind the enslavement to custom stands the slavery of the evil spirits."[47] In his doctoral dissertation, Ratzinger admitted the discomfort any modern reader must feel at Augustine's lengthy discussion of these demons as inhabiting the "air," the realm apparently midway between heaven (gods) and earth (men) as conceived within the "ancient image of the cosmos."[48] Ten years later, he had arrived at a new and more political reading of that same discussion. On the basis of Augustine's antithesis of the Christian martyr to the pagan "hero," where the "hero" is mythically described as a son of the goddess of the realm of "air," and where the martyr is said to have conquered the demonic powers of the "air," Ratzinger says: "Here the conviction is manifestly being expressed that the demons are what 'hangs in the air,' the anonymous powers of a particular spiritual climate, according to which man orients himself and by which he lets himself be overpowered. . . . [T]he Christian martyr, meanwhile, is the one who has not oriented himself by these powers, by common opinion, by what 'one' thinks, but rather has overcome all these things through faith in the greater power of God."[49] When political theology consecrates custom and "common opinion" in the name of political well-being, it effects our enslavement to those anonymous forces (political, economic, and psychological) that already dominate the "climate," the air, of our existing community and that hide behind the "fantastic masks" of its traditional divinities.[50] Those masks have been ripped away thanks to the courage of the martyrs, whose willingness to die for the one true God has been the political force driving the demonic pagan gods out of Rome.[51] And the subsequent "political and military successes" of some Christian emperors show moreover that "one does not need to run to demons in order to achieve such [worldly success]: there is no necessity that politics should be demonic, that it should be grounded on lying and contempt for right; rather, it can prosper even on the basis of truth and justice."[52] Roman political theology would seek to hobble the enormous spiritual strength manifested by the Christian martyrs, whose willingness to die for "truth and justice" was already anticipated by "martyrs" of the philosophic tradition such as Seneca and Socrates, but who have managed to change the world as no philosophic martyr ever did.[53] An abandonment of the gift of freedom that the Christian martyrs have given the world,[54] a return to religiously sanctioned complacency in the face of the demonic aspects of our social-political life, ought to be recognizable as a loss to humanity from any point of view.

These two points exhaust Ratzinger's summary of Augustine's critique of the Platonic "conception of the *polis*." Yet as powerful as these two critiques may be in many respects, they are not likely to seem adequate to anyone who sympathizes with Platonic political philosophy. If the Platonists did not themselves believe in the existence of the gods they were defending, then why should they be stung by Augustine's accusation that they were consecrating political utility over truth? Surely they had known that they were doing so, and had had what they considered to be good reasons for it. And would these Platonic philosophers really be satisfied with Ratzinger's claim that Constantine or Theodosius had now established Roman politics "on the basis of truth and justice"—a claim that moreover goes beyond anything Augustine actually says about these emperors?[55]

It is not clear to me whether Ratzinger was moved by these questions during the first ten years of his scholarly career, during which he produced the studies of Augustine from which almost all my references to this point have been taken. What is clear is that after a second decade had passed since his dissertation, there appears in his writings a new and deeper understanding of aspects of Platonic political philosophy to which the earlier studies had made no reference, and to which his attention appears to have been first drawn by Ulrich Duchrow's *Christenheit und Weltverantwortung* (1970).[56] If we turn to the passages of Ratzinger's later works that reflect this new understanding of Plato, we will find what we need in order to complete his picture of Augustine's engagement with Platonic political thought and to see what questions about Augustine it opens up for us.

## The Platonic Roots of Political Theology

We should begin with the depiction of Plato's philosophy that Ratzinger said in the 1970s could be found "everywhere in theological as well as philosophical treatises," and which unfortunately continues to be accepted today even among many scholars of Augustine's political thought.[57] According to this collection of what he calls "Plato-clichés," our spirit is trapped in the prison of our fleshly body, to be released at last when we die; Plato is an "individualistic and dualistic thinker . . . who denies all that is earthly and teaches humans to flee into the beyond"; and there is an unbridgeable gap between spirit and matter, between the rational and irrational parts of the soul, between the "invisible-divine" and the "concrete-political," and between the theoretical and practical lives, with a consequent need for us in each case to cling to the former while avoiding or "suppressing" the latter.[58] Certain passages in Ratzinger's own earlier works, particularly his doctoral dissertation, appear to be still indebted to some of these "clichés."[59] In any event, by the 1970s he has recognized that "the true orientation and goal of Plato's thought is completely misunderstood" when one reads it through this "familiar schematic of Platonism."[60] In the case of such apparent "dualisms" as spirit and matter or theoretical and practical, Plato's philosophy in fact seeks not to divide these aspects of human life from one another but precisely to reintegrate them into a harmonious whole.[61]

Of particular importance to our inquiry is the apparent dualism of "orientation toward the invisible-divine and toward the concrete-political," the overcoming of which Ratzinger says is not only one goal but *the* goal of Plato's entire philosophy. The term "Platonic political philosophy" can almost even be called redundant, since Plato's philosophy as a whole has an "eminently political character."[62] "Plato's thought . . . is in fact constructed around precisely the goal of making the *polis* possible again, of a new grounding for politics."[63] For in "the sixth and fifth centuries B.C.," according to Ratzinger, the subtle and sometimes not-so-subtle critique of the traditional gods that had lain dormant for centuries within Greek literature suddenly "took the open form of rational critique" at the hands of the sophists, who rejected the common way of life prescribed by the traditional gods and proposed instead a natural-right teaching based on the advantage of the stronger. The "spiritual crisis" of this period of "Enlightenment," which was by no means confined to Greece and even left its mark on biblical literature, became in Greece a "political crisis as well."[64] (We have seen above why the rational questioning of the traditional gods would have led to a greater political crisis in Greece than elsewhere in the world: Greece is the original home of the *polis*, the complete human community that unites the religious and political as perhaps no other community ever has done, so its politics is linked particularly closely to its religiosity.[65]) Plato "seeks to respond to this political crisis, which is in truth an intellectual crisis," by offering a new interpretation of "natural right" as the true justice that is grounded in Being itself, an interpretation that is no longer "individualistic" like that of the sophists but rather "becomes a new grounding for the political and makes the *polis* as a community newly possible." The whole of Plato's philosophy, "constantly in search of the rightful and just political community," "circles around" his single "basic theme" of a "justice" that is grounded in reality and truth—a theme that informs all the other topics he treats, from cosmology to psychology.[66]

As for the results of this Platonic search, Plato chose to convey his insights only through various "mythical and political representations," "images" that he is "constantly switching" on his readers, and "varied and metaphorical sketches that ultimately resist any systematization," thus leaving us "a philosophic landscape rich in problems."[67] Still, certain basic aspects of Plato's political thought are clear enough. One is that he shared and even further advanced a critique of the city's traditional gods similar to what had already been popularized by the sophists: he never "tries to reestablish the shattered mythical world."[68] He does offer a "religious grounding" of his political-philosophic project through certain traditional myths, which his dialogues reinterpret and refashion so that they conform more closely to his own philosophic thought.[69] But this is hardly a reactionary project, since it represents an attempt "to abolish the classic Homeric *mythos* and replace it with a new *mythos* in accord with *logos*"—which the old *mythos* was not, as the *Euthyphro* among other Platonic dialogues makes unmistakably clear.[70]

Another point is that political justice in Plato's view cannot exist outside of a community grounded on the full "integration" of the human soul's various parts in their proper order, with this integration entrusted to human intellect or *nous*, the highest of those parts, which Ratzinger defines as man's "capacity to perceive the actual standards of Being itself, [man's] organ for the divine." "Only the truth can validly bind human beings, and thereby produce freedom and right in their inner unity."[71]

A final point is that Plato's own description in the *Republic* of the "ideal State," from which Ratzinger appears to be drawing most of these observations, must be understood not as an actual political program with any hope of realization, but as what Wilhelm Kamlah calls a "utopia" in the "classic" sense, namely a hypothetical community through which "justice, the ideal standard of law, receives a thoroughgoing formulation in its purest form possible, so that through this theoretical experiment we find critical standards by which to measure political reality."[72]

Unlike Ratzinger's studies of Augustine, these summaries of Plato contain almost no textual references to Plato himself, so Ratzinger's interpretation of Plato is much harder to assess. Nonetheless, although I find even the details of his interpretation almost universally convincing, we can bracket many of those details and still agree on at least two points relevant to our understanding of the Platonists whose "conception of the *polis*" Augustine opposed. First of all, by treating religion primarily as a communal rather than an individual phenomenon and defending the *polis* as the exemplary human religious-political community, Platonists such as Cicero and Varro were indeed keeping alive central aspects of Plato's own thought that Neoplatonism had threatened to obscure.[73] For Plato, "the *polis* remains a *polis*" even at the peak of its (utopian) philosophic reform.[74] This is of great importance for understanding Augustine, who saw Christianity as having made it impossible for the *polis* to remain a *polis*.

Second, insofar as they are Platonists, it would be grossly unfair to claim that men such as Cicero and Varro, who accepted political theology's "canonization of custom over against truth," simply considered it a matter of "indifference" whether their city's cultic practices signified truths or falsehoods about the gods. The young Ratzinger had tried to make such a claim, arguing that Varro's "norm of religion is not God but the *civitas*," and that Varro's wish that he could replace the traditional Roman "civil theology" with something more closely resembling philosophic "natural theology" only demonstrates Varro's "own indifference with respect to all theology," that is, Varro's radical distinction between "cultic religion" on the one hand and metaphysics or physics on the other.[75] The young Ratzinger had moreover tried to claim that Varro was in this respect only reproducing a widespread pagan view, according to which religion essentially consisted not in "faith but [in] worship; what one believes or thinks while practicing it is a matter of complete indifference."[76]

But even the young Ratzinger had difficulty maintaining consistently this psychologically implausible claim about pagan religion.[77] And within fifteen years, he would come to assert that humans do "unavoidably" and "necessarily" care about the truth of their religion, at least wherever their "consciousness has attained a certain maturity." The "rational critique" of the traditional gods had therefore in fact led (as we have seen) to a serious "spiritual crisis" in the ancient world, for the Socratic-Platonic search for the truth about the city's gods corresponds to a natural desire of every human being.[78] *Pace* the younger Ratzinger, it seems clear that precisely Varro's desire to purify Roman "civil theology" through an approximation to philosophic "natural theology," and his regret that under existing circumstances there was "no possibility" of doing so in a more radical way, show that far from asserting a radical separation between cult and metaphysics,[79] Varro adhered to what the later Ratzinger identified as the genuinely Platonic belief that real political reform should be measured by the "standards" set forth in the utopian *Republic* (which describes an entire religious-political community regulated by the *nous* that grasps the truth about the divine). Varro's "reformative intention to bind [Roman civil theology] henceforth more to the philosophers' teaching on God" shows his recognition of the true goal of Platonic utopianism, namely "the measuring of present-day politics by the highest political standards and thereby the maximal approximation of the state to the norm of justice" described in the *Republic*.[80]

If all this is the case, then why would Platonists in the tradition of Varro and Cicero be defending the false gods of Rome against Christian monotheism—a monotheism that they would surely have regarded as, at the very least, a closer approximation to their own philosophic "natural theology" than was the existing Roman "civil theology," heavily based as the latter was on the fantastical "poetic theology" of their uneducated ancestors?[81] The answer becomes evident from Ratzinger's accurate summary of Augustine's own interpretation of Varro: there was in Varro's own judgment "no possibility" of reforming the traditional Roman theology any more than he was already doing, because he would not have been able to bring the entire community along with him in such a reform.[82] The Platonic effort to achieve the "maximal" approximation of politics to the true standards of justice must always respect the limits of political possibility; these limits are indeed what make the Platonic "utopia" a utopia rather than a realistic political program. Augustine's famous insight into the "enduring imperfection of the state, or more precisely of the states, in this world"[83] was old news to his Platonic predecessors. In fact, in answer to his critique of their political theology, they would apparently have thrown this insight back at him. One can hardly blame Rome for worshiping false gods once one sees that, before it could cease doing so, it would have to either become the utopian city of Plato's *Republic* or cease to be a *polis* (i.e., cease to be united in its religious worship).

This brings us back to Ratzinger's observation that Augustine's political thought in effect demanded that the *polis* cease to be a *polis*. We are now in a better position to clarify that observation by articulating the "conception of the *polis*" to which

Augustine's polemic against paganism had to respond. According to this conception as interpreted by Platonic philosophy, any human community, including and above all the political community, is a genuine and binding community only to the extent that it is held together by a common perception of the divine, or of the truth of Being. It is not to be expected that any earthly political community will ever fully live up to this standard or perhaps even come close to it. Nonetheless, this standard does allow one to distinguish major gradations between better and worse communities, and a true Platonic philosopher will always feel obligated to "return into the 'cave'" of public service in order to nudge his own community in a better direction.[84] At least one important aspect of the true standard for politics is the relative truth of the images of the divine that the community publicly worships. The world contains a wide range of falsehoods, from the enlightened myths of the Platonic dialogues to the crazy and immoral fables of "poetic theology," and so some political theologies are much better than others. If the community ceased publicly to worship anything at all—if it were no longer bound together by even an attempt at common perception of the divine—then it would abandon even the attempt to approximate itself to the standard of full and true justice, which would be contrary to the whole reformative intention of Platonic political thought. To be sure, as Augustine emphasized, Platonic philosophers did convey to many of their students and readers their critique of the gods of the city. It would then be more precise to say that they apparently wanted the political community to be held together by common acts of *external* worship, even if not all the community's members (especially not the best among them) would put their hearts and minds into that worship. A higher level of intellectual purity in communal worship must not be pursued in a way that would jeopardize the whole community's unity in that worship.

Ratzinger's own ecclesiological interest in Augustine leads him to emphasize the following aspect of Augustine's answer to this Platonic "conception of the *polis*." The true religious community, in whose name Christians reject the religious claims of the Roman *civitas*, is indeed also a *polis* but one of a different sort, namely the *civitas dei*, for which Ratzinger cannot think of a better translation than "*polis* of God."[85] Like the "literal" *poleis* of Rome and of the Old Testament commonwealth, the City of God is "characterized by the fact that at its heart is worship" of the divine. Unlike those *poleis*, the City of God cannot be found anywhere on earth, for even the visible Catholic Church can be identified with it only "spiritually" or "pneumatically."[86] The visible Catholic Church, which though not identical to the City of God is indeed the true revelation on earth of that City, is bound together by visible (sacramental) worship just as the "literal" classical *polis* is.[87] And not all of the Church's members put their hearts and minds into that worship: it is essential to her existence as a this-worldly community that she includes many sinners who partake only externally in her sacraments without receiving the grace that these signify.[88] Yet despite these similarities, the Church does have one apparent advantage over the *polis* from the point of view of Plato himself. Because of her transpolitical character, the Church's proclamation of the truth about God is not bound within the same limits of political "possibility" that constrained Varro in his reformation of Roman religion. She can, and indeed must, speak the truth about the divine without worrying about whether the entire (earthly) city will find that truth acceptable.[89] "In the Church there shines once again all the brilliance of the ancient *polis*, which had once been worth the *eusebeia* of her inhabitants, and which has now been brought to a final definitiveness."[90]

## The Limits of Ratzinger's Scholarship on Augustine

For the self-understanding of the Christian Church, it would be difficult to overstate the importance of these conclusions. Nonetheless, they could hardly be fully satisfying to the Platonic philosophers with whom Augustine is engaging here. For these men were well aware of transnational philosophical movements—not on the scale of Christianity, but still real—that were united by common opinions about the divine. The "individualistic-cosmopolitan" thought of Stoicism as later summarized by Seneca (whose "*civitas* is the *civitas philosophorum*") viewed philosophers of all countries as united into a merely metaphorical *polis* on account of their virtue and hence their relationship to the divine, which distinguished them from the "masses" of "every 'empirical' community" and so made it impossible that they should ever be identified with any earthly city.[91] Varro and Cicero had each drawn on Stoicism in other aspects of their thought,[92] so their rejection of its understanding of the *polis* in favor of the Platonic understanding must be assumed to have been a conscious one. It is therefore not clear that they would have been impressed by the Christian Church's promise to spread truths about the divine while undermining the religious unity of the *polis*. Based on what we have seen, they might well ask: if cultic worship is no longer to play a major role (or perhaps any role at all) in holding the political community together, then what *will* hold that community together? How is human political life to be reconceived and reshaped if it is no longer to be so closely identified with human religious life? And how can this reconceived and reshaped politics respond to the Platonists' own analysis of politics, according to which any attempt to improve on the old *polis* will produce only some inferior human community?

To questions like this, Ratzinger offers some answers of his own that do draw on his readings of Augustine, but he never claims that they are Augustine's own answers.[93] In fact, Ratzinger considers it a "limitation" of Augustine's political thought that (unlike his many students in the Middle Ages) Augustine never sought to offer any "actual positive foundation for the earthly city," concentrating instead on distinguishing the church from that city in order to preserve the "unpoliticizable *proprium* of faith."[94] The most that Ratzinger says Augustine ever offered in the direction of "later centuries' positive concept of the state" was a recognition (which he attributes to Augustine without citation) that the "earthly city" of the new Christian-Roman state, like that of the Old Testament commonwealth, "without doubt" cannot fairly be called a *civitas diaboli*, even though he admits that some passages in Augustine suggest that the term *civitas diaboli* refers to the earthly city as such.[95] For the Christianized Roman empire has in common with the ancient Jewish commonwealth that on the one hand it forbids any sacrifices to demons, whereas on the other hand most of its members worship God only for the sake of earthly rewards and so do not worship him in truth.[96] It is not clear to me where the young Ratzinger got his confidence that an earthly city that has outlawed literal demon worship must no longer be a *civitas diaboli*: later he would admit and even emphasize that demonic forces can be just as dominant in what he calls "post-Christian paganism," which appears after Christianity's own successful critique of the gods has compelled demonic forces to drop their religious "masks" and "show themselves in their true secularity."[97] But in any case, Ratzinger is surely right to point to an important commonality between the Old Testament commonwealth and the Christian state (however one may understand the term "Christian state").[98] Both are "earthly cities" that manifest at least some visible reverence for the true God, and both therefore force us to raise the question of precisely to what extent the "demonic" element can or cannot be driven out of earthly politics. We have seen that the Platonists seem to have simply assumed it never could be, and that Augustine is somewhat harder to pin down: on the one hand he praises the martyrs for delivering us from the political power of demonic forces, and on the other he gives no explicit indication that supposedly Christian "earthly cities" offer any exception to his famous and resounding critiques of earthly cities as such. Much more work would have to be done in order to see to what extent he really believes the demonic can ever be banished from any earthly city.

Ratzinger clearly also has a point in saying that Augustine's thought offers little in the way of "positive" political guidance, at least compared to medieval thinkers who wrote whole treatises on government. But his point seems to me somewhat overstated, and it arguably reflects the limitations of his own studies of Augustine more than any limitation of Augustine's thought itself. For if the rest of Ratzinger's observations about Augustine's relation to Platonic political thought are true—and I believe that in general they are—then it staggers the imagination to believe that Augustine can have made such a serious break with these thinkers, to whom he was so close in other respects, without leaving behind some indications of his grounds for doing so and of his response to the objections they certainly would have made to such a break. A genuine response to these objections would require at least some suggestion as to how politics ought ("positively") to be conducted after the death of the *polis*. Certainly, Augustine's indications on this point may require some detective work to find: even the central place of the Platonic "conception of the *polis*" in Augustine's "critical engagement with paganism," as Ratzinger has uncovered it, is hardly obvious from a superficial reading of *De civitate dei* and is still insufficiently noted by most scholars of Augustine's political thought. Despite the impression his polemics sometimes give, Augustine did not actually think it appropriate to discuss every possible objection to Christianity out loud and in public.[99] Nonetheless, for readers motivated to seek out Augustine's answers to the questions that Platonic political thought raises about the Christian religious-political revolution, Augustine all but promises (assuming that all the foregoing analysis is true) that those answers are somewhere to be found in his books:

> In [writing] books, . . . this duty is not to be neglected: that when we ourselves have once perceived something true, we must, no matter how difficult it is to understand and no matter how much effort of disputation this will cost us, convey it to the understanding of others—assuming that [they] have a desire to learn, as well as the mental capacity to pick up what the teacher merely intimates when he is concerned with the evidence of his teaching and not its eloquence.[100]

From the point of view of the student of Augustine's political thought, the greatest merit of Ratzinger's studies of Augustine is that he pointed the way to an extensive study of Augustine's "intimations" of his real disagreements with Platonic political thought, a study that Ratzinger himself never undertook.

## Possibilities for Future Study

What would this study look like? Here we are fortunate to have some idea already, for anglophone scholarship on Augustine is currently experiencing a small renaissance of thoughtful work illuminated by the question of his relation to ancient and especially Platonic political thought. One need look no further for examples than all my colleagues' admirable essays in this volume. This is because by a strange coincidence, another twentieth-century Augustine scholar came independently to many conclusions about Augustine similar to the ones this chapter has derived from Ratzinger's writings. Ernest L. Fortin, to whose intellectual guidance all of us in this volume are indebted, made Augustine's relation to Platonic-Ciceronian political thought the major theme of his writings on him.[101] Although they both attended the international *Augustinus Magister* conference in 1954, Fortin barely ever refers to Ratzinger's scholarship, Ratzinger never refers to Fortin's, and I have found no evidence that either influenced the other. Fortin takes his understanding of Platonism almost entirely from Leo Strauss and Allan Bloom, whereas Ratzinger relies for his on the Tübingen school of Wolfgang Schadewalt—although it is remarkable what similar conclusions about Plato the two arrive at from such different starting points. Fortin never demonstrates from Augustine's own texts, as I have been arguing that Ratzinger does, the importance of the "intellectual engagement with paganism" to Augustine's self-understanding as a Christian. On the other hand, Fortin seems simply to assume this importance, and unlike Ratzinger he does actually undertake some of the comparative work of which (I have argued) Ratzinger leaves one wanting to read more. I am tempted to say that the main conclusion of this chapter is simply that students of Fortin and of Ratzinger ought to pay more attention to one another as they advance what ought to be their common project of coming to understand Augustine as he understood himself. But in the interest of advancing that project, I will offer a few more concrete suggestions for future study.

One striking feature of Fortin's work on Augustine is its insistence on the importance of his early works, which are too often neglected thanks to the influence of the "developmental" reading popularized most recently by Peter Brown.[102] Ratzinger's dissertation begins with a fairly sympathetic account of several of the early works,[103] but there are several others that his writings never or barely refer to. Two in particular stand out as touching on the themes whose importance to Augustine he has shown. The first, *De vera religione*, has a great deal to say about religion in its relation to both philosophy and (less obviously) politics. Sometimes dismissed as a Neoplatonic anti-Manichaean polemic, this work in fact begins with a cuttingly ironic depiction of the problem faced by all the ancient philosophers whose metaphysical doctrines conflicted with the public theology of the city: they would worship the gods in common with the "people" (*populus*), then deny the gods' existence "in private, with the people (*populus*) still listening."[104] *De vera religione* then compares Plato's ability to spread his own doctrines with Christ's much greater ability to spread similar doctrines, contrasts philosophic esotericism with Christian veracity, and describes the social structure of the transpolitical Christian religion, including its basic similarities to and differences from the religion of the Old Testament.[105] It also offers a lengthy discussion of the effect that the true Christian religion is meant to have on the souls of its adherents: the contrast with "carnal" pagan religion is nearly always visible in the background and occasionally comes to the foreground, including in a several-paragraph peroration exhorting readers not to fall into paganism, and in an earlier comparison between the "carnal" life led by a citizen of even a "well constituted earthly city" and the "spiritual" life of the Christian who follows "heavenly laws."[106] Few if any works of Augustine's offer such a close engagement with the questions that Ratzinger's writings leave us with.

Another area of fertile ground for future studies is book 1 of *De libero arbitrio*, whose importance Fortin highlighted but which he himself treated in only a brief and surprisingly unsatisfactory way.[107] In this book, Augustine articulates—for the first time in Western intellectual history that I am aware of—a clear distinction between the "eternal" law of God on the one hand and the "temporal" law of all earthly cities on the other, with the latter understood as limited in its scope but necessary for the sake of "peace and human society."[108] Although Ratzinger never once refers to this book, its distinction between the "two laws" is an essential presupposition of that Christian refashioning of the *polis* whose importance he has pointed to, and this book offers rich material for a better understanding of that refashioning. The book's distinction between the "two laws" comes at the culmination of a dialogue between Augustine and his student Evodius, who at earlier points in the dialogue had seemed either hesitant about drawing such a distinction or confused about its scope.[109] This dialogue is thus Augustine's only literary depiction of how a Christian citizen can be brought to accept the basics of Augustinian political thought, and so is indispensable as a guide to the moral and psychological preconditions of the revolution in civic self-understanding that Ratzinger shows him defending against his pagan critics. Furthermore, the same dialogue professes to lay out the intellectual steps by which Augustine himself had, as part of his intellectual conversion to Christianity, been delivered from confusions similar to those Evodius now exhibits.[110] Since many of these confusions concern the nature of political or "temporal" law, this book at least sketches for us the engagement with legal and hence political philosophy that Augustine had had to undertake in order to convert to Christianity—an engagement that would presumably shed further light on his post-conversion view of Platonic political philosophy.[111] Moreover, that engagement appears not as a direct response to Plato but rather as a dialogue with the more ordinary moral and civic views held by Evodius—the type of dialogue on which Plato himself had built his own philosophic views, as Ratzinger emphasizes.[112] It thus shows how Augustine responds to Plato precisely by imitating the Socratic attempt to ascend from the cave of common opinion into the light of the truth. Finally, the character Evodius illustrates vividly how even an earnest and educated Christian who considers himself above the guidance of earthly laws tends nonetheless to remain under their spell, deriving from them the very moral understanding on whose basis he considers himself superior to that guidance.[113] In other words, Evodius overestimates how much his Christianity has really revolutionized his relation to his political community. He is therefore particularly interesting as a piece of evidence that Ratzinger may have somewhat overstated the practical significance of the Christian political revolution: Ratzinger's statements about how Christianity "negated the [pagan] self-understanding of the state and thereby also its spiritual foundations" are indeed grounded in the letter of Christian doctrines, but through his character Evodius, Augustine sketches for us how those doctrines actually play out in the lived experience of Christian citizenship.

Of course one can also never exhaust *De civitate dei*, and several chapters of this volume already illustrate how Fortin has been inspiring a new wave of scholarship sensitive to Augustine's dialogue with pagan philosophy in his *magnum opus*. I will mention here just one aspect of the text to which Ratzinger's work encourages us to direct further attention. Even while drawing his sharp distinctions between the *civitas dei* and the earthly city, Augustine offers both explicit and implicit treatments of how life *within* the earthly political community ought to change as a result of Christian revelation—or as Ratzinger put it, treatments of what Christianity's "meaning should be for life in this world," of what it can offer to "this our own history."[114] Book 1, for example, gives answers to this question, including the following: compared with pagan Rome, Christian Rome can expect somewhat more humane conduct toward those seeking asylum from the still horrific conduct of conquering armies, an increase in public admiration for a Regulus at the expense of the admiration for a Cato, a decrease in the shame attached to rape victims, and a decrease in publicly sanctioned obscenity.[115] The whole of Augustine's longest work is littered with politically relevant observations of this kind. If more of it could be interpreted with a view to what it says about the conduct of actual politics (as for example Ratzinger strikingly interpreted its teaching on the "demons" of the "air"), we could acquire a better sense of what Augustine thinks the Christian revolution ought to mean for political theory and practice.[116] We could therefore take significant steps toward answering the question, posed but not answered by Ratzinger, of the extent to which Christianity makes it actually (realistically) possible to expel the influence of the demonic from politics. In this regard it would also be helpful to supplement *De civitate dei* with those letters and sermons that show Augustine living out the concrete effects of the Christian revolution, speaking as a bishop to Christians holding political responsibility about the role that their faith ought to play in their discharge of that responsibility.[117]

Many other works of Augustine's also deal, less centrally but still significantly, with themes closely related to his debate with Platonic political philosophy and have yet to be treated by either Ratzinger, Fortin, or their students. I will offer just a few examples. Fortin does point occasionally to the political-philosophic importance of Augustine's two works on lying, *De mendacio* and *Contra mendacium*.[118] These works treat some politically charged dilemmas (including an early version of the "Nazis at the door" example), while their conclusions state that the most "capital" of all lies is one "having do with religious doctrine."[119] One would be caricaturing patriotic Platonists such as Varro and Cicero only slightly if one said that they opposed lying in all cases *except* those having to do with religious doctrine, about which they thought wise men were indeed civically obligated to lie. Augustine's works on lying thus clearly have some importance for the understanding of his disagreements with Platonism. Or again, in *De bono conjugali*, Augustine speaks at length not only about the virtues of Christian marriage but also about the institution of marriage as it exists "in all nations and among all men," of whose "human society" it is "the first natural link." He sketches some points of comparison and contrast between this social-political marriage as regulated by the "laws of the gentiles" and sacramental marriage "in the city of our God" on earth.[120] In one key passage on the obligation of marital fidelity (including or even primarily within Christian marriage), Augustine goes so far as to explain its universally binding character by comparing it with "rules of civil law," which one must not break even when one could achieve something useful by doing so.[121] And the same analogy between marital obligation and political law comes up in *De adulterinis conjugiis*, which speaks repeatedly of the obligation of marital fidelity as a "law" binding on Christians, and again compares it to the less rigorous but still serious demands on marital fidelity made by good political laws "for the sake of the dignity of the earthly city."[122] The close connection between piety and the family in Platonic political thought makes these works another promising starting point for comparison.

Or if we wish to follow Ratzinger's suggestion that Augustine's treatment of the Mosaic law sheds light on his understanding of the possibilities and limits of a politics influenced by Christian monotheism, the clearest place to look would be the *De sermone domini in monte*, which is unusually helpful in this regard since it consistently discusses the Mosaic covenant according to its "literal" meaning as a political law rather than according to its "spiritual" meaning as a type of the Church. A major theme of Augustine's commentary is Jesus's contrast between the "lesser righteousness" embodied in the excellent Mosaic political law and the "greater righteousness" to which Jesus calls his transpolitical band of followers.[123] Of course, the work also famously interprets the Sermon on the Mount's "greater righteousness" as being much less opposed to the demands of ordinary political life (including oaths, punishments, private property, harming enemies, worrying about tomorrow, and judging others) than the Sermon might appear on the surface.[124] But this only brings us back to the question of just how much Augustine thinks that Jesus's teaching can actually change the conduct of earthly politics. In that light, it is of political interest when Augustine insists that the Christian teaching is "not contrary" to even the literal Mosaic law *qua* political law, since for example a law permitting divorce and remarriage does not ever command Christians to avail themselves of that permission.[125]

Finally, to return to the early works, the Cassiciacum dialogues and early anti-Manichaean polemics ought to provide ample material for a comparison between Augustine's thought and Platonic political philosophy. Michael Foley's chapter in this volume points to many of the Ciceronian and otherwise politically relevant aspects of the Cassiciacum dialogues; Ratzinger points out the essential similarity between Augustine's early engagement with the pseudo-philosophy of Manichaeism and his later engagement with the genuine philosophies of paganism.[126] One must also add what Ratzinger does not seem to have noted, namely that Augustine's overcoming of Manichaeism already presupposed the extensive engagement with political philosophy tersely summarized in book 1 of *De libero arbitrio*.[127] In light of *De libero arbitrio*, we have to say that Augustine's early critiques of Manichaeism already reflect the results of the engagement with Ciceronian thought which Ratzinger seems to have thought Augustine did not undertake until later in his career.[128]

These, along with many other avenues of interpretation opened up by the trailblazing work of Ratzinger (and Fortin), will ultimately lead to satisfying answers only insofar as the scholars traveling on these intellectual paths are able to uncover traces of the dialogue that Augustine was conducting with Platonic political thought while he himself walked those paths. Ratzinger's work therefore shows the need for Augustine scholars to push back, as many Fortin students are already pushing back, against the lamentable ignorance of the Platonic political tradition that currently bedevils the majority of scholarship on Augustine's political thought. Here the clearest place to start is Cicero. As fragmentary as our texts of Cicero's are, many of the ones we have are already crying out to be compared with Augustine's: the treatment of Cato and Romulus in *De civitate dei* has precursors in *De officiis*, as does the whole treatment of morality throughout *De sermone domini in monte*, and the *Soliloquia* has a nearly explicit reference to book 1 of the *Tusculan Disputations*,[129] to name only a few and to say nothing of Augustine's many references to Cicero by name. Yet it is rare to find Augustine scholars who treat Cicero's texts with anything like Augustine's own respect for the man of whom he said, "I would never be so arrogant as to compare myself to Marcus Tully in industry, attentiveness, ingenuity, or learning."[130] How many Augustine scholars take seriously Augustine's claims, for example, that Cicero's skepticism was merely an exoteric doctrine to keep his true Platonic metaphysics from being corrupted through vulgarization? Or that it should be obvious to any reader of *De natura deorum* that the Stoic Balbus does not really believe in the Roman gods whom he seems there to defend vigorously?[131] How many, when they do draw comparisons between Augustine and Cicero, devote any of the effort to unpacking the latter's texts that Augustine visibly devoted to unpacking Varro's?[132]

Still, given the limitations of our Ciceronian texts, at some point an understanding of Augustine's relationship to Platonism requires scholars to move beyond those and other Latin texts to their original Platonic sources.[133] Fortunately we now possess Plato in the complete form that Cicero himself had access to, rather than the extremely fragmentary form in which Augustine could have read excerpts from him in translation. It is admittedly a dangerous scholarly enterprise to compare Augustine with an author whom he knew only at one degree of separation. But perhaps Plato is correct in that risking certainty in exchange for clarity is sometimes a "noble risk."[134] I will offer just two examples. Ratzinger shows that the Platonic political theology with which Augustine engaged rested ultimately on the fundamental metaphysical claim that, as Augustine quotes Apuleius, "no god mixes with a human being": this claim makes the gods "religiously inaccessible." It also explains why the god of Platonic metaphysics was thought an unsuitable object of worship for any human community outside the city of the *Republic*, thus forcing the Platonists to rest content with the false and more or less demonic gods worshiped in existing cities.[135] The young Ratzinger appears to have understood Apuleius's metaphysical claim in the light of the "clichés" of Platonic dualism that the older Ratzinger came to reject.[136] If we are to reject those clichés, as I believe we should, then we are left wondering what Plato and his heirs really meant by this claim. Apuleius himself offers little help in understanding it. But Apuleius took it from Plato's *Symposium*, as he more or less says.[137] Even if we know that Augustine never read Plato's *Symposium* firsthand—if this metaphysical claim is as important to Augustine's opponents as Ratzinger argues it is, then does anyone wishing to understand Augustine's response to paganism have a better option than studying the (notoriously difficult) *Symposium* and looking for any echoes of it in Augustine's writings? Or again: in the passage containing his famous dictum "an unjust law is no law at all," the character Augustine in *De libero arbitrio* brings up three different laws, all of which sanction some form of homicide whose justice might be questioned, and asks whether these are just laws. Of these three laws, the first and second also appear as the second and third in a similar list of five laws within the legal code of Plato's *Laws*.[138] This could be a coincidence. Or it could be that Augustine was drawing on a similar list that Cicero had reproduced in the section of his own *Laws* treating homicide, which we have lost. Either way, until the complete *De legibus* should turn up in some fortunate manuscript trove, how can Augustine scholars do anything but make the best use we can of Cicero's Platonic source? In light of the centrality of Platonism to Augustine's thought, it is hard to see what alternatives we have.

If I can summarize what I have shown Ratzinger's works on Augustine to be arguing, it is that a sympathetic critique of Platonic political philosophy is central to Augustine's understanding of earthly politics; that his understanding of politics is central to his engagement with paganism; that his engagement with paganism is crucial for his ecclesiology; that his ecclesiology is at the heart of his theology; and that his theology represents one of the very few peaks of self-understanding within the history of the Christian church. Certainly there are points on which one can dispute Ratzinger's analysis of Augustine. But if one does accept even most of that analysis, it seems to me that one will have difficulty avoiding the conclusion (which I believe Fortin shared) that for anyone interested in understanding the human meaning of the Christian proposition, there are few more urgent activities than undertaking a rigorous comparison of Augustine to the tradition of Platonic political thought. Like any difficult scholarly undertaking, this one will be best pursued in common. I wish therefore to conclude by emphasizing again that my own tentative suggestions as to where one might wish to begin it are of much less importance than the fundamental direction for new Augustine scholarship that Ratzinger points us toward. Others can seek answers to Ratzinger's questions in many ways that I have not been able to list here, and this volume already offers many fruits of such seeking. May it produce many more.

# Notes

1. See esp. Joseph Ratzinger, *Werte in Zeiten des Umbruchs. Die Herausforderungen der Zukunft bestehen* (Freiburg: Herder, 2005); *Wendezeit für Europa? Diagnosen und Prognosen zur Lage von Kirche und Welt* (Einsiedeln: Johannes Verlag, 1991); *Kirche, Ökumene und Politik. Neue Versuche zur Ekklesiologie* (Einsiedeln: Johannes Verlag, 1987), 137–243.

2. Michael J. S. Bruno, *Political Augustinianism: Modern Interpretations of Augustine's Political Thought* (Minneapolis: Fortress Press, 2014), 120–27, 262–63. The only other brief references to Ratzinger that I am aware of in twentieth-century scholarship on Augustine's political thought (outside of mere literature reviews) are made in R. A. Markus, *Saeculum: History and Society in the Theology of St. Augustine* (Cambridge: Cambridge University Press, 1970), of which only one (126n1) refers to any statement about Augustine's political thought.

3. Ratzinger, *Wendezeit für Europa*, 96–97. The citation is to Joseph Ratzinger, *Die Einheit der Nationen. Eine Vision der Kirchenväter*, 71–103 (cited by original page numbers), reprinted in *Gesammelte Schriften, Bd. 1. Volk und Haus Gottes in Augustins Lehre von der*

*Kirche*, ed. Gerhard Ludwig-Müller (Freiburg: Herder, 2011), 555–607. All translations are my own. The later Ratzinger cites several other sources in support of his interpretation of Plato, but only his own earlier monograph in support of the connection between Plato and Augustine. Ratzinger sometimes uses the term *Staatsphilosophie* and at other times *politische Philosophie*; I translate both as "political philosophy."

4. Ratzinger, *Wendezeit für Europa*, 93–97, citing the famous *De civitate dei* 4.4. See Augustine, *De Civitate Dei*, 2 vols., ed. B. Dombart and A. Kalb (Stuttgart: Teubner, 1993).

5. See Ratzinger, *Einheit der Nationen*, 28.

6. Joseph Ratzinger, *Volk und Haus Gottes in Augustins Lehre von der Kirche* (St. Ottilien: EOS Verlag, 1992), 185; see also 125. This work is reprinted, with original page numbers, in Ratzinger, *Gesammelte Schriften, Bd. 1*, 43–418.

7. Ratzinger, *Volk und Haus*, 185, 328.

8. Ratzinger, *Volk und Haus*, 185n1.

9. Ratzinger, *Volk und Haus*, xvi–xviii. For similar criticisms see *Volk und Haus*, 222n8, 288n23, 293n43a.

10. Ratzinger, *Volk und Haus*, 2–43, esp. 22n33.

11. Ratzinger, *Volk und Haus*, 124–26; for Manichaeism see also *Volk und Haus*, 22, 26n10, 130n6; for Donatism, *Volk und Haus*, 103–6, 127–35.

12. Joseph Ratzinger, "Herkunft und Sinn der Civitas-Lehre Augustins. Begegnung und Auseinandersetzung mit Wilhelm Kamlah," in *Gesammelte Schriften, Bd. 1*, 437–38; *Volk und Haus*, 205–18.

13. Ratzinger, "Herkunft und Sinn," 421–22; *Volk und Haus*, 276–78.

14. Ratzinger, "Herkunft und Sinn," 420–22; *Volk und Haus*, xvi–xvii, 121–23; *Einheit der Nationen*, 100–104.

15. This is the theme of Ratzinger's entire dissertation, whose assigned topic was the role played by the concepts "people of God" and (less importantly) "house of God" in Augustine's understanding of the Church (*Volk und Haus*, xii–xiii). For his conclusions on the relation between the two Testaments, see *Volk und Haus*, 296–309. On the "theocratic" character of the Old Testament, see *Volk und Haus*, 123, 300, 302; *Einheit der Nationen*, 83–84.

16. Ratzinger, *Volk und Haus*, 123, 57–58, 65, 93, xvi; on Augustine's stature see *Volk und Haus*, xii, 43. For more on the importance of this question of the two Testaments, which is in the background of nearly all of Ratzinger's published works, see Joseph Ratzinger (Benedict XVI), *Jesus von Nazareth, Bd. 1.* (Freiburg: Herder, 2007), 131–60; *Kirche, Ökumene und Politik*, 235–40.

17. Ratzinger, *Volk und Haus*, 158. I use "critical engagement" or "intellectual engagement" to translate the untranslatable term *Auseinandersetzung*.

18. *Volk und Haus*, 125.

19. *Volk und Haus*, 124–25: see 185–328.

20. *Volk und Haus*, 185–86. See also 129n5 on Augustine's "apologetic against paganism (philosophy)."

21. Joseph Ratzinger, *Einführung in das Christentum* (Munich: Kösel-Verlag, 1968), 104–7.

22. Ratzinger, *Volk und Haus*, 223–25, 7–8.

23. *Volk und Haus*, 8–43; for greater detail see Joseph Ratzinger, "Der Weg der religiösen Erkenntnis nach dem heiligen Augustinus," in *Gesammelte Schriften, Bd. 1*, 511–29. On the contradictions see *Volk und Haus*, 45, and cf. 149–51 with 298–99; "Weg der religiösen

Erkenntnis," 527. The young Ratzinger took the common twentieth-century view that Augustine never became fully "conscious" of the change that had taken place in his own thought since his early writings: see *Volk und Haus*, 45–46, 155n73, 227, 245n21, 303n18. His dissertation does also offer biting criticisms of Heinrich Scholz for attempting a somewhat more condescending "reconstruction" of such supposedly "tragic" contradictions in Augustine's thought (*Volk und Haus*, 277n5).

24. *Volk und Haus*, 274n30.

25. *Volk und Haus*, 263n5.

26. See Thomas Harmon's chapter, "The Few, the Many, and the Universal Way of Salvation," in this volume.

27. *Volk und Haus*, 167, 318.

28. Ratzinger, "Herkunft und Sinn," 431.

29. Ratzinger, *Volk und Haus*, 262–64, with the many references to Cicero at 255–62; also *Volk und Haus*, 294n44 on Cicero and 239 on Varro.

30. *Volk und Haus*, 42 (citing *De ordine*, 2.18.48), 263–64, 294; "Herkunft und Sinn," 430. For Ciceronian sources see *Volk und Haus*, 258–59, 294n44. See Augustine, *Contra Academicos, De Beata Vita, De Ordine, De Magistro, De Libero Arbitrio*, ed. W. M. Green and Klaus-Detlef Daur, Corpus Christianorum Series Latina 29 (Turnhout: Brepols, 1970).

31. Ratzinger, *Volk und Haus*, 170–71, 188–89.

32. Ratzinger, "Vorwort," *Gesammelte Schriften, Bd. 1*, 8; see also *Einheit der Nationen*, 70–72.

33. Ratzinger, "Herkunft und Sinn," 430.

34. Ratzinger, *Volk und Haus*, 266. See also Daniel Strand's chapter, "*The City of God* and Roman Sacral Politics," in this volume.

35. Ratzinger, *Einheit der Nationen*, 70–72, 80–84. On the compatibility of philosophic monotheism with polytheism, see Joseph Ratzinger, *Gott des Glaubens, Gott der Philosophen. Ein Beitrag zum Problem der theologia naturalis*, ed. Heino Sonnemans (Trier: Paulinus, 2006), 26–28, and somewhat more crudely, *Volk und Haus*, 6–7, 271–75.

36. Ratzinger, *Einführung in das Christentum*, 81; *Kirche, Ökumene und Politik*, 191.

37. Ratzinger, *Einheit der Nationen*, 24, 28; *Einführung in das Christentum*, 81; see also Joseph Ratzinger, *Glaube—Wahrheit—Toleranz. Das Christentum und die Weltreligionen* (Freiburg: Herder, 2004), 137.

38. Ratzinger, *Einheit der Nationen*, 71–72; *Kirche, Ökumene und Politik*, 195, 209.

39. Ratzinger, "Herkunft und Sinn," 430–31. This is not to deny that metaphysical disagreements may to some extent have underlain the political disagreement: see again *Einheit der Nationen*, 71–72, with *Gott des Glaubens*, 34–35, and *Einführung in das Christentum*, 108–12.

40. Ratzinger, *Volk und Haus*, 325n4.

41. *Volk und Haus*, 220.

42. Cf. again Ratzinger, *Einheit der Nationen*, 80–84.

43. On Varro and "political theology" see Ratzinger, *Volk und Haus*, 267–71; *Glaube—Wahrheit—Toleranz*, 133–37.

44. Ratzinger, *Einheit der Nationen*, 72–73. At *Einheit*, 104, Ratzinger suggests, citing the historical work of Gustave Bardy, that even some Christians were joining the political cries for the restoration of the old gods.

45. *Einheit der Nationen*, 74–75.

46. *Einheit der Nationen*, 75n79; *Volk und Haus*, 267–68.

47. Ratzinger, *Einheit der Nationen*, 75–76.

48. Ratzinger, *Volk und Haus*, 191–94.

49. Ratzinger, *Einheit der Nationen*, 96–97, citing *De civitate dei* 10.21. Ratzinger refers to a monograph by Heinrich Schlier to support the view that this "existential" interpretation of an "originally cosmographical statement" is even true to the intentions of the New Testament authors as well (*Einheit*, 96n111).

50. See Ratzinger, *Einheit der Nationen*, 77.

51. *Einheit der Nationen*, 95–97; *Einführung in das Christentum*, 81, 83.

52. Ratzinger, *Einheit der Nationen*, 89.

53. Ratzinger, *Kirche, Ökumene und Politik*, 160–61; on philosophic martyrs see *Kirche, Ökumene und Politik*, 218; *Wendezeit für Europa*, 93; *Einheit der Nationen*, 13–14, 62; Joseph Ratzinger, *Eschatologie. Tod und ewiges Leben* (Regensburg: Friedrich Pustet, 2007), 72.

54. On this gift see Ratzinger, *Kirche, Ökumene und Politik*, 137–39, 181.

55. The citation for this claim, at *Einheit der Nationen*, 89n101, is to *De civitate dei* 5.24–26 on the Christian emperors. There Augustine says in fact only that these emperors prove that *individuals* can be politically successful without being in thrall to demons, not that an entire city can be (see esp. *De civitate dei*, 5.25, at the beginning).

56. See Joseph Ratzinger, Review of *Christenheit und Weltverwantwortung*, by Ulrich Duchrow, in *Gesammelte Schriften, Bd. 1*, 683–91, esp. 685. Duchrow is the only secondary source to which all of Ratzinger's later discussions of Plato refer.

57. Ratzinger, *Kirche, Ökumene und Politik*, 218. In 2006, Ratzinger seemed to think that the field of theology had made only limited progress in the battle against this "entirely schematized" misunderstanding of Platonic (and more generally Greek) thought: see *Eschatologie*, 196.

58. Ratzinger, *Eschatologie*, 68, 72; Review of Duchrow, 685.

59. Cf. Ratzinger, *Einheit der Nationen*, 71; *Volk und Haus Gottes*, 15–20, 40–43.

60. Ratzinger, *Eschatologie*, 72.

61. Ratzinger, Review of Duchrow, 685; *Eschatologie*, 118.

62. Ratzinger, Review of Duchrow, 685.

63. Ratzinger, *Eschatologie*, 72.

64. *Eschatologie*, 70–71.

65. In the memorable phrase from Xenophon, *Anabasis* 3.2.13, "The freedom of the *poleis* in which you [Greeks] were born and raised" is shown in that "you prostrate yourselves before no human master, but only before the gods." See Xenophon, *Anabasis of Cyrus*, ed. E. C. Marchant (New York: Oxford University, 1904).

66. Ratzinger, *Eschatologie*, 71–72, 118–19; *Kirche, Ökumene und Politik*, 218; review of Duchrow, 685.

67. Ratzinger, *Eschatologie*, 72, 119; *Kirche, Ökumene und Politik*, 218.

68. Ratzinger, *Eschatologie*, 71.

69. *Eschatologie*, 71–72, 119.

70. Ratzinger, *Einführung in das Christentum*, 104; *Glaube—Wahrheit—Toleranz*, 178–79.

71. Quoted in Ratzinger, *Wendezeit für Europa*, 94–95.

72. Ratzinger, *Kirche, Ökumene und Politik*, 211–12.

73. Even the younger Ratzinger had seen this to at least some extent: see the vivid contrast between Plato and Neoplatonism drawn at Joseph Ratzinger, "Die Kirche in der Frömmigkeit des heiligen Augustinus," in *Gesammelte Schriften, Bd. 1*, 506–7, as well as the passing reference to Plato's religious concept of the city at *Volk und Haus*, 265n1.

74. Ratzinger, *Kirche, Ökumene und Politik*, 219.

75. Ratzinger, *Volk und Haus*, 267–71.

76. *Volk und Haus*, 219.

77. Cf. *Volk und Haus*, 241n14 (the "popular opinion" as to the "reality" of religious sacrifices), 266 (the Romans' "faith of the fathers"), and 274 ("their faith").

78. Ratzinger, *Einführung in das Christentum*, 104–5, 107; *Glaube—Wahrheit—Toleranz*, 177–79. At *Glaube—Wahrheit—Toleranz*, 134–35, Ratzinger explicitly cites his dissertation and corrects two of its passages that had made the untenable claim about a radical split between "faith" and "cult" in ancient paganism.

79. Cf. again Ratzinger, *Volk und Haus*, 267–71.

80. *Volk und Haus*, 271 (in apparent contradiction to the conclusion drawn in the next sentence); *Kirche, Ökumene und Politik*, 212.

81. See Ratzinger, *Volk und Haus*, 268–69; *Glaube—Wahrheit—Toleranz*, 134.

82. Ratzinger, *Volk und Haus*, 267, citing *De civitate dei* 4.31 and 6.4 (quoted in part at *Einheit der Nationen*, 72n76). I am relying on the original Augustine passages for my interpretation of the "possibility" that Ratzinger identifies as the constraint on Varro.

83. Ratzinger, *Einheit der Nationen*, 97.

84. See Ratzinger, *Werte in Zeiten des Umbruchs*, 60.

85. Ratzinger, "Herkunft und Sinn," 429n29.

86. "Herkunft und Sinn," 436–39. Ratzinger summarizes here the conclusions of large parts of his doctoral dissertation: see *Volk und Haus*, esp. 136–84, 205–18, 276–309, 322–28.

87. Ratzinger, *Volk und Haus*, 168–69, 175–77, 304–5; "Herkunft und Sinn," 438–39.

88. Ratzinger, *Volk und Haus*, 137–49.

89. *Volk und Haus*, 23–35.

90. Ratzinger, "Frömmigkeit," 507.

91. Ratzinger, *Volk und Haus*, 260–61; see also *Einheit der Nationen*, 13.

92. For Varro, see *Volk und Haus*, 267; *Einheit der Nationen*, 80n85.

93. See my "Ratzinger on the Augustinian Understanding of Religious Freedom," *Communio: International Catholic Review* 44, no. 2 (2017): 296–322.

94. Ratzinger, review of Duchrow, 690–91; *Kirche, Ökumene und Politik*, 190–91.

95. Ratzinger, *Volk und Haus*, 314n10; "Herkunft und Sinn," 431n34.

96. See Ratzinger, *Volk und Haus*, 301–4, 314n10; "Herkunft und Sinn," 436.

97. Ratzinger, *Einführung in das Christentum*, 80–83.

98. Ratzinger gives some conflicting indications about this term, stating at one point that "an actual Christianization of public life as such is not an actual concern of Augustine's": *Volk und Haus*, 317n17; see similarly *Einheit der Nationen*, 101–3.

99. See Augustine, *De sermone domini in monte*, ed. Almut Mutzenbecher (Turnhout: Brepols, 1967), 2.20.67–69.

100. Augustine, *De doctrina christiana*, in *De Doctrina Christiana, De Vera Religione*, ed. Joseph Martin and Klaus-Detlef Daur, Corpus Christianorum Series Latina 32 (Turnhout: Brepols, 1962), 4.9.23.

101. Bruno, *Political Augustinianism*, 105–6; see Ernest L. Fortin, *The Birth of Philosophic Christianity*, ed. J. Brian Benestad (New York: Rowman & Littlefield, 1996), 1–122; *Classical Christianity and the Political Order*, ed. J. Brian Benestad (New York: Rowman & Littlefield, 1996), 1–105 (esp. 32–33), 117–50, 199–222.

102. See, *inter alia*, Fortin, *Birth of Philosophic Christianity*, 95–114. On the developmental reading as applied to Augustine's political thought in particular, see my "Augustine on the Moral Significance of Human Law," *Revue des études augustiniennes et patristiques* 61 (2015): 275–79.

103. Ratzinger, *Volk und Haus*, 1–47, although cf. note 23 above.

104. Augustine, *De vera religione*, 1.1–2.

105. *De vera religione*, 1.3–17.34.

106. *De vera religione*, 18.35–55.113, esp. 26.48–49, 5.98–55.112. I believe this is the earliest use of the actual phrase "earthly city" in Augustine's writings, although a grammatically interchangeable phrase appears at the earlier *De libero arbitrio* 1.32.108 (see Burns, "Moral Significance," 276).

107. See Fortin, *Classical Christianity*, 8–11, 205–9. Both treatments strikingly neglect Fortin's (and to a lesser extent Ratzinger's) admonitions on the importance of distinguishing between the statements of different characters in a dialogue where only one character represents the author: cf. Fortin, *Birth of Philosophic Christianity*, 44–46, 99–102; Ratzinger, *Volk und Haus*, 32n30. In a forthcoming MS, I offer my own interpretation of book 1 of *De libero arbitrio*.

108. Augustine, *De libero arbitrio*, 1.31.106–32.112.

109. *De libero arbitrio*, 1.6.14–7.19, 1.9.25–10.26, 1.12.35, 1.13.41, 1.15.48–50.

110. *De libero arbitrio*, 1.4.10–11.

111. See Adam Thomas's chapter in this volume, "The Investigation of Justice in Augustine's *Confessions*," on the importance of Augustine's preconversion wrestling with the issues discussed in book 1 of *De libero arbitrio*.

112. See Ratzinger, *Eschatologie*, 71–72, 118–19; *Glaube—Wahrheit—Toleranz*, 203–4, 128; *Werte in Zeiten des Umbruchs*, 114–15.

113. See Burns, "Moral Significance," 273–98.

114. See again Ratzinger, "Vorwort," *Gesammelte Schriften, Bd. 1*, 8; *Wendezeit für Europa*, 46–47 (on the same question more generally).

115. Augustine, *De civitate dei* 1.1–7, 1.15–16, 1.18–19, 1.23–24, 1.32.

116. Many helpful steps in this direction have recently been taken by Pierre Manent, *Les metamorphoses de la cité: Essais sur la dynamique de l'Occident* (Paris: Flammarion, 2010), 292–397. Manent shares most of Ratzinger's observations about the character of the ancient city and Augustine's critique of it (see *Les metamorphoses*, 273–92).

117. An excellent anthology of these and similar writings of Augustine's can be found in E. M. Atkins and Robert J. Dodaro, eds., *Augustine: Political Writings* (New York: Cambridge University Press, 2001).

118. Fortin, *Birth of Philosophic Christianity*, 31–33; see also Ryan Balot's chapter, "Truth, Lies, Deception, Esotericism: The Case of St. Augustine," in this volume.

119. Augustine *De mendacio*, in *De Bono Conjugali, De Adulterinis Conjugiis, De Mendacio*, et al. (Vienna: Tempsky, 1900), 13.22–23, 14.25.

120. Augustine, *De bono conjugali*, 17.19, 24.32, 1.1, 3.3, 7.7–8.7.

121. *De bono conjugali*, 14.16.

122. On the Christian "law" against adultery see Augustine, *De adulterinis conjugiis*, 1.14.15, 1.17.18, 1.18.22, 2.8.7, 2.9.8, 2.10.9, 2.20.21. For contrasts between the "law of Christ" and the "laws of the world" made by the "earthly city," with the latter including "Roman laws" and even the "old law of God" given by Moses, see *De adulterinis conjugiis*, 2.8.7, which demands that some of these political laws should change; 2.9.8 and 2.10.9, which seem to grant the inevitability of a gap between others of these laws and Christ's law; and 2.15.15, which could plausibly be read either way.

123. See Augustine, *De sermone domini in monte*, 1.1.2 on the contrast between "greater precepts for the sake of the kingdom of heaven" and "lesser precepts for the sake of an earthly kingdom."

124. *De sermone domini in monte*, 1.17.51–52, 1.19.56–23.80, 2.16.53–19.66.

125. *De sermone domini in monte*, 1.14.39.

126. Ratzinger, *Volk und Haus*, 130n6, and the citations given above at note 11.

127. See above, and cf. *De libero arbitrio*, 1.4.10–11 with *Volk und Haus*, 4–5. At one point Ratzinger makes a claim about the early works (review of Duchrow, 687) that appears to ignore the existence of *De libero arbitrio*, 1.31.106–32.108.

128. Cf. *Volk und Haus*, 261. See, e.g., Ratzinger, *De Moribus Ecclesiae Catholicae et De Moribus Manichaeorum*, ed. John B. Bauer (Vienna: Hoelder-Pichler-Tempsky, 1992), 1.8.13 (Christ's answer to Cicero's question).

129. Cf. Augustine *De civitate dei* 1.24 with Cicero *De officiis*, ed. M. Winterbottom (New York: Oxford University, 1994), 1.112, 3.99–115; cf. Augustine *Soliloquia*, ed. Wolfgang Hörmann (Vienna: Hoelder-Pichler-Tempsky, 1986), 2.13.23, with Cicero *Tusculanarum disputationum*, ed. J. E. King. (Cambridge: Harvard University, 1988), 1.34.81–47.111.

130. See Foley, "Cicero, Augustine, and the Philosophical Roots of the Cassiciacum Dialogues," *Revue des études augustiniennes* 45 (1999): 51–52, citing *Contra academicos* 3.16.36. Fortin students tend to be the welcome exceptions to this rule. See Foley, "Philosophical Roots"; Manent, *Metamorphoses de la cité*, which integrates a careful treatment of Augustine's political thought into a deeply sympathetic treatment of his political-philosophic predecessors and successors (especially Cicero); and Veronica Roberts Ogle's chapter, "Augustine's Ciceronian Response to the Ciceronian Patriot," in this volume.

131. Cf. Augustine, *Contra academicos* 3.17.37–20.43; *De civitate dei* 4.30. Even the young Ratzinger appears skeptical of what, as he notes, Augustine considered to be "obvious" interpretations of Cicero's and Varro's hidden meanings: see *Volk und Haus*, 273n24.

132. See Augustine, *De civitate dei* 6.4.

133. Douglas Kries's chapter, "Augustine's Imitation in the *Confessions*," in this volume offers an example of how this can be done.

134. See Ratzinger, *Eschatologie*, 119, citing Plato, *Phaedo* 114d. See Plato *Phaedo*, ed. E. A. Duke et al. (New York: Oxford University Press, 1995).

135. Ratzinger, *Einheit der Nationen*, 71–83; *Gott des Glaubens*, 23–28; *Glaube—Wahrheit—Toleranz*, 133–36.

136. See Ratzinger, *Einheit der Nationen*, 71–72, 80–81.

137. Apuleius, *De deo socratis*, ed. Alois Goldbacher (Vienna: C. Geroldi Filium, 1876), 4, 6; see Plato, *Symposium*, ed. John Burnet (New York: Oxford University Press, 1901), 203a.

138. See Augustine, *De libero arbitrio* 1.11.33, and Plato, *Laws*, ed. John Burnet (Oxford: Oxford University Press, 1907), 874b–d.

# Contributors

Ryan K. Balot is a professor of political science and classics at the University of Toronto. He is the author of several books and a number of articles on Greek and Roman antiquity. His latest book is *Courage in the Democratic Polis: Ideology and Critique in Classical Athens*. His current research focus is Plato's *Laws*.

Daniel E. Burns is an associate professor of politics at the University of Dallas, a fellow at the Catholic University of America's Institute for Human Ecology, and a member of the Neuer Schülerkreis Joseph Ratzinger / Benedikt XVI. He writes on the relation between religion and citizenship in authors including Cicero, Augustine, Farabi, More, Locke, the American Founders, and Joseph Ratzinger. He has also published in the *American Interest*, the *New York Times*, and the *Washington Post*.

Peter Busch is an assistant professor in the Augustine and Culture Seminar Program and the Department of Political Science, Villanova University. His research and teaching address classical and modern political philosophy, the thought of St. Augustine, and the education that is possible when the two intersect in the soul of Augustine's readers. He has published several recent papers and articles on these subjects.

Richard J. Dougherty is the chairman of the Politics Department and director of the Graduate Program in Politics at the University of Dallas. He is a contributor to *Augustine Through the Ages: An Encyclopedia* and to the three-volume *Oxford Guide to the Historical Reception of Augustine* and has recently republished (with Thomas Neumayr) Charles McCoy's *The Structure of Political Thought*. His *Oxford Bibliographies Series* entry on *The City of God* is forthcoming in 2019. In 2016 he served as a visiting professor in the Department of Comparative Political Science at the Katholische Universität Eichstätt-Ingolstadt, Bavaria, Germany.

Michael P. Foley is an associate professor of patristics in the Great Texts Program at Baylor University. He received his PhD in systematic theology from Boston College and he is the editor or author of several books, including Frank Sheed's translation of Augustine's *Confessions*; *Ever Ancient, Ever New: Ruminations on the City, the Soul, and the Church: Collected Essays of Ernest L. Fortin*, volume 4; and the four-volume Cassiciacum Dialogues of St. Augustine.

Thomas P. Harmon is an associate professor of theology at the University of St. Thomas in Houston, Texas. He has published essays in *Gregorianum, New Blackfriars,* and *Pro Ecclesia.* He is coeditor, along with Roger W. Nutt, of *Wisdom and the Renewal of Catholic Theology: Essays in Honor of Matthew L. Lamb.* His research interests include St. Augustine, St. Thomas, the interplay of faith and reason, and Catholic Social Teaching.

Douglas Kries is a professor of philosophy at Gonzaga University in Spokane, Washington. His research and writing is devoted especially to Latin medieval political philosophy; he also maintains an interest in classical French liberalism. His books include *The Problem of Natural Law* and *Augustine: Political Writings* (with Michael Tkacz and Ernest Fortin). His publications have appeared in such places as *The Review of Politics* and *The American Catholic Philosophical Quarterly.* He is currently working on a book on Robert Bellarmine.

Ashleen Menchaca-Bagnulo is an assistant professor of political science at Texas State University. She studies the civic republican tradition with a special focus on religion, women, and race. She has served as a James Madison Program William E. Simon Postdoctoral Fellow in Religion and Public Life at Princeton University, as a resident fellow in the Stockdale Center for Ethical Leadership at the US Naval Academy, and as the Postdoctoral Teaching Fellow in Western and American Political Thought in the Tocqueville Program at Furman University.

Veronica Roberts Ogle is an assistant professor of philosophy at Assumption College. Her research focuses on the intersection between theology and political philosophy in classical and Patristic thought, and as such, she works across disciplinary lines, having published in *Perspectives on Political Science, Journal of Religious Ethics,* and *Augustinian Studies.* She is currently working on a book manuscript entitled "A World Besieged: Politics and the Earthly City in Augustine's *City of God.*"

Daniel Strand is an assistant professor of ethics in the Department of Leadership and Warfighting at the Air War College. Prior to his appointment he was a postdoctoral fellow at Arizona State University (2015–19) in the History Department and the Program in Political History and Leadership. At the Air War College he teaches courses on the Just War tradition, moral theory, and applied ethics. Strand's research interests include the political and moral theology of Augustine and the Augustinian tradition, ethics and foreign policy, the Just War tradition, bioethics, and moral theory. He is the author of the forthcoming *Gods of the Nations,* a historical study of Augustine's political theology in *City of God.* He has published articles and book chapters on Augustine, Hannah Arendt, and the ethics of euthanasia.

Adam Thomas is a 2018–19 James Madison Program Postdoctoral Research Associate at Princeton University. His work focuses on the foundations of law, justice, and constitutionalism in Cicero, Augustine, and Thomas Aquinas. He is currently at work on a manuscript titled "Cicero, St. Augustine, and the Politics of Virtue," which revives the shared Ciceronian-Augustinian conception of politics in light of virtue in order to clarify our political moment and the Church's relation to the political order. Previously, he was the T. W. Smith Postdoctoral Fellow in Western and American Political Thought at Furman University's Tocqueville Program. He received his PhD in Political Science from Boston College.

# Index